INTRODUCTION TO
ORGANISATIONAL
BEHAVIOUR

INTRODUCTION TO ORGANISATIONAL BEHAVIOUR

Richard Pettinger

First published 1996 by
MACMILLAN PRESS LTD
Houndmills, Basingstoke, Hampshire RG21 6XS
and London
Companies and representatives
throughout the world

ISBN 0–333–63919–7 hardcover
ISBN 0–333–63920–0 paperback

A catalogue record for this book is available
from the British Library.

10   9   8   7   6   5   4   3   2   1
05   04   03   02   01   00   99   98   97   96

Copy-edited and typeset by Povey–Edmondson
Okehampton and Rochdale, England

Printed in Great Britain by
T.J. Press (Padstow) Ltd, Padstow Cornwall

Contents

List of figures, tables and boxes

■ Figures

■ Tables

■ Boxes

Preface

There is a direct relationship between the long-term commercial success achieved by organisations from all parts of the world – 3M, McDonald's, Nissan, Sony, Marks & Spencer, Body Shop – and the approach adopted to their human aspects of management. Without exception, these organisations respect and value their people, both for themselves and for their contribution to success. Levels of expectation are high. Commitment to continuous training and development is required and expected and all staff participate. There are high and specific standards of performance, conduct and behaviour, and a distinctive ideology that all are required to adopt when they join.

These organisations are versatile and resilient in both expertise and behaviour. Versatility is essential to be able to identify and respond to opportunities as and when they arise, and to generate the flexibility and dynamism required as the result. Resilience is required because the progress of organisations is composed of both successes and failures (for example, the Sony Betamax video recorder and player was a commercial and global failure, yet the Sony Corporation remains highly regarded, respected – and profitable).

More generally, economic turbulence, the globalisation of business, technological change, the advance of knowledge, competitive pressures and continuous reappraisal of the nature of public services have caused all aspects of commercial and government organisations and their activities to be questioned. There are two fundamental concerns.

The first of these is increasing expectations on the part of consumers for high-quality, reliable and durable products and high-quality services. The advance of competition and the ever-increasing choice available in all areas adds fuel to this. Except in the case of primary monopolies, consumers may satisfy their needs and wants from products and services provided from all parts of the world. The commitment to buy the indigenous product only remains as long as it meets the standards of similar items from elsewhere.

The other concern is the relationship between organisations and their people: their staff or employees. The lifespan of organisations themselves (and also their expertise and technology) is getting shorter. Old jobs are demolished or rejuvenated, new jobs are created and may themselves have a highly limited life. Organisations are no longer providers of lifetime employment; and neither may an individual expect to be able to pursue a single occupation or career based on expertise gained at an early age. Careers, especially those that offer regular progress upward through hierarchies, are becoming obsolete.

From this arises, in turn, a fundamental reappraisal of the relationships between organisations, staff and customers. On the one hand, organisations have to be able to survive in order to build effective commercial relationships with their markets. On the other, this is only possible if organisations concentrate on developing and enhancing the skills, knowledge, attitudes, behaviour, qualities and expertise to make this possible.

Further, the intensity of competition now means that attention is constantly paid to improving administration, processes, procedures and support functions to ensure that they operate effectively and in support of the core purpose, and that they take up as few of the organisation's resources as possible.

This is the context for the study of organisational behaviour and a grasp of this is essential at the outset if successful understanding is to be achieved.

The purpose of this book is to present and illustrate the main aspects and features of human behaviour in organisations. The first two chapters establish and discuss a basis on which effective study of organisational behaviour is based. Successful organisations are not created in isolation from the rest of the world, and neither can they operate in isolation. Successful organisations are those which interact, influence and respond effectively to constraints placed upon them by their environment. Chapters 3, 4, 5 and 6 discuss the main aspects of individual behaviour that those working within organisations must under-stand if they are to be able to engage in successful and effective human relationships. Without these the organisation and pursuit of fully profitable and effective workplace relations are impossible. Chapters 7, 8, 9, 10, 11 and 12 illustrate and analyse the elements and features faced by all people in any form of organised situation: communication, authority, leadership, working in groups, conflict and the prevalence of politics. Chapters 13, 14, 15 and 16 broaden the discussion further to cover the major internal pressures and constraints which face organisations and which may be both barriers and drives to engage in particular activities in distinctive ways. Chapters 17 and 18 bring the coverage full circle, establishing likely influences on organisations in the future and underlining current lessons, both absolute and those drawn from what is currently regarded as best and most effective practice.

The hypothesis (insofar as there is one) is that an understanding of basic human behaviour is essential to the creation of effective and successful organisations; that steps can, should and must be taken to influence skills, knowledge, attitudes and behaviour; and that this in turn positively influences total performance. There is therefore clearly a body of knowledge, skill and understanding required on the part of all those who seek to create and direct organisations and manage and supervise those who work within them; and on the part also of those who have dealings on their behalf with the outside world, especially with customers and the wider community. The approach taken in this book is fundamentally managerial, but it also offers an introduction to the study of human behaviour in organisations to those with little or no previous understanding of the field. It seeks to present highly complex patterns and elements of human behaviour in ways that are intelligible to a wider audience and to break down the barriers and mystique perceived by those who come to the subject for the first time.

The book is therefore intended as an introduction from which those who read may go on and develop a deeper understanding. It is intended to be of special value to undergraduates on full-time university courses that include elements of organisational behaviour or other related introductory units.

It will be of value also to those in human resource and personnel functions; to accountants, lawyers, teachers, chartered secretaries, administrators, information technologists, senior secretaries and personal assistants, and those working in supervisory, administrative and similar roles and functions. It is intended to be especially useful to people in these functions who are pursuing professional qualifications and certificates or diplomas in management courses. It should be of general value also to practising managers who wish to develop an understanding of their people and improve the effectiveness of their management of their human resource.

RICHARD PETTINGER

▌Acknowledgements

Many people helped in the preparation of this book.

I am especially grateful to Bev Nutt, David Kincaid, Andrew Scott, Graham Winch, Victor Torrance and Barbara Young at University College London; to Paul Griseri at London Guildhall University; to Margaret Malpas and Sandra Madigan of Malpas Flexible Learning Ltd; to Kelvin Cheatle of the Royal Philanthropic Society; to Ram Ahronov; to Frances Kelly; and to Rebecca Frith, who typed and edited the manuscript. I am also indebted to Stephen Rutt, Jane Powell, Tracy France, Keith Povey and Gail Sheffield at the publishers for their constant help, advice and guidance.

RICHARD PETTINGER

CHAPTER 1

Introduction

Organisational behaviour is concerned with the study of the behaviour and interaction of people in restricted or organised settings. It involves understanding people and predicting their behaviour, and a knowledge of the means by which their behaviour is influenced and shaped.

Organisations are bodies or entities created for a stated purpose. They may consist of one or more people. In the case of the sole trader or single operator, he needs to builds relationships with suppliers, contractors, customers, clients and the community. For those that consist of more than one person, internal as well as external relationships have to be created and maintained. Organisations therefore consist of individuals; groups; and relationships. Objectives, structures, systems and processes are then created to give direction and order to activities and interactions.

Organisational behaviour is thus of great concern to anyone who organises, creates, orders, directs, manages or supervises the activities of others. It is also of concern to those who build relationships between individuals, groups of people, different parts of organisations and between different organisations, for all these activities are founded on human interaction.

Organisational behaviour is therefore concerned with:

- the purposes for which organisations are created;
- the behaviour of individuals, and an understanding of the pressures and influences that cause them to act and react in particular ways;
- the qualities that individuals bring to particular situations;
- the creation of groups (collections of people brought together for given purposes);
- the background and context within which activities take place;
- relationships and interactions with the wider environment with other organisations and groups;
- the management and ordering of the whole and its parts into productive and effective work relationships.

■ The background of organisational behaviour

Organisational behaviour is not a natural or absolute science, and neither is it a distinctive field of study. It draws on a range of disciplines and is viewed from a variety of perspectives. Rather than provide an absolute or perfect body of knowledge and expertise, each of these offers a different point of view on the whole, so that as complete an understanding as possible may be built up. Consideration of organisational behaviour from each standpoint indicates both the broad context, and also some of the specific areas of concern.

Moreover, each discipline and perspective is incomplete and imperfect. Each is in itself an ever-developing and enlarging field. However, this at least indicates why a full understanding of organisational behaviour has not yet been achieved and the context in which studies in the field are to be seen.

■ Disciplines

The main disciplines that contribute to the study of organisational behaviour are as follows. In summary, they are concerned with the capabilities and potential of people; influences on capabilities; the attitudes and behaviour of people; influences on behaviour; the organisational context; organisational processes and the execution of work; and interaction with the environment.

Psychology concerned with the study and understanding of human personality and behaviour, the traits and characteristics of individuals; their perceptions, attitudes, values, beliefs and motives; their goals and priorities; their capabilities and potential.

Sociology concerned with the study of behaviour in groups; influences on this behaviour; interactions between groups; the extent to which people organise themselves and the ways in which they do this; processes of socialisation (the ordering and limiting of individual behaviour by groups and the environment); the creation of norms, rules and regulations.

Anthropology concerned with the study of large groups, nations and cultures; global beliefs, customs, ideas and values; the wider processes of socialisation (for example, through religious activities, caste systems, aristocracies, technocracies).

Economics concerned with the study of the ordering, use and distribution of the world's resources; of gathering and using these to best effect in particular situations and in the pursuit of stated aims and objectives.

Ethics concerned with the establishment of absolute standards; these relate above all, to the nature of interpersonal relationships and interactions, and these include standards of honesty, integrity, probity, value, esteem and respect.

Mathematics and statistics concerned with the need to prove absolutes and facts wherever possible; to give a basis of certainty to particular situations; to provide the means by which logical and demonstrable conclusions can be drawn from bodies of knowledge and research.

Each of these disciplines offers a different point of view and contributes to understanding; none, however, offers the complete picture. The major problem is the inability to arrive at absolute facts and conclusions. This is in direct contrast to the study of physics, mathematics, mechanics, chemistry and biology, each of which is capable of:

- absolute and logical reasoning;
- the combination of components and variables to produce certain and predictable results;
- consistent relationships between variables through time and space that are incapable of being reinterpreted due to differences in nationality or location;
- capability of validation and demonstration through experimentation.

None of the disciplines indicated has this certainty, predictability, validity or reliability. People do not behave in consistent or rational ways. Every situation is unique, and so it is impossible to recreate the conditions under which one experiment took place in order to repeat it. Rather than controlled experimentation, organisational behaviour investigations rely on observed experiments, case studies, the analysis of documentation and the use of qualitative investigations and questionnaires to provide the information with which they arrive at their conclusions.

1. Observations and observed experiments are subject to perception and interpretation; the use of the senses; and the ability to take in enough of a particular situation to form a sufficient understanding on which judgements can be made.
2. Observed experiments are limited by the ability of researchers to design hypotheses and devise means for testing these in ways that are capable of being validated.
3. The study of case histories and examples are subject to perception and judgement, except where cause and effects can be directly related (for example, where £10.00 was made because 10 items were sold at £1.00 each).
4. The analysis of documentation is subject to the knowledge, quality and judgement of those who originally produced the documents, as well as being subject to the interpretation of those currently using them.
5. Questionnaires: the use of questioning and questionnaires is limited by the capabilities of the researchers to define their purpose, ask the right questions, interpret and analyse the responses and draw conclusions from the information and material gained. Limitations are also produced by situational factors, individual priorities and perspectives. These are continuously being influenced by their environment and can quite legitimately provide a different set of answers to the same questions within moments if their circumstances suddenly change.

   (a) Their responses are influenced by the ways in which they are questioned.
   (b) The response to written questionnaires is affected by their length; the number of questions; the nature of questions asked; the ways in which these are asked; the length of time required to complete the questionnaire; the length of time at the disposal of the individual; the responses of others if these are known; the language used; the extent of interest of the individual in the material; the visual

presentation of the questionnaire (or the interviewer); the amount of space or time given for each answer.

(c) The response to oral questioning is also influenced by the media used (face-to-face or telephone); whether it is an individual or group situation; time constraints; the attitude of the questioner; the personality of the questioner; the importance of the subject matter to the interviewer and interviewee; the extent of mutual respect; appearance, manner, dress; speech patterns and emphases on different words.

BOX 1.1   Research Methods and Organisational Behaviour

The disciplines and perspectives from which organisational behaviour is studied indicate various limitations on effective research and inquiry, and constraints which have to be accommodated. These are as follows.

Observation

Observation is limited by the standpoint of the observer. This may take any of the forms described below.

- **Unobtrusive:** in which the researcher identifies patterns of behaviour and activity without actually coming into contact with those being observed. An example of this is the study of clocking on cards to identify patterns of attendance and non-attendance among different groups of staff.
- **Removed:** in which the researcher observes the target group, either through a two-way mirror or else on video or film.
- **Non-participative:** in which the researcher is physically present in the particular setting but otherwise takes no active part in the proceedings. She confines herself to observing and reporting what actually occurred.
- **Participative:** in which the researcher explains her role in the situation and in which she may be asked for comments, criticisms and views as matters unfold.
- **Active:** in which the researcher becomes an employee or full group member, adopting the job and roles in order to gain first-hand knowledge and experience. This may be overt (in which case everyone knows why the researcher has joined the group) or covert in which the researcher is to all intents and purposes an ordinary member, and the rest of the group have no knowledge of her real purpose). The covert method is much more likely to lead to the other members continuing to act and behave as they always do. However, there are ethical implications to be considered, especially if extreme and, above all, unacceptable results are observed.

Experimentation

Experiments are used to test hypotheses – establish the veracity, integrity and certainty of a given proposal or point of view – arising, either from the disciplines or perspectives indicated above. These consist of the following.

- **Control:** the equivalent of setting up a laboratory and using elements to produce results in the same way as other sciences. The problem with controlled organisational behaviour experiments is that people usually know that they have been placed in an artificial situation for a given reason, and therefore tend to react to the fact of the experiment, rather than as they would elsewhere.

- **Piloting:** the conduct of a pre-test or pre-experiment in order to establish or disprove the basic veracity of the hypothesis.

- **Interaction:** the evaluation of the effects of one element (variable) on others. These may be observed in controlled and/or uncontrolled situations. In many cases the researcher will look at both in order to provide a basic veracity before taking the hypothesis into a wider situation. The effects of other variables may then also become apparent or be observed, or inferred.

- **Comparisons:** where results obtained in one situation are compared with those from others. This leads to analysis of the similarities and differences, and the effects of these on the results.

- **Limitations:** as indicated above, almost anything may limit the effect and integrity of organisational behaviour research. Limitations are also placed by the particular expertise and capability of the researcher. Organisations may, for their own reasons, be unwilling to commission or allow research to take place if it is likely to produce uncomfortable or threatening results; or when results are achieved that are uncomfortable or threatening, these may not be acceptable.

Validity, reliability, predictability

The main problem with organisational behaviour research and experiments concerns these limitations. Scientific experiments are capable of being constructed and reproduced in all situations in the certain knowledge that the results will always be the same: that they are both predictable and reliable and therefore valid. For organisational behaviour, no two situations are alike and it is impossible to recreate the same situation twice. Where the experiment is repeated with the same group of people in the same situation the following day, the results may quite legitimately vary, dependent upon the states of mind of the participants, what had gone on in the intervening period, and any outside interventions (for example, domestic arguments, booking a holiday, or a good or bad game of football or tennis could all affect the state of mind of individuals at work the following day).

Reliability and predictability therefore have margins of error and uncertainty within which results are achieved. Validity therefore, tends to be qualitative and judgemental rather than quantitative, though statics and other quantities are produced in this research. It is an evaluation of the conclusions drawn from the research, rather than the research itself which constitutes validity.

(d) Responses are also conditioned and limited through the responder not knowing the answer to questions or only knowing a part of it; they may also tell the interviewer what they think they want to hear, or what they think the answer should be; they may lie; they may give no answer; they may give an answer at variance with their own views or understanding because they perceive that this is expected of them; or they may just make something up.

(e) Responses are also conditioned by wider situational factors and constraints; matters of confidentiality; the use to which the information is going to be put; any opportunities or threats that are known or perceived to arise as the result of giving particular answers.

This has all then to be interpreted and analysed by others. Because there is no absolute basis or certainty, reception is subject to the expertise of the receivers and also matters of familiarity, credibility and acceptability, all of which are highly subjective.

This is the context in which the disciplines used in researching and investigating organisational behaviour are used. The picture is further complicated by the range of more general points of view from which organisations may be seen. These are as follows.

Structures and edifices	The analogy here is with buildings. Indeed, the physical premises often represent the hierarchical and value structure: for example, top managers on the top floor or away from the noise and bustle of production.
Aims and objectives	This is where relationships are drawn or inferred between the design of the organisation and the purposes for which it was designed.
Stability	This is where the future of the organisation is viewed in terms of its past history, its traditions, long standing areas of activity, achievements and reputation. This also often includes a community role as the provider of regular and constant employment in the particular locality or with certain skills and expertise.
Dominance–dependency	This concerns the general state of relationships between the organisation and its employees and also between particular groups. These relationships may be based on each or all of the following:

   (a) authority: the ability of one group (for example, supervisors) to get others (for example, workers) to carry out work because of their position;
   (b) function: the ability of one group to get others to work in particular ways because of their particular expertise;
   (c) economic: the ability to persuade people to work because of their need to earn money and support themselves;
   (d) social: the ability to persuade people to a particular point view because it is held to be right or important.

Restriction	This concerns the ability to guide, order and organise people in the pursuit of stated purposes (that is, to restrict their freedom to act as they might otherwise choose to do). It refers to the extent and perspective by which rules and procedures are drawn up and applied.
Creativity	This refers to the fact of continuous development that individuals (and therefore their organisations) are forever enlarging their knowledge, skills, capabilities and experiences, and that organisations have this ever-increasing fund at their disposal if they so wish. It also includes the approaches used to address issues and solve problems, and the presence or otherwise of inventiveness and imagination.
Interaction	This concerns the totality of the relationships that exist. It includes relations between and within individual groups, departments, divisions and functions; between different positions in the hierarchies; between different types and levels of expertise. It also refers to the interactions between work and non-work, between people and their work, between the organisation and other organisations, and the organisation in its wider environment.
Psychological contract	This concerns the extent to which a psychological bond (as well as a contract of employment) is deemed or perceived to exist between organisation and employees. It has implications for wider concerns for individual welfare, loyalty, identity and commitment.
Stakeholders	This refers to everyone who has a particular interest in the well-being of the organisation. Stakeholders are: staff, potential staff, former staff (especially those dependent on the organisation for references or a pension), customers, clients, shareholders, other backers, directors, governors, the community, influential figures.
Effectiveness	This refers to the need to maximise and optimise resources and to pursue aims and objectives successfully. This is concerned with the tangible (providing goods and services for sale at a profit and, in public service terms, meeting demands in full), and the intangible (generating levels of expectation, satisfaction and confidence among customers and clients so that they will return in the future).
Managerial	This refers to the ability to plan, organise, coordinate and control activities in the pursuit of effective performance. It refers to the ability to get things done through other people, arranging and ordering equipment, processes and materials, and designing work and organisational forms for this purpose.
Means and ends	This refers to the relationships between what is done and why, and the ways in which things are done and why. This concerns the nature and standard of the relationship between an organisation and its people, managers and staff, and levels of understanding, compliance

and acceptance of purposes. It has implications for organisational policies, ethics and integrity. It also normally directly relates behaviour and performance effectiveness.

Employment This refers to the basis of the employment relationship. The main strands of this are hiring people because there is work to be done which they can do, and giving opportunities for progress, enhancement, variety and development (in personal, professional, occupational and economic terms). In the past, some organisations sought to offer lifetime employment, guaranteeing that there would be no lay-offs or redundancies. Others tried to create complete stability and certainty based around permanent technology, skills, output and quality. Currently, both positions are untenable.

Conflict This refers to the adversarial or confrontational view taken of employment relations. It is based on a combination of mistrust and occupational status and personal differentials. It normally implies a proliferation of rules and regulations, administrative processes and the means of institutionalising and formalising conflict.

Cooperative The cooperative perspective takes the view that success and effectiveness are most likely to come about where people are encouraged and directed to work with each other for the good of the organisation and, by implication, for the good of each other and themselves. This can only be achieved through the creation of a harmonious environment, equality of opportunity and treatment, clear communications and well understood aims and objectives.

Case histories This refers to lessons learned and conclusions drawn from extensive studies of organisations and situations. These are then used as the basis for evaluating success and failure and may hold (or be perceived to hold) wider lessons for other organisations and situations.

BOX 1.2　Organisation Metaphors

Morgan (1986) adopted an analogical or metaphorical way of viewing and understanding organisations. These are as follows.

Machines

Organisations can be designed as if they are machines with orderly relations between clearly defined parts. This can provide the basis for efficient operation in a routine, reliable and predictable way. Machine organisations function better in a stable and protected environment.

Organisms

Organisations are seen as behaving like living systems in the same way as biological mechanisms.

Brains

Viewing organisations as brains involves thinking about them as inventive, rational, flexible and creative.

Cultures

This is where organisations are made up of their own distinctive sets of ideology, values, rituals and systems of belief and practice.

Political systems

Means are required to create order and direct people; organisations are therefore concerned with authority, power, superior–subordinate relationships, reporting relationships and the resolution of conflicts of interest.

Psychic prisons

This view identified the behavioural constraints and psychological boundaries placed around people and groups in particular situations.

Flux and transformation

As everything around them is constantly changing, so organisations must continually adapt and improve in response to this and in order to survive.

Instruments of domination

The power relations within organisations, the ability of individuals in groups to impose their will on others.

Morgan's purpose in drawing up these contrasting metaphors is to aid the understanding of the complex nature of organisational life and to cast a fresh light on the dynamics and components of organisational behaviour. Morgan points out that these metaphors are not fixed categories and are not mutually exclusive. An organisation can be a mix of each with one or more dominating. Combinations would normally be expected to change over periods of time.

■ Conclusions

Understanding the behaviour of organisations arises from combining the elements of the sciences or disciplines indicated with a number of more general and overtly subjective assertions. The total picture is incomplete, ever-changing and constantly developing. The drive is therefore towards as complete an understanding as possible rather than towards absolute enlightenment. This understanding is based on the application of methods of research and inquiry that are capable of contextual evaluation. This also concerns the validation and reliability of results and conclusions, especially when the divergent and conflicting nature of the different perspectives is considered. Ultimately, conclusions and predictions about human, and therefore organisational, behaviour are always subject to measures of uncertainty and interpretation.

CHAPTER 2

The organisation and its environment

■ Introduction

Organisations are created on the basis that more can be achieved by people working in harmony and towards a stated purpose than by individuals acting alone. It is also more efficient and effective to specialise in seeking to serve or fulfil a given set of wants or needs. Resources – technology, expertise, information, finance and property – can then be commanded and ordered for the stated purpose. Activities can be determined, coordinated and controlled.

The result of this is that society is more or less founded on a highly complex and all-pervading network of organisations, each of which serves a given purpose and all of which serve the entire range of purposes required. Organisations pervade all aspects of life: economic, social, political, cultural, religious, communal and family. They serve needs and essentials (food, shelter, health, education, water, energy and communications), as well as wants and choices (cola, cinema, football). They serve these needs and wants from before the cradle, through every aspect of life until after the grave.

An organisation is any body that is constituted for such a given purpose, and which then establishes and conducts activities in pursuit of this.

For those who work in them, organisations form a distinctive and significant part of society. Human beings generally both need and enjoy the company of other people. Organisations fulfil social as well as technical, occupational and professional needs.

Those who interact with organisations – as customers, clients and suppliers – require a positive relationship based on satisfaction, expectation and value.

From this, it becomes apparent that there is a great complexity in the relationships between organisations: between organisations and their place in the wider environment, between those who work within them, and between organisations and those who come to them from products and services.

This may be summarised as the relationships between organisations, people and the environment. It is now necessary to consider in more detail the factors and components that affect these relationships. These in turn form the basis of understanding the ways in which people behave in organisations and the creation of effective and successful behaviour in organisations.

Organisations may be considered from a variety of different points of view, including:

- legal status and formal regulation;
- primary beneficiaries (those for whom the organisation is especially important for some reason);
- approach and attitude to staff;
- psychological contract, or the nature and level of mutual commitment between organisation and staff.

■ Legal status

The main forms are as follows.

1. **Sole traders**, in which individuals set themselves up as a going concern and put their own resources into it. People who do this are entitled to receive any profits or surpluses accrued; and are also responsible in full for any losses.
2. **Partnership**, in which two or more people establish themselves as a going concern as above.
3. **Limited company**, in which the organisation is based on the private sale of shares which provides it with a financial and capital base. The company is given its own life and entity in this way and it receives any profits made and is responsible for making good any losses. The liability of shareholders for any losses is limited to the extent of their share ownership.
4. **PLC or corporation**: basically the same as for a limited company but where shares are offered for sale to the general public on a recognised stock exchange.
5. **Friendly or mutual society**, in which the benefits accrued by activities are distributed among members as agreed between them.
6. **Cooperative**, usually constituted as a company or partnership in which everyone involved has a stake (financial, physical or psychological).
7. **Public bodies and public corporations**: central, regional and local government functions to provide essential public services and ensure adequate infrastructure, transport and communications for the society at large.
8. **Quangos** (quasi autonomous non-governmental organisations) are autonomous entities funded by government grant and constituted for a particular purpose.
9. **Charities**, funded by donations and other receipts for stated purposes; these funds are then distributed to the areas with which the charity is concerned. Charities must be registered with the charity commissioner in order to carry out activities in this way.

■ Primary beneficiaries

Primary beneficiaries are those people for whom the organisation is especially important or for whom it was constituted. A primary beneficiary approach requires organisations to be looked at as follows.

1. **Business organisations**, where the primary beneficiaries are shareholders and staff, and where the benefits accrue from providing products and services required by customers and clients.
2. **Utilities**, where the primary beneficiary is society at large. Utilities include gas, electricity, water, transport, post and telecommunications organisations.
3. **Public service organisations**, where the primary beneficiaries are particular client groups drawn in because of their characteristics and which include provision for the homeless, destitute, elderly, disabled and handicapped (some of these functions are also carried out by charities).
4. **Cooperatives**, where the primary beneficiaries are all those who work in them, and a cooperative coordinates its business from the point of view of this mutual commitment and identity.
5. **Convenience organisations**, where the primary beneficiaries are those who avail themselves of the organisation's products and services on the basis of convenience. This includes village shops and amenities. A form of this is also to be found in those organisations that take a 'just in time' approach to the purchase of raw materials.
6. **Institutions**, where the primary beneficiaries are those who avail themselves of the institutions services and facilities, or who are sent there (for whatever reason) by society. Examples include schools, colleges – and prisons.
7. **Mutual benefit associations**, where the primary beneficiaries are the members (these include trade unions, churches, political parties, clubs, friendly societies and cooperatives).
8. **Service organisations**, where the primary beneficiaries are the clients who come to use its services for stated reasons, or when they need them on particular occasions. Examples include hospitals and the fire service.
9. **Bodies for the regulation of society**, constituted by government and given the means and wherewithal to act in the interests of the members of the society. The main examples of these are the police and the military.
10. **Common general organisations**, where the primary beneficiaries are the general public. These include police services and also education, health and social services.

■ Approach to staff

Organisations may also be viewed from the standpoint from which they regard their staff. They may be categorised in the following ways.

1. **Unitary**, in which the aims, objectives, hopes, fears, aspirations and ambitions of the individual must be harmonised and integrated with those of the organisation, and where necessary subordinated so that the overall purpose of the organisation remains the main driving force.
2. **Pluralist**, in which the organisation recognises the divergence and often conflicting aims, objectives and drives of the people who work for it. Organisations that take

this view normally include opportunities for personal and professional (as well as organisational) fulfilment. The basis is that by recognising this divergence and attending to all needs, the organisation's needs will be satisfied.

3. **Cooperative**, in which the organisation establishes a psychological and behavioural basis of partnership and involvement based on the value of the contribution that everyone is to make.

4. **Confrontational**: an adversarial approach to staff. This is based at best, on the recognition that harmony of objectives is impossible, which leads to the creation of systems and processes for the containment and management of conflict. At worst it is based on mistrust and coercion, often stemming from a lack of genuine value placed on staff.

■ Psychological contract

Organisations may be viewed from the nature of the psychological contract that they engage in with their staff. This is the result of implications and expectations that arise as the result of the given organisational, occupational, professional and personal relationships in specific situations. They vary between all organisations and situations and may be summarised as follows.

1. **Coercive**, whereby the relationship between organisation and staff, and also organisation and customer, is founded on a negative. An example of this is prison: the prisoners are there against their will. It is also present where sections of the community are forced or pressurised into using a monopoly or near-monopoly for an essential commodity or service (for example, electricity, telecommunication, petrol and fuel). It also can be present in institutions such as schools and colleges where the children or students attend because they are required to do so by the society.

2. **Alienative**, whereby the relationship between staff and organisation is negative. This has traditionally applied to large and sophisticated organisations and especially to those staff working on production lines and in administrative hierarchies where they have no, or very little, control over the quality and output of work.

3. **Remunerative**, whereby the relationship between staff and organisation is clearly drawn in terms of money in return for efforts and attendance. It is normally to be found as the dominant feature where there is also a low level of mutual identity between staff and organisation.

4. **Calculative**, whereby the staff have a low commitment to organisation goals and a high commitment to current levels of earning and satisfaction. It is again a key feature of the wage–work bargain for production and administrative staff. For those with high levels of professional and technical expertise, the calculative relationship is based on the ability to practise, the need to find an employer and outlet for those skills and individual drives to serve and become expert.

5. **Normative**, whereby the individual commitment to organisational purpose is very high. This is found in religious organisations political parties and trade unions. Some business organisations also set distinctive standards of policy and practice. It is

effective as long as the wage – work bargain itself is sound and the organisation accepts a range of obligations and responsibilities to ensure that it is maintained.

Viewing organisations from a variety of positions in these ways indicates the background against which aims and objectives are to be drawn up. It also indicates the source of some of the limitations and constraints that have to be taken into account when considering the capabilities of organisations and the nature and relationship of these with the purposes that are to be pursued.

■ Organisational goals, aims and objectives

However constituted and from whatever point of view they are considered, all organisations have purposes: goals, aims and objectives, their reason for being. These provide the essential foundation on which the organisation is to be built. Some essential features of aims and objectives should therefore be defined.

■ Clarity

Aims and objectives should be specific and capable of being understood and accepted by all those who are to be engaged in their pursuit.

■ Measurable

Aims and objectives provide the measures against which success and failure are to be evaluated. The clearer the means of measurement, the more accurate the assessment; and then the easier it is to establish why something has been successful or why it has failed (as well as the fact of the matter).

■ Capability

Organisations combine resources – human, technology, financial and other equipment – to pursue their goals. The purpose is to maximise and optimise usage of those resources. Inadequacy of resources leads to loss of capability. Surfeit of resources leads to waste and profligacy. This may also lead to incapability caused by a loss of drive or urgency: if too many resources seem to be available, those concerned may feel no need to maximise/optimise performance.

■ Timescales

These act as a general discipline on the organisation as specific performance indicators on groups and individuals (see also Box 2.1).

BOX 2.1   Timescales

It is useful at this stage to indicate the nature of the relationships between organisations and pressures of time. Time acts in different circumstances as a motivator, stressor, resource constraint and performance constraint; and as a measure of organisation effectiveness and efficiency.

Periods

1. **Short**: concerned with the present and immediate future and around which activities can normally be mapped and planned precisely and accurately.
2. **Medium**: concerned with the period beyond the immediate future in which a good idea of the likely nature and range of activities can be given; and these can be planned and mapped with some degree of certainty.
3. **Long term**: concerned with the future as far as it can genuinely be foreseen. The long term refers also to the ability of the organisation to continue to be effective and/or remain in profit. It is also a reflection of the extent of confidence that it has in its own continuity.

Because of the globalisation of business and public activities, and the changing nature of technology, work and patterns of work, time periods (especially the medium to long term) are getting shorter. It is currently not possible to plan in detail for a five-year period in any sector. This is because such plans are overtaken by events, technological advance, loss of market, gain of new markets and global events (for example, the ending of the Cold War). All of these can and do come about very quickly, nullifying careful and painstaking plans and schemes of work that have been drawn up to give the organisation a long term measure of certainty. While absolute definitions of short, medium and long term vary between organisations and between departments and functions within them, any meaning ascribed to 'long term' is unlikely to be much further into the future than two years.

The main exception to this is the need to keep a diary of events for the distant future: for example, that a production line is to be replaced in five years' time, or that a building will require particular maintenance in ten years' time. Both presuppose however, that the particular organisation will still exist in that time and that it will still own the particular items and continue to have a use for them.

Understanding

Short and medium term periods are much easier for any individual to grasp, recognise and understand. If something is to happen by the end of the week, there is a very clear understanding. If something is to happen in three years' time, the individual experiences something between vague awareness, on the one hand, and a lack of concern until towards the end of the period on the other.

This can be very damaging and stressful. If, for example, an organisation says that it will bring in a performance-related pay scheme in 18 months' time, people are caught between the contrasting perceptions of

'If it is such a good idea, why wait 18 months, why not bring it in now?'

and

'If it is not such a good idea, why are we having it at all?'

More generally, a lack of confidence is produced among the people who work in organisations that do produce highly detailed plans for the long term future which then have to be changed on a regular basis. The eventual outcome normally bears little resemblance to that which was mooted in the first place.

Motivation

Time acts as a motivator when it is sufficiently precisely stated as part of the framework in which jobs and tasks have to be carried out. Again, it acts as a demotivator when this is not sufficiently clear or recognisable. The relationship between time and task is therefore important. The time allowed must be sufficient to carry out the work: if it is insufficient, the work will simply not get done; if it is over-sufficient (for example, if someone is given six months to produce a simple two-page report) it may still get left until the last minute.

Language

Language clarifies the time factor. Use of phrases such as 'a matter of urgency', 'a matter of importance' and 'as soon as possible' give impressions of concern and priority but not full understanding. Use of phrases such as 'by 3 o'clock', 'by the end of this month' and 'by February' leave no room for misunderstanding at all.

■ Efficiency and Effectiveness

P. F. Drucker defined these as:

efficiency is doing things right;
effectiveness is doing the right thing.

Efficiency is therefore concerned with performance during the task and attention to best use of resources. Effectiveness is concerned with the end result; it may also be concerned with resources, especially where these constitute the building blocks of the eventual outcome.

BOX 2.2   Successful Objectives

A useful acronym is SMART. SMART objectives should be:

- Specific
- Measurable
- Achievable
- Recognisable
- Time constrained

This is a useful summary of much of the discussion so far.

The greater the presence of each element, the more certain the organisation is of its purpose. Where one or more of these is not present, there are normally questions over the general success and effectiveness of performance.

Aims and objectives are normally broken down into sub-aims and objectives, and this leads to the basis on which work is structured. In turn, this leads to the identification of the types of individuals required and their skills, knowledge and qualities and the organisation of people into groups, departments, divisions and functions. Establishment of clarity of purpose at the outset is therefore essential if this range of activities is itself to be effective.

BOX 2.3   Aims and Objectives: Examples

The Good

'to increase sales by 30% by the end of the year'
'to increase output from 1 tonne to 3 tonnes by the end of the month'

The great advantage of writing things in this way is that they are clearly and easily understood; they fulfil the SMART criteria. The main problem arises when they are seen as ends in themselves rather than as means to an end.

The Bad

'to promote the social well-being of groups with physical, mental and environmental handicaps to enable them to function as far as possible as a community and within the community of their choice'

This is imprecise and unintelligible and draws people away from it rather than towards it. The approach clouds rather than clarifies issues.

On the other hand, producing objectives in this way at least gives opportunities for improvement. This could be rewritten as 'the establishment of the following facilities and services . . . by a given deadline, for people with physical, mental and environmental handicaps'

The Ugly

'to seek to maintain our position as far as possible within the foreseeable future'
'to seek to maximise opportunities as and when they arise'
'to seek to provide a range of services for the customer or client group as and when these are required'

Objectives written in this way are insidious and destructive. Overtly the language used is positive; in reality nobody is bound to anything. Invariably this means the organisation itself has lost its sense of purpose and direction. Such objectives become a barrier to effective performance rather than an instrument for its achievement.

BOX 2.4   Organisational Performance

Organisational performance may be classified under the following headings.

1. **Steady-state**: the conduct of day-to-day activities, routines and tasks; the creation of structures, systems, rules and procedures to ensure that these continue; the creation of stability and confidence.
2. **Innovative**: the drive to continuously improve all aspects of the organisation and its work; seeking improvements in efficiency and effectiveness; seeking new products, opportunities and markets; seeking new and better means of staff management, organisation and development.
3. **Pioneering**: the drive for radically new activities and markets; the drive for radical new technology, its uses and applications; the drive for radically new means and methods of organisation, staffing and management.
4. **Crisis**: the handling of emergencies, problems and dramas when they occur; the structuring of activities and resources to ensure that there is a balance between being able to meet crises when they do happen or taking steps to ensure that these occur as infrequently as possible; the avoidance of crisis management (lurching from one emergency to another); the recognition and addressing of the likely and actual components of crises in the given situation.
5. **Strategic and directional**: concerned with the organisation, its purposes, goals and overall aims and objectives; the monitoring, review and evaluation of these and of the activities organised and structured in their pursuit; attention to the success and effectiveness – and profitability – of performance; taking remedial action where required. Strategic and directional performance also includes attention to the nature and mix of steady-state, innovative, pioneering and crisis aspects indicated above.

This can then be related to the different headings under which objectives are classified. In general, these are a combination of the following elements.

1. **Strategic**: concerned with overall direction of the organisation and the focus for all other activities.
2. **Operational**: concerned with the effectiveness of day-to-day activities in pursuit of the strategic.
3. **Behavioural**: concerned with the human aspects of the organisation, management and supervisory style and the aura of general well-being.
4. **Ethical**: concerned with particular standards of operation and interaction, the ways in which staff, customers, the community and the environment are treated and the general level of respect in which they are held.
5. **Attitudes and values**: the psychological focus of the organisation and requirements and expectations placed on staff and customers.
6. **Superior and subordinate or supporting aims and objectives**: the interrelationship, harmony and unit of purpose and drive between overall aims and the goals set for departments, divisions, functions and individuals.

■ Other boundaries

Other boundaries around overall purposes, aims and objectives are as follows.

1. Policies, representing the ways in which the organisation seeks and determines to operate, and the standards (especially of honesty and integrity) that it sets for itself. These normally refer to:
   (a) attention to staff and staff relations;
   (b) attention to customers and customer relations;
   (c) attention to community and community relations;
   (d) attention to the environment and waste disposal;
   (e) standards of image, marketing and public relations;
   (f) the promotion of equity and equality;
   (g) the extent of commitment to product and service quality, and customer satisfaction.

2. Specific operational constraints, the interaction with suppliers, distributors and customers; any legal constraints; the effects of internal and external pressure groups and vested interests.
3. The preferences and drives of shareholders and other stakeholders, especially in terms of the nature of the results required and the deadlines for these.
4. The nature of expertise required. Where persons of high professional or technical qualifications are employed, there is often a potential conflict between their commitment to the organisation and to their profession or occupation.

5. Ethical and social constraints. These are based on the norms, values and standards of the wider society and communities in which activities are to be conducted; and also the extent to which the organisation itself is, or seeks to be, a good citizen.
6. The need for discipline, guidance and motivation on the part of staff and the creation of support functions, procedures and processes of supervision and management for these reasons.
7. Competitive pressures: the need to compete for business, work and customers; and the need to compete for staff and resources. Competition for staff and resources may have both external and internal constraints.
8. Cooperative pressure: the extent of dependency on other bodies and organisations (such as suppliers or distributors; also banks and other sources of finance; any other particular expertise required); the extent to which other bodies are allowed to influence the direction and purpose of the particular organisation.
9. Relationships between means and ends, and the priority that is placed on each; the extent to which people and groups are rewarded for hard work (means) as distinct from effective or productive work (ends); the views taken by the organisation of success and failure.

These constitute the main constraints within which organisations have to set their aims and objectives if they are to be effective. It is impossible to work in isolation from these except in the very short term and where a monopoly on the particular product or service is held.

BOX 2.5 Management by Objectives

The concept of management by objectives grew out of the attention given by Drucker and others to the need for establishing means by which the success and failure of managerial performance could be measured. It also provided the means for focusing on results rather than activity, by translating corporate objectives into measures of individual, group and departmental performance. It concentrated on the following aspects.

1. Key tasks, key results, performance standards and area of activity. It also provided for control data, and the availability and use of information against which task performance could be measured. These were established in both quantitative (measurable) and qualitative (not so easily measurable) areas.
2. Work improvement plans, setting key tasks against action plans, target dates, and again using control data to monitor performance.
3. Regular performance reviews based on participation and agreement and concentrating on future directions as well as assessment of the present.
4. Potential reviews and previews, based on concepts of career development and succession planning, and concerned with the capability and likelihood of success in the next job (whatever that was to be). This included attention to training and development needs, as well as attention to performance outputs and requirements.

The main pitfalls and criticisms of the approach are as set out below.

1. It tends to cast activities in stone unless attention is also paid to the need for flexibility, dynamism, adaptability and responsiveness.
2. It tends to assume a state of stability over the period; the process is easily disrupted in practice by changes in superior–subordinate relations, new work demands and priorities, operational constraints and crises, or changes in technology and work practices.
3. It can be very bureaucratic and time-consuming to establish. This tends to reinforce the perception that once established, it has to be religiously followed because so much time and so many resources have gone into setting it up in the first place. People do not like to perceive that their time has been wasted.
4. It focuses on objectives in ways that leave little room for judgement or initiative.

Much of this clearly summarises both the boundaries within which aims and objectives are to be established and the problems inherent in doing so. In the UK much of the work that has been done in this area comes from the activities of John Humble, who saw management by objectives as the means of integrating organisational goals of growth, profit and effectiveness with managerial activities to ensure the unity of purpose required. In public service terms, this translated into terms of reliability, coverage and efficiency, as well as management morale.

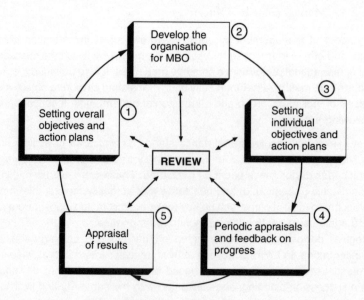

Figure 2.1   Management by objectives (MBO)

■ Tangible and intangible objectives

P. F. Drucker (1955, 1990) identifies tangible and intangible objectives these are classified as follows.

Tangible

• Market standing, reputation and position, sales performance.
• Innovation, enterprise, pioneering, research and development, general attention to the future.
• Productivity and output performance.
• Use of physical human premises, capital and other financial resources.
• Productivity, profitability and effectiveness.

Intangible

• Managerial performance and development.
• Worker performance and attitude.
• Public responsibility.

Attention is necessary in each area. While the balance will vary between organisations, neglect in any one area is likely to weaken the whole. It is also designed to ensure that the organisation is not blinded by extremes of performance in one area to the detriment of the others. For example, excellent sales performance may lead to feelings of complacency and lack of attention to the need for new products when the current range becomes obsolete. Conversely, poor sales performance may be seen in isolation as a crisis; or, as long as the rest of the activities are considered to be fundamentally sound, this may lead to a focusing of managerial attention to bring this aspect of performance up to the standards of the rest.

The basis is therefore:

• to give a clear statement of direction to the organisation and all its departments and functions;
• to indicate proper courses of action and standards of attitude and behaviour;
• to indicate what effective performance is in all areas, and to indicate the means and measures by which this is to be judged and evaluated;
• to provide a rationale for removing that which is unproductive and failing to contribute;
• to indicate areas of responsibility, authority and accountability.

A feature of organisations and groups that fail to perform effectively is that they are not clear about their general purpose or why they have been allocated particular work.

Aims and objectives should therefore be stated precisely (even in the intangible areas). If this is not possible, it usually means that the purpose or focus of activities has not been properly thought out. Also, if aims and objectives are written down, people can refer to them when necessary. This again tends to lead to a clarity of forethought. Above all, if they are wrong they provide a basis for change and an indication of alternative courses of action.

Aims and objectives should be positive and demanding, rather than negative or coercive. They should reflect the need to motivate and to improve and progress. They should be stated in ways that everyone affected both understands and can identify with; and again, in areas of poor or reduced performance, it is likely that a lack of understanding will be one of the contributors to this.

Drucker (1986b) wrote about this as follows.

1. Goals should be written down to give greater credibility and to serve as a visual reminder.
2. Goals should be positive and not negative.
3. Goals should have precise aims and targets.
4. Goals should be personal and related directly to members of departments; they should reconcile and acknowledge the conflicting and divergent purposes that everyone has in being there.
5. Goals should be specific, quantifiable and measurable.
6. Goals should be challenging, motivating the department and its individuals to work harder, more effectively and more productively than in the past.
7. Goals should be realistic and achievable.
8. Goals should be prioritised.
9. Goals should be understood, accepted and valued by everyone.

■ Limitations

The limitations on effectiveness begin where any of the SMART features are not apparent or complete. Further problems arise when the following are either dominant or not capable of being reconciled with overall purpose.

1. The drive for volume of work rather than quality or effectiveness. This is exacerbated where rewards are given for volume. This is satisfactory only as long as competitive position can be maintained on the basis of volume and as long as some level of profit is achieved. It is invariably unsatisfactory in the long term unless accompanied by drives for quality and effectiveness.
2. Lack of attention to supposedly non-quantifiable aims and objectives, especially for managers, administrators and support functions. At its most positive this gives those categories of staff considerable latitude to exercise judgement, initiative, creativity and enthusiasm and these are the usual excuses cited by organisations that fail to

address the problem of establishing effective aims and objectives for these categories of staff. More usually however, it is a symptom of failure to structure and direct these activities in the organisation's best interests and harness the qualities indicated in this pursuit. The invariable result is that managers set and pursue their own agenda, achieving high rewards for themselves and minimum-to-satisfactory levels of success for the organisation.

3. Displacement occurs where the work itself becomes the overriding aim. Attention becomes focused on length rather than effectiveness of attendance; volume rather than quality or purpose of work; day-to-day activities, clearing the in-tray and invariably the backlog; attention to immediate tasks and requests; attendance at meetings.

4. Operational and political influence of interest groups increases at the expense of their productive output. This tends to put pressure on resources and stress on individuals and groups. Internal competition for resources becomes a resource-consuming process and an objective in itself.

5. Adherence to, and operation of, procedures and rule books becomes a goal in itself. Focus is therefore placed on compliance and conformity rather than effectiveness.

6. Goal conflict is not addressed or reconciled. Such conflicts often occur as the result of differing pressures and strains (for example, professional commitments, administrative requirements; production and maintenance; production and sales). They are compounded where more than two different elements are present.

7. Compliance is not achieved. This is either because the required attitudes and standards are not recognised or valued, or because those working in the organisation place no value on the overall purpose and the work is not carried out in its pursuit.

■ Decision-making

Decisions are taken at all levels: strategic and policy; operational, divisional and departmental; managerial and supervisory; and individual. Whatever the level, there are certain fundamental considerations to be considered if the process is to be effective and successful. There are also different stages which have to be understood and followed.

Decision-making is a process as well as a linear activity. It is dependent upon effective systems.

Current decisions and patterns of decisions arise from that which has previously occurred and the present situation. Decisions taken at present have direct impact and implications on the future. Decisions taken, for example, in a marketing department, have implications for, and effects on, production, sales, human resource management, purchasing and supplies. Decisions taken by a human resource department (for example, when new staff are taken on) have implications for the subsequent performance of the organisation.

This is the context in which elements of the process are considered. These are as follows.

1. PROGRESSION   2. PROCESS

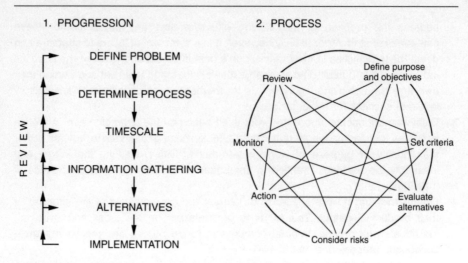

Figure 2.2   Decision-making: model and process

■ **Problem or issue definition**

This is the starting point of the process. Once this is defined, the likely effects and consequences of particular courses of action can begin to be understood. Failure to do this may lead to considerable waste of time, effort and resource.

■ **Process determination**

Much of this depends on culture, structure, environmental and other pressures on the organisation or department involved. It also depends on ways of working and the personalities and groups involved. There may also be key groups – staff, customers, vested interests, pressure groups – who must be consulted on particular matters. Not to do this, in spite of the fact that the decision may be 'right', is likely to minimise or even nullify the whole effect.

■ **Timescale**

Time is involved heavily in process determination. There is also a trade-off between the quality and volume of information that can be gathered and the time available to do this. The longer the timescale, the better the chance of gaining adequate information and considering it and evaluating it effectively. However, this also increases the cost of the eventual course of action. On the other hand, a quick decision may involve hidden extras at the implementation stage if insufficient time has been spent on the background.

■ Information gathering

Very few decisions are taken with perfect information; conversely, decisions made without any information are pure guesswork. Both quality and volume of information are required; and means for the understanding, evaluation and review of that which is gathered are also essential.

■ The alternatives

The result of the process is that alternative courses of action become apparent. At the very least there is always the choice of doing nothing.

■ Implementation

This is the point of action. It arises as the result of working through each of the previous elements. The choice made affects future courses of action; as well as the choice, the reasons for which it was made should be understood.

This is an attempt to provide a rationale for courses of action that often have to be taken in ways that are not fully logical. Part of the purpose is therefore to recognise where the non-rational elements lie and, in recognising these, how they can best be accommodated. It is not a prescription for providing perfect decisions. It is rather the means by which opportunities and consequences of following particular courses of action may be understood, assessed and evaluated.

■ Decision-making: other factors

■ Risk and uncertainty

Uncertainty occurs where no information exists. This in itself underlines the need to gain as much knowledge and understanding as possible in advance of choosing a particular course of action. However, there is an element of risk in all decision-taking. This is reduced by the quality and volume of information available, and the accuracy of its evaluation.

■ Participation and consultation

This is necessary where a wide measure of support from among the workforce community or public at large is required. The purpose here is to generate understanding and acceptance of courses of action.

It may also be necessary to consider:

- legal constraints, affecting all aspects of business and organisation practice;
- public interest, public pressure, lobby and special interest groups;
- economic, social and political groups, including consumer groups, environmental lobbies, local and public authorities, public agencies and statutory bodies, industrial lobbies and staff representative bodies;
- committees and other formally constituted boards.

■ Organisational adjustment

This is where the process is limited or constrained, based on each of the factors indicated. The normal result is that the organisation alters, adjusts or limits its activities in some way as the result.

Sufficient time and resource must be set aside to deal with these, if what is proposed is to be supported and accepted.

Effective decisions are therefore arrived at through a combination of the preferred and chosen direction, together with recognising and accommodating a means by which this chosen direction can be made successful. A large part of the consultation, participation, staff and public communication processes are directed at generating understanding and acceptance of particular courses of action. Organisations must accept that everyone is much more likely to follow a course of action if this is understood. If they do not understand what they are being asked to do, people tend either to reject the matter outright, or else to view it with suspicion and uncertainty.

BOX 2.6   Satisficing

Many of these limitations were first identified by H. A. Simon (1969) as parts of the process of achieving satisfactory performance or satisficing. Simon identified three levels of performance, as set out below.

Excellent: high achievement, output, quality leading to high levels of profit effectiveness and satisfaction. This was in reality achieved by very few.

Unsatisfactory: low and unacceptable achievement, output, quality and volume leading to losses, inefficiency, ineffectiveness and dissatisfaction. This would be remedied by training, development (disciplinary activities where necessary) and greater management focus on acceptable performance.

Satisfactory: achieved by most and producing acceptable levels of output, volume, quality and leading to steady acceptable – and therefore satisfactory – levels of profit and effectiveness. In practice he found this was an acceptable and likely state of organisation performance. It included attention to volume rather than quality of work; and the freedom of managers to set their own agenda as long as organisation objectives were met at least partly. It recognised that organisations would tend not to try to measure the overtly unquantifiable. Satisfactory performance was apparent where the organisation continued to exist for a long period of time.

He coined the word satisficing to explain this. It is defined as 'the ability to achieve satisfactory performance'. This also influenced decision-making processes; managers would tend to take decisions based on the ability to achieve some measure of satisfaction rather than seeking high levels of performance which were not always achievable (especially where the latter had high attendant risks or requirements for increases in commitment that could not always be made).

■ Failure

As stated above, a key ingredient of performance failure is insufficient attention to establishing a clarity and understanding of purpose at the outset. Other features are now identified.

1. Insufficient attention to the behavioural aspects of operations, above all in creating effective and suitable conditions and support systems as the basis for carrying out the work. This also includes insufficient attention to the need to motivate and value the staff engaged in the work.
2. Insufficient attention to the quantifiable performance requirements of management and to the establishment of proper aims and objectives in managerial, administrative and support functions.
3. Prioritising short-term results at the expense of the long term future together with the overconsumption of resources in this way. This normally occurs because the organisation can see easy results if it pursues the short-term course. It also occurs because of the need for triumphs on the part of a key figure or particular department.
4. Artificial constraints and deadlines, driven by budget systems and reporting relationships, requiring energy and resources to be used in non-productive and

often counter-productive activities, rather than as a check on continuous performance.

5. Establishment of priorities for reasons other than performance effectiveness and especially for reasons of publicity, kudos, status and the demands of key figures for their own purposes.

6. Setting unreasonable deadlines for the achievement of particular objectives.

7. Casting plans, aims and objectives as 'tablets of stone' so that once they are written they are never to be changed or modified.

8. Failure to recognise that which cannot be controlled and which may nevertheless have great effects on organisational activities. This includes changes in customer demands and expectations; legislative changes; the activities of competitors; loss of sources of supply; change in relationships with distributors; and so on.

9. Complacency, often based on a long history of success, continuity and achievement in the past, and which tends to lead to feelings of infallibility and immortality. This leads to loss of commitment to purpose, loss of focus and an idea of what constitutes truly effective performance.

10. Attention to means rather than ends and the confusion of hard work with productive work. Sheer volume of work therefore becomes the measure of performance rather than the purpose for which it is being conducted. Or, to quote a former Chief Executive of the Cadillac Car Company: 'Any fool can learn to stay within budget. But I have met only a handful of managers in my life who could draw up a budget that is worth staying within.'

■ Systems

A system is a collection of interrelated parts and components which form a whole. Typical organisation systems are production, communication and electronic data systems. Systems may first be defined as either closed or open, and then as formal, informal or networks.

■ Closed

Closed systems are those that are self-contained and self-sufficient, and do not require other interactions to make them work. There are very few systems that are genuinely closed. Some domestic central heating systems are more or less closed. In these cases the components are assembled. The system is switched on and must operate continuously or else break down. Even in these cases they are dependent upon being fed a constant supply of energy to ensure continuity of operation. They are also dependent upon maintenance, both to prevent break-downs and to make repairs when faults occur.

■ **Open**

Open systems are those that require constant interaction with their environment to make them work (see Figure 2.3). The characteristics are:

(a) the need to provide inputs and energy to make sure that the process – the system – is able to operate (inputs and energy come from elsewhere in the environment);
(b) the discharge of outputs – production waste and energy residue and exhaust – into the environment;
(c) the operation of the system itself as the conversion process.

Inputs (External)	Process The System	Outputs
Expertise Supplies Components ⟶ Resources Energy Demands	Technology Expertise ⟶ Energy	Products Services ⟶ Waste Exhaust

Figure 2.3   An open system

■ **Formal**

Devised and developed by the organisation with specific purposes in mind and with the view that effective operations are dependent upon those that are put in place.

■ **Informal**

Devised by individuals and groups to facilitate their own place and well-being in the organisation and to fill those gaps left by the formal approach.

■ **Networks**

The combination of formal with informal networks are normally based on human interaction and information exchange (and sometimes information hoarding and trading). Their purpose is to support both the operations of the organisation and also to ensure the continuity and stability of the position of individuals and groups.

Organisation systems may now be shown as in Figure 2.4. They convert human activity, energy, information resources and components of raw materials into products and services, usable information, by-products and waste.

INPUT	PROCESS	OUTPUT
Raw Materials	Technology	Finished goods
Energy	Applied expertise	Services
Expertise →	Applied information →	Waste →
Components	Coordination	Exhaust
Information	Planning	
Demand	Control	
Ideas	Supervison	
Inventions		

Figure 2.4   Organisation systems

■ Main systems

Main systems are those devised to ensure that the organisation can pursue its core purposes successfully. They are normally the production services and information systems essential to well-being and success. They may be largely:

● human or social, where achievement of the core purpose depends greatly on interactions between people;
● technological, where achievement of the core purpose depends greatly on the output of large volumes of items;
● socio-technical, in which the interaction between the two is critical.

In practice, a mix of the social and technical invariably occurs. The system itself consists of the combination of technical and social components (see Figure 2.5).

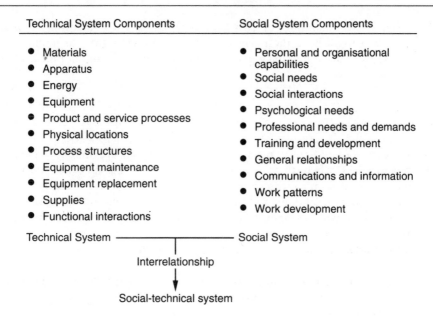

Technical System Components	Social System Components
• Materials	• Personal and organisational capabilities
• Apparatus	• Social needs
• Energy	• Social interactions
• Equipment	• Psychological needs
• Product and service processes	• Professional needs and demands
• Physical locations	• Training and development
• Process structures	• General relationships
• Equipment maintenance	• Communications and information
• Equipment replacement	• Work patterns
• Supplies	• Work development
• Functional interactions	

Technical System ——————— Social System

Interrelationship

Social-technical system

Figure 2.5   Socio-technical systems

■ Support systems

These are devised in the same way in order to harmonise and order the rest of the work to ensure that the prime activities are provided with the resources and sub-activities necessary to remain effective.

■ Maintenance systems

These are devised in order to prevent any blockages occurring and to put these right when they do happen. Maintenance systems require attention to both social and technical aspects. A part of organisation and individual development is concerned with maintaining the human resource. This includes attention to morale and commitment, as well as skills, knowledge and expertise.

Technological maintenance consists of regular servicing of equipment, depreciation and replacement. It also includes the purchasing and introduction of new hardware and software, and the training and development of staff so that it can be used effectively.

Systems for the handling of customer complaints are also forms of maintenance and should have the purpose of putting things right and maintaining standards; and also of making a general contribution to the development of the effectiveness of work.

■ Crisis systems

These are devised and put in place on the basis that they are seldom to be used, but nevertheless when they are required they can be speedily energised. Emergency systems are clear examples of this. So also are systems for the handling of operational input and distribution breakdowns and hiatuses, and in these cases these will normally consist of hot-line arrangements for emergency supplies, activities and distribution.

In this context, the specific concerns of systems are:

- production and service outputs and the management of operations and projects;
- research and development, innovation and concern with the future;
- maintenance functions;
- attention to resource management matters and activities including culture formation and development;
- marketing, public relations and other activities concerned with building images and giving impressions of quality and confidence;
- sales and distribution – the delivery of products and services to market;
- purchasing and supply – ensuring regularity and required volume of inputs;
- resource gathering, organisation and prioritising;
- the means of conflict resolution, containment and management;
- communication and information.

For all systems to operate effectively the following characteristics must be present.

1. **Energy**: required to give the systems life, make them work and continue.
2. **Returns**: part of the returns on output will be used to ensure the fresh flow of inputs into the processes.
3. **Steadiness and stability**: most systems work best to a steady flow of work rather than having to accommodate peaks and troughs; if peaks, pressures and overpressures do occur, steps should be taken to recognise these, establish the reasons for them and, where possible, carry out remedial and modifying action.
4. **Balance**: of input, process and output to ensure a steady flow of work and the avoidance of blockages and bottlenecks.
5. **Flexibility and adaptability**: concerned with the ability to respond effectively to changes in the environment, markets, perceptions and tastes; and to structure the work so that speedy responses can be made when necessary.

6. **Coordination and control characteristics**: to ensure that as far as possible steadiness and balance are maintained and to take remedial action where peaks and troughs start to become apparent; also to ensure the maximisation and optimisation of resources at each stage.
7. **Equifinality**: the concept that similar outputs can be achieved from a variety of systems and processes; that there is no one right way of doing things; that there are many different routes to the same destination; that no one person's system, process or approach will be right in all situations.

■ Managerial systems

At their best these start with the performance of others. They are created to provide a process for evaluation of performance, organisation adaptation, coordination of activities and taking decisions.

1. **Evaluation of performance**: the actual performance of the system will be evaluated through constant monitoring and review, and the results achieved analysed to show why success has been achieved and where and why any failures have occurred. This will also indicate general areas for attention, capabilities for improvements and progress, and it will also include establishing the reasons for success so that these may be built on for the future in other areas.
2. **Adaptation and change**: this is concerned with the future of the organisation, the development of structures, attitudes, values, skills, knowledge and expertise for the purpose of achieving aims and objectives and planning for longer-term strategies and directions.
3. **Coordination and control**: this is the harmonisation process, the ordering of the disparate and divergent elements, conflict resolution, balancing and ordering of priorities and resources.
4. **Decision-making**: this is attention to the processes by which effective decisions are made and the elements that contribute to this.

For effective performance in each of the processes to take place, a systematic approach is required. This is to ensure that sufficient attention is paid and examination of each area takes place on the basis of depth and breadth of knowledge, so that in turn a full basis of judgement, analysis and assessment is achieved and ensured.

■ Organisations in their environment

As no organisation exists in isolation from its environment, the nature and extent of the relationship and interactions must be considered (see Figure 2.6).

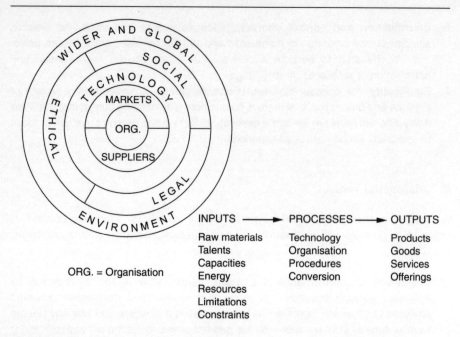

Figure 2.6   Archetype model of the organisation in its environment

Source: Katz and Kahn (1978).

Organisations are subject to a variety of economic, legal, social and ethical pressures which they must be capable of accommodating if they are to operate effectively. In some cases there are strong religious and cultural effects, and also local traditions which must be capable of effective harmonisation. More specifically, organisations need access to workforces, suppliers, distributers, customers and clients; and to technology, equipment and financial resources.

Relationships between organisations and their environment may be simply summarised as:

- **environment domination**, especially overwhelming legal, social and ethical pressures and also those that relate to any strong local histories and traditions;
- **organisation domination**, where the environment is dependent on the organisation for the provision of work, goods and services.

This must then be seen in the context that the best organisation–environment relationships are generated where measures of general responsibility are attached to each. If the environmental pressures are too great, or somehow otherwise unacceptable to the organisation, it will eventually relocate elsewhere. If the organisation takes an expedient or cavalier view of its involvement in the particular area, it will be rejected by those who live there. The picture is further complicated by the fact that all organisations interact with other organisations that are also part of their own environment and they influence these, and are influenced by them.

There is therefore a range of capabilities by which the organisation influences its environment, and vice versa. A framework may be put around this as follows.

1. Those factors that can be controlled and those that cannot. The latter category normally includes global and international interactions, other political factors, the actions of governments, and the effects that all these bring to economic and social activities.
2. Those areas where the organisation has greatest influence in the relationship and where the environment has greatest influence.
3. Those areas that lead to greatest cooperation between the two and those that tend to cause conflict between the two.
4. The degree of certainty and permanence of the relationship between the two, and the ways in which this is to be nurtured and maintained in order to ensure continuity and permanence.
5. The degree of interdependence between the two, and the extent to which one is dependent on the other.
6. The degree of stability and turbulence that exists in the environment, and the ways in which this affects organisations.
7. The degree of sensitivity of the environment to the actions of organisations, and vice versa.
8. The nature and mixture of these and their relevant importance will clearly vary between organisations and their environments and between organisations in the same location; much of this is dependent upon the nature of the work carried out by particular organisations and the pressures and priorities of the environment.

Moreover, the environment has to be seen from a variety of points of view. It is likely to be a combination of markets, infrastructure, locations, activities, social and political pressures (and vested interests and pressure groups). This in turn varies according to context. For example, an environment may be Warwickshire, mining, Indonesia, the Pacific Rim, Southern Africa, the south-east, the computer sector, London or Oxford Street; it may be the health service, the school system, share shops or town centres. Each has its own validity and influence at different times. Organisations may further describe a variety of different environments with which they interact for varying reasons: the term 'catchment area' will mean different things dependent upon whether they are currently considering staff, supplies, customers, distributers, backers and bankers.

Above all, the environment is overwhelmingly competitive. At different times organisations compete for staff, customers and resources. Based on choice, competition may be any of the following.

Overt	The choice between two or more similar items for the same price, two or more similar items at different prices or different items. This type of choice is made by organisations deciding whether to hire one individual in preference to others to fill a particular post; or by an individual deciding to take up one post and not others. Also constitutes a form of competition.
Covert	Choosing a particular item, job or activity because of feelings of well-being that the individual expects to accrue from owning it; the rejection of an item, job or activity because its possession is not valued; making choices as means to ends rather than as the end in itself.
Opportunity cost	Choosing one item, activity or job means that others also on offer cannot be bought, taken up or fulfilled.
Rational	Buying something or doing something because there is 'a logical reason': for example, buying a Picasso painting for £2 at a market stall knowing that it can be sold for £30 000 is logical in economic terms; taking up a job with a bank knowing that it will lead to the opportunity to work overseas also indicates a line of logical reasoning.
Irrational	Doing something for 'illogical reasons' (for example, buying a suit knowing that it is never going to be worn).
Socialised	Doing or buying something because of strong social pressures: for example, becoming an army officer because that is what everyone else in the family/peer group has done; working to particular standards because it is driven by the need for acceptance by the peer group rather than economic maximisation.
Something and nothing	There is, moreover, always the choice to reject. This is where, for example, individuals turn down 'the perfect job', 'the perfect holiday', 'the perfect car' on their own grounds, whims, 'reasons' and prejudices.
Demands	Organisations make demands on their environments and vice versa. These may be summarised as:

- organisational demands: for workforce, resources, access, transportation and distribution; education, training and development; primary resources (gas, electricity, water, telecommunications and fuel); they make demands for customers and clients; they make demands for confidence and continuity of relationship; they make demands for security, health and maintenance services;
- environmental demands: for work, money to be spent elsewhere in the community, on access, support and sponsorship for schools, clubs and other local institutions; for honesty and openness; for good relationships, for confidence, for continuity; the environment expects also that organisations will take care and trouble with the disposal of waste, and other aspects of pollution such as noise and lighting; the environment expects relationships with organisations to be positive and beneficial.

There is, therefore, a very broad and complex picture to be understood. Only if this is achieved, however, can successful and effective organisations be designed and produced, and systems devised that enable them to interact efficiently and effectively with their environment.

■ Contingency approaches

Contingency approaches indicate the context in which effective organisations are devised and designed. Burns and Stalker (1961) defined the contingency approach as 'the most appropriate system for a given set of circumstances'. While this may appear a statement of the obvious, it does indicate the important relationship between appropriateness and circumstances, and that effective (appropriate) organisations cannot be designed in isolation from their situation. It is first necessary to recognise the twin concepts of divergence and integration.

Divergence and integration can be seen at three levels: between an organisation and its environment; between different organisations; and within organisations (see Figure 2.7). Some parts of the relationship between organisations and the environment are based on the reconciliation of conflicting demands. Other parts are based on a stated or implied mutuality of interest. The problem is therefore to recognise where the mutuality lies and the extent of this as the basis by which the points of conflict can then be addressed. Some factors may be distinguished.

The more dynamic and diverse the environment, the greater the degree of differentiation and specialisation required within organisations to cope with its

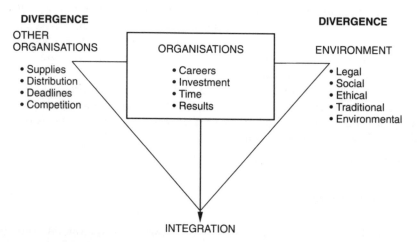

Figure 2.7   Divergence and integration pressures

demands. High degrees of integration are also required (a) to build up effective working relationships with each part of the environment and (b) to harmonise differing and often divergent efforts within the organisation itself.

Less dynamic and more stable environments require high degrees of interaction to ensure that the stability is preserved. A major cause of conflict (see Chapter 11 below) is lack of communication and understanding caused, in turn, by lack of attention to continuing relationships.

The more dynamic and diverse the environment, the greater the likelihood of misunderstandings and conflict occurring. In these situations, a proportion of organisation resources is therefore likely to be required to ensure that these can be tackled effectively when they do arise.

■ Contingency approaches within organisations

Within organisations, Lawrence and Lorsch (1967) identified divergence as set out below:

- different groups of labour and expertise; sections of the workforce, departments, divisions and functions; skills, knowledge, attitudes, behaviour and experience;
- goals, targets, aims and objectives;
- timescales and time spans for the achievement of the targets, aims and objectives, and also the sub-activities and functions on which they were dependent;
- interpersonal, interdepartmental and interfunctional relationships, and those between peers, subordinates and superiors;
- departmental structures.

Integration was achieved as the result of devising systems and procedures that encouraged or enabled people to cooperate and collaborate so that the different and often conflicting demands and priorities implicit in this list could be reconciled. This included attention to management and supervisory styles, rule books and procedures, and industrial relations and staff management systems.

It also made reference to degrees of interdependence, the extent to which one function's ability to operate effectively was based on the efforts of others; or where the work output of one group constituted the input of another. This also became a means of building positive relationships. It may be shown as interdependence chains (see Figure 2.8).

■ The Aston Group

The work of the Aston Group consisted of research into the organisation and its environment in the late 1960s. Based at the University of Aston, Birmingham, it included attention to both variables and context.

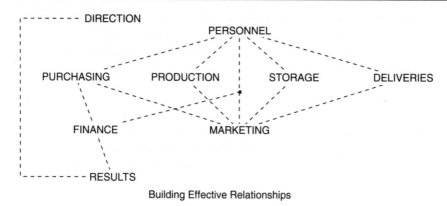

Building Effective Relationships

Figure 2.8 Interdependence chains

■ Variables

1. The degree of specialisation of the workforce, the nature of division and allocation of work.
2. The degree of standarisation and production and support activities; the content and use of procedure.
3. The degree of formalisation through the use of rules, channels of communication, hierarchies and reporting relationships.
4. The degree of centralisation, decentralisation and delegation.
5. The structure of the organisation: the length of the hierarchy, the degree of compartmentalisation, the means by which interdepartmental relationships were established or divided.

■ Context

1. The size of the organisation and its work groups and the balancing of primary (production and sales), support and administrative functions.
2. The technology used and the impact that this had on organisation design.
3. The ownership history and traditions of the organisation and its workforce, its location and relationships with its community.
4. Its markets.

■ Conclusions

The main conclusions drawn were that historically:

- larger size tended to lead to greater degrees of specialisation (and therefore a greater propensity for conflict);

- larger size tended to lead to greater efforts towards standardisation and formalisation with the stated interest of ensuring adequate levels of control;
- larger size tended to lead to greater devolution and decentralisation, the need to delegate measures of authority.

It was therefore possible to identify the type and nature of an organisation from an assessment of the variables within the given context (see Figure 2.9), and likely sources of pressure, strain and conflict could be inferred. More generally, as an organisation grew, it could be predicted with a certain amount of accuracy what form that growth would take and the fact that attention

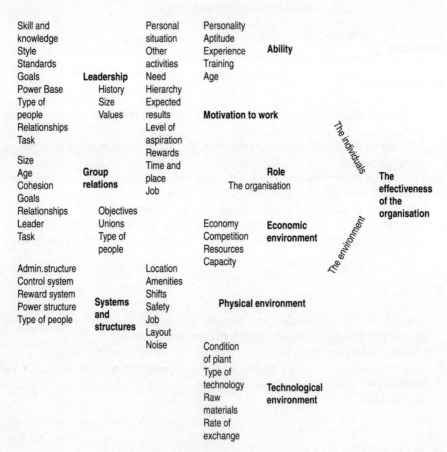

Figure 2.9   The context and composition of organisations

Source: Handy, 1990

would be necessary to structure, specialisation, reporting relationships and rules and procedures as the growth took place. This in turn would indicate the likely functional and operational factors that would need to be integrated.

The contingency approach has implications for all aspects of organisational behaviour. Leaders, groups, teams and individuals cannot exist in isolation from each other or from the wider environment. For all these, therefore, situational knowledge and understanding is required so that the qualities they bring can be harmonised and integrated effectively.

Some conclusions and inferences may be drawn.

1. There is clearly no best way to organise; as the environment changes so systems, aims and objectives must be flexible and responsive.
2. The environment changes in both predictable and unpredictable ways; it changes in ways that can be controlled and influenced and in ways that cannot be controlled and influenced; the problem for managers lies in the extent of their understanding of their environment and in their ability to anticipate the unexpected by building systems that are capable of accommodating these pressures.
3. Because of the nature of the relationship with the environment, organisations require to spend time on external issues, assessing and understanding the environment, and the changes and turbulence within it.
4. Each input–process–output cycle changes the nature of the organisation's social and technical resources, presenting an opportunity to strive for optimisation and improvement.
5. Above all, the environment is dynamic and not static or rigid, allowing for limitless opportunities for change to occur; investment in environmental adaptation and transformation are as essential to success as investments in capital, equipment and staffing. The more complex and turbulent the environment, the more essential this form of investment becomes.
6. Environmental, technological and social changes are the primary causes and inspiration for organisational improvement.
7. Legal and ethical constraints constitute the main limitations placed on the activities of organisations. These require that specific approaches are adapted to all aspects of activities in order to meet standards prescribed by law or laid down by the prevailing values and morals of society.

The purpose of this chapter has been to summarise and indicate the various forms of organisation, the different points of view from which they may be considered and the wider context in which they operate. No organisation operates in isolation from, or without reference to its environment. The environment provides staff, customers, resources, technology and equipment, and also confidence and expectations: the context in which successful and effective activities take place.

■ Questions

For a village primary school; city hospital; refuse disposal organisation; airport; mass production car factory:

1. summarise the environment, the pressures and the constraints that are imposed and have to be accommodated.
2. draw up SMART short-, medium- and long-term aims and objectives for each. State how these should be measured for success/failure.
3. what steps should each of these organisations take to create, maintain and improve harmonious relationships with their community and environment?
4. to what extent does each of these organisations dominate its environment; and to what extent is each dominated by its environment? What are the main implications of this for the creation of effective organisations in these circumstances?

CHAPTER 3

Perception

■ Introduction

Perception is the process by which all people limit their views of the world. Perception is essential because of the amount of information, signals and cues with which the senses are constantly assailed. The total is not capable of assimilation because it is constantly changing and developing and because of the constant nature of human activity. A process of some sort is therefore clearly necessary by which this is first limited and then transformed into something that is useful and usable.

The process by which individual perception is developed is both learned and instinctive. Some of it comes from the senses – sight, hearing, touch, taste and smell. Some of it also plainly comes from instinct: one's view of what is edible is clearly coloured by how hungry one is.

That which is learned comes from a combination of civilisation and socialisation. This gives rise, above all, to moral and ethical codes by which behaviour is regulated. It also gives rise to the formation of norms, expectations, customs and etiquette. It forms the basis for concepts of fashion and desirability and the need for achievement.

Other influences on perception arise from specific elements such as situational factors, peer group pressure and value judgement (especially success and failure).

Perceptions are also heavily influenced by media and business activity. Marketing is directed in large part to the formulation of positive and acceptable impressions. Much human resource activity is taken up with influencing people's perceptions of others as they interact in work situations. Control functions are desirable in order that organisations may understand the state of their status and progress. Primary activities such as manufacturing or service provision must be undertaken in such a way that those conducting them understand to a greater extent at least what is being done, how and why.

Perception is therefore clearly a primary human activity. A general understanding is required by anybody who wishes to assess and evaluate human behaviour. In working situations and above all for those who have people to manage, this level of understanding is critical to successful managerial and organisational performance. In order to illustrate this, it is first necessary to identify some of the means by which human beings limit and define their view of the world. These processes are needed in order to be able to assess those people, places and situations with which we come into contact and make predictions about them. We need to be as familiar and comfortable with these as possible.

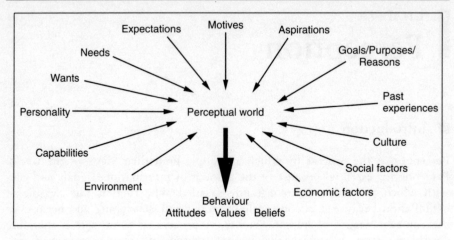

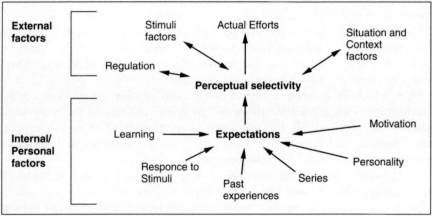

Figure 3.1   Relationships between perception, behaviour, attitudes and values

Source: from Huczynski and Buchanan 1993

In unfamiliar situations people will latch on to anything that is in some way familiar. Thus, for example, the first time traveller to Kenya may put the temperature in the following terms: 'It is hotter than Paris/Tokyo/London/Brussels/New York.' Initial conversation in the West between strangers covers a quick range of 'weather, home, job, family, sport, car' until some common ground is found. Football is (apparently) the universal and common interest of the male world; children are (apparently) the female equivalent.

It is finally at this stage necessary to recognise the general limitation that perception and the processes which contribute to it are placing upon people. In a way this is the greatest barrier of all to an understanding of this area. People do not like to be reminded of failings or shortcomings. They see their own view

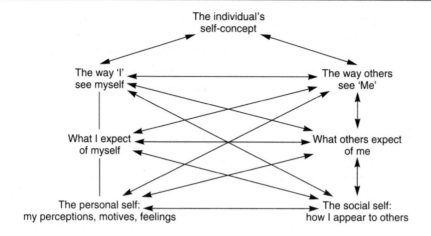

Figure 3.2   The basis of interpersonal perception

Source: C. Rogers (1947).

of the world as perfect; in disputes over things that have happened the refrain 'I know what I saw' is commonplace. Where two or more people 'know what they saw' time and energy is often wasted on arriving at 'the truth'. In reality, 'the truth' is the sum of all the versions of events, and not just one of them.

An understanding of the basic concepts outlined here is critical to the successful assimilation of all the other elements explained in the book.

BOX 3.1   Wages at Nuclear Power Stations: A Good Deal?

In the 1960s the UK Central Electricity Generating Board (CEGB) built nuclear power stations in remote parts of the UK. Many of the staff, especially the technical, semi-skilled and unskilled, were to be drawn from rural, coastal and often remote communities. Stations brought additional income and work to these areas.

The first attempts to recruit people from these communities consisted of offering a high salary (about £15 000 in 1996 terms) in return for which the staff concerned would work rosters determined by the station directorate. Hours would be flexible and extensive time-off arrangements in lieu would be afforded to those having to work nights, weekends and public holidays.

Take-up of this arrangement was so low that the CEGB returned to the drawing board. The organisation came up with a basic wage of £7 000 per annum (also at 1994 values) and extensive and complicated rostering arrangements that required overtime, shift pay, attendance, inconvenience and call-out allowances. The total to be earned by the staff concerned was to be between £13 000 and £15 000, provided that the overtime and so on continued to be forthcoming. Without exception the demand for jobs in the communities involved exceeded supply, in spite of the fact that the offer was worse than the original. But the perceptual barriers were overcome and those involved felt themselves to be getting a better deal. This was the reason for the success of the latter approach.

■ Comfort and liking

Comfort and liking occur when elements and features accord and harmonise with each other. Instant rapport is achieved when initial perceptions – strong characteristics, halo effects (see below) – coincide, meet expectations and lead to an initially productive relationship. This is developed as people become more familiar with, and knowledgeable about, each other and about situations and circumstances.

The greater the continuing coincidence, the greater the harmony and accord, and the more flexible the boundaries of this become. For example, if the initial impression of someone is that they are a 'smoker' this may lead to discord; if the relationship then develops in strong and positive ways, the smoking becomes less and less relevant and easier to accommodate.

Discomfort and dislike occur when the elements are in discord. This is usually founded in strong and contradictory initial and continuing impressions. For example, in response to a job advertisement, a beautifully prepared and overtly substantial curriculum vitae (CV) may arrive; when the individual is called for interview, he turns out to be scruffy; and discomfort and dislike occurs because expectations are not met. To the unwary, the person has turned from a potential employee into someone to be got rid of as quickly as possible. In practice, everyone has contradictory characteristics and those with whom they come into contact have to reconcile these in order to build up a comfortable picture.

BOX 3.2 Perceptual Errors

The sources of error in person and situational perception include:

- not collecting enough information;
- assuming that enough information has been collected;
- not collecting the right information; collecting the wrong information;
- assuming that the right information has been collected;
- seeing what we want and expect to see; fitting reality to our view of the world (rather than the reverse);
- looking for in others what we value for and in ourselves;
- assuming that the past was always good when making judgements for the future;

- failure to acknowledge and recognise other points of view;
- failure to consider situations and people from the widest possible point of view;
- unrealistic expectations, levels of comfort and satisfaction;
- confusing the unusual and unexpected with the impossible.

The remedies are:

- understanding the limitations of personal knowledge and perception; that this is imperfect and that there are gaps;
- decide in advance what knowledge is required of people and situations and set out to collect it from this standpoint;
- structure activities where the gathering of information is important (for example, this should apply to all interviews, research activities, questioning, work organisation, use of technology);
- avoid instant judgements about people, however strong and positive, or weak and negative, the first impression may be;
- avoid instant judgements about organisations, whether as customer or employee;
- build expectations on knowledge and understanding rather than halo effects, stereotypes and self-fulfilling prophecies;
- ensure exchanges and availability of good quality information;
- ensure open relationships that encourage discussion and debate and generate high levels of understanding and knowledge exchange;
- develop self-awareness and understanding among all staff;
- recognise and understand the nature of prevailing attitudes, values and beliefs – and prejudices;
- recognise and understand other strong prevailing influences – especially language, nationality, culture and experience.

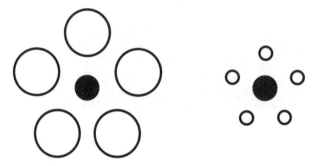

(a) Which black spot is larger?

Figure 3.3a   Perception: illustrations *continued over*

(b) Old lady or young girl?

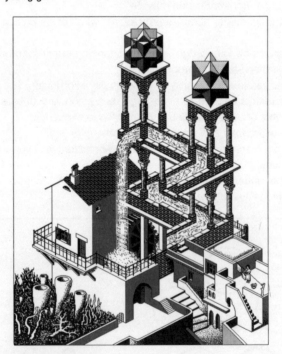

(c) Water flowing up and down?
Source: C. Escher/Cordon Art © 1995

(d) A farmer was asked how many animals he had on his farm
   'Well,' he replied, 'I have 233 heads and 843 legs. Work it out from that.'

Figure 3.3   Perception: illustrations

■ Inference

People infer or make assumptions about others and about things, situations and circumstances based on the information available and their interpretation and analysis of it. Simple forms of this are found in stereotyping and the halo effect.

It becomes more complex when these effects cannot be seen in isolation (see Boxes 3.3 and 3.4). It is not possible to define attitude from behaviour or performance from attitude; it is only possible to infer this. This means that while it is possible to predict to a certain extent, there are too many uncertainties and the full range of actual results remains possible and available and should be considered.

Extreme forms of inference are jumping to conclusions and 'gut reactions', in which quantum leaps are made about the outcome of something from a limited range of information available. In each case the individual selects those elements before them with which they are familiar and places her own interpretation of the likely or 'logical' (*sic*) outcome based on her knowledge and understanding of what happened before when these elements were present. The range of misunderstandings possible is virtually limitless (see Box 3.4). There may be three elements out of six present with which the individual is familiar; or this may be three out of ten; three out of forty; or three out of 100. In each case it is the familiar three which form the basis of judgement.

BOX 3.3 'Good Morning'

Two men were walking from the organisation's car park to their place of work. On their way, they passed their manager walking in the opposite direction. One of the men said 'Good morning' to the manager in a cheery voice. The manager grunted, mumbled something and walked on. The other man turned round and put his tongue out at the manager's receding back.

What is the attitude of the men to their manager?

BOX 3.4 Jumping to Conclusions and Gut Reactions

1. The old school tie: if from the same school, familiar and positive; if from a different school, subject to instant interpretation.
2. You play golf; I play golf; therefore you are like me.
3. You play golf; I play golf; I am a successful manager; therefore you are/will be a successful manager.
4. Football has hooligans; you like football; therefore you are a hooligan.

5. Mick Jagger has long hair; you have long hair; therefore you are like Mick Jagger.
6. Men with beards are hiding something; Richard Branson has a beard; therefore he is hiding something.
7. He has a firm handshake; I have a firm handshake; therefore I like him.

■ Halo effect

This is the process by which a person is ascribed a great range of capabilities and expertise as the result of one initial impression of an overwhelming characteristic. As stated above, the person who has a firm handshake is deemed to be decisive. A person with a public school education is deemed to be officer material. The person who can play golf is deemed to be an expert in business.

The converse of this is the horns effect (the halo apparently comes from heaven; the horns therefore clearly originate elsewhere). This is whereby a negative connotation is put on someone or something as the result of one (supposedly) negative characteristic. Thus the person with the soft handshake and lisp is perceived to be soft and indecisive. Anyone who wears fashions from a past era is deemed to be eccentric or old fashioned.

Excellent examples of this clearly abound. Kim Philby was able to act as a Soviet spy for 20 years with ease because nobody in the British establishment believed that anyone with his impeccable credentials could possibly be anything other than a pillar of the aforesaid establishment. Richard Branson is perceived to be dynamic and iconoclastic partly because of the clothes that he wears and the style with which he presents his company in the media. Apples sold at Marks & Spencer must be good because they are shiny and bruise-free.

BOX 3.5   Jumping to Conclusions Again

The book *Recruitment and Selection* by Clive T. Goodworth is dedicated 'to all those who can spot a good chap as soon as they walk into the room. And to all those who suffer as the result.'

You are about to appoint somebody to a junior managerial post. All candidates are equally qualified. One is a married woman of 26 who has no children; one is a married man of 29 with two children; one is a single man of 30; the fourth is a divorced woman of 38 with teenage children. On the basis of the information given which one would you appoint to the job and why?

■ Stereotyping, pigeonholing and compartmentalisation

It is a short step from the halo effect to developing a process of stereotyping, pigeonholing and compartmentalisation. This occurs at places of work whereby, because of a past range of activities, somebody is deemed to be that kind of a person for the future. This may both enhance and limit careers, activities and organisation progress dependent upon the nature of the compartmentalisation. In any case it gives specific and limited direction. A person who has worked overseas for a multi-national corporation for a long time may have difficulty getting a job back at Head Office because he has been pigeonholed as 'an expatriate' and may be perceived to have difficulties should he be required to conform to the Head Office norms and practices.

■ Self-fulfilling prophecy

Self-fulfilling prophecy occurs when a judgement is made about someone or something. The person making the judgement then picks out further characteristics or attributes to support her view and edits out those do not fit in. (See Box 3.6).

BOX 3.6   Self-Fulfilling Prophecy: Examples

If you want people to be trustworthy, trust them. If you want people to accept responsibility, give them responsibility.   (R. Semler, 1992)

People will behave as they expect those in charge would behave in the same situation. The *Herald of Free Enterprise* sank because the staff perceived that it was important to set sail in spite of the fact that the bow doors were not closed. When the ship turned over the hunt was for scapegoats, not mistakes. (Brass Tacks BBC2: 1989)

Universities have adopted systems of numbered exam papers. This is so that those who mark the papers see what is actually written rather than what they expect to see written by particular students to whom they can put a name and therefore a set of perceptions.

■ Perceptual mythology

This occurs where myths are created by people as part of their own processes of limiting and understanding particular situations. A form of rationale emerges, which is usually spurious.

Thus, for example, people will say such things as 'I can tell as soon as someone walks in the door whether he can do this job', or 'I always ask this question and it never fails', or 'I never trust people in white shoes/white socks/ with moustaches/with tinted glasses' in order to give themselves some chance of understanding and therefore mapping the person who stands before them.

People also use phrases such as 'in my opinion' and 'in my experience' for the same general reasons, but more in support of general views of the world's stereotypes and business developments.

The third manifestation of this is in relating the present situation to some-thing that happened in the past or elsewhere. The line of argument becomes 'X did this and it worked and so we should do it and it will work for us'; or 'It happened like this in 1929 and so this is the way to do it in 1995'; or, more insidiously, 'We had to do things like this in my day and it never did us any harm and so this is how it has got to be done now.'

It is a short step from this to comparisons, again often of dubious value. Industries publish league tables of company performance by business volume, business value, wage and salary levels, numbers employed and so on. These are then used to justify and explain a range of other issues of varying degrees of relevance and substance. Companies, for example, say 'We are sixth in the league' or 'We are in the same boat as the rest of the industry' or 'We are no worse than anyone else', without attaching any rationale to any of the points made.

One of the most notorious comparisons made in the UK was the attempt in the 1970s to establish a comparator for school teachers for the purpose of assessing a correct level of pay. The group chosen to compare them with was airline cabin staff. This was done on the basis that 'They too were dealing with people for the whole of their working day.'

Above all, this part of the process illustrates the difficulties involved. On the one hand, each of the examples given in this part is flawed at best and spurious at worst. On the other hand, people have to limit their intake of information, stimuli and cues in some way and provide themselves with a means of understanding. At this stage, therefore, the main lesson to be drawn is in the recognition of this and limitations attached.

■ Personal mapping and constructs

In this process people, situations, activities, images and impressions are being fitted into the perceived map of the world in ways which can be understood, managed and accommodated. The information thus gathered is broken down into constructs or characteristics which may be categorised as follows.

1. **Physical**: by which we assume or infer the qualities of the person from their appearance, racial group, beauty, style, dress and other visual images.
2. **Behavioural**: whereby we place people according to the way they act and behave or the ways in which we think they will act and behave.

3. **Role**: whereby we make assumptions about people because of the variety of roles they assume; the different situations in which they assume these roles; their dominant role or roles; and the trappings that go with them.
4. **Psychological**: whereby certain occupations, appearances, manifestations, presentation and images are assumed to be of a higher order of things than others (part of this is also sociological). This reflects the morality, values and ethics of the society of the day as well as the environment and organisation in question.

This part of the perception process aims to build up a picture of the world with which the individual can be comfortable. Comfort is achieved when people and situations are perceived to have complementary characteristics or constructs. Discomfort occurs when characteristics and constructs are contradictory. For example, there is no difficulty placing an individual who is kind and gentle in the perceptual map. There is difficulty, however, in being comfortable with an individual who is both kind and violent.

■ Closure

Closure occurs where an individual sees part of a picture and then completes the rest of it in her mind; or hears part of a statement or conversation and then mentally finishes it off. It also occurs as part of the process of exclusion. Based on halo effects and stereotyping, a picture is completed around the strong trait and everything else is omitted or excluded; the picture is closed around the desired or understood trait.

■ Proximity

Proximity is based on the desire to understand and be comfortable with that which is close at hand: to be at ease in the immediate environment. Matters which cause discomfort therefore assume importance, often out of proportion to their actual effect.

Proximity also concerns the tendency to group people or items that are physically close into groups. Those who work in the same office, for example, are seen as a group; and if one or two continually raise grievances, the whole may come to be seen as a collection of trouble makers.

■ Intensity

Perception is affected by extremes of heat, cold, light, darkness, noise, silence, colour, taste, touch and smell. People who wish to stand out from the crowd wear bright or other eye-catching colours. People who move from the city to the country notice the contrast between the noise and bustle of the one and the peace and quiet of the other.

■ **Attribution**

Attribution is the explanation put by individuals on behaviour or activities. Attribution may be:

- rational: 'You burnt your hand because the plate was hot';
- pseudo-rational: 'He is a bully at work because he has a difficult home life';
- empathised: 'In her place I would have done the same thing';
- mythological: 'This was how we always used to do it and it worked then'.

Whether rational or not, attribution gives people a point of reference for their actions and for those of others. It also helps in the attaining of comfort and satisfaction, enabling people to explain – to themselves at least – why they continue to work in particular occupations, ways, situations, or with particular people.

■ **Situational factors**

People react differently to the same stimuli according to the given situation. If someone is rude, for example, the response to this varies depending on whether the transaction is taking place at home, at school, at the shops or at work. In the latter case especially, mechanisms are required by organisations to deal with these and similar situations so that behavioural aspects are satisfied and so that business is not lost. This is also a large part of the particular context or background of events. It also varies according to the nature of the organisation involved and the relationship with it (whether one is a member of staff or customer, for example).

■ **Confidence**

The greater the confidence and understanding between two or more people or between persons and their environment, the more effective and successful their behaviour. Persons who have complete confidence in each other speak in direct language. Persons who do not must couch what they say in safe phrases to avoid giving offence. Closely related to this are the behavioural components of confidence: elements of security, constancy, honesty and trust.

■ **Past history**

In organisation behaviour terms this is especially important when one has been (or is) both a customer of the organisation and also its employee. Both relationships influence the effects of the other. An understanding of this is essential on the part of universal public service organisations such as post offices, schools, hospitals, transport services and department stores. In these cases new people who come to work in them must have a proper induction and orientation at the outset of their period as an employee, otherwise they will behave as they perceive others to do so or as a reflection of their own past experiences as a customer or client.

■ Trappings and furnishings

When an individual visits a particular place its initial appearance influences the rest of the transaction. Opulent, thickly carpeted and expensively furnished offices are designed to give the impression of confidence and permanence (they may also give messages of corporate extravagance and waste). Trappings and furnishings are also used to influence such situations to the advantage of the person in control and to the detriment of those who come into them as juniors or customers.

■ The messenger

Messages from one quarter may be unacceptable; the same message delivered by someone else may be eagerly accepted. For example, organisations use consultants and arbitrators in order to put across difficult or contentious issues. What may be unacceptable coming from the organisation 'Chair' has the perception and feeling of an objective seal of approval if it is delivered by an outsider.

■ Language

In general, threatening and coercive approaches to people and other negative language normally produces worse responses than if the approach is positive. According to the language used, therefore, people perceive situations as opportunities, challenges or a chance to progress; or as threats, risk and uncertainties. More generally, the more direct, clear and unambiguous the language used, the greater the general and positive response generated.

■ Fashions and fads

These are current and transient influences on behaviour. They are important in the context that they are 'today's triggers' and are to be understood as such. When something passes out of fashion it loses this influence: indeed, it may become something to divest. A fine example of this is to be found in the antiques trade (whether, for example, something is to be regarded as tatty old furniture or as a priceless commodity).

■ Social regard

People receive recognition – positive and negative – for everything that they do. The extent of the positive or the negative directly influences the way in which they do it. Negative jobs, activities and pursuits have therefore to be addressed in words and phrases such as troubleshooting, crisis management, problem-solving and consulting. This is to be seen also in more general terms. Different societies place differing levels of general regard on particular types of behaviour and attitude and this influences the behaviour of organisations in turn.

■ Human response

Perception is a continuous process. Transitions from the negative to the positive take place very quickly (as does the reverse) and as the result of particular stimuli. For example, the spouse of the person who is late home from work is angry because of his lateness; anger turns to concern when she is told that the spouse has been in a car crash; concern turns to relief when it is established that he is not hurt.

Transitions also occur from the positive to the negative very quickly. For example, the person who walks unhurt from a bad car crash may initially feel lucky to have escaped with her life; this view turns quickly to anger when she finds out that the accident was caused by a drunk driver.

■ Selective focus

This is a part of the stereotyping and halo effect processes. The individual searches for evidence of the given halo effect in other attributes and behaviour of the person or situation in question. Evidence in support of this is accepted; evidence that counters it is rejected.

■ Modification

The reality of what actually occurs or is said is modified by reportage, summary and time lags as well as through the senses of those receiving the messages or witnessing the events.

Distortion is that part of modification which occurs when a message has to pass through a number of different stages or relayers to reach its destination. This occurs naturally and is emphasised when one of the stages or relayers takes active steps to distort it for his own ends. Different emphases are also given to different parts of the message according to ways in which they are transmitted or received.

■ Other influences on perception

The following, more general, influences may also be distinguished.

■ Repetition

The repetition of a message or an event gives currency, familiarity and validity. This may subsequently become a barrier to change.

■ Familiarity

This is the outcome of repetition and also of continued exposure and involvement in given situations. The most positive form is comfort; the negative is complacency. It is a general bonus, however, in the generation of organisational format (such as for memos, reports and letters). It has great importance in the development of a house style for general communication purposes.

■ Authority, responsibility and position

These relate to the person giving the message. This influences the propensity of the receiver to accept or reject it. A person who understands well the strength or weakness of her own position in this regard is always likely to be a more effective communicator than one who does not.

■ Emotions

Feelings of anger, antagonism, mistrust and disregard emphasise the tendency to reject. At the very least, therefore, any such feelings present or potentially present in a given situation are to be recognised at the outset and at least neutralised where possible.

The greatest of all emotional barriers in organisations is pride. Nobody likes to lose face or to have it made plain that they were wrong. Neither do others wish to be associated with someone who is forced to be seen as defeated, to back down, or to climb down from a given position.

This is especially important in the understanding of the conduct of workplace disputes and grievances. It is important in the understanding of why projects that are plainly doomed to failure are nevertheless allowed to proceed. In each case the alternative – withdrawal – is an admission of failure. It is seen as such and is therefore unacceptable from a variety of points of view.

The converse of this, the accentuation of the positive, the generation of enthusiasm, is also not an end in itself. This is where feelings of infallibility can be generated if the emotion becomes too strong.

■ Levels of recognition

This concept is highly complex. Levels of recognition are formal and informal. They also exist in organisations at corporate, departmental, divisional, group and individual levels. They are further complicated by the existence and recognition of professional bodies, employers' associations and trade unions.

The other dimension to this is the acceptance or rejection spectrum. This include concepts of denial; and of the recognition of something but refusal to accept it.

BOX 3.7   *A Bridge Too Far*

In a scene from the film *A Bridge Too Far* recognition level is graphically illustrated. The film is the story of the wartime Arnhem landings of 1944. In this scene the general in charge (played by Dirk Bogarde) is presented with photographic evidence that if he goes ahead with the projected plan it will fail. In the scene he stands in front of the photographs and denies their existence. He reinforces this with a question to the subordinate who produced the photographs: 'Are you saying that we should abort this plan because of the existence of three photographs?'

■   **Visibility**

Much is made of visibility as an instrument of the generation of effective organisational behaviour throughout this book. Visibility is the cornerstone of so much. It is a prerequisite to effective communication. It greatly helps in the generation of confidence, familiarity and interaction. It underlines levels of honesty, trustworthiness and straightforwardness. It helps develop both professional and personal relationships between those involved. There are therefore both general and specific benefits to be gained from an effective face-to-face relationship.

The converse is also true. Lack of visibility is both a perceptual barrier in itself and also compounds others that are present, such as general feelings of disregard, distrust and dishonesty for example. Misunderstandings occur least often and are most quickly and easily sorted out at the face-to-face level. Where this is not present, such misunderstandings invariably take longer to resolve and may quickly become disputes and grievances.

■   **Comparison**

Comparison is a part of the process of perceptual mapping. Some comparisons are precise and exact (this glass is fuller than that; she is better qualified than he is, for example). Others are less so and may be based on a range of opinion (informal or otherwise), expectation and prejudice. Some comparisons are valid; others not.

Comparisons also have the added value of helping to meet the expectations of people in certain situations. If one company has a bigger percentage pay rise than another, its staff tend to be happy. If the pay rise is lower, staff tend to be unhappy. Organisations therefore tend to seek out and emphasise those comparators that present them in their best light.

The standpoint from which the comparison is made is also to be considered. For example, the statement that bankers earn more than teachers is valid only if a simple comparison of earnings is being considered. It does not prove or disprove that one job is better or worse than the other. For other aspects, therefore, other equivalent comparators have to be identified and addressed.

It is also usual to put weightings on different comparators when trying to arrive at satisfactory, complex and valid comparisons. The process at least recognises the difficulties involved and proposes steps towards addressing them, even if it is unlikely that they are to be entirely resolved.

People	Service
• appearance, dress, hair, handshake • voice, eye contact • scent, smell • disposition (positive, negative, smiling, frowning) • establishing common interest/failure to do so • courtesy, manner • age	• friendliness (or lack of) • effectiveness • speed • quality • confidence • value • respect • ambience • appearance
Objects	Organisations
• design • colour/colours • weight • shape • size • materials • purpose, usage • price, value, cost	• ambience • welcome • appearance • image and impression • technology • care • respect for others • confidence • trust

This is a useful (but by no means perfect or complete) means of compartmentalising the cues and signals which are present when coming into any situation or into contact with someone for the first time. There are certain to be contradictions and contra-indications. It is essential to recognise and understand this in order to understand, in turn, the impact and influence of first impressions.

Figure 3.4   First impressions

■ **First impressions**

First impressions count: this is received wisdom throughout the Western world. It applies everywhere (see Box 3.8). Yet first impressions are plainly misleading: prima facie you must know less about someone after 30 seconds than after 30 minutes. Yet overwhelmingly the converse is highly influential and this should be understood.

Above all, the first impression gives a frame of reference to the receiver. The appearance, manner, handshake and initial transaction is the writing on a blank sheet. Before there was nothing; now there is something on which to place measure and assess the other. The impact is therefore very strong. It is essential to recognise this. The consequence of not doing so is that a one-dimensional view of the individual is formed, and everything which is contrary to that dimension or which indicates complexities, other dimensions and qualities are edited out.

■ Editing

This part of the process is referred to above. In general terms it is that part of the perception process that reconciles all conflicting signals and cues. In its simplest form it involves the rejection of that which does not conform to the overwhelming view of the person's situation or place. Otherwise it may be reconciled as a larger-than-life character, as we have seen above.

BOX 3.8   First Impressions

Telephone contact. The contact and manner of greeting afforded over the telephone is an extremely important prerequisite to effective interaction. If this is unsatisfactory, unproductive and destructive, efforts and energies are used in the inquest into it and into rectifying any damage that is done. The same may be said for handshakes, facial expressions, appearance and dress.

■ Expectations

People go into every situation and transaction with a purpose. The fulfilment of this is their expectation. Expectations are measured in hard material terms, soft behavioural terms and a combination of the two.

Hard	goods for money
Soft	courtesy, honesty, trustworthiness, value
Combination	value for money: a combination of the measurable (the money) with the unmeasurable (value)

■ Meeting expectations

When expectations are met people are satisfied. This applies to all those who come into contact with a particular organisation: staff, customers, clients, the community, the media and other stakeholders.

The community also expects a general positive response to itself from playing host to particular organisations. The output of expectation is therefore satisfaction in whatever terms that is to be measured.

Other expectations may be distinguished.

1. **Expectation as a customer**: of value for money; of utility and reliability of products and services; to be treated with courtesy and accuracy.
2. **Expectation as a shareholder or stakeholder**: of the longevity, stability and profitability of the organisation; of steady and increasing returns on investment; of strength of positive reputation.
3. **Expectation as a staff member**: to be treated well and fairly; to be paid well and on time; to have prospects for advancement; to have pay and rewards increased; to participate in the success of the organisation; to be treated with respect; to receive accurate and up-to-date information.

Fulfilment of expectations is a key feature of the motivation of the individual. This is the basis of expectancy theories and motivation (see Chapter 5). Marketing activities generate the expectation that particular needs and wants are to be satisfied through the use of products and services indicated. Part of the recruitment and selection process is concerned with setting out a range of expectations that may be satisfied if the individual is to come to work for the organisation. Much of what is usually called industrial relations is concerned with meeting the more general and universal human expectations, and having access to information and being kept abreast of developments in particular situations.

■ **Exceeding expectations**

Generally expectations are exceeded in the very short term only. It occurs when the outcome of a particular situation, performance or product, or the result of a transaction is more positive (or brings a greater level of satisfaction) than was anticipated at the outset. The invariable result of this is the setting of a new level of expectation in regard to the particular activity in question. This becomes the norm by which these events will then be measured in the future; if there is then a reversion to the original level of performance or output, dissatisfaction will be engendered.

BOX 3.9 Perceptual Defence Mechanisms

People build defences (blocks or refusal to recognise) against people or situations that are personally or culturally unacceptable, unrecognisable, threatening or incapable of assimilation. Perceptual defence normally takes one or more of the following forms.

1. Denial: refusal to recognise the evidence of the senses.
2. Modification and distortion: accommodating disparate elements in ways which reinforce the comfort of the individual.
3. Change in perception: from positive to negative or from negative to positive, often based on a single trait or characteristic becoming apparent which was not previously so.
4. Recognition but refusal to change: where people are not prepared to have their view of the world disrupted by a single factor or example. This is often apparent when people define 'the exceptions to the rule'.
5. Outlets: where the individual seeks an outlet (especially for frustration or anger away from its cause). For example, browbeating a subordinate offers a sense of relief to someone who has previously been browbeaten themselves by their superior.
6. Recognition thresholds: the higher the contentiousness or emotional content of information, the higher the threshold for recognition (that is, the less likely it is to be perceived readily).

■ Failing to meet expectations

This is where satisfaction is not achieved, the output is revealed in loss of business, increased customer complaints and loss of reputation. It is also revealed in heightened levels of disputes, grievances, accidents and absenteeism.

■ Adaptation

Adaptation is 'perception as a continuous process'. Our view of the world is influenced directly by the circumstances and surroundings in which we find ourselves. Part of the process also relates to priority levels: what is important now; and what is important for life, work, leisure, and so on.

BOX 3.10   Perception

1. When people exhibit strong and conflicting characteristics, the general response on the part of the rest of the world is to reject or mistrust them, as accommodation and acceptance require an understanding of the limitations of perceptions at the point of meeting and dealing with them.
2. A combination of the various perceptual processes is to be found in the 'pre-conceived idea' and 'pre-judged case'. What invariably happens is that a situation arises to which an individual can bring different familiarities and experiences to different aspects. He then reconstructs these, for good or ill, to the matter in hand, and jumps to a conclusion and solution to it.

3. It is possible through the observation of an individual's activity and behaviour, to infer her attitude. It is not possible to prove it; and, if this is the overriding requirement of the moment, further action must be taken in this regard to overcome these inferences and gain a true picture.

4. The adaptation process is constantly in action. People overrespond to someone who is polite if the last six others that they have met have been rude. A person driving home in a rush from work may fear the wrath of his partner if he is late; if he crashes the car in so doing, the driver immediately feels lucky to be alive; the feelings of the person waiting for him change from anger to anxiety and then relief.

5. There is also the question of 'construct reconciliation' to be addressed. Examples of this include reconciling the brilliant performance of an actor with his own personality; the radical politician or religious leader with that of one's next-door neighbour or travelling companion; the children's matinee idol with the boor who refuses to sign autographs.

In general, a grasp of the basic principles of perception on the part of those in managerial roles at least enables the questioning of certain supposed 'rules' and 'facts'. It should be part of the process of generating a healthy scepticism and genuinely inquiring mind when faced with such perceptual 'absolutes'.

Adaptation is therefore the process by which our view of the world and our relationships with it and within it, and its people and its organisations, establishments and events, constantly change. It is based on a combination of expectation and anticipation, knowledge, actions, previous experience and the continuing development of particular situations. It is accentuated by the other perceptual effects indicated above.

Adaptation is positive and negative and a constant process. It is accentuated by priorities, crises and constantly changing circumstances.

For example, an individual who is waiting for a train may become agitated if the train is late, especially if she has to get somewhere else quickly at the other end. When the train finally arrives, it is crowded, dirty and noisy and she has to stand. She therefore starts thinking of alternatives (car, coach). The train makes up time on its journey and arrives 20 minutes early. She therefore has time for food and drink before going on to her appointment. The overall feeling becomes one of satisfaction because the speed of service and time of arrival were the highest priority. The other factors simply contributed to the nature of the situation at the particular point of time.

BOX 3.11　Adaptation

A passenger survey carried out by one of the world's leading global airlines was rendered virtually useless because those who commissioned it overlooked this simple point. The survey questionnaire was given to passengers to fill in during long-haul flights and handed in at the end. It covered the service offered by the cabin staff, range of goods on sale, quality of the food, comfort of the accommodation and general feelings about the flight.

Since the survey was carried out on the actual flight, the airline received only average feedback when everything had gone more or less smoothly. The feedback was highly negative when small things had gone wrong. Twenty minutes' discomfort in flight was reported as a major negative, implying a threat to life and limb. Lack of instant response to demand for service was regarded as sloppy and symbolic of a poor attitude. One item in the food offered would colour the entire perception of food quality, especially if this was poor or not to the liking of the individual passenger.

In summary, the results were based on the constant adaptation of the passengers in respect of each occurrence rather than their wider perceptions and feelings of satisfaction.

BOX 3.12　Conveying Real Attitudes (1): Language

There are a great variety of words and symbols that define the actual view held by those that use them in regard to those about whom they are used.

1. 'These people': different and inferior groups, classes, tribes and families. It is a favourite phrase of politicians describing groups whom they would rather not have to deal with (such as the poor, the homeless or the socially disadvantaged).
2. 'Workers', 'workforce': always used by directors. A variation of this is to be found in the Annual Report: 'Staff are our most valuable resource.'
3. 'If you don't want this job there are X million unemployed who do': this phrase is never used in a satisfactory, or productive or harmonious situation; the question of whether the person has a low level of value simply does not arise.
4. 'We conform to legal requirements; we meet legal minimum standards; we meet particular directives': especially where the organisation concerned is hiding behind the letter of the law rather than assuming absolute responsibility for its own activities.

BOX 3.13   Conveying Real Attitudes (2): Symbols and Differentials

Job titles

A   Typist, clerk, worker operative.
B   Assistant manager, manager.
C   Crew, gang, cast.

Status

Hourly, clock, salary, levels and nature of supervision, industrial relations, management style, job titles, location, manuals and procedures.

Trappings

Cars, car phones, personal computers, offices, personal assistants, personal departments, staff officers, furniture and furnishings, personal facilities (fax, toilet, lift).

Behavioural differentials

Forms of address, separate canteens, designated car parking spaces, executive dining rooms, workers' canteens, location by floor.

Procedural differentials

Dependent upon: occupation, job title, department, division, location, etc.

The cover-up/openness syndrome

Dealing with mistakes and errors, scapegoating, use of (and failure to use) phrases such as 'We have made a mistake'; or 'I was wrong'.
   Dress codes, dress allowances, the use of uniforms, overalls; universality or differential.

Address codes

Referring to staff by first and last names, job titles and rank.

BOX 3.14   Managerial Job Adverts

'. . . you should be self-motivated, imaginative and able to persuade and influence at all levels . . .'

'. . . our innovative and proactive approach in all areas of HR means we are introducing new policies and systems . . .'

'. . . the competitive salary is pitched at a level attractive to the highest calibre individuals and you will receive the excellent company benefits you would expect from a leading financial services organisation . . .'

'. . . you must be a professionally qualified graduate with at least five years' relevant experience . . . creative, commercially driven and self-motivated, you are capable of designing and implementing original solutions to business issues . . .'

'. . . highly visible, highly challenging and highly rewarding, this position requires at least five years' experience in a significant personnel function, gained in a fast-moving environment . . .'

(Samples taken from *People Management*, 20 April 1995.)

■ Conclusions

Perception is the basis on which everyone forms their understanding of the world. People make interpretations of others that they meet, and places and situations that are encountered by combining each of these elements indicated to produce their own individual picture, which they can then understand and be comfortable with.

Perception is affected by repetition and familiarity. Something or someone who is always present acquires the illusion of permanence. Routines and habits are formed by organising activities and interactions into regular patterns based on a combination of expectation and near certainty.

Perception is affected by the context in which individuals are placed. There is a great range of responses to the request: Please do this for me. This depends on who has made the request and under what circumstances, whether it was a manager, subordinate, child, spouse, customer, waiter, barman; whether the person to whom the request was made was feeling well, ill, good or bad-tempered, calm or stressed; the tone of voice in which the request was made; whether it was a work or social situation; and what had gone on immediately beforehand.

Perception is affected by the characteristics of perceiver and perceived. The greater the knowledge of perception on the part of people and organisations, the greater the mutual understanding likely to be generated; and, where problems do arise, the greater the potential for addressing these effectively. Personal characteristics affect the type of characteristics likely to be seen in others, their levels of importance and whether these are or should be negative or positive. Those being perceived greatly influence the views of the perceiver through their visibility (appearance, manner, dress, speech) and through their status and role (either in the given situation or in a wider context). The simplest form of this is a conversation between two people; this becomes much more complex where the conversation is between more than two people, and more complicated still where this is in a new or unknown situation.

The purpose here has therefore been to draw attention to the nature and imperfection of perception and its processes. This forms the basis of being able to understand all individual behaviour, and the ability and need to reconcile different, and often conflicting, characteristics and aspirations, motivation, drives and desires.

■ Questions

1. To what extent have the initial impressions that you formed about your current colleagues remained the same? To what extent have they altered and why?
2. Choose a series of public figures – politicians, actors, actresses, sports and media personalities – and identify the key characteristics presented by them. What else do you infer from these about their personality and capabilities? How much of this can be proven or demonstrated, and how much must remain inferred or assumed?
3. (a) Consider the scenario in Box 3.5. What assumptions and inferences have you made about each of the four persons?
   (b) Given that nobody would make up their mind about anything on this quality and volume of information, what other information would you need and how would you go about gathering and validating it?
4. Identify the main aspects of your own perceptual mythology. Identify examples that both confirm and deny your perceptual mythology. What conclusions can be drawn from this?

Attitudes, values and beliefs

■ Introduction

Attitudes are the mental, moral and ethical dispositions adopted by individuals to others and the situations and environments in which they find themselves. They can be broken down into the following components.

1. **Emotional**: feelings of positivity, negativity, neutrality or indifference; anger, love, hatred, desire, rejection, envy and jealousy; satisfaction and dissatisfaction. Emotional aspects are present in all work as part of the content, working relationships with other people, reactions to the environment, and the demands placed on particular occupations.
2. **Informational**: the nature and quality of the information present and the importance that it is given. Where this is known or widely understood to be wrong or incomplete, feelings of negativity and frustration arise.
3. **Behavioural**: the tendency to act in particular ways in given situations. This leads to the formation of attitudes where the behaviour required can be demonstrated as important or valuable; and to negative attitudes where the behaviour required is seen as futile or unimportant.
4. **Past experience**: memories of what happened in the past affect current and future feelings.
5. **Specific influences**: especially those of peer groups, work groups and key individuals,such as managers and supervisors. These also include family and social groups, and may also include religious and political influences.
6. **Defence**: once formed, attitudes and values are internalised and become a part of the individual. Any challenge to them is often viewed as a more general threat to the comfort of the individual.

■ Values

Values are the absolute standards by which people order their lives. Everyone needs to be aware of their own personal values so that they may deal pragmatically with any situation. This may extend to marked differences between individuals or between an individual and demands of the organisation. Conflicts of value often arise at places of work; anything to which people are required to ascribe must recognise this and, if it is to be effective, must be capable of harmonisation with the values of the individual. These values may be summarised as follows.

1. **Theoretical**: where everything is ordered, factual and in place.
2. **Economic**: making the best practical use of resources; results-orientated, the cornerstone of people's standards and costs of living.
3. **Aesthetic**: the process of seeing and perceiving beauty; relating that which is positive and desirable or negative and undesirable.
4. **Social**: the sharing of emotions with other people.
5. **Integrity**: matters of loyalty, honesty, openness, trust, honour, decency; concern for the truth.
6. **Political**: the ways and choices concerning the ordering of society and its sub-sections and strata.
7. **Religious and ethical**: the dignity of humankind; the inherent worth of people; the morality – the absolute standards – of human conduct; this includes specific beliefs and the requirements of particular religions.

■ Shared Values

A clear set of values or direction offered by an organisation to its people, its customers and environment gives a clear sense of identity. The adoption of shared values is central to the generation of high levels of commitment and motivation among those who work in organisations. Recognising that people bring a diverse range of qualities to an organisation is essential. Giving a clear corporate purpose that is both above individual aspirations, and also accommodates them is a major function of the articulation of shared values. This is also instrumental in structuring particular ethical and moral stances that are taken.

Attitudes and values are affected by:

- past experiences and interactions with the given person, people or situation;
- continuing experiences and interactions;
- perceptions and levels of general understanding;
- the presence of, and understanding of, the particular rules, regulations and other limitations with which these are bounded;
- particular mental and physical aspects;
- levels of identity with the others involved and with the situation;
- the extent to which the people/situation are known or unknown;
- aspects of risks and uncertainty;
- levels of active or passive involvement;
- positive aspects (the extent to which something good and productive is certain or expected to come out);

- negative aspects (the extent to which something negative and unproductive is certain or expected to come out);
- any strong or prevailing moral, ethical or social pressures;
- general degrees of comfort (usually again based on levels of knowledge and understanding).

Attitudes are not easy to define precisely. The attitude of one person is capable of being inferred over periods of time and from certain patterns of behaviour or from particular interactions; it is not possible to prove.

Organisations take steps to identify and formulate the attitudes required of their people. This particularly refers to the positive aspects – emphasising the levels and nature of regards that are to happen, the commitment and effort necessary, the mutual confidence and respect between organisation and its people. This arises from the view that positive attitudes are based on high levels of mutual understanding and confidence. There is a strong predisposition on the part of those involved in any situation to seek the positive. People reject the unknown or approach it with fear and trepidation, precisely because it is unknown. When translated into organisation and work situations this also occurs, and the result is a lack of clarity or positive commitment and approach – negatives prevail because the positive has not been made clear. If this is allowed to persist people will find their own positive approach to the particular matter which may or may not coincide with that required by the organisation.

The best and most positive attitudes are therefore formulated by attacking each of the elements indicated above as follows.

1. Setting past experiences and interactions aside and placing emphasis on the current and continuing, by paying attention to and ensuring absolute standards of behaviour, approach, form of interaction, personal and interpersonal respect, esteem and value. This also refers to familiarising people with their situation and environment; again, on the basis of generating as great a level of understanding as possible.

2. Recognising the effects of general perceptions and levels of understanding; people will complete their own perceptual picture if this is not done for them. This means attention to the levels, nature, volume and quality of information available and how it is delivered; and also general environmental and situational familiarity and understanding.

3. Attention to the positive rather than the negative. This is underpinned by management style, nature of organisation/staff interactions, clarity of overall purpose and the sub-aims and objectives that support this, the language used in the organisation and between its people. This also means placing the emphasis on rewards and opportunities rather than punishments and threats.

4. Attention to the rules, regulations and other limitations to ensure that these reinforce the positive standards set, that they give clarity and understanding to all those that they affect, that the boundaries of situations and opportunities are well

defined, and that the consequences of transgression are suitable to the situation and evenly applied to everyone.

5. Attention to the work of individuals based on setting required operational standards and ensuring that these are met, resolving problems as they arise. This normally means ensuring visibility of supervision and continuous personal contact, which in turn generates the personal and positive relationship between superior and subordinate.

6. Identifying and removing as far as possible those aspects which are regarded as threatening. This means attention to that which people do not know and which they need/want/would like to know. This is the organisational behaviour equivalent of threat reduction. The greater the level of threat the more negative the response in this context in terms of time taken by people in mulling things over, wondering what is going to happen, creating imaginary scenarios and hypothetical outcomes. This is removed by recognising where the gaps in knowledge lie and filling them.

7. Gaining active rather than passive involvement. This means attention to the nature of the working relationship to ensure that people are valued and respected, and that the organisation has high expectations of them. The lower this level of expectation, the lower the general level of respect held and this is compounded by loss of self-esteem on the part of the people. Positive attitudes are generated by setting high and positive levels of involvement and commitment.

8. Reinforcing what is said and promised with delivery. If high levels of pay are promised they must be made. If equality of opportunity is offered to all staff it must be forthcoming. If sanctions are put in place for particular breaches they must be universally applied and people who transgress must be punished.

9. Reinforcing the positive with delivery. Given that people have a strong predisposition to identify with the positive, they will identify with good quality products and services, a good quality of working environment and life, good quality work colleagues and high levels of commercial (or public service) success and effectiveness.

10. Attention to any absolute standards required. These are to be spelled out at the commencement of employment so that nobody is in any doubt where they stand and what is required of them. This applies in all situations to health and safety, and emergency practices and procedures. It should also apply to matters of general integrity, respect and equality of treatment and opportunity. Some organisations also set other absolutes: Nissan and Sanyo and other Japanese organisations in the West have very strong attendance patterns and absence and sickness management, while the Body Shop requires all its staff to work on environmental concerns and projects and other public service activities one day per month.

11. Attention to prevailing moral and social pressures (this may include religious pressures also). The organisation requirements are to be harmonised with these and effective working relationships are to be achieved. This means ensuring that the organisation contributes to the general quality of life of the community and that the pressures that it places on its staff are capable of being harmonised with these. It also means having respect for the history and traditions of particular regions and communities and recognising their strength. Anything that denigrates these is liable

to cause hostility and rejection; while anything that builds on these, recognising their strength and value is much more likely to be accepted.

12. Attention to mutuality of interest in the given situation. This involves the recognition that people have personal as well as professional and occupational objectives, and that organisations have their own goals, and that these both complement and contradict each other. The problem lies in reconciling and harmonising these so that what is achieved covers, as far as possible, the full range. Where this is not recognised people tend to take refuge in professional and other technical expertise, identity and advancement at the expense of that of the organisation, and this in turn contributes to general disharmony, fragmentation of purpose and loss of general motivation.

13. Attention to information flows, in terms of both volume and quality, to ensure that as few gaps as possible are left in what people need and want to know. This is above all in terms of organisational performance and well-being. It also includes attention to individual performance in terms of understanding, aims and objectives, feedback; and the ways in which this performance is to be enhanced, improved and rectified and how problems are to be solved.

14. Attention to clarity of purpose, both overall and in terms that relate to particular departments, divisions, functions and individuals. Each is required to contribute to the whole in operational terms. From an organisation behaviour point of view, positive attitudes are enhanced when people know or perceive that they make their own distinctive and critical contribution; and negative attitudes are generated when this clarity is not apparent.

15. Attention to particular attitudinal barriers and constraints. These are present, or potentially present, in all situations. They consist of:

    (a) fear – of the unknown; misunderstood or badly understood situations and people; lack of information;

    (b) discrepancy – past histories, traditions and values in terms of those now required;

    (c) outside influences – family and friends; peer groups; professional associations and trade unions; and those who hold particular forms of influence such as dominant personalities, overmighty subjects, desired peers and other associations.

16. Attention to job and work satisfaction. This means considering:

    (a) the work itself, the ability to provide variety, enhancement, improvement, interest, respect, commitment and development; and the ability to provide tangible/output success and achievement;

    (b) pay and rewards, in terms of absolute amounts payable; and also to be seen in terms of the psychological contract of giving reward in terms of the value contribution and commitment of time, expertise and energy;

    (c) supervision and management style, and the extent to which this enhances/ diminishes job and work satisfaction; the work of Herzberg (see Chapter 5) suggests that supervision and management style is less likely to enhance satisfaction when it is right, but very likely to enhance dissatisfaction when it is wrong (for example, when it is dishonest or confrontational);

(d) co-workers, in terms of the extent to which they are technically expert and socially supportive.

17. Attention to the basic human needs of pride, esteem, value and worth. The problem is not so much with the work, but with the approach taken by the organisation in its division and allocation and in the styles of supervision under which it is carried out. This is emphasised by:

(a) the nature of the working environment, whether clean or dirty, high or low quality; general levels of ambience; approaches to matters of operational necessity (for example, the degree to which extremes of noise, heat, cold, dust, repetition of tasks are recognised as affecting general attitudes and the steps taken to remedy these);

(b) the extent to which supervision is driven by operational factors with attention to volume and quality of output, and the measures taken to ensure that the required levels are achieved (the greater the emphasis on efficiency and effectiveness of production and performance, the greater the contribution to positive attitudes);

(c) negative attitudes are generated when management and supervision style is (or is perceived to be) coercive, confrontational, rule driven; and where people are pulled up for breaches of rules and regulations rather than failing to meet performance targets. This is not to say that people should not be pulled up for these breaches, but the best attitudes prevail where these are related directly and principally to standards of performance and standards of respect.

In summary, therefore, the lesson for organisations lies in recognising the nature of influences on attitudes and taking steps to ensure that in the given situation these are positive. There is a range of interventions that can and should be made to influence attitudes and these both feed off and reinforce each other. The result is therefore either a positive and upwards spiral generating ever-stronger identity and commitment; or a negative and downward spiral, creating fragmentation and alienation.

The result of this is the creation, in turn, of a positive mutuality of interest as the basis for productive work and employment. Where this prevails, many of the institutions of staff management and administration can be simplified and streamlined. This especially applies to personnel welfare and industrial relations departments, and to those functions which would otherwise be needed to draw up and administer complex rules and regulations. The positive result of this is compounded because it frees up these resources that would otherwise be consumed in these activities for other purposes.

■ Formation of attitudes

The elements indicated are adopted by individuals in their own unique ways to form their own distinctive attitudes. The main processes that are involved are listed below.

1. Their propensity to accept rather than reject those of the group (including the organisation) to which they seek to belong; they have a high degree of potential compliance.
2. Their perception of the future relationship as being productive, effective, profitable and harmonious (people do not willingly enter a situation if they have no expectational perception of this; people are more willing and likely to enter situations, the greater the likelihood of this being achieved; and people will avoid situations where these elements are neither present nor apparent).
3. Relating past experience to current and future situations, relationships and environment; positive experiences tend towards the formation of positive attitudes; negative experiences tend towards the formation of negative attitudes.
4. Availability and completeness of information; availability includes access and clarity; completeness includes reference to key and critical gaps; and also to the value and usefulness of that which is available.
5. The general state of organisational well-being, the general state of the individual and the relationship and interaction between the two.
6. Other pressures, including the views of peers, co-workers, superiors, subordinates, family, friends; and economic, social, legal, moral and ethical pressures. These are likely to include sweeping generalisations, prevailing or received wisdom, opinions and prejudices (opinions formed without full reference to available facts) and, again, from the variety of sources indicated.
7. Any myths and legends present in the particular group or situation. For example, the statement that 'The person who holds job X or sits in office Y always gets promoted first/never gets promoted at all' puts behavioural and psychological pressures on each situation.

Each part of the process is present in the promotion and development of all attitudes, though the mix varies between particular situations and individuals. The mix also changes as people come into and go out of organisations and their groups. Also, by seeking to move, individuals may require (or perceive themselves to require) to change their attitudes in order to stand any chance of being successful. The attitude may change again, depending on whether or not they were able to make the move, and if they did, whether or not this was successful.

■ Adjustment of attitudes

This is the development of attitudes (positive and negative) in a given situation. The processes by which adjustment is achieved are similar to those above. They tend to reinforce what is already present.

Problems occur when a radical adjustment is either required, or else is to be imposed. The first response to such an adjustment or shift is often simply to shut it out; those affected do not believe the evidence before them.

Adjustment therefore works best where the prevailing attitudes are being developed rather than radically transformed. Where a radical change of attitude is required, it is much better from the point of view of generating effective organisational behaviour and interpersonal and intergroup relations if it is tackled as a major change.

Positive	Negative
• Equality of opportunity and treatment • Saying what is meant, meaning what is said • Identifying and solving problems • Clarity of purpose • Unity of purpose • Reward of achievement, loyalty and commitment • Openness of management style • Particular standards set at outset • Absolute standards for everyone • High and equal value placed on all staff • Recognition of every contribution • Pride in the organisation • Identity with the organisation • High levels of esteem and respect for staff • Clarity of communications • Harmony • High quality information • Open personal relationships • Open operational and professional relationships	• Inequality of opportunity and treatment • Expediency • Victimisation, scapegoating • Lack of clarity • Fragmentation of purpose • Rewards based on favouritism and infighting • Remoteness and distance of management style (both physical and psychological) • Standards allowed to emerge • Different standards for different groups, departments, divisions and individuals • Different levels of value placed on different staff groups • Lack of recognition • Lack of pride in the organisation • Lack of identity; rejection of identity • Low levels of esteem and respect; variations in levels of esteem and respect according to occupation, department, division and function • Lack of clarity of communications • Hostility • Low quality information

Figure 4.1   Influences on attitudes: summary

■ Beliefs

Beliefs are the certainties of the world. They may be any of the following.

Absolute	Based on such things as mathematical fact; night following day; mortality and taxation.
Near absolute	Based on seasonal changes; the continuous development of knowledge and awareness; the continuous technological and social development.
Acts and articles of faith	Based on the certainty of God; and often underpinned by religious allegiance and the following and adoption of the teachings of those who pronounce in the name of God; this may also extend to the adoption of social and political creeds.
Other strong ethical and moral standpoints	Relating to honesty, trustworthiness, right and wrong.
Strong illusions and perceptions of order, permanence and stability	Often founded on long steady-state factors.

Beliefs are the psychological cornerstone of the lives of people. They provide the foundations and framework upon which people order and structure the rest of their lives. They are internalised to the heart and soul of the individual, providing the basis for other attitudes, values and chosen behaviour.

Forcing and imposing belief changes on people is very traumatic for those who are to be affected. Religious persecutions and the willingness of people to die for their beliefs indicates the extent of this. People would rather lose their lives than their beliefs. (Frederick Forsyth describes this trauma as being akin to 'a china vase hit by an express train.')

From an organisational behaviour point of view it is clearly possible to make the rational case that as there is no such thing as an eternal organisation, there is therefore no question of individuals believing in it. However, individuals may create a relationship very akin to belief, especially if they work in the same situation for a long time and where the relationship is mutually productive, effective and harmonious. Any change in this (especially sudden change) is therefore in turn akin to the trauma indicated above. Moreover, people internalise particular aspects of the organisation, coming to believe (or nearly believe) in the given standards of honesty, trustworthiness, and high ethical and moral standpoints. In these cases when it becomes apparent that they are illusory the same degree of trauma is felt.

BOX 4.1   Beliefs

Bank of Credit and Commerce International (BCCI)

This bank collapsed in 1991. It followed a long history of allegations of fraud and participation in the laundering of drug money, and illicit armaments deals and sales. This was so extreme that most of the staff working in the bank simply shut it out. They could not accept that their organisation could possibly be corrupt in this way. When the bank finally closed, following the removal of great volumes of its money and assets, many of the staff went into (and remain in) deep shock that this could have happened – to them.

Maxwell

When Robert Maxwell drowned in September 1992 it became apparent within days of his death that he too had left behind a dubious legacy. Many of the staff of the *Daily Mirror*, the newspaper that he owned, simply left, taking jobs anywhere else to put the knowledge that they had worked for a thief and the trauma of this behind them. Until his death, Robert Maxwell had gone to a lot of trouble to cultivate an image of being a larger than life character, based on his past history of having escaped from the Nazi invasion of his homeland of Czechoslovakia, his arrival in the UK as a refugee, the brilliant military record that he had gained during the Second World War, his creation of a global publishing empire, and his subsequent election as a Labour MP.

In more general terms, much trauma has been caused to individuals who joined organisations on the basis of permanence and, after relatively long periods of stability and order, found themselves suddenly surplus to requirements during redundancy and reorganisations. The problem lay on the one hand, with the fact that the illusion of permanence had been shattered and this was combined with the fact that most organisations did little to prepare their people for the reality that the relationship was not permanent and that changes would occur; they did little to prepare people for the arrival of these changes. In effect, they did nothing to generate any understanding of the fact that the illusion of permanence was indeed just an illusion.

The lesson for organisations and individuals therefore lies in the necessity and ability to create and maintain a working relationship based on honesty, integrity and clarity. This means above all, recognising and reconciling the following points:

- that individuals have beliefs;
- that they seek a set of certainties in their lives and tend towards belief when the illusion of certainty and permanence is fostered;

- that the organisations in which they work, and to which they commit a substantial part of their time, energies, expertise and talents (and therefore forgo the opportunities to use these elsewhere and in other ways) tend to give a measure of certainty and permanence.

The nature of the relationship, if it is to be truly honest and effective therefore needs to be contextual. This means creating a relationship which satisfies the need for some degree of permanence and at the same time setting out the boundaries of this, which normally means addressing questions of flexibility and dynamism and the willingness to change, develop and adapt. Permanence therefore becomes something to which individuals have their own direct and active contribution to make: it is not solely dependent on organisation provision.

Above all, there is the need to recognise the difference between attitudes, values and beliefs and to ensure that these are distinguished. This, in turn, is to make certain that people's beliefs are kept separate from their attitudes and values; that whereas organisations have a legitimate role in the shaping and influencing of attitudes and values, the requirements to adopt and internalise the organisation as an act of faith is undesirable and potentially devastating for the individual.

◼ Socialisation

Socialisation is the process by which individuals are persuaded to behave in ways acceptable to their society, family, social groups and clubs. This also applies to work organisations and their groups, departments, divisions and functions. Effective socialisation results in compliance and conformity with the values, beliefs, attitudes, rules and patterns of behaviour required. While this does not necessarily mean that individuals must adopt everything to the point of total faith and commitment, successful integration only occurs if they can at least acknowledge and respect these as boundaries and constraints within which they can work and operate.

For this to occur the group's attitudes, values, beliefs, behaviour and rules must be capable of being accepted by the individuals that seek to join or who are required to join. They tend therefore to reflect the prevailing customs of the wider society and to be in harmony with general ethical and social pressures.

On the other hand, socialisation should also leave enough space, latitude and freedom for individuals to express themselves in the given setting. Too great a restriction leads to frustration. At the other extreme, a lack of clear under-standing of these standards leads to lack of focus and purpose leaving the individual in a void, and this can be just as harmful and stressful as over-restraint.

Socialisation takes place from the moment of birth. It is conducted in the early years by parents and family, schools and colleges, religious institutions, sports and leisure clubs. By the time individuals arrive in work they have therefore been subject to a great variety of pressures and influences. The problem for organisations lies in their ability to build on this and create conditions that are both acceptable to individuals and also ensure that productive and effective work can take place.

This problem is greater with mature employees who may arrive at an organisation after experience in many others. They will already have formed their own ideas about high standards, best practice and optimum ways of working, and this in turn leads to the need for effective orientation at the outset of the new job. Where an employee comes to a new organisation after a long stay in a single place of work, the problem is greater still because the new employee's only recent (possibly his only other) point of reference is the place that he has just left. For whatever reason, positive or negative, the person is coming into a new situation for the first time in a long while and great care is needed to ensure that he settles in quickly and effectively. This also applies to those returning to work after long periods of absence (because of previous job loss or family commitments, for example).

Effective organisations' socialisation processes tackle this by addressing their own needs from the point of view and perspective of the individual, and engages positive feelings in him/her. If an organisation sets its standards and expectations out clearly at the start, the individual is in no doubt about the expectations placed upon him and the ways in which he is to use his talents and

Organisation	Individual
• Productive effort	• Comfort
• Effective workforce	• Warmth
• Effective individuals	• Belonging
• Effective groups	• Contact
• Continuous development	• Success
• New talents and energies	• Fulfilment
• Work harmony	• Achievement
• Expectations	• Professionalism
• Job proficiency	• Expectations
• Professionalism	• Rewards
• Success	• Training and development
• Value	

The lists represent two sides of the same coin. Organisation socialisation is designed and devised to bring them together, to match up and harmonise the pressures. Some of these pressures are convergent, others divergent; all must be integrated and interrelated as far as possible.

Figure 4.2   Social needs

qualities. This also generates the beginning of a relationship based on mutual respect and identity.

This underlines the importance of adequate and effective induction and orientation programmes. Too many organisations and their managers still neglect this, believing it to be a waste of time, cutting into their other priorities; or else they have simply never learned to see it as an investment, the return on which is a committed and effective employee; and, if this is really successful much of the process is achieved over a relatively short period of time.

■ Learning

Learning is the process by which skills, knowledge, attitudes and behaviour are formed and developed. It takes place as the result of education, training, socialisation and experience. Learning also occurs as the result of conditioning and restriction, whereby the individual is persuaded to adopt, and ultimately accept, guidance, regulation, conformity and compliance in particular situations.

BOX 4.2   Behaviourist and Cognitive Learning

Two contrasting views of learning may be distinguished, behaviourist and cognitive.

Behaviourist

The behaviourist (or stimulus response (S–R)) theory states that series of actions and movements are learned as responses to particular stimuli. Learning is (in part at least) a form of conditioning; and this is reinforced by feedback. Feedback may either be positive and rewarding, or negative and punitive. The effect of positive feedback is to increase desired behaviour. The effect of negative feedback is to reduce undesired behaviour.

Positive   For example, if an employee receives praise for doing good work she will tend to do good work as often as possible in order to receive the praise as often as possible.

Negative   If a supervisor is angry every time work is poor or late, the employee will tend to do good work and on time in order to avoid the anger.

The result may therefore be very much the same – that good work is done on time – but the means by which this has been learned (and also often the attitude and approach) are very different. The overall view is that people learn and repeat behaviour that has positive and favourable consequences and avoid that which has negative and undesirable consequences.

The approach is extremely useful in:

- the organisation of learning and adoption of routines;
- establishing forms of address between colleagues;
- standards of dress, appearance, time-keeping;
- some on-the-job training, especially concerning the use of machines, computers and technology;
- establishing effective emergency procedures and ensuring that these are followed.

For the approach to be effective, reinforcement – both positive and negative – must be consistent and continually applied. For example, emergency procedures (such as fire drills and building evacuations) only remain effective if continually practised and rehearsed. Standards of dress and behaviour are only effective if they are enforced and if recalcitrants are taken to task.

Cognitive

The cognitive approach takes a broader view. It states that learning occurs as the result of different responses to the great variety of cues and stimuli that are present. To be effective, learning must take account also of individual personality, perception and motivation; these all contribute to the disposition of the individual to learn.

The operation of feedback, rewards and punishments is also more complex than that indicated by the behaviourist approach. The key lies in the volume of value and information available to the individual and the ways in which this is received, understood and processed in relation to behaviour. Rather than a conditioned series of movements, behaviour is learned through mental processes and retained in the memory. It is reinforced by expectations, the anticipation of rewards and achievements. It is adaptable: knowledge and skills learned from one situation can be reprocessed or repositioned in order to understand and be effective in another. The cognitive approach also recognises creativity, invention and imagination as elements present in learning: for example, in the ability to solve problems, improve operations and activities.

Feedback is also seen as a continuous process rather than as a series of events. This may take the following forms.

1. **Current**: taking place during the task performance, controlling and modifying it as it proceeds.
2. **Delayed**: where the effectiveness (or otherwise) of the performance is not clear, apparent or measured until sometime afterwards.
3. **Internal**: in which individuals evaluate, judge and assess their performance themselves.
4. **External**: in which the performance is evaluated, judged and assessed by others.

5. **Cooperative**: in which the performance is assessed jointly by the individual and others.
6. **Environmental**: in which the performance is modified, directed or limited by interactions with the wider situation.

Finally, the cognitive approach takes into account the view that people naturally and continually strive to improve their knowledge, skills, abilities and understanding of every situation in which they find themselves.

■ Ability to learn

Individuals learn at different rates, times and stages in their lives. Some people acquire new knowledge, skills and qualities easily, while others struggle to learn the very basics of the same things. This is based on a combination of the following.

1. The desire and motivation to learn brought about by the individual's own needs and drives, usually in the expectation that this will bring success, rewards, enhanced potential and expertise, marketability; and also increased esteem, respect and status.
2. The quality and suitability of the learning and teaching methods (including the quality of instruction).
3. Pressures to learn placed on individuals by others – including organisations – to enable them to acquire the knowledge, skills and qualities required by them in the individual; and also to adopt the attitudes, values and behaviour required in order to be comfortable in the particular situation.
4. Specific drives and requirements such as the onus placed on individuals in particular occupations to keep abreast of new developments and initiatives in their field.
5. The nature of the individual's attitude and disposition to acquire new skills, knowledge and qualities.

The result is to increase the range, depth and interactions of thoughts, ideas and concepts, as well as skills, knowledge, attitude, behaviour and experience; to increase the ability to organise and reorganise these; and to order them in productive and effective activities (whatever that may mean in the particular set of circumstances).

The cycle illustrates the importance of the relationship between behaviour, action, and experience. It also emphasises (testing and experience) the need to reinforce abstract learning with practice and performance.

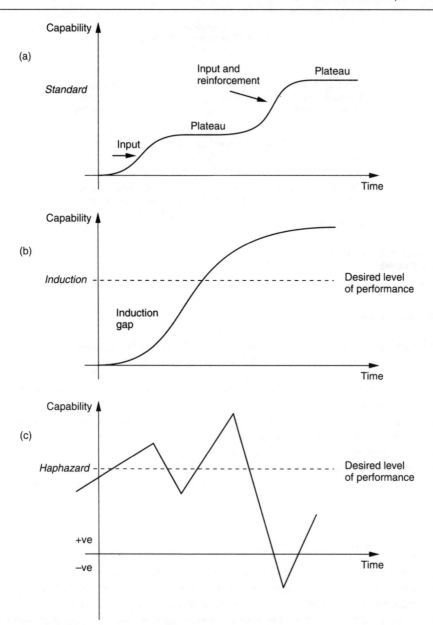

(a)   Theoretical, based on rational and ordered input, familiarisation, practice and reinforcement.

(b)   The theory of induction – time taken at the outset leads to long-term high levels of performance.

(c)   The theory of non-induction and non-training, based on trial and error.

Figure 4.3   Learning curves

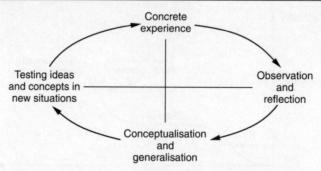

The cycle illustrates the importance of the relationship between behaviour, action and experience. It also emphasises (testing and experience) the need to reinforce abstract learning with practice and performance.

Figure 4.4   Learning cycle

Source: Kolb (1985)

■ Retention

The ability to retain and internalise that which has been taught and learnt is based on a combination of the following factors.

1. The ability to practise and use, and become proficient in that which has been taught and learned.
2. Its actual value once it has been taught and learned (as distinct from its perceived or anticipated value before it was learned).
3. The regularity and frequency with which it is to be put to use.
4. The rewards that are to accrue as the result.
5. The punishments and threats that occur if learning does not take place (this is especially important in the acquisition of attitudes, values and behaviour, and in conforming to rules and standards).

This is usually called learning reinforcement. Reinforcement may be:

•   continuous, in which case the learning is soon internalised;
•   intermittent, in which case it is likely to become important from time to time only and may lead to the need for revision, retraining and refresher courses;
•   occasional, in which case the learning is likely to have been of general or marginal value only.

More generally still, learning, acquiring and becoming proficient in new skills and qualities normally leads to enhanced feelings of personal confidence and self-respect. It enhances flexibility of attitudes and approaches. It is also increasingly likely that it will bring greater general perceptions of worth and value to the organisation.

■ Feedback

Feedback is essential on all aspects of performance leading to enhanced general levels of understanding, confidence and support. Related specifically to learning, feedback is best in the following circumstances.

1. When it is positive rather than negative, in that it enhances the general concept of progress to which learning is supposed to contribute. Negative feedback is best as a 'nuclear deterrent' (that is, it is present, but is never to be used). It is normally to be applied to persistent failure to accept and conform to necessary rules, rather than because of failure to learn skills and knowledge.
2. When concentrating on processes as well as results so that individuals both know their results and also understand why they have succeeded or failed.
3. When delivered as near to the conclusion of the learning as possible and then followed up with opportunities to apply that which has been learned and for this also to be incorporated into the feedback process.
4. When continuous in general, so that any problems with what has been learned that subsequently become apparent or any later decline in performance, can be quickly rectified.

■ Mentoring and coaching

This is where the feedback role is enhanced and developed into active interest in the progress of individuals. Mentors and coaches may be assigned to individuals or an individual may be encouraged (or directed) to seek them out. The mentor or coach then becomes an integral part of the development of that person (and therefore of the organisation) agreeing and implementing development strategies with him and seeking out opportunities and openings. The individual's learning therefore becomes a partnership between the individual himself and the mentor or coach (and therefore also the organisation).

Mentoring and coaching needs both high priority and adequate resources if it is to be effective. It is most likely to be successful where a form of organisation development or learning culture has been adopted (see Chapter 14).

■ Learning styles

Individuals have preferred learning styles. For some this may be very marked; they can only learn in one particular way and other methods have little effect.

Honey (1986) identifies four preferred learning styles as follows.

Activist   Concentrating on learning by doing and via direct experience, and through considering the results of trial and error so that performance may be improved next time.

Pragmatist   Concentrating on that which is possible and practical and of direct application to given situations.

Theorist   Concentrating on why things are as they are and investigating theories and concepts that form the background to this.

Reflector   Concentrating on assessing and analysing why things have turned out in particular ways and using this as the basis on which to build understanding.

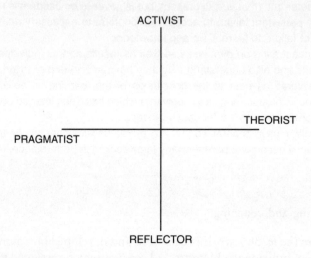

This spectrum was devised by Honey and Mumford to identify the preferred learning style. By completeing a questionnaire and plotting the results the respondent would

(a) identify those activities likely to be most and least beneficial;
(b) identify those areas which needed working on, so that full benefit from all activities could be gained.

Figure 4.5   Preferred learning styles

Honey and Mumford designed a questionnaire, the purpose of which was to identify under which of these four headings an individual's preferred learning style fell. The results would then be used to ensure that the individual understood why she tended to learn some things better than others; to seek out those activities that were best suited to her preferred learning style; and to develop her lesser and least preferred areas of preferred learning to enhance her total learning capability.

Other aspects of preferred learning style may be identified:

● the influence of rewards and outcomes;
● economic factors (career and payment enhancement);

- peer, professional and social group expectations;
- the nature of the material and the means by which it is taught/learned;
- the quality of the teacher;
- time factors.

There are also some absolutes. For example, eventually someone who wishes to know whether he can drive a car will have to sit in a car and drive, however much of a theorist he may be. Similarly it is not possible to be an effective leader of people if there is no basic understanding of why people behave in different ways in different situations (and different ways in the same situation), however much of a pragmatist a person may otherwise be. This underlines the need to broaden the preferred learning style into an individual learning style that can accept effective input and information from as wide a variety of sources and means as possible.

■ Individual development

In absolute terms, individual development is not optional. The world no longer allows people to acquire an education and training for life during their childhood and adolescence and then apply it for the rest of their time. Skills and knowledge become inadequate and obsolete at all levels and in all fields over short periods of time, and in many cases these periods are getting shorter.

Training and development are therefore becoming ever more central to the wage–work bargain. The organisation that fails to develop its staff loses competitive edge and advantage; undertrained and underdeveloped staff become uncompetitive and obsolete, and unmarketable when they seek to change jobs and broaden their horizons.

The primary purpose is therefore to enhance skills, knowledge, qualifications and expertise through the use and application of the great variety of means and methods available, and which are indicated in Box 4.3. If this is to be successful the following must be clear.

- aims and objectives, and measures of success/failure;
- positive motivation of both trainers and trainees;
- rewards must be perceived and available;
- benefits in terms of personal, professional and organisational performance and objectives must be met;
- it must be capable of reinforcement of the workplace;
- it must be current and relevant;
- it must have organisational and managerial support;
- it must be planned and integrated into the workload of the individual and have priority and importance at the time when it takes place;
- it should be part of a total package and process of continuous learning and development;

- it should be evaluated afterwards by all interested parties, both in the short term and also into the future.

BOX 4.3   Training Methods and Techniques

1. Classroom: lectures, talks, seminars, day-release, block-release, full-time study, professional updates, briefings and discussion groups.
2. Laboratory and workshop: for the development of precise practical and scientific skills and the ability to practise and apply these in safe situations, leading to the ability to practise these in real situations.
3. Project work: for the purposes of problem-solving and developing the capabilities and experience of those undertaking the projects.
4. Secondments: to develop and broaden the experience of staff and to ensure a regular supply of fresh ideas and flexible attitudes into different organisation activities.
5. Competencies training: specifically targeted at the 'can do' elements of work; in the UK this includes the gaining of recognised technical and professional competencies and the awarding of National Vocational Qualifications.
6. Open distance learning: whereby the student is given a framework or objectives to work to and sets her own agenda, timetables, goals and learning methods within the broad programme.
7. Mentoring, coaching and counselling: and other one-to-one relationships with key employees for the purpose of developing them into very high performers (see below).
8. Role plays, case studies, computer-based activities and other interactive forms of learning: these give the opportunity to generate a measure of reality or to consider a version of it with a view to recognising, observing and analysing particular behaviour/activities/situations in order to broaden an understanding of the consequences of particular courses of action.
9. Outward bound and other outdoor activities: generally perceived to be of greatest value in the assessment and development of leadership, strategic and operational characteristics and in the formation of confidence, trust and mutuality in work groups and teams.
10. Skills updates and other short-term targeted activities: again, these are used in both the technical field (for example, computer software) and in the behavioural (for example, leadership, presentation skills and decision-making ability). It is essential that these are capable of being reinforced when the learner returns to work.
11. High-cost seminars and professional association programmes: the main purpose of these is normally to create a forum where persons from similar occupations or organisations can meet and exchange ideas supported by a modicum of structured input (for example, from experts in the particular fields).

There is a great range of material and opportunities available to all those concerned with the development of organisations and employees. There is also a great range of opportunity available to employees as they pursue their particular expertise. All methods used should relate to the matters in hand, performance gaps and development requirements. They are to be viewed as part of a process to be built upon and developed for the future (rather than as ends in themselves). The obligations of the organisation, learners and teachers vary in each situation. The responsibility does not – this remains always with the organisation and teacher.

If this is to be achieved, organisations must also consider individual development from the point of view of:

- organisation requirements, the need and drive for enhanced current and future performance;
- professional and expertise requirements, the need for individuals to enhance and improve their general skills, knowledge and expertise;
- personal drives and preferences.

Other points may usefully be made.

1. Individuals must be motivated to learn. This motivation arises from a combination of personal and professional or occupational circumstances, drives and needs and the requirements of the organisation.
2. Learning and development are part of the general commitment to each other made by organisation and individual. The organisation is entitled to expect the individual to learn; and the individual is entitled to expect training and development.
3. Whatever is learned must be capable of recognition and measurement so that performance standards can be set and identified.
4. The better understood the activity, the stronger the motivation and drive to learn. It is often necessary to break complex tasks and practices down into smaller parts to avoid facing the trainee with too much to grasp at one time.
5. Feedback is essential to reinforce understanding, expertise and commitment. Current or immediate feedback is much better than delayed feedback: the greater the delay, the greater the loss of meaning and impact.

BOX 4.4 Continuous Professional Development

Continuous Professional Development (CPD) is the name given to the formalised requirement to undertake regular and current training and development activities. The requirement is placed on members and graduates of professional bodies and institutions to ensure that they keep abreast of current developments, best practice, new and improved standards of performance and new knowledge coming into their particular field. Increasingly, it is a condition of continued membership that individuals complete a certain number of days (or some other volume) of designated CPD. While the standards and content of this varies widely, there is an increasing organisation commitment required, at least in the matter of giving time off for staff to attend events.

Many professions and the best organisations have always required this of their staff and members. Doctors, lawyers and engineers have also been consulted and engaged on the basis of their current (rather than historic) knowledge and expertise. The current drive is to get organisations to recognise the importance of this to all staff; for people of all types and levels of expertise to understand its importance and value; and for providers to deliver a combination of regular quality and relevant training and development.

■ Conclusions

Forming and nurturing the required attitudes and values clearly requires a broad knowledge and understanding of all the factors and elements indicated. If this is to be effective, the following must be present.

1. Identification of the required attitudes and values, together with the reasons why these are desirable and ensuring that these are capable of being supported and adopted by all those concerned.
2. Taking positive steps to reinforce them in the ways in which the organisation and its departments, divisions and functions operate and penalising any shortfall.
3. Recognising the effects of all training and development activities on attitudes and values, whatever the training and development is overtly concerned with. Attitudes and values are shaped, developed and reinforced by all learning activities, as is the general mutual relationship and commitment between organisation and individual.
4. It is also necessary to recognise that attitudes, and especially negative attitudes, emerge whether or not they are shaped and influenced by the organisation. Where the organisation has no influence on attitudes, these are formed by other pressures, especially peer, professional and social groups.
5. Positive attitudes help to provide a harmonious and open working environment, and increase general levels of motivation and moral. Negative attitudes tend to reinforce any stresses and strains, such as poor working relationships, lack of trust and value.
6. Attention to workplace attitudes, especially at the induction stage, helps employees to adopt and find the place required of them in their environment. It helps to provide a clear mutual understanding between organisation and employee, and is one of the cornerstones of the working environment. Above all, as organisations strive for ever-greater levels of flexibility and responsiveness, building these characteristics as positive and valuable attitudes is essential.

■ Questions

1. Outline the extent to which the following influence the attitudes of participants towards their organisation.
   - (a) MBA programmes studied part-time while employed from the point of view of being both directly sponsored, and also of having to pay one's own fees.
   - (b) Attending a week-long middle management seminar at Harvard Business School, USA.
   - (c) Attending regular training activities based at the place of work.
2. Discuss the view that, as everyone has their own individual preferred learning style, structured induction programmes are a waste of time.
3. What are the major contributors to negative attitudes and negative influences on attitudes, and how should these be treated within organisations?
4. Produce an outline training and development programme for the next 12–24 months for yourself. This should include aims and objectives, training methods, learning outcomes, and the means by which you would evaluate it for success/failure.

CHAPTER 5

Motivation

■ Introduction

Motivation is a reflection of the reasons why people do things. All behaviour has a purpose (often several). All behaviour is therefore based on choice: people choose to do the things they do. Sometimes this choice is very restricted (sink or swim, for example). Sometimes, again, it is constrained by the law (for example, stopping the car when the traffic lights are red). And again, it is constrained by the norms and processes of society: for instance, people tend to wear smart clothes to a party where they know that everybody else will be well dressed. In each case however, there is a choice, though the propensity and encouragement and direction to choose one course of action rather than another in the examples given is strong, if not overwhelming.

■ Definitions

Huczynski and Buchanan (1993) defined motivation from three perspectives: in terms of the goals towards which human behaviour is directed; as the process through which those goals are pursued and achieved; and the social factors involved.

Luthans (1986) sees motivation as a combination of needs, drives and incentives. Motivation is defined as 'a process that starts with a physiological or psychological deficiency or need that activates behaviour or a drive that it is aimed at a goal or incentive'.

Mullins (1993) summarises motivation thus: the underlying concept of motivation is some driving force within individuals by which they attempt to achieve some goal in order to fulfil some need or expectation. Mullins also distinguishes between *extrinsic* motivation (related to tangible rewards such as money), and *intrinsic* motivation (related to psychological rewards such as the sense of challenge and achievement).

Motivation is therefore both limited and directed by the situations and environments in which people find themselves. This is the general context in which people set their targets, ambitions, purposes, drives, goals, aims and objectives as marks of achievement and success. These are pursued in anticipation of the rewards – financial, social and behavioural – that their achievements are to bring. Satisfaction occurs when the targets set bring the anticipated rewards. Dissatisfaction occurs when the rewards are either not forthcoming, or else do not meet expectations.

The salient features identified thus far should now be considered in more detail.

Goals and ambitions	These must be present, and both realistic and achievable if satisfaction is eventually to occur. Problems arise when the goals set are too low (leading to feelings of frustration), or too high (leading to the constant lack of achievement). They must also be acceptable to the individual concerned – in terms of self-image, self-worth, and self-value – so they are likely to be positive and based on the drive for improved levels of comfort, capability and well-being. They must also be acceptable (or at least not unacceptable) to the society and environment in which the individual lives and works, and capable of being harmonised and integrated with them.
Recognition	A critical part of the process of developing self-esteem and self-worth lies in the nature and levels of recognition accorded to the achievement of particular goals. The need for recognition itself therefore becomes a drive. Individuals thus tend to pursue goals that will be recognised and valued by those whose opinion and judgement is important to them, such as family, friends, peers and social groups, as well as work organisation. Dissatisfaction occurs when this recognition is not forthcoming.
Achievement	The components of achievement are the anticipated and actual rewards that the fulfilment of a particular goal brings. High levels of achievement occur where these overlap completely. High levels also normally occur where real rewards exceed those that are anticipated. Low levels occur where the anticipated rewards are not forthcoming; this devalues the achievement. High or complete achievement is normally seen and perceived as successful. Low achievement or failure to achieve is seen and perceived as – a failure.

From this in turn, other aspects of motivation become apparent.

The need for success	People tend to aim their sights at what they know they can do or think they can do, or think that they may be able to do, so that success is forthcoming. Genuine successes, victories and triumphs enhance feelings of self-esteem and self-value; failures diminish these.
The need to be recognised and valued by others	This is a combination of pursuing things that individuals know or perceive will be valued by those around them (as stated above) and also of seeking out those who will value the achievements for themselves.
The need to develop and improve	This is a positive statement of need. If satisfaction is not forthcoming in one field, individuals are likely to lose interest and find something else to pursue. As well as matters of comfort and well-being, it also

includes broadening and deepening experience and variety of life (including working life). Moreover, includes developing new skills, capabilities and interests with the view to pursuing personal potential as far as possible.

These are social and behavioural needs, wants and desires; they are influenced, developed and conditioned by societies and organisations, and groups within them. They are based on more fundamental human needs.

The need and instinct for survival	When individuals are hungry or thirsty, their prime motivation is for food or drink. When people are cold, their instinct is to find warmth and shelter. When the life of an individual is under threat (for example, from war or disaster), the instinct is to take actions that preserve life.
The need and instinct for society and belonging	This is a reflection of the need for esteem, warmth and respect. More fundamentally, it is the need to belong, to interact and to have personal contact with those with whom the individual has identity, respect, liking and love. It also includes being drawn to those who have similar hopes, aspirations, interests and ambitions.
The need to be in control	This is the ability to influence the actions and feelings of others; and the ability to influence the environment, to make it comfortable and productive in response to the particular needs, wants and drives. Control is a function of purpose: the organisation and arrangement of particular resources (including other people) for given reasons.
The need to progress	This is a reflection of the capacity to develop, to enhance knowledge, skills and capability. It includes:

(a) economic drives for better standards of living, quality of life and enhanced capacity to make choices;
(b) social drives to gain status, respect, influence and esteem as the result of enhanced capability and economic advantage;
(c) personal drives reflecting ambition and the need to maximise/ optimise the potential to achieve;
(d) opportunistic drives, the identification and pursuit of opportunities that may become apparent and attractive to the individual;
(e) invention and creativity, the ability to see things from various points of view and create the means by which quality of life can be enhanced.

Development, adaptation and creativity are also features of the needs for survival, society and control. They are a reflection of the extent to which individuals are able to influence their ability to survive, belong to and control their environment.

Except at the point of life and death, when the instinct for survival is everything, these needs constitute part of the wider process of adaptation and interaction. At given moments therefore, some will be stronger than others; there is no linear progression from one to the next.

BOX 5.1   Achievement Motivation Theory: D. C. McClelland

Much of the background on which the nature of motivation is based was organised and summarised by D. C. McClelland. Working in the 1950s and 1960s he identified the relationship between personal characteristics, social and general background and achievement.

Persons with high needs for achievement exhibited the following characteristics:

- task rather than relationship orientation;
- a preference for tasks over which they had sole or overriding control and responsibility;
- the need to identify closely, and be identified closely, with the successful outcomes of their action;
- task balance: this had to be difficult enough on the one hand to be challenging and rewarding; to be capable of demonstrating expertise and good results; and gaining status and recognition from others, while on the other hand it needed to be moderate enough to be capable of successful achievement;
- risk balance: in which the individual seeks to avoid as far as possible the likelihood and consequences of failure;
- the need for feedback on the results achieved to reinforce the knowledge of success and to ensure that successes were validated and publicised;
- the need for progress, variety and opportunity.

Need for achievement is based on a combination of:

(a)   intrinsic motivation – the drives from within the individual;
(b)   extrinsic motivation – the drives, pressures and expectations exerted by the organisation, peers and society.

It is also influenced by education, awareness, social and cultural background, and values.

One potential problem was identified in relation to the appointment of high achievers to highly responsible managerial and supervisory positions. Because the higher achievement tended to be task- rather than relationship-driven, many did not possess (or regard as important) the human relations' characteristics necessary to get things done through people.

BOX 5.2   Self-Actualisation

Self-actualisation is a key concept in the understanding of human motivation. First used by Maslow and Schein (see below), it refers to people's ability and drive to realise their full potential, to progress as far as possible and to be fulfilled; and also for this to be recognised and valued by others. The concept addresses the need for challenge, responsibility, variety and pride in work and achievement as well as the technological or professional expertise. Again, the ability to fulfil potential is affected by society, cultural background and norms and values.

Two views of self-actualisation are taken. The first is that self-actualisation is available only to the very few. It is limited by the inability to develop sufficient qualities and capabilities for this to take place. This is due to the limitations of the social background of many people and, above all, of education, training and other means by which skills, knowledge and expertise are developed.

The second view is that self-actualisation is achievable by almost everyone in their own particular circumstances. Whatever the limitations placed by society and education, individuals nevertheless exhibit a range of capabilities and qualities which have the potential of being harnessed and developed in the pursuit of highly rewarding lives in their own terms. Self-actualisation is therefore an individual and not an absolute process.

The latter view currently holds sway. It is of particular value in understanding that everyone has needs for respect and esteem; and that whatever the nature, level or content of work carried out, they will tend to seek variety and enhancement if this is at all possible; if it is not possible in the workplace, people will seek it elsewhere. This view tends to militate against traditional and classical organisation features of task specialisation and administrative hierarchies which expect individuals to restrict their capabilities, work as directed and operate machinery and systems, rather than develop and use their capabilities and talents to the full.

BOX 5.3   Passivity and Activity

The transformation of the individual from a state of passivity to one of activity is based on a theory of personality development which argues that, as an individual's personality matures, highly structured organisations are unsuitable places in which to work. Argyris (1957) identified seven dimensions along which the individual develops towards psychological maturity.

1. An individual moves from a passive state as an infant to an active state as an adult.
2. An individual moves from a state of dependency as an infant to a state of relative independence as an adult.

3.   An individual has limited behaviour as an infant but complex and sophisti-
     cated behaviour as an adult.
4.   An individual has short, casual and shallow interests as an infant but deeper
     and stronger interests as an adult.
5.   An infant's time span and perspective is very short; their concentration span
     is very short (it involves only the present); with maturity this widens into
     conception of past and future.
6.   An infant is subordinate to others and becomes a peer, equal or superior as
     an adult.
7.   Infants lack self-awareness and self-control; adults are self-aware and
     capable of self-control.

This is a theory of personality development, presenting the view that highly
structured and formalised organisations are therefore unsuitable places in which
to work. There is a fundamental lack of harmony – or congruence – between the
needs of the individuals and the drives of the organisation. This tends to get worse
as the organisation becomes more sophisticated and as its rules, procedures and
hierarchies grow, and also as the individuals concerned seek to progress
themselves. This leads first to restriction, then frustration, and finally, to conflict.
Frustration and the potential for conflict are greatest at the lower levels of the
organisation, where the ability to work independently is most restricted. It is also
apparent where people at any level of the organisation and of any level of
professional or technical expertise (or lack of it) believe themselves to be
restricted in their potential to achieve by unnecessary and unproductive rules,
procedures and systems.

From whatever point of view the matter is considered, the relationship between
organisation and people is fundamentally unsound. The conclusion is that
organisations create the conditions for disharmony and unproductiveness themselves by placing so many limitations on the potential and drives of their people.
Staff apathy and lack of effort is the inevitable result of this approach to structuring
and organising work. Effectively, therefore, people are expected to behave in
these negative ways.

■ Major theories of motivation

■ Rensis Likert: System 4

Likert's contribution to the theories of workplace motivation arose from his
work with high-performing managers; that is, managers and supervisors who
achieved high levels of productivity, low levels of cost aud high levels of
employee motivation, participation and involvement at their places of work.
The work demonstrated a correlation between this success and the style and

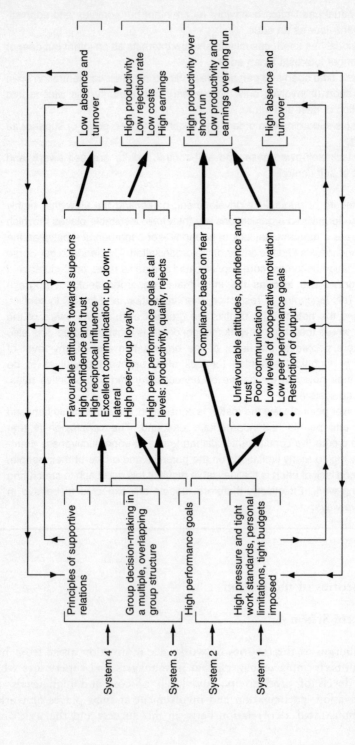

Figure 5.1 System 4

Source: Likert (1961)

structure of the work groups that they created. The groups achieved not only high levels of economic output and therefore wage and salary targets, but were also heavily involved in both group maintenance activities and the design and definition of work patterns. This was underpinned by a supportive style of supervision and the generation of a sense of personal worth, importance and esteem in belonging to the group itself.

The System 4 model arose from this work. He identified four styles or systems of management.

System 1: Exploitative Authoritative, where power and direction come from the top downwards and where there is no participation, consultation or involvement on the part of the workforce. Workforce compliance is thus based on fear. Unfavourable attitudes are generated, there is little confidence and trust, and only low levels of motivation to cooperate or generate output above the absolute minimum.

System 2: Benevolent Authoritative, which is similar to System 1 but which allows some upward opportunity for consultation and participation in some areas. Again attitudes tend to be generally unfavourable; confidence, trust and communication are also at low levels.

In both Systems 1 and 2, productivity may be high over the short run when targets can be achieved by a combination of coercion, bonus and overtime payments. However, both productivity and earnings are demonstrably low over the long run; there is also manifestation of high absenteeism and labour turnover.

System 3: Consultative, where aims and objectives are set after discussion and consultation with subordinates; where communication is two-way and where teamwork is encouraged, at least in some areas. Attitudes towards both superiors and the organisation tend to be favourable especially when the organisation is working steadily. Productivity tends to be higher, and absenteeism and turnover lower. There are also demonstrable reductions in scrap, improvement in product quality, reduction in overall operational costs and higher levels of earning on the part of the workforce.

System 4: Participative, in this system three basic concepts have a very important effect on performance. These are the use by the manager of the principle of supportive relationships throughout the work group referred to above; the use of group decision-making and group methods of supervision; and the setting of high performance and very ambitious goals for the department and also for the organisation overall.

Likert saw the various management systems as having causal, intervening and end result variables.

The causal variables are independent variables which determine the course of developments within an organisation and the results achieved by it; and also management policies, decisions, business and leadership strategies, skills and behaviour.

Intervening variables are those which reflect the internal state and health of the organisation. These include loyalties, attitudes, motivations, performance goals and their achievement, the perceptions of all members and their collective capacity for interaction, communication and decision-making.

End-result variables are the dependent variables reflecting the achievements of the organisation in terms of its productivity, costs, efficiency, product quality and earnings.

System 4 was Likert's favoured system. His research demonstrated that the principles and attitudes prevalent in System 4 could and should be applied to all types of organisation.

■ Abraham Maslow: a hierarchy of needs

Abraham Maslow was a behavioural scientist whose researches led him to depict a hierarchy of needs which explained different types and levels of motivation that were important to people at different times. This hierarchy of needs is normally depicted as a pyramid (see Figure 5.2). The hierarchy of needs works from the bottom of the pyramid upwards showing the most basic needs and motivations at the lowest levels and those created by, or fostered by, civilisation and society towards the top of it. The needs are as follows.

1. **Physiological** – the need for food, drink, air, warmth, sleep and shelter; that is basic survival needs related to the instinct for self-preservation.
2. **Safety and security** – that is, protection from danger, threats or deprivation and the need for stability (or relative stability) of environment.
3. **Social** – that is, a sense of belonging to a society and the groups within it: for example, the family, the organisation, the work group. Also included in this level are matters to do with the giving and receiving of friendship; basic status needs within these groups; and the need to participate in social activities.
4. **Esteem needs** – these are the needs for self-respect, self-esteem, appreciation, recognition and status both on the part of the individual concerned and the society, circle or group in which they interrelate; part of the esteem need is therefore the drive to gain the respect, esteem and appreciation accorded by others.
5. **Self-actualisation** – that is, the need for self-fulfilment, self-realisation, personal development, accomplishment, mental, material and social growth and the development and fulfilment of the creative faculties.

Thus was the hierarchy of needs outlined. Maslow reinforced this by stating that people tended to satisfy their needs systematically. They started with the basic, instinctive needs and then moved up the hierarchy. Until one particular group of needs was satisfied, a person's behaviour would be dominated by

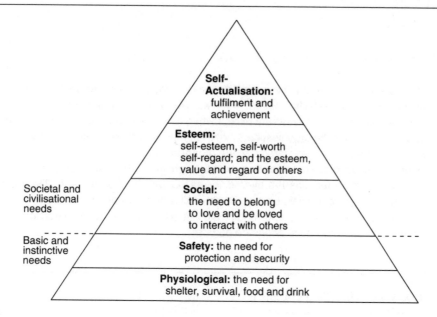

Figure 5.2 A hierarchy of needs

Source: Maslow (1960)

them. Thus the hungry or homeless person will look to their needs for self-esteem and society only after their hunger has been satisfied and they have found a place to stay. The other point that Maslow made was that people's motives were constantly being modified as their situation changed, and in relation to their levels of adaptation and other perceptual factors; this was especially true of the self-actualisation needs in which having achieved measures of fulfilment and recognition, people nevertheless tended to remain unsatisfied and to wish to progress this further.

Maslow's work was based on general studies of human motivation, and as such was not directly related to matters endemic at the workplace. However, matters concerning the last two items on the pyramid, those of self-esteem and self-actualisation, have clear implications for the motivation (and self-motivation) of professional, technical and managerial staff in organisations.

■ Douglas McGregor: Theory X and Theory Y

McGregor identified two distinctive sets of assumptions made by managers about employees. From this he articulated two extreme attitudes or views and called these Theory X and Theory Y. His thesis was that in practice most people would come somewhere between the two except in certain circumstances.

□ *Theory X*

This is based on the following premises.

1. People dislike work and will avoid it if they can. They would rather be directed than accept any responsibility; indeed, they will avoid authority and responsibility if possible. They have no creativity except when it comes to getting around the rules and procedures of the organisation. Above all, they will not use their creativity in the pursuit of the job, or the interests of the organisation.
2. People must be forced or bribed to put out the right effort. They are motivated mainly by money, which remains the overriding reason why they go to work. The main anxiety concerns personal security, which is alleviated by earning money.
3. People are inherently lazy and require high degrees of supervision, coercion and control in order to produce adequate output.

BOX 5.4   'They Don't Want It'

One of the most insidious of managerial nostrums is the assertion that the staff do not want responsibility, involvement, advancement and growth. The counter-assertion made is that this is simply not true. Any group of people given the choice between being bored, alienated and disaffected, or not, will take the latter always. This extends to all places of work. The idea was perversely reinforced by the 'Affluent Worker' studies of the 1950s and 1960s. These identified widespread and enduring alienation among the workforce and the value of earnings accrued at work in the pursuit of out-of-work activities. The trade-off was therefore that this form of working relationship was only to be endured as long as opportunities away from work continued.

□ *Theory Y*

This is based on the premise that work is necessary to everyone's psychological growth. People wish only to be interested in work and, under the right conditions, they will enjoy it. People gain intrinsic fulfilment from it. They are motivated by the desire to achieve and to realise potential, to work to the best of their capabilities and to employ the creativity and ingenuity with which they are endowed in the pursuit of this.

People direct themselves towards given accepted and understood targets; they will seek and accept responsibility and authority; and they will accept the discipline of the organisation in the pursuit of this. People will also impose self-discipline on both themselves and their activities.

Whatever the conditions, management was to be responsible for organising the elements of productive enterprise and its resources in the interests of economic ends. This would be done in ways suitable to the nature of the organisation and workforce in question; either providing a coercive style of management and supervision, or arranging a productive and harmonious environment in which the workforce can and will take responsibility for directing their own efforts and those of their unit towards organisational aims and objectives.

■ Frederick Herzberg: two-factor theory

The research of Herzberg was directed at people in places of work. It was based on questioning people in organisations in different jobs, at different levels, to establish:

(a)   those factors that led to extreme dissatisfaction with the job, the environment and the workplace: and

(b)   those factors that led to extreme satisfaction with the job, the environment and the workplace.

The factors giving rise to satisfaction he called motivators; those giving rise to dissatisfaction he called hygiene factors (see Figure 5.3).

The motivators that emerged were: achievement, recognition, the nature of the work itself, level of responsibility, advancement, and opportunities for personal growth and development. These factors are all related to the actual content of the work and job responsibilities. These factors, where present in a working situation, led to high levels and degrees of satisfaction on the part of the workforce.

The hygiene factors or dissatisfiers that he identified were as follows: company policy and administration; supervision and management style; levels of pay and salary; relationships with peers; relationships with subordinates; status; and security. These are factors that, where they are good or adequate, will not in themselves make people satisfied; by ensuring that they are indeed adequate dissatisfaction is removed, but satisfaction is not in itself generated. On the other hand, where these aspects were bad, extreme dissatisfaction was experienced by all respondents. Organisations that failed to provide adequate hygiene factors tended to have high levels of conflict, absenteeism and labour turnover and low general morale.

The work of Herzberg has tended to encourage attention on such factors as: good and adequate supervision which encourages and extends the workforce rather than restricts it; job satisfaction which can often be increased through work restructuring, job enrichment and job enlargement programmes; and the setting and achieving of targets and objectives based on a full understanding of what they are and why they have been set. Some organisations have also

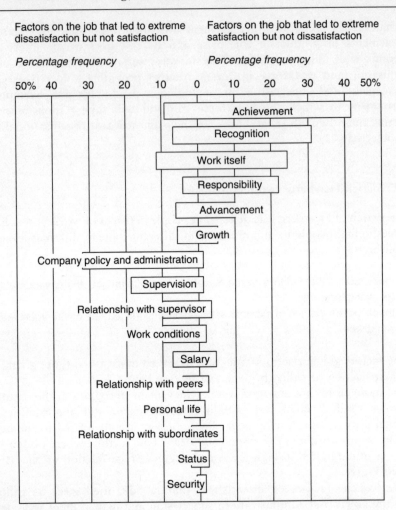

Factors on the job that led to extreme dissatisfaction but not satisfaction

Factors on the job that led to extreme satisfaction but not dissatisfaction

Percentage frequency

Percentage frequency

50% 40   30   20   10   0   10   20   30   40 50%

Achievement

Recognition

Work itself

Responsibility

Advancement

Growth

Company policy and administration

Supervision

Relationship with supervisor

Work conditions

Salary

Relationship with peers

Personal life

Relationship with subordinates

Status

Security

Figure 5.3   Two-factor theory

Source: Herzberg (1960)

concentrated on removing the dissatisfiers or hygiene factors to ensure that causes of intrinsic dissatisfaction with the workplace and its environment are minimised.

Both the Theory X/Y and the hygiene factor concept require further emphases. If the bases of these studies are accepted there are substantial steps that organisations and their managers can take in order to remove or limit propensities for dissatisfaction and demotivation. These include attention to the following:

1. Management style, attitude and approach to staff; this should be based on integrity, honesty and trust, whatever the nature, limitations or technology concerned in the work itself.
2. The working environment, which is to be comfortable, functional and suitable in human terms, again whatever the operational constraints and limitations may be.
3. General factors of status and importance which ensure that every member of staff is respected, believed in, treated equally and given opportunity for change, development and advancement within the organisation.
4. Effective and professional operational relationships between members of staff that in turn promote profitable and successful activities across the entire organisation. This includes recognising the existence of barriers and potential conflicts between departments, divisions and functions and taking steps to provide effective counters to these.
5. Administrative support and control processes and mechanisms should be designed both to make life easy for those working at the front line, while at the same time providing the necessary management information. This particularly refers to the nature and effectiveness of the roles and functions of corporate headquarters and the relationships between these and the front-line operations indicated.
6. The work itself, and how it is divided up. There is particular reference here to those parts of the work that are looked upon with disfavour but which nevertheless must be carried out adequately and effectively (see above).
7. Security of tenure. This ensures that people are employed on a continuous basis as far as that is possible. At the same time steps have to be taken to ensure that there is a steady and open flow of information, so that when changes do become necessary the staff concerned are both forewarned and positively responsive.

■ V. Vroom: expectancy theories

In essence, this approach to motivation draws the relationship between the efforts put into particular activities by individuals, and the nature of the expectations of the rewards that they perceive they will get from these efforts.

This is clearly centred on the individual. It relates to the ways in which the individual sees or perceives the environment. In particular, it relates to his view of work, his expectations, aspirations, ambitions and desired outcomes from it, and the extent to which these can be satisfied at the workplace or carrying out the occupation in question. For example the individual may have no particular regard for the job that he is currently doing but will nevertheless work productively and effectively at it and be committed to it because it is a stepping stone in his view to greater things; these are the expectations that he has of it and this constitutes the basis of his efforts and the quality of these efforts. This is compounded, however, by other factors: the actual capacities and aptitudes of the individual concerned on the one hand, and the nature of the work environment on the other. It is also limited by the perceptions and expectations that the commissioner of the work has on the part of the person who is actually carrying it out. There is a distinction to be drawn between the effort put into performance and the effectiveness of that effort: hard work, conscientiously carried out, does not always produce effective activity; the effort has to be directed and targeted. There has also to be a match between the rewards expected and those that are offered; a reward is merely a value judgement placed on something offered in return for effort and if this is not valued by the receiver it has no effect on that person's motivation (see Figure 5.4).

There has consequently to be an understanding of the nature of the motives and expectations of the individual, related to an ability to satisfy these on the part of the organisation if it is to address effectively the issue of motivation. The approach required is therefore to take both an enlightened and specific view of what constitutes job satisfaction (rather than assuming that it exists, or exists in certain occupations at least); and an understanding of the processes of percep-

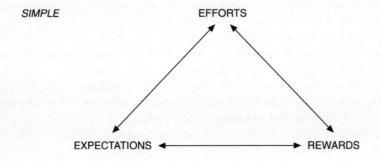

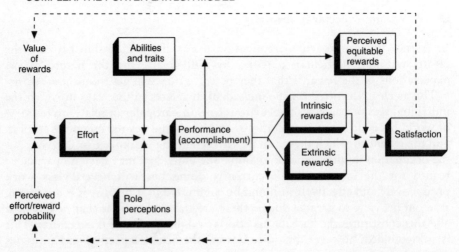

Figure 5.4   Expectancy theory

Source: from Luthans (1986)

tion and the nature of reward in relation to the aspirations of those conducting the work.

The components of the expectation–effort–reward mixture are as follows.

Personal ambition
The inner drive to make progress and the rewards that this progress brings with it. These are in terms of increased prosperity and disposable income (and by extension, the uses to which that disposable income is put: the larger car, larger house, prestigious address, foreign holidays, higher-quality food and clothing, private education, better health care). These are to be seen also in terms of the status and esteem afforded by this: the feeling of well-being that accrues from, for example, the prestigious address or the children in private education.

Professional ambition
The drive and desire to make it to the top of the chosen occupation, to become an expert (and to be regarded as such by both peers and the public at large). This includes the drive for constant self-improvement and self-development, pushing at the boundaries of the chosen field.

Situation
The ability of the situation to provide the rewards expected and anticipated. This is constantly unfolding and changing. The situation that may have once been attractive to the individual can change quickly, particularly as the result of reorganisation. The situation may or may not bring the expected rewards. It may open up other opportunities that are either perceived or not perceived as opportunities. The individual may have gone into the situation with a variety of objectives and the situation perhaps satisfies one or several of these, but not all.

Performance
This is the nature of the work in question, both present and future. Individuals inevitably are required to carry out a variety of tasks. They tend to gravitate towards those which are seen to produce a greater level of desired rewards. This may be at the expense of tasks which are just as essential but which do not carry the same motivational factors in regard to the persons in question.

Perception
It follows from all of this that most of the drive comes from within the individual rather than being imposed or directed. The genesis is therefore what the individual feels or perceives to be important and worthwhile. Satisfaction derives from within, and from the successful completion of activities that lead to this, rather than from the achievement of organisational targets *per se*. If one accepts the expectation model, therefore, it follows from this that organisational targets and work methods are to be dovetailed with individual expectations and aspirations for the best results. Indeed, to pursue it to its extremes, the source of organisational targets must be the satisfaction of those people working within it and to these ends.

BOX 5.5   Motivation, Achievement and Rewards

An alternative view of the expectation–effort–reward mixture consists of restating this as motivation, achievement, rewards. Drives for particular goals are enhanced by the capability to achieve them and the rewards which are to accrue as the result.

These rewards are a combination of the following factors.

1. **Economic:** monetary pay for carrying out the job, for special achievement for responsibility and accountability; this is expected to continue and improve in line with the relationship between organisation and individual, both in terms of current and future occupations and also loyalty and commitment. Economic rewards meet the needs and expectations of individuals, and also reflect the value in which they are held by the organisation.

2. **Job satisfaction:** intrinsic rewards attained by individuals in terms of the quality of their work, the range and depth of expertise used and the results achieved.

3. **Work content:** the relative contribution to the output of the organisation as a whole and the feelings of success and achievement that arise from this. As stated elsewhere, operating a small part of the production process or administrative system tends to be limited in its capability to satisfy this part of the requirement for achievement.

4. **Job title:** certain job titles give images of prestige as well as a description and summary of what the work is, and the respect and esteem in which it is held by the individual and her peers and social circles.

5. **Personal development:** the extent to which the individual's capabilities are being used (or limited in their use); and the extent to which alternative means of achievement and reward may become apparent through the development of both current and new expertise.

6. **Status:** the relative mark of value placed on the individual's rank, role, expertise and job by those whose views and opinions they value. This invariably includes those of the particular organisation, because of the nature of the continuing relationship between the two. It is also likely to include again, the views of social and professional circles.

7. **Trappings:** these are the outward marks of achievement and success, material and visible benefits by which others can recognise its extent. They include:

   (a) benefits – such as cars (both the fact that a car has been issued and also the value of the car itself); other business technology; business trips; sabbaticals; course and seminar attendance; health care (they are marks of achievement when presented in professional and social circles);

   (b) autonomy – the ability of individuals to set their own patterns of work; to come and go as they see fit, to work from home; to attend the place of work at weekends or other quiet periods in order to be able to work without interruptions (as distinct from having to attend during the same time as everyone else); to make work arrangements based on sole individual judgement without reference to higher authorities; to exhibit absolute, professional or technical expertise and judgement;

(c) secretaries, personal assistants and personnel departments – normally integral to the nature of the work, they also constitute a trapping insofar as they are an outward representation to the rest of the organisation of the value and importance of the individual's work;

(d) accessibility – in many organisations, the inability to get to see someone, either because of their rank or because of their workloads, constitutes a mark of achievement (often perverse).

The problems associated with these do not lie in their validity. This is not an issue since they are based on perceptions, expectations, the wider situation and the individual drives that accumulate from the achievement and possession of these. They rather indicate the organisation's capability of recognising the extent to which its employees need and want them, and its ability to satisfy them in these ways.

The other aspect that requires consideration is the need to build positive motivators into all work.

It is therefore the responsibility of all organisations to find means of giving recognition, giving opportunities for growth and advancement and measuring achievement. This extends to front-line production and service activities as well as professional occupations. It involves taking a broad and enlightened view of what the whole purpose of the work is. Advocates of efficient but alienative traditional production and service methods point to the reductions in unit costs that are achieved by these, but usually take no account of the consequences of that alienation: absence, turnover, disputes and grievances and the additional levels of supervision that go with these. Above all, such approaches take no recognition of the resource base that is required to support these negative activities.

BOX 5.6 'The Need to Know'

This is one of the most damaging and demoralising of phrases. It is used inevitably by top managers of organisations in describing the extent and volume (that is, the limitations) of information that the rest of the staff are deemed to require. Organisations which take a prescriptive view of this demoralise and alienate the rest of their staff.

Protagonists of 'the need to know' cite commercial confidentiality as the overwhelming reason for this approach. On the one hand, plainly, organisations have to protect their commercial position. This has to be balanced against what a genuine business secret is. Very little that is described as such, by such organisations, has any impact on business performance once the particular information emerges. Genuine business secrets and genuine needs for confidentiality are few and far between, and are limited to information about individuals or about a genuinely new invention.

■ Edgar Schein: a classification of humankind

Schein classified people as follows.

1. **Rational economic**. People are primarily motivated by economic needs. They pursue their own self-interest in the expectation of high economic returns. If they work in an organisation they need both motivation and control. As they intensify the pursuit of money they become untrustworthy and calculating.

    Within this group, however, there are those who are self-motivated and have a high degree of self-control. This is the group that must take responsibility for the management of others. They also set the moral and ethical standards required.

2. **Social**. People are social and gregarious beings, gaining their basic sense of identity from relationships with others. People will seek social relationships at the place of work and part of the function of the work group will be the fulfilment of this necessity. The role of management in this situation is therefore greatly concerned with mobilising the social relationships in the pursuit of operational effectiveness and drawing a correlation between productivity and morale; and also in taking an active interest in the development of the work group.

3. **Self-actualisation**. People are primarily self-motivated. They seek challenge, responsibility and pride from their job and to maximise the opportunities that these bring. They are likely to be affected negatively by organisational and management style, external controls, scarcity of resources and other pressures. They will develop their own ways of working and objectives, and integrate these with those established by the organisation.

    The inference is that this is strongest among professional, technical, skilled managerial staff. However, all work groups have tended towards higher levels of motivation and morale when given a greater degree of autonomy at work.

4. **Complexity**. People are complex and sophisticated. People have 'varieties' of emotions, needs, wants and drives driven by personal circumstances, interactions and adaptation. They have many differing, diverse and contradictory motives which vary according to the matter in hand and the different work and social groups in which they find themselves. They will not fulfil every need in any one situation, but rather require a variety of activities in order to do this. They respond to a variety of stimuli according to needs and wants at a given moment. Schein's view of 'complex man' in organisations is that of a psychological contract, based on mutual expectations and commonality of aspirations. It is therefore a psychological partnership.

■ The Hawthorne studies

The Hawthorne studies were carried out between 1924 and 1932. They took their name from the Hawthorne Works of the Western Electrical Company at Chicago where the research was conducted. The original objective was to ascertain the relationships between the physical working environment and operational productivity. However, the main findings were in terms of the social environment of work: membership of groups, both formal and informal; relationships between workers and supervision; relationships between workers and organisation; and the degree of attention and interest shown by the organisation to its staff.

The work was carried out by George Elton Mayo (1880–1949), an Australian academic. He was Professor of Industrial Research at Harvard Business School, and an authority on industrial fatigue, labour turnover and accidents, and health and safety. He was called in by the Western Electrical Company to advise on the results of a study that had already been carried out by the company into the effects of lighting on productive output and staff morale. One group – the core group – had the lighting levels in which it had to work varied; the other, the control group – had constant lighting levels. The output of both groups rose consistently over the period of the experiment (1924–7). The output of the core group rose whether the lighting levels were increased or diminished. The output of the control group (where the lighting levels remained constant) also rose.

Mayo was first called in to explain this. The conclusion was that the experiment indicated a general relationship between levels of output and interest taken in the people carrying out the work. He then conducted four further experiments.

□ *Relay Assembly Test Room (1927–9)*

The purpose was to assess the affects of different physical conditions on productivity. Six female assemblers formed themselves into a group and were given a room – the relay assembly test room – in which to work. At first, they continued to work their usual 48 hour week (including Saturdays) with no breaks. Changes were introduced, including stoppages for lunch and tea and rest periods, and production went up; and, when the breaks were withdrawn, production went up again.

This result is what is usually known as 'The Hawthorne Effect'. It was concluded that the women were responding to special treatment. The breaks were incidental. They had selected themselves to be the group; they were the centre of attention; they had a good relationship with the researchers from Harvard Business School; and by being placed in a separate room they felt special and distinctive, with increased morale and self-worth.

☐ *Employee Attitude Interviews (1928–30)*

In all, 20 000 of the company's employees were interviewed with a view to finding out what they really felt about their work, patterns of supervision and relationships with the organisation, and the relationship between these aspects and staff morale. Interviewers initially asked employees highly structured questions about how they felt about their work; and this was later extended to cover general complaints and grievances (the ability to 'sound off' about the company). The questioning also extended to family and social issues.

The results led to an assessment of relative satisfaction and dissatisfaction of work based on:

- social organisation of the company, both formal and informal, including the formation and membership of cliques and other groups;
- organisational policies and directives;
- the position, work content and status of the individual;
- outside demands and commitments placed on employees.

Each element contributed to levels of satisfaction and dissatisfaction. Above all, relationships with others – both within and outside the organisation – were critical to the formation and maintenance of positive attitudes.

☐ *Bank Wiring Observation Room (1932)*

The bank wiring observation room experiment was to pursue further the finding in the employee attitude interviews that there was a high degree of informal organisation and clique membership. In this case, 14 men were removed from the production lines and put in a separate observation room. The project lasted six months and observed the work itself, work organisation and formal and informal groupings.

The findings were as follows.

1. The group quickly developed its own norms and behaviour, and set its own standards of output. These should neither be too high nor too low.
2. There was overwhelming social pressure for everyone to conform to this, usually through the use of sanctions, ridicule of anyone who tried to work too fast and pressure on those who worked too slowly.
3. The company would be told that results were both steady and satisfactory, whatever the actual output achieved.
4. The group never worked to its full capacity in spite of productivity incentives that were available. Members perceived that if they did, the bonus rates would be cut to match the new increased levels of output, and that they would have to work harder for less.
5. Interventions of supervisors and inspectors to try and increase output were ineffective.

The conclusions from this phase were:

(a) the need to be part of the work group is very strong;
(b) the pressures to conform to the norms and standards of the group (as distinct from those of the organisation) are very strong;
(c) attitudes are shaped and influenced by the group, both between members and also in relation to the work;
(d) these pressures and needs are strong motivators, especially in the ways of working and its organisation. The individual is more responsive to peer pressure than organisational and managerial incentives and exhortations.

☐ *Personal interviews (1936)*

This was a return to the employee attitude format indicated above: again it encouraged people to discuss problems, air grievances and say what they felt about organisation–worker relationships. It led to enhanced priority being given to management and supervisory training, especially in human relations. This was to try to develop the need for attention to the social side of work group organisation and direction on the part of those in responsible positions. This was so that the groups themselves would become more responsive to organisational requirements which could then be matched and harmonised with the social needs and pressures of group members.

The main general conclusion of these studies demonstrated that social factors at work were quite as important as monetary rewards and adequate working conditions. They also indicated the source of motives, drives and pressures that are placed on the individual and which both limit and channel their energies.

The following strands of motivation to work may be identified.

1. The motivation to seek out particular types of work, the determination to follow a particular career, to work in particular sectors, occupations, trades, professions and crafts.
2. The motivation to apply for specific jobs, with specific employers, to complete the application process and to subject oneself to the recruitment and selection processes.
3. The motivation to accept job offers, to accept the salary/occupation/prospects mixes of particular organisations.
4. The motivation to turn up for work on the first day.
5. The motivation to turn up for work on the second day and to continue turning up on a daily basis; and to start and continue to produce effective and successful work on behalf of the organisation.

There is therefore clearly plenty of need for attention to this. Conversely, there is plenty of opportunity for things to go wrong, for the individual to lose interest in the organisation. Above all, there is the necessity to recognise the organisation's obligations, to motivate its people, and to understand what motivates them, and the overwhelming extent to which the process is influenced by what it does (and does not do). The process of attraction and retention is to be viewed from this standpoint. The process of attitude and value formation of generating a mutual identity and interest, begins to take place at this point of contact. It takes place in both positive and negative terms: that is, a negative mutual identity may be formed in the same way as positive (as, for example, where the individual receives a bad initial contact or a bad job interview). This is exacerbated when the individual has been a customer or client of the organisation in question (for example, a retail chain, hospital, other public service); or where, for example, someone goes to work for a company whose products they have previously or currently owned (for example, a car or electrical goods company).

The hypothesis is that the organisations which understand the importance of this and get it right ensure a better flow of quality staff ready, willing and able to use their talents and expertise in pursuit of the objectives of the particular organisation and to work as directed in this pursuit.

From the point of view of the organisation, a good part of this involves deciding upon an absolute view of what constitutes work and jobs. A traditional scientific management view is that it is to be divided and compartmentalised as much as possible so that the individual becomes expert at a tiny occupation and can carry it out perfectly every time.

The administrative/hierarchical view is that systems and procedures are developed by which organisations are to be steered and directed and that hierarchies provide both order for organisations and careers for individuals.

The overwhelming problem with both such views is that of motivation. At the unskilled level people are required to suborn completely their persona in the pursuit of their occupation; while those operating in the hierarchy tend to focus on that which is necessary to advance their own careers rather than that which is good for the organisation, its customers and clients. Both hierarchies and mass production lines are staff intensive and therefore expensive. This is exacerbated by the fact that hierarchies tend to be non-productive and non-contributory. Problems thus arise in both production lines and hierarchies associated with achievement, identification, satisfaction and value, all of which contribute to the motivation of the individual, and which by their absence contribute to their alienation. Those working in such situations therefore tend to operate in ways that suit themselves, that make life bearable, and that enable progress from one job to the next to be achieved rather than in the interests of the organisation in question.

■ Job and work design

The issue therefore is the need to reconcile the organisation's often conflicting operational, personal and professional requirements into sets of activities – jobs and occupations – that are effective, productive and satisfying. There is an instant general self-test or ready-reckoner in this. If the organisation is experiencing morale problems, jobs and occupations can be queried along these lines to try to find a way into the particular problems.

There is also the point that job titles are in themselves demeaning and dissatisfying. Titles such as typist, dustman, operative (and their politically correct alternatives of clerical assistant, refuse executive, crew person) are issued by organisations as proof of status as much as occupational indicators.

It is within this context that job enrichment, job rotation, job enlargement and empowerment activities are to be considered. If carried out effectively, motivation and commitment can be generated in any staff or occupational group, whatever the working situation and provided that the behavioural satisfaction aspect is also addressed. It must also be noted that the converse is true: where jobs and occupations are not effective, productive and satisfying, demotivation and demoralisation occurs whatever the interests inherent in the particular profession may be.

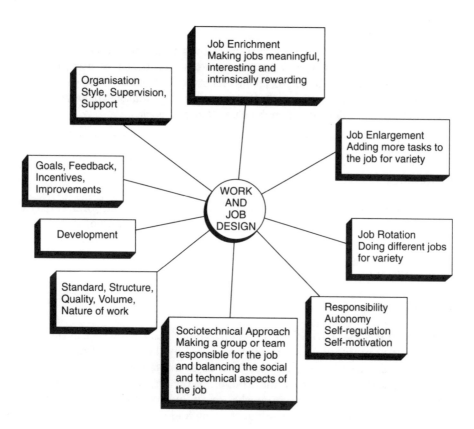

Figure 5.5   Job design

The other prerequisites for effective job and work design are the existence of effective channels of communication, the presence of constant feedback, and absolute knowledge of results. The outcome of these is a clarity of purpose, both of the occupation in question and also of the context in which they are carried out.

BOX 5.7   The Bad Bits

A part of this involves basic recognition that jobs and occupations invariably have bad bits. Activities such as cleaning, maintenance, working away from home and basic administration have to be dealt with in ways that at least ensure that they are bearable.

A spread of these activities on an egalitarian basis normally assumes this, as long as everyone involves genuinely takes their share.

Flunkeys

The alternative to this clearly is to employ persons specifically for the purpose of carrying out the unwelcome or demeaning tasks. The benefit of doing this is normally justified because it frees up the rest of the staff in order to do what they are good at. In practice, the inevitable result is an organisational hierarchy with different types of value placed on the different occupations.

■ Rewards

Organisations reward their employees in a variety of ways and for a variety of reasons. It is essential to establish at the outset the parameters of this.

Thus, people understand what the essential elements of performance are, how these are to be achieved, who is to assess what has been achieved and what the rewards are.

■ Promotion

At this point it is useful to reflect on a salient point made elsewhere in the book, that the use of promotion as a reward is limited by the ability of the person in question to do the job to which he is to be promoted. Forms of reward are rather to be seen as satisfactory and valuable to the organisation and motivating to the employee. The person who wishes to attain promotion is therefore to be obliged to undertake aptitude testing, training and development in order to be confirmed as suitable for the proposed new job. The best organisations set promotion in this context. It is not to be offered as a right but as an achievement based on capability.

BOX 5.8   Promotion (1)

Traditional organisations badly misplace promotion as a reward. For example, tennis players do not aspire to be senior tennis players, director tennis players, stadium or tournament controllers. Their winning of tournaments and related earnings reflect their status and quality.

Similarly, there is no reason why a human resource officer should expect to be a senior human resource officer or director of human resources by virtue of promotion and expectation. As with the tennis example, the reward that is available to that person should be based on capability.

Also, as with the tennis example, those players that do become tournament directors tend to be those who are not able to reach the top as players. However, failure to reach the top along the one path does not of itself constitute the requirement to open up others on the part of the sector in question. Neither does it mean that because an individual cannot pursue a path based on excellence, a path based on rank must be opened up to her.

To complete the comparison, many (probably most) tennis players earn more than those who organise the competitions in which they play. There is no reason why this cannot be translated into the world of business and public organisations. The excellent and high achieving nurse, teacher, sales person, operative or software engineer should be able to achieve high earnings, high rewards and be measured as a high achiever as the result of their expertise rather than the outward manifestation of their job title.

BOX 5.9   Promotion (2)

The fundamental organisational problem of pursuing promotion strategies for staff rather than expertise is the need to divisionalise and compartmentalise work in terms of precise job functional structures. Quite apart from anything else, this is directly contrary to the overwhelming drives for flexibility, dynamism and responsiveness required of organisations in the 1990s and beyond.

The complexities thus created will feed off themselves also. Work needs to be structured and designed to fit into the structures and hierarchies, and this leads to work structuring departments being devised along the same lines. Those in functional areas require the same opportunities for advancement, and so the promotion structures and hierarchies tend to be similar across all departments and divisions, again usually in spite of necessity. The potential for blockage barriers on costs and inefficiencies is compounded.

Rewards may be either extrinsic (material, visible and tangible, such as money and trappings) or intrinsic (sources of professional, personal and occupational satisfaction).

They may also be a combination of the two. Job titles are a form of this. They signify a part of the individual's ready-reckoning process: the personal, professional and occupational measure of progress. This is also very often important in organisational *realpolitik*, where the possession of a particular title constitutes the key to the next set of doors. The reason why the title has been conferred may also be both apparent and necessary, for prestige and recognition. It is indeed necessary for such things as qualification to practise (especially prevalent in the public professions, and also construction and engineering) and insurance (where a specifically designated officer is required in particular circumstances).

Rewards are therefore a major means by which organisations set and maintain their standards of activity, attitude and behaviour. It is important to establish what they are given for. This covers the area of achievement, success, loyalty and conformity, and relates both to individual and team performance.

Each organisation sets its own reward mix within these broad boundaries. The relationship between motivation, effort and reward from the organisation's point of view is thus clearly indicated. Those working there are shown the pathways to achievement in the particular situation. The opportunity is afforded either to accept or reject these pathways.

Demotivation and disaffection occurs when the pathways are not clearly indicated or if the achievements at their end are not then duly rewarded. This also happens in individual cases where they were taken on by the organisation or given tasks to do within it on the basis of misunderstandings of what was expected or what the rewards were to be. It is essential to be clear about this. There is no point, for example, in recruiting or retaining task-oriented staff in situations where rewards are for loyalty and time service (or vice versa). Where specific achievements are required, these are to be stated in clear and unambiguous terms and rewarded accordingly.

BOX 5.10   Rewarding Groups and Individuals

The view is increasingly being taken that there are few genuinely solitary occupations (those where the performance of one is not in some way dependent upon the performance of others). This is compounded by the view currently prevailing that there are now no surplus or spare members of staff in organisations.

If this view is accepted, then clearly every contribution is vital. Everyone should therefore share in any rewards to be achieved. Professional cricket teams, for example, put all awards for individual performance into a team pool. Bowlers may not take wickets without the support of fielders. Excellent batting performances are achievable only as long as the particular batsman has partners.

The only exceptions to this are exceptional performances, such as the achievements of Brian Lara in 1994 in setting both the highest international and first-class scores.

Differentiating the value of performance between individuals within teams leads to resentment and jealousy, and invariably becomes counter-productive.

The outcome of this view is two-fold. In the first place it reinforces the identity of everyone concerned with the particular organisation (and therefore the extent of dissonance if things go wrong). It further requires the recognition that star sales performances, for example, cannot be achieved without the support of excellent products, which must be of the right quality and design. Star sales staff cannot be recruited without excellent human resource performance. Star sales calls cannot be made without excellent scheduling, secretarial, clerical and administrative support. Viewed in this way, the contribution of everybody is important.

The converse of this is the requirement for a clear understanding of the aspirations of the particular staff employed. It is no use offering rewards for achievement if the staff concerned value continuity and longevity with rewards based on loyalty, and vice versa.

Any reward must be issued if the person or team concerned has fulfilled all the requirements necessary to achieve it. The reward should be issued promptly and with gladness and satisfaction on the part of the organisation to its staff.

Written in this way, it appears trite in the extreme; yet organisations across the world are notoriously bad at this. Those that do it invariably stand out as beacons of both motivation and profitability. They are a roll-call of the world's finest organisations of the mid-1990s – McKinsey, International Management Group, AC Milan, Virgin Atlantic, McDonald's, Nissan.

If you do not say what you mean, if you do give mixed and obfuscated messages in regard to the availability of payment of rewards, the staff will not believe that they will be paid. If you do not pay when you should, you take active steps to alienate the staff and destroy morale. This is all universally understood and accepted, yet organisations still persist in pursuing this path.

BOX 5.11   Rewards and Language

There is nothing that is guaranteed to demotivate and demoralise more than the inclusion of phrases such as 'There are only *x* increments available'; or 'We will pay you for excellent performance provided that there is money in the budget'. The worst example of all is 'We acknowledge your performance as excellent, but we are going to rate it as mediocre because otherwise we would have to find extra money for you'.

This last happened to a colleague in 1991. She transformed her area of work, turning it from a hopeless morass into a strong, integrated and professional team. Her boss gave her an excellent rating. This was rewritten by her area director (that is, her boss's boss) into a mediocre because there was no money in the budget to pay for the excellent rating.

■ Motivation and rewards

Money – in the form of wage and salary – is the reward for performance, especially, and ideally, effective and successful performance. Wages and salaries are paid by organisations to individuals to reward them for bringing their expertise into the situation and for their efforts. The payment made must therefore reflect:

- the level of expertise brought by the individual and the ways in which he has been required to apply it;
- the quality and intensity of effort;
- the effectiveness of individual performance; and the effectiveness of overall performance;
- the value that the organisation places on the presence of the particular expertise;
- the value placed by the individual on her expertise;
- the expectations of the individual for particular levels of reward;
- the anticipation of continuity and improvement in reward levels.

These must then be set in a wider context.

Herzberg makes the point that money is of limited value as a motivator even where pay levels are good, but that it is very demotivating when pay levels are bad and do not meet expectations.

■ Perceptions

There is a strongly perceived relationship between pay and job importance. A chief executive who declares an annual salary of £20 000 will be widely considered not to have a great deal of responsibility or authority. A marketing officer on £80 000 a year will be generally perceived to have a responsible and high powered job. This now extends to the individual: if people perceive themselves to be on 'only £x' it affects their self-esteem and self-worth because it is a statement of limited value. The converse is also true: where people can state that they are on 'good money' this underlines feelings of high value.

■ Continuity

In conditions of relative stability and permanence, people are more disposed to accept a trade-off between current levels of reward and the certainty of continuity. In the UK over the period from 1945 until the late 1970s, this was virtually explicit in many organisations: while at no stage would reward levels be particularly high, they would be steady, would gradually improve, and would last the whole of one's working life and beyond by paying a retirement pension.

In times of turbulence and uncertainty the drive is for higher immediate rewards, part of which is a hedge against the vagaries of the long-term future.

■ Economic rent

This is the term used to describe the necessity to pay particular rates (usually high) for scarce skills, knowledge and expertise. It is further enhanced where the particular expertise is required at short notice, possibly involving a consultancy or sub-contract arrangement.

■ Value

Given that people are employed on the basis that there is work required of them, and that they are therefore of value, pay levels and methods should reflect this.

These levels should be as high as possible as a part of maximising the long-term confidence and quality of relationship. Organisations may also legitimately take the view of 'high wages for high levels of commitment and hard work' when pay levels are raised.

BOX 5.12 'High Wages for High Levels of Commitment and Work'

The stark truth behind this as a statement of the value of the working relationship is clearly illustrated by considering its comparisons and contrasts.

1. 'Low wages for high levels of commitment and hard work' will only work if there are prospects for increased reward levels (so people are effectively investing in their own future) or where the work is based overwhelmingly on intrinsic factors and commitments (for example, voluntary service overseas, and see also the Samaritans' advertisement on p. 124).
2. 'High wages for low levels of commitment and hard work' is profligate. It is only remotely valid when it is used as a one-off payment as a prelude to some form of change. It is nevertheless often found in the country club cultures of head offices of large and sophisticated organisations.
3. 'Low wages for low levels of commitment and hard work' constitutes a valueless, unproductive and ultimately destructive relationship. Low level officials of the Communist Party in the former USSR had their own proverbial version of this: 'We pretend to work and they pretend to pay us.'
4. Japanese organisations in the UK adopt the position of ensuring that they are the top payers in their sectors and good-to-high payers in their locality. In

return for this the staff are required to be fully flexible and to undertake any job that the company requires of them.

5. At the other extreme, the low pay–low value equation is nearly always underpinned by managerial attitudes that indicate 'If you do not want the job, there are *x* million others who would love it'.

The wage–work bargain is therefore a psychological, as well as economic, relationship.

The levels of pay and value also quite legitimately indicate expectation levels. The higher the level of pay, the greater the levels of expectation placed on the employee; and the more disposed the employee is to accept these raised levels of expectation.

■ Comparisons

Ultimately pay comparisons between different jobs in different organisations are spurious. However, they have a very strong psychological drive. If one person is receiving a particular salary for carrying out a given job, and then finds out that 'the same job' in the neighbouring firm carries a salary of double what they receive, they become dissatisfied and frustrated. If a vacancy then occurs at the neighbouring firm, the person may then put in for it and even get the job, only to find out that the nature, volume, content and commitment in the new job are nothing like the old.

■ The going rate

This occurs where the problem of comparison is overcome by setting local, regional and national rates for the same (or very similar) generic occupations. It applies especially to public professions (for example, teaching, nursing and social work); while the job content and application of expertise may vary widely between establishments, the job output and expertise required are very much the same.

This also applies to pay rises. If one sector or occupation gets a rise of 5 per cent for example, then those in others that get only 4 per cent will tend to feel slighted, while those who get 6 per cent will tend to feel that they have done rather well. Percentage rises in general also underline the value – or lack of value – placed on categories of staff. A low percentage therefore tends to give feelings of being undervalued or unvalued, even where the percentage may be known to reflect a low rise in the cost of living and seek only to compensate for this.

■ Equity and equality

The converse of comparisons is the application of principles of equity and equality within and across organisations. The term 'equal pay, for equal work, of equal value' is widely used and is a legal (as well as moral) obligation in the UK.

Problems arise when a particular expertise is only available on terms that will break the principle. Some organisations, including some that are very successful and effective will break their salary and reward structures if they find their need for the individual and his qualities to override other considerations. Others will find alternative approaches: for example, Arsenal Football Club, in the early 1990s, found that their ability to attract the very top players from overseas was limited because the Club refused to break its salary structure to accommodate the very high levels of demand of the foreign stars.

More generally, the presence or absence of equality and equity in rewards is indicative of the general relationship between the organisation and its employees. Where there is no or little equality, this always means that different levels of value are placed on categories of employees for whatever reason. Those who lose out know that they are undervalued or unvalued, at least in comparison with others, while even those who benefit understand the inherent lack of integrity of the relationship.

■ Expectations and obligations

Problems are greatly reduced in the money area where expectations and obligations are clearly set out, understood and accepted by both organisation and individual at the outset. Problems occur where the individual has not understood the nature of effort required to achieve rewards; and where the organisation has not made clear (either through ignorance, accident or deliberately) the levels of effort and commitment that it requires (see Figure 5.6).

People in particular organisations have expectations of payment methods. For example, a sales person may expect all or part of her reward to be in the

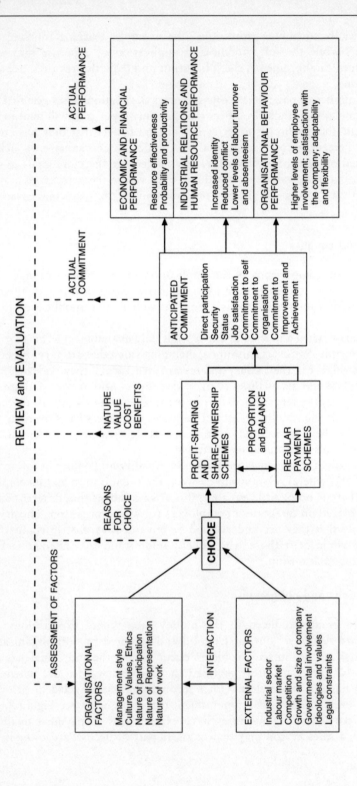

Figure 5.6 The relationship between pay and performance

form of bonus or commission because this has worked well for her in the past. She therefore perceives herself to be able to earn much more through this means than through a simple salary, and to control her own earnings level. Operative and clerical staff may expect part of their work to be paid as overtime; this is again perceived to enhance the ability to earn and also underlines the intrinsic feeling of value (based on 'You are so important to us, you must stay and work, we cannot possibly allow you to go home yet – and we will pay you extra'). Problems occur in these areas when the facility is introduced, institutionalised, becomes expected and is then withdrawn.

BOX 5.13 Frustration

Frustration occurs when the relationship between expectation, effort and reward is skewed for reasons outside the individual's control. It is caused by a range of factors.

1. The removal of anticipated rewards during the effort phase. For example, an individual may pursue qualifications in the expectation, anticipation – even near certainty – that he will receive job promotion, enhancement and opportunities when he has finished his course. Towards the end of the course, if the organisation is taken over, or moves into new fields, or if the individual's superior changes jobs, the reward disappears.
2. The cancellation of anticipated rewards through arbitrary (or even rational) action by the organisation. To take a similar example, the achievement of qualifications may have led in the past to pay rises, and then there is a change of policy during the course of the individual's studies and the rewards are now no longer available.
3. When promised or indicated opportunities for training and development do not materialise, for whatever reason.
4. When the intrinsic satisfactions afforded by the job do not meet the wider needs (especially esteem and economic) of the individual. This has occurred in recent years in the UK with public services and occupations such as teaching, nursing and social work.
5. When the nature of opportunities afforded and anticipated do not match up, based on misperceptions on either part.
6. When the individual knows or strongly believes that she is not being offered the opportunities that her talents and qualities merit; and this occurs especially when the individual feels that this is as a result of the perceptions of their superior.
7. Where opportunities are simply not available, causing individuals to have to look elsewhere for their future prospects.
8. Restriction of the capability to act by rules, regulations and procedures.

■ Pay and motivation as a process

Each element and factor indicated contributes to the pay and reward process. By the very nature of the continuity of the wage–work bargain, this in itself is a continuous process. As such it requires constant attention and maintenance. If this is not done, people perceive that they are being taken for granted and if this persists, it leads to feelings of being neglected.

1. With regularity, consisting of regular and frequent reviews; stated occasions for rises; stated levels or criteria for rises and improvements; and ensuring that these are paid in full on the required dates.
2. Rewarding enhanced performance, either because people have developed and enhanced their skills, knowledge and expertise and therefore their value to the organisation; or because the organisation has had a successful, effective and profitable year. In the latter case especially, there is a current consensus that the staff of organisations should receive their fair share of the rewards that have been generated by their efforts. This applies equally to the best public services and not-for-profit activities, rewarding staff from the proceeds of enhanced effectiveness of performance (for example, an enlargement of jobs or workload which enables the organisation to reduce staff levels), or from other efficiencies and savings (for example, in premises charges or through the simplification of procedures).
3. Issuing regular symbols of value. Part of this includes praise and recognition. Genuine recognition is enhanced through the use of small, creative, varied and frequent rewards issued to everyone regardless of rank, status or occupation, and based on the total contribution of everyone to organisational performance.

BOX 5.14   Monetary Rewards as Symbols of Value

Presents
Many organisations give presents to their staff on a variety of occasions. This includes Christmas presents (for example, hampers); birthday and wedding presents (usually a small cash payment or vouchers); and on the birth of children to employees.

'Thank yous'
An Amsterdam bank gave all its employees everywhere in the world $200 at the end of 1993 and an extra day off to go and spend it to thank them for their record efforts over the previous year.

   A retail chain increased its staff discount from 15 to 20 per cent as a reward for a record-breaking year in 1990; and the following year, when profits were down, it maintained the new staff discount level.

Subsidies

These usually take the form of free or heavily subsidised meals, snacks, tea and coffee. This is often extended also to include travel, the payment of taxation or the lease on company cars, occupational health and private health schemes (often extended again to include the employee's immediate family).

One-offs

These consist of special awards, honoraria and other discretionary activities. They are normally given for truly exceptional performance, suggestions and initiatives that make a significant gain or saving to the organisation; and to inventions and improvements that are adopted and commercialised.

Their true value lies in their application, which must be fair and equitable; and available and payable to everyone who makes such contributions. They must be valuable in the context in which they are offered. They must be distinct from the general reward package (except in the case of subsidies). They exist to reward extra achievement, devotion, commitment, loyalty and results. They must be offered from the point of view of absolute integrity or else they will be seen as favours.

BOX 5.15   Other Symbols of Value

Trips and Outings

These work best when the entire workforce is taken or sent on a visit somewhere. The purpose is to reward both achievement and commitment, and also loyalty. It also enhances the general relationships between staff and may help to break down such barriers as exist at the workplace. Some organisations do this on a regular basis (for example, the Saga Holiday Company fly all their staff for a short break to the Mediterranean during the winter months), while others simply aim to put on a certain amount of events over the year (which may consist of short breaks, theatre concert trips, or sports events such as football, cricket matches and race meetings).

Shut Downs

These work best where they are additional to (rather than a part of) the annual holiday entitlement of the staff. They may be enhanced by offering subsidised holidays at particular venues, available to as many staff and their families as wish to take advantage.

Dinners and Dances

These are opportunities for all staff to gather together and congratulate themselves on the organisation's performance over the previous period. They work best when they are compulsory (though where general identity and motivation are high, attendance is likely to be high anyway). Some organisations also encourage the staff to bring their partners. They may include guest speakers and cabaret, although each of these has to be good and well received by everyone or else they will feel that they have been slighted.

Work Variety and Enhancement

This is a symbol of value when it is offered and available to everyone on an equitable basis (rather than as the province of certain departments or a chosen few). It usually consists of the opportunity to pursue ideas and initiatives, conduct project work, be educated and trained according to personal goals and ambitions, and to make visits and introduce initiatives as the result.

The main purpose here is to strengthen the bond and positive feelings of respect between the organisation and staff, and between the different members and groups of staff. These activities create positive attitudes where they are offered honestly (and create negative attitudes where they are seen to be favours). More generally, they address and enhance the quality and interest of working life, extend and enhance the perceptions of people, and (in the case of work variety and enhancement) extend and develop the horizons and potential of the people.

---

4. Ensuring that pay levels are kept up to the organisation's own absolute standards and taking remedial action where this has been allowed to slip as soon as possible. Further, it may have been necessary in the past to reduce or depress pay levels for reasons of organisation performance; when things get back on track, the staff should be rewarded for their loyalty and commitment over the difficult period.
5. Never losing sight of the absolute value of the staff to the organisation and their need to be valued, of which one of the main manifestations is the nature and level of financial reward over the long term.

This constitutes a basis of the relationship between motivation and money. Some general points should now be made. Monetary reward does not make a job more satisfying or interesting except in the very short term, though it may, and does, lead to high levels of commitment (again, especially over the short term) if the individual has an overriding need to earn. Moreover, lack of adequate financial reward for a job that is otherwise very satisfying leads to frustration and stress as the individual struggles to reconcile the conflicting pressures of loving the job but not being able to afford to stay in it.

Table 5.1 Payment methods and motivation

Method	Aspects of Motivation
Weekly cash wages	Meets traditions and expectations of industrial and commercial sectors and other parts of society also.
Monthly salary into bank account	May be status attached to being 'salaried'.
Time rate	Encourages attendance for particular periods; overtime may be desired and available outside set times.
Piece rates	Encourages production volume (and possibly also quality and deadline achievement).
Flexitime	Encourages attendance, especially where there is the opportunity for overtime or time off once sufficient time has been accrued.
Commission, bonuses	Relates performance output to payment level.
Profit-related pay	Relates to organisation performance and payment levels; difficulties lie where profit levels are outside the control of the staff.
Performance-related pay and merit pay	Relates own performance to payment levels; difficulties lie with setting, assessing and validating performance objectives and targets, especially in unquantifiable areas.

BOX 5.16 Attendance and Other Bonuses and Allowances

These have been used in many forms and in a variety of situations over the years. At their best, they reward (or give the perception of rewarding) special efforts and commitments such as working at night, at weekends and over bank and public holidays and away from home (however, see the power station example in Box 3.1).

In many other cases, however, they simply demonstrate the limitations of this approach, and the consequent limitation of money as a motivator if other types of reward and achievement are not present.

1. The bank room wiring operators at the Hawthorne Works actively conspired against the organisation's bonus system because they perceived that it would be changed to their disadvantage if they demonstrated the full capacity to which they could work.
2. In the 1970s, the UK National Coal Board went through a phase of offering 50 per cent of attendance pay to the miners if they turned up for four days. The other 50 per cent would be payable only if the staff attended on the fifth day. It had no effect on attendance patterns. This approach was copied by the Rootes/Chrysler and British Leyland car manufacturing companies and also had no effect.

3. In the 1980s and 1990s, the Allied Irish Bank gave an additional week's holiday to every member of staff who took no time off for sickness during the previous year. Once people had had a day's sickness, they therefore would tend to take at least another five working days to ensure that they did not miss out anyway.
4. In the 1970s and 1980s, Batchelor's Food Company undertook a policy which stated that anyone who was more than 10 minutes late for work would lose half a day's pay. The result was that anyone who was more than 10 minutes late – whether at the start of the day or returning after lunch – would simply take the rest of the period off.

BOX 5.17   Profit-related Pay

The purpose of relating pay to profit is part of the process of targeting the reward package and also the motivation and commitment effort. By combining the two elements, the line of reasoning is that all staff are both focused on the purposes for which they are supposed to be working and that they also assume a positive stake in its commercial success.

Profit-related elements come in two main forms. The simplest of these is to allocate a percentage, or proportion, or amount from the surplus generated by the organisation, and to share this out. For maximum equality, this will be as a percentage of salary to everyone. The other approach is to offer shares and equity in the organisation; the employees therefore become investors in their own future.

The relationship between profit, ownership, commitment and pay is a constant theme of the Excellence Studies. In the UK, the Bell–Hanson Report of 1989, researching 113 publicly quoted companies, found that profit-share companies out-performed others by an average of 27 per cent on returns on capital, earnings per share, and profit and sales growth.

For best results, the scheme must be believed in, valued and understood by all concerned. The overall purpose of profit-related pay is to reward effort and achievement on the part of the staff. Staff must also clearly understand that this payment will be forthcoming if the organisation has a good year; and that it will not be forthcoming if for any reason the organisation has difficulties or does not make profits.

Above all, profit-related pay is never to be used as a means of cutting wage and salary bills. Its purpose is to target these and to reward efforts, not penalise them. Its general effect is to put up wage and salary bills and, as stated in the text above, this both raises the expectations of the individuals concerned, and is also a quite legitimate means by which the organisation can raise its expectations of the individuals.

■ Conclusions

The standpoint taken is that people work better when they are highly motivated and there is a direct relationship between quality of performance and levels of motivation; the volume and quality of work declines when motivation is lower or when demotivation is present. The need to motivate and be motivated is continuous and constant. Some specific conclusions may be drawn.

1. Motivation comes partly from within the individual and partly from the particular situation. It is therefore both constant and subject to continuous adaptation.
2. Value, esteem and respect are basic human requirements extending to all places of work and all occupations (and, indeed, to every walk of life). The key features of this are the integrity of relationships, levels of knowledge and understanding, general prevailing attitudes (whether positive or negative) and the nature of rewards, including pay.
3. All people have expectations based on their understanding of particular situations, and they will be drawn to, or driven from these in anticipation of rewards and outcomes.
4. People respond positively to equality and fairness of treatment, and negatively when these are not present.
5. People respond positively to variety, development and opportunities when they know or perceive it to be in their interests to do so. They are less likely to respond to genuine opportunities if they do not understand or perceive them as such.
6. People respond positively when they know the attitudes, behaviour, values and ways of working required; and negatively or less favourably when these are not apparent or not strong.
7. People need constant attention to their individual wants and needs and will seek this from many sources, including work. If the work is demotivating, they will seek it elsewhere.
8. The key to positive motivation is the establishment of a high level of mutual trust, commitment and responsibility. The main obligation here lies with the organisation. Individuals may be expected to respond positively when these are present. They may not be expected from individuals when the organisation is itself uncommitted to this, or where it takes an expedient, confrontational and adversarial view of its staff.

■ Questions

1. Outline the advantages and disadvantages of engaging in job enrichment and job enlargement programmes for unskilled operative and clerical staff. How are these to be measured for success or failure?
2. In what circumstances does the 'Theory X' view of the world apply? In these circumstances, what actions can be taken by managers and individuals to improve the quality of working life?

3. Identify different forms of pay structure and payment arrangements made by organisations, and the effects – both positive and negative – that these have on staff. Identify the key feature of pay scales that successfully reward and motivate people.

4. To what extent is the motivation to work (i) similar and (ii) different in respect of (a) factory staff; (b) doctors; (c) charity volunteer workers; (d) professional sports players (those not at the very top of their chosen sport); (e) hospital administrators?

CHAPTER 6

Personality and roles

■ Personality

Individual personality may be defined as 'the total pattern of traits and characteristics, of thoughts, emotions, attitudes, values, behaviour and beliefs, and attributes and qualities, and their interactions'. Since the strength, presence and interaction of these varies between individuals, each individual is unique. The concept of personality also embraces perception, motivation, aspiration, learning and development. It is therefore necessary to recognise at the outset that human personality is highly complex and that steps must be taken by organisations to understand the characteristics, interactions and complexities exhibited by their people (and those who are potentially their people) if an effective working relationship is to be produced. Some useful distinctions may be made at the outset.

■ Traits and characteristics

From an organisational behaviour point of view, the purpose is to identify those traits and characteristics necessary to produce effective activity and harmony of relationship and to seek these among the individuals who come (or who would like to come) to work. The important traits are:

(a) strong, dominant and frequently exhibited;
(b) weak and less frequently exhibited;
(c) overriding, often based on emotional response to particular situations (for example, aggression, shyness, anger, temperament);
(d) positive/negative, often related to general disposition, attitude to work, approach to problems.

■ Influences on personality

These clearly start at birth and include the formation and internalisation of attitudes, values and beliefs, skills, knowledge, qualities and attributes. The sources of influence include family, school, peer groups, social groups (for example, guides, scouts), location and environment; and also any particular political, religious and ethical factors that may be present. Strong personalities – for example head teachers, priests, guiders and scouters, as well as managers – may also have effects and influences on individuals and as individuals.

The organisational behaviour interest lies in the extent to which these influences are compatible with the requirements and demands that are to be placed on the individual during the course of his work. There is also the interaction between the individual, other members of staff and the personality of the organisation to be considered.

■ The two-sided self

This is the combination of how individuals see and perceive themselves with how they are seen and perceived by others. Dissonance occurs where the two are seriously at variance, or where one strong characteristic is perceived to be positive by the individual and negative by others: for example, where temperamental extremes are considered to be integral to creativity by the individual and boorish by those who observe them.

BOX 6.1   Personality and Generalisation

'People will behave in the future as they have behaved in the past.' (Farnsworth)

'People who are unpunctual are likely to be bad time keepers.' (Huczynski and Buchanan)

'I am a complex personality. You cannot have a great footballer without the temperament.' (Eric Cantona)

■ Emotions

In organisational behaviour terms, emotions are important in relationship to the rest of the personality, especially where these are strong, distinctive and overriding traits. In some situations and for some jobs and roles, emotional involvement is very important. In others, it is necessary that emotions are submerged in the pursuit of occupational excellence and quality. Otherwise extreme emotional outbursts and signs of loss of control have to be seen in the context of whether these can be accommodated in the given job or role.

■ Defence and offence mechanisms

□ *Defence*

Defence mechanisms are developed by individuals in response to the unknown and where they are going into unfamiliar or threatening situations. The individual exhibits characteristics that are her response to the need for information, to be able to assess the situation and to reduce any inherent threat.

Examples of this are formality (when dealing with strangers), rejection (when dealing with change), and aggression (when dealing with threats or defending an untenable position). In general, defence mechanisms are responsive.

□ *Offence*

Offence mechanisms are apparent when an individual has problems and issues to address and for which he must take the initiative. These include planning and organising, investigation, and confrontation, and are based on dealing with issues and problems which are known and understood (or at least believed to be so). In general, offence mechanisms are dynamic.

■ Qualities, talents and attributes

These are the physical and mental capabilities of the individual. All people bring some of their capabilities into all situations. It is the relationship between those that are demanded in the given situation in relation to the range offered by the individual that is important here. For example, a qualified airline pilot who can also cook and make tea and coffee is clearly qualified to be a catering assistant, but whether she would want to be one would need careful consideration on the part of both the individual and also any organisation which might be thinking of offering her a job as a catering assistant.

BOX 6.2   Identification of Qualities, Talents and Attributes by Organisations

This is the basis on which person specifications are drawn up. It is the identification of qualities, talents and attributes which are deemed necessary to carry out particular sets of activities effectively. This then becomes the basis on which job selection is based.

The process is most likely to be successful when those qualities, talents and attributes are easily observable and identifiable, and can be proven or tested. It is less likely to be successful if they have to be inferred or based on a short conversation or part of an interview.

The initial concern is therefore to recognise the presence and interaction of each of these aspects. Some are complementary, others contradictory. Some are positive, others negative; some may be regarded as positive in one situation and negative in others. This complexity requires that those responsible for the design and staffing of organisations and for dividing and allocating work are able to recognise the key and critical elements of each aspect when it comes to assessing qualities and behavioural requirements in order to fill job positions and to have a harmonious and productive workforce.

BOX 6.3   Personality and the Work of H. J. Eysenck (born 1916)

The work of Eysenck has produced a distinctive approach to the assessment of personality.

Clusters and sets of traits

The argument is based on the assessment that possession of one particular trait is likely to mean that a further discernible set is also present. Everyone possess a discernible and identifiable number of traits. Where trait 1 is present, then traits 2 and 3 are likely to be present also; where trait 1 is not present, then traits 2 and 3 may not be present either, or may be weaker.

Hierarchies of traits

This develops the argument a stage further. Where one trait is strong or dominant then others may be expected or inferred. Where one trait is weak, then others may be expected.

The result of this is the identification and formulation of personality types based around the clusters and hierarchies.

The extroversion–introversion dimension

Extroversion, spontaneity, sociability: extroverts are strong and tough-minded. They need constant arousal and stimulation. They are sociable, need and enjoy the company of others, do not enjoy their own company and have a wide circle of acquaintances. They seek excitement and uncertainty, take risks, act impulsively and display their emotions. They are optimistic, care-free and active. They can be aggressive and quick tempered. Eysenck identifies a cluster of seven traits that contribute to extroversion:

- active
- irresponsible
- practical
- social
- risk-taking
- impulsive
- expansive

Introversion, inhibition, unsociability: introverts are tender-minded. They experience deep feelings and strong emotions. They do not need the regularity or intensity of stimulation. They tend to be quiet, retiring and withdrawn. They are happy with their own company. They plan, organise and order their lives. They are pessimistic. They suppress their strong emotions.

Eysenck identifies a cluster of seven traits that contribute to introversion:

- inactive
- restrained

- careful
- responsible
- controlled
- reflective
- unsocial

The neuroticism–stability dimension
Neuroticism/instability: neurotics are emotional and anxious. They tend to have a low opinion of themselves. They tend to be disappointed, pessimistic and depressed. They worry about things that may never happen. They are easily upset and angered. They are obsessive and conscientious. They have a high degree of self-discipline. They have a high propensity to accept the authority and discipline of others. They are orderly and upset by disorder and uncertainty. They seek to blame others for the shortcomings of the world. They blame themselves for their own shortcomings. They have active (often overactive) consciences.

Eysenck identifies seven traits that cluster to form neuroticism:

- low self-esteem
- lack of autonomy
- anxiety
- guilt
- obsessive
- unhappy
- hypochondria

Stability/adjustment
Stable individuals are self-confident, self-reliant, assertive and optimistic. They resist and overcome fear. They are realistic. They solve problems as and when they arise. They look to the future rather than the past.
Eysenck identifies traits that cluster to form stability:

- high self-esteem
- calm
- freedom from guilt
- casual
- healthy
- happy
- self-contained

Eysenck believes that personality is largely inherited and that the effects and interactions of others, and of the environment, are therefore limited. One can thus identify personality type early in life.

From an organisational behaviour point of view, personality type can be identified early in working life. Assessment of the match of personalities that are and were effective in certain occupations can be made with those present or with those who are coming in to work in the organisation.

■ The desire for achievement

Desire for achievement is a basic human drive in most societies. The problem lies in the definition of achievement which means something different to each individual: for example, money, status, power, helping others, a large house, invention and creativity, excellence in a chosen field (social or occupational). For organisations, the problem lies in what they mean by achievement, where the contribution of individuals to that lies and in attracting the right types of individual to ensure that this happens.

Individual desire for achievement is based on:

- economic pressures, the need to support a continuity and quality of life;
- social pressures, exerted by peers, friends, family and relations;
- esteem and value, what the individual regards as important, and what is regarded as important by others;
- status afforded by both self and others to particular achievements;
- association, with particular organisations, groups, expertise and activities;
- individual pressures, the need to live up to (or down to) particular expectations from different parts of society.

The desire for achievement in work situations is based on:

- the nature of the work itself, variety, routines, technical expertise;
- the value of the work to self, the organisation, peers, customers, clients and the community;
- the relative need for development, new opportunities and horizons;
- the need of the individual to demonstrate a range of abilities and qualities;
- the need to be seen as excellent, to be highly thought of in a range of areas;
- the need to complete that which has been commenced; dislike of leaving things unfinished;
- the need for working relationships to be operationally productive and effective as well as friendly;
- time, the need to get things done as quickly as possible; to avoid things being dragged out.

BOX 6.4   The Need for Achievement

People with a low need for achievement are concerned more with security and status than with personal fulfilment. They are preoccupied with their own ideas and feelings. They worry more about their self-presentation than their performance.

People with a high need for achievement tend to have the following character-istics:

- they prefer tasks in which they have to achieve a standard of excellence, rather than simply carrying out routine activities;
- they prefer jobs in which they get frequent and clear feedback on how well they are doing to help them perform better;
- they prefer activities that involve moderate risks of failure (high-risk activities lead to failure, low-risk activities do not offer challenge or an opportunity to demonstrate ability);
- they have a good memory for unfinished tasks and do not like to leave things incomplete;
- they can be unfriendly and unsociable when they do not want others to get in the way of their performance;
- they have a sense of urgency, appear to be in a hurry, to be working against the clock and have an inability to relax.

This seems to be broadly consistent with our popular or intuitive understanding of what the need for high achievement actually is.

From: Huczynski and Buchanan (1993).

In general, the higher the desire for work achievement, the more likely it is that the individual will use those items in the second list to meet the pressures indicated in the first. Their desire for achievement is based on task achievement, personal development, excitement and challenge. The rewards accrue as the result of knowing that organisation, peers, customers and clients have been well served.

The lower the desire for achievement at work, the greater the likelihood that individuals are concerned with security, status, the regard and esteem in which they are held by others, social pressures and the pressures of association. Their desire for achievement is based on their own preoccupations and feelings and the presentation of self to the rest of the world.

■ Roles

In simple terms roles are combinations of behaviour and activities that are undertaken by individuals in given situations (see Figure 6.1). This is in turn set against a backcloth of the variety of expectations that go with each role. The source of these expectations is overwhelmingly a product of the particular community and society in which the individual lives and works.

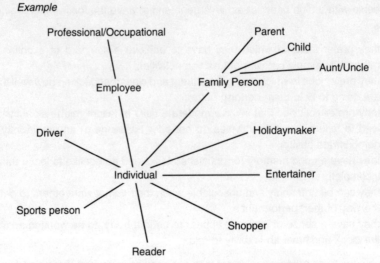

Example

Each role has expectations, pressures, rewards and consequences. There are overlaps between each and measures of honesty, discord and conflict.

Figure 6.1   Individual roles

■ Role sets

People have a great range and variety of roles. Some of these are dominant, some subordinate. Some of these are constant; some are continuous; some are intermittent; some are short term, others long term. The total number of roles adopted by the individual constitutes the role set.

It is useful to compartmentalise roles in this way in order to establish a basis for the understanding of the ways in which people behave in the different situations indicated. Often this behaviour is contradictory – the bullying manager for example may also be a loving parent – and it is necessary to be able to understand and explain the reasons (or a set of reasons) for this.

A further glance at Figure 6.1 indicates the great variety, complexity and sophistication of this. The promotion of effective general organisational behaviour can only be achieved if steps are taken to harmonise and reconcile these complexities and the inherent stresses and strains.

■ Role definition

It is useful to indicate the source of this at the outset. A few roles are universal. Titles such as President, King or Emperor have different meanings in different parts of the world. The main sources of definition are social and occupational.

The social indicates those such as parent, son and daughter in which the particular obligations and activities implicit and explicit are defined by the particular society in which those concerned are living and which are precisely associated with the role titles.

Occupational roles give definitions within particular organisations. The actual role, however, varies between organisations. Titles such as manager and technician are universally applied but subject to specific interpretation. They are in turn subject to interpretation by the society in which these managers and technicians also live.

BOX 6.5   *The Mikado*

Ko-Ko:	It seems that the festivities in connection with my approaching marriage must last a week. I should like to do it handsomely and I want to consult you as to the amount I ought to spend on them.
Pooh-Bah:	Certainly, in which of my capacities? As First Lord of the Treasury, Lord Chamberlain, Attorney General, Chancellor of the Exchequer, Privy Purse, Private Secretary or First Commissioner of the Police?
Ko-Ko:	Suppose we say as Private Secretary.
Pooh-Bah:	Speaking as your Private Secretary, I should say that as the City will have to pay for it, don't stint yourself.
Ko-Ko:	Exactly, as the City will have to pay for it. That is your advice.
Pooh-Bah:	As Private Secretary. Of course, you will understand that as Chancellor of the Exchequer I am bound to see that due economy is observed.
Ko-Ko:	Oh! But you said just now, don't stint yourself, do it well.
Pooh-Bah:	As Private Secretary.
Ko-Ko:	And now you say that due economy must be observed.
Pooh-Bah:	As Chancellor of the Exchequer.
Ko-Ko:	I see. Come over here where the Chancellor can't hear us. Now, as my solicitor, how do you advise me to deal with this difficulty?
Pooh-Bah:	Oh, as your solicitor, I should have no hesitation in saying chance it.
Ko-Ko:	Thank you. I will.
Pooh-Bah:	If it were not that, as Lord Chief Justice, I am bound to see that the law isn't violated.
Ko-Ko:	I see. Come over here where the Chief Justice can't hear us. Now then, as First Lord of the Treasury?
Pooh-Bah:	Of course, as First Lord of the Treasury, I could propose a special vote that would cover all expenses if it were not that, as Leader of the Opposition, it would be my duty to resist it tooth and nail. Or, as Paymaster General, I could so cook the accounts that, as Lord High Auditor, I should never discover the fraud. But then, as

> Archbishop, it would be my duty to denounce my dishonesty and give myself into my own custody as First Commissioner of Police.
>
> Ko-Ko: That's extremely awkward.
>
> (From W. S. Gilbert, *The Mikado*.)

The role is therefore a combination of:

- who you are;
- what you know;
- what you can do;
- what you want to do;
- what is important and of value to you;
- economic factors;
- social factors;
- who you work for;
- who works for you;
- whom you associate with;
- who associates with you;
- what is expected of you and by whom;
- what you expect of yourself and why;
- prospects and progress;
- situational factors;
- ethical factors;
- specific constraints (for example, legal).

Roles differentiate between people, activities, social segments and sectors. Roles vary between work, family, social and community situations.

■ Background

The following elements are also to be considered. They provide useful general supportive information. They also identify points of inquiry and assessment when trying to establish why the adoption of some roles is successful and why others are rejected.

Comfort   This is a combination of the capability of the individual to carry out the role with the levels of esteem, reward and satisfaction placed upon it. This includes material rewards. It also includes general levels of respect and regard.

Expectations   This is where particular roles are adopted or sought in the expectation of the comfort indicated above. These include again material rewards, respect and regard. The individual experiences disappointment if these rewards are either not forthcoming or else do not carry these expected benefits. Role titles indicate expectations and reinforce them. They also indicate bench marks of assessment (she is an excellent captain; he is not a good manager).

Harmonisation
The individual requires the ability to harmonise the work, family, social and community elements indicated. It is incumbent upon organisations to understand this.

Organisations must further understand that if they place heavy demands on their staff, especially in terms of long working hours or working away from home, those involved will start to form social relationships at the place of work.

Clashes occur when conflicting demands are placed by each of the four areas. For example, the parent who is under pressure from both children and job, who is also a local councillor and sports club captain, is likely to experience role clash at some point. Individuals devise their own means of reducing the levels of stress and strain.

Reconciliation
This is required by those who interact with the same people in each of the four areas. It occurs, for example, where the work subordinate is the captain of the sports team in which the workplace senior also plays (this is compounded where one or both of these relationships is adversarial).

Progression and growth
There is the need to recognise that some roles grow and develop and others wither and die. There are implications for this. Individuals may outgrow the job, the organisation and possibly also the marriage and family. Conversely they may not be able to keep pace with the growth of these. In each case the role, relationship and interaction changes causing stresses and strains.

Knowledge
The packaging of activity and behaviour into roles enables quick assumptions about someone to be made. The knowledge that someone is a teacher, doctor, railway porter or bar tender enables a quick summary. This is the basis both for understanding and misunderstanding.

Status
Roles indicate status and relative worth in a particular context. This is both occupational and social. Status may also be progressive: junior manager, for example, indicates a point on a promotion or progression ladder that in time leads to middle, and top manager.

Status may also be acquired as the result of behaviour. This applies especially to the informal aspects of roles (where, for example, the junior wins an argument with the senior).

■ Roles within roles

Each role identified carries other elements. For example, Handy identifies the roles of the manager as:

● executive planner, policy-maker, expert, controller of rewards and punishments, arbitrator, exemplar, representative of the group, scapegoat, counsellor, friend and teacher.

This list may be extended to include:

● guardian, teacher, disciplinarian, friend, leader, cook, first-aider, arbitrator, exemplar, general resource, fountain of authority and wisdom.

In some cases this may also include:

● energiser, personality, teacher, idol, advertisement, star, trend and fashion-setter.

The same breakdown can be carried out on all main roles.

Roles diverge, conflict with, and contradict each other, as well as being complementary. They require reconciliation and prioritising. At different times one will take precedence over the others. Some role elements are a continuous part of a main role, while others are present for parts of the time only.

■ Limiting factors

At the workplace each role is limited and constrained by the culture, structure, organisational and operational features of a particular situation. Thus, for example, the role of finance officer differs between a hospital, a car company, a legal practice and a charity even though the title may be the same.

There is also the interaction between the working and non-working roles of the individual in question to be taken into account, and the relevant importance placed on each. Societies place particular values on the different roles that take place within them and accord different measures of esteem, status and value to those carrying them out.

There are also more general and global influences to be considered. These include the extent and value of any expertise specific to the role in question and the skill, knowledge, aptitudes and technology that go with it. There are also ethical and moral (sometimes religious) aspects to be taken into account, together with any specific and distinctive social values.

Roles may usefully be clarified under the following headings.

□ *General categories*

Family: mother, father, son, daughter, uncle, aunt, grandparent, niece, nephew, cousin, taxi, cook, teenager, child, consumer, customer, servant, adult.

Work: defined by job title, profession, training, location, hours of work, freedom or otherwise to operate, autonomy/direction, creativity/regimentation.

Social: neighbour, friend, sportsman/sportswoman, gardener, dog walker, taxi (again), organiser, servant, consumer.

Community: American, Japanese, school governor, customer, pillar of community, councillor, elder, organiser.

Formal: by any of the titles indicated above.

Informal: on an *ad hoc* basis and normally behavioural in orientation.

□   *Behavioural aspects*

Workplace examples are as follows.

The bully: either physical or psychological; with particular categories of staff (especially junior); threatening and menacing; abusive and harassing.

The braggart: normally a self-publicist; if boasting on the organisation's behalf braggarts normally put themselves in the spotlight also.

The barrack room lawyer: leader of the informal organisation and sometimes also an influential figure in the formal, especially if the management involved is weak or insecure.

The clown or comedian: a useful safety valve for the group in which they exist. Clowns attract attention and stories about themselves. The role may be hard to shake off. Clowns are often regarded both as irritant by the organisation and also with measures of envy and jealousy.

The devil's advocate: questions and queries everything and is constantly looking for flaws; it is a useful, valuable, even essential role but it is also a major irritant to top managers and those trying to get pet schemes and projects off the ground.

The film star: looks, acts, sounds, plays the part; is always immaculately dressed; has all the relevant trappings; problems arise only when asked to be the part.

The eccentric: eccentrics are accommodated because of qualities and expertise that they also bring; eccentricity is also the means by which a reputation or distinction may be achieved (provided that it is at least perceived to be attached also to results); it is rationalised as being colourful or larger than life.

Scoutmaster/scoutmistress: develops the next generation of talent for the organisation; is accommodated as long as this does not threaten the current equilibrium, *modus operandi* or vested interest.

The advocate/lobbyist: a chaser of causes, some lost and others not; may also be a whiner and whinger; has strong moral and ethical principles, often at variance with those of the organisation.

The peacemaker: has a rich supply of oil to pour on troubled waters and consequently often adds pollution to the problems that already exist. The worst form of this is the person who sees no evil, hears no evil and speaks no evil.

The scapegoat: attracts blame for everything that goes wrong in the given situation; may go out of his way to do this in order to gain identity (however corrupted or toxic this may be).

Much of this is reflected in the definition of team and group roles explored in Chapter 10.

☐ *Trappings*

Dress: designer labels; colour coordinates; prestige labels (for example, Armani and Gucci); fashion labels (for example, Reebok, Nike); dress imitation (of the top management, for example); cheap, expensive, or special clothing (for example, tuxedo).

Possessions: make, model and year of car; domestic hardware and technology (see also below); may also include spouse, children, mistress, lover, friends and associates.

Fashions and fads: appearance; self-presentation; job title; also includes dress and possessions and may include spouse, children, mistress, lover; belonging to the right clubs and associations and groups; taking part in the right activities.

Technology: car (again); hobbies and interests, make and model of kitchen appliances, television, audio and video, home computer.

The elements of title, behaviour and trappings thus combine to indicate the particular role set. They also give off particular perceptions and expectations to those with whom they interact. This is part of the wider perceptual process.

Above all, however, it indicates the complexities, issues, inconsistencies and uncertainties that are key and continuous features of human behaviour (and therefore clearly of organisation behaviour).

■ **Role Signs**

Role signs make clear what the individual's role is at a given time. The main signs used are:

☐ *Uniforms*

The most universal and widely used form of role signs is the uniform. In particular, these identify both the wider role and also the place in the hierarchy of the individual. They furthermore give an impression of comfort, confidence, knowledge and capability. They give legitimacy to the range of activities with which the role is concerned. They are also a general point of reference: anyone wearing a uniform is assumed to have a general range of capabilities. By donning the uniform, responsibilities and expectations are then required of the individual in question.

□ *Other dress elements*

These indicate and reinforce the other roles carried out. The dress of the holiday-maker, the student, the wedding guest and the stockbroker reinforces the role and identity in each case.

There is also present in this a combination of quality, status and esteem. The wearing of the colours of sports clubs (Barcelona, Toronto Blue Jays), designer labels (Reebok, Nike), or manufacturers' labels (St Michael) all reflect this.

There is also the highly functional: the overalls of the motor mechanic, the safety helmet and shoes of the builder. There is finally the dress element of the traditional: the garb of the cleric, the purdah of the Muslim women, the wig of the UK judge.

□ *Titles*

These are to be regarded in similar ways. Titles are a combination of situational factors, the relative importance placed on the role by the society in question and a measure of progress and status of the individual to which reference has already been made. Elements are therefore a combination of status, esteem, function and tradition. This is illustrated in Box 6.6.

BOX 6.6   Titles

Social: Mr, Mrs, Dr, Reverend.
Specific: Your Excellency, Your Grace, Mr President.
Traditional: Hon. Sec., Hon. Treasurer, Club Captain.
Organisational/functional: Chief Executive, Officer, Assistant Manager, Salesman.

A different way of looking at this is as follows.

Shirley Jones, for example, is known as:

- Shirley, to the fellow directors of the company of which she is a director;
- Mrs Jones, to the teacher of her two children at the school to which they go;
- Shirl and SJ, to the hockey club for which she plays;
- Sally, to the Samaritans for whom she works on a voluntary basis;
- Dr Jones, at the surgery where she works as a part-time locum three weekends a year covering for ex-colleagues who are on holiday;
- Shirley J, to distinguish her from Shirley Martin and Shirley Young at the amateur dramatics society to which they all belong.

☐ *Place*

People behave differently according to the place, location and environment in which they find themselves. Away from the place of work, the Chief Executive Officer has no formal authority over those who work for her. Such a person may indeed, for example, accept authority from one of her work subordinates who is the captain of the local sports team to which they both belong (see above).

Location is worth an additional mention here. Two main manifestations of these are at places of work, whereby one's office location is an indication of relative status; and one's home address which is also liable to connotations of class, opulence and status.

☐ *Symbols*

The phrase 'status symbol' is used throughout the Western world. The symbols in question are specially reinforced status and esteem aspects of particular roles. In work situations this includes the make and model of the company car; clothing; the size, appearance and location of the office; the furnishings used in the office; even the personal staff employed (secretary, personal assistants); all these exude status, reflect importance and outward measures of regard, and (sometimes) achievement. Where these are not present this reflection is, or can be, adverse.

Away from work other symbols include: the name of the school to which the children are sent; places visited on holiday; possession of property; shows, plays and films visited; sports and leisure achievements and clubs.

☐ *Rituals*

Some rituals are role signs; or, more precisely, they reflect and underline moves by the individual from one role to another.

This may happen on a regular basis: the person who changes from working clothes to leisure wear when they return home each day signifies that he has finished his work and is now a domestic animal.

It may signal a major transformation. For example, the wedding ceremony clearly identifies the change of role for the two persons concerned.

This also applies in working situations. A clear and useful by-product of organisational selection and promotion processes is the behavioural transition through which those involved pass as a result. This indicates again, a move from the previous role, a past role to the future.

☐ *Longevity*

A major role sign is its duration. Reference was made in passing to this above. Some roles gain legitimacy or authority through longevity – 'She has been Chair for 20 years' or 'He has 20 years' experience.' The converse may also be applied: 'She is new to the job; give her a chance.' The distinction may again be drawn between working and non-working situations. In the former roles are deemed to have degree of permanence, stability and continuity. Away from work, there are those such as holiday-maker which are easily assumed and regular; and those such as husband, wife, son or daughter and so on which are taken on for life.

☐ *Recognition*

The role signs must be recognised and therefore be capable of recognition. Their major requirement is clearly to be easily identifiable in whatever form they come. Each group of signs indicated above must be distinctive if it is to be successful.

The converse is also worth stating. For example, receptionists who treat the important guest at the workplace with indifference invariably do so because they have not recognised him, because the signs and symbols exuded by the visitor were not clear. Lack of distinction and lack of recognition tend to lead to confusion, disappointment and even embarrassment and anger.

The coverage also indicates their general value and usefulness. Role signs are universally required as part of the wider perception processes as well as for specific situations. Roles that are not clearly signed are the source of confusion and dissonance.

It is clear from this that there are strong complex and conflicting influences present. The major lesson is in the understanding of this. People adopt and aspire to work roles as part of their wider role sets and as a reflection of what is important to them. The effective and successful creation of work roles must both reflect and accommodate this.

It is also clear from this that roles give identity. Again, if this is to be successful, this identity must be positive. People need roles of which they can be proud and with which they can be happy and confident. These roles, after all, are a critical part of the process by which those holding them are to be placed, mapped and identified by the rest of the world at large and the particular society in which they live.

Further, the different roles feed each other and feed off each other. They constantly interact. Satisfaction as a parent, for example, is enhanced by feelings of well-being as the holder of a particular job and diminished if the job is considered or perceived to be bad or negative. Total well-being only arises when there is harmony across the entire role set, or at least as much of it as possible.

It is also necessary to draw attention to misunderstanding, misconception and complacency. This arises most often where the organisation is completely certain and confident of its own well-being and ceases to pay attention to the needs of those working within it. This form of neglect may be purely benign; in all events it requires constant positive and active attention.

It is also necessary, finally, to recognise the fluid, ever-changing and ever-developing nature of all roles, both inside and outside work, and their constant and sophisticated interactions and interrelations. Roles may not therefore be precisely defined or designed. They must be set in the broader framework indicated. Mechanisms must be established by organisations for coping with the inevitable resultant ambiguities, stresses, strains, dysfunctions and conflicts.

■ Role uncertainties and ambiguities

These arise when there is a lack of clarity as the precise nature of the role or roles at any given point. They relate to:

- uncertainty about aims and objectives, resulting in uncertainty/lack of clarity as to what constitutes successful and effective performance;
- uncertainty about job/task/occupational boundaries in terms of extent, range and depth of coverage, quality of performance (especially where this is not easily or precisely measured);
- uncertainty about the nature of commitment expected/anticipated/required, including areas of responsibility, authority and accountability;
- uncertainty of expectations arising from misconceptions at the outset; expectations placed on the role by the individual which are not met in the ways anticipated; expectations of others;
- uncertainty of relationships within the group, between groups and across the whole organisation;
- uncertainty of prospects, development, enhancement and advancement;
- uncertainty of stability, continuity and confidence.

Each contributes to a lack of clarity of relationship and expectations, and is a source of potential stress and conflict. They may also give rise to clashes, anger, lack of confidence and respect.

Uncertainties may also arise where an individual has a complex and often conflicting role to perform. Managers and supervisors are invariably subject to this as they carry out (and must reconcile) roles of leader, direction, organiser, planner of work; confidante, friend, recruiter, developer, promoter, disciplinarian and dismisser to and of the staff. Integrity of relationship is called into question where the pursuit of one role leads to effects on the others. For example, if the manager has disciplined a member of staff for some reason, should this affect subsequent opportunities for development and advancement; should weaknesses identified at performance appraisal lead to disciplinary measures? If it is not clear where each role begins and ends, those affected may not act in appropriate ways – and individual may always see their manager or supervisor as ready to discipline them, even when the latter is supposed to be carrying out the role of friend or confidante.

■ Incompatibility

Incompatibility arises when an individual is unable to carry out the role. This is normally either because she lacks the capability or because she is unable to perform it in the ways required.

The first is exemplified by the 'Peter Principle' – promotion to the level of incompetence – whereby someone is given a job or task for which he has no aptitude or capability.

The second is to be found for example, where a supervisor is required by her superior to run a highly structured operation and where the staff prefer and are used to a more relaxed and less formal style.

Incompatibility is also to be found where values and beliefs are called into question. A supervisor may be required to discipline or dismiss a member of staff and find himself unable to do so because he believes it to be wrong. If the rest of the group also believe that it is wrong, this will adversely affect the supervisor's future relationships with the other group members.

■ Overload

This occurs where the individual is required to take on:

- too much work, too many tasks;
- too much responsibility, authority and accountability;
- too much pressure, stress and strain;
- incompatibility, as above.

The result is either that all of the work is unsatisfactory; or that some of the work is effective at the expense of the rest; or that some aspects are not covered at all.

Overload can only be sustained in the short to medium term (while the organisation is getting through a crisis for example). Continued overload normally leads to loss of performance, loss of achievement, and damage to the health of the individual.

■ Underload

Underload occurs where there is not enough in the role to keep the individual happy and satisfied. This is normally related to feelings of:

- undervalue, including where the individual feels that she is being underpaid and underrewarded; and also where her contribution is not being fully recognised;
- underperformance, where the individual feels that he could be going on to better and higher things;
- not being needed, a lack of confidence in the quality, worth and contribution of the work itself;

- lack of feeling on the part of the organisation for the well-being of the staff, or on the part of superiors for subordinates;
- loss of self-respect, self-esteem and the esteem and regard of others;
- external and internal pressure, a consciousness on the part of the individual that she is capable of doing far better and of achieving much more; this is compounded when peers, friends, family and acquaintances all believe the same thing.

This may clearly have nothing to do with absolute volumes of work. Indeed, it is most likely to hinge on the individual's perceptions of his own capabilities and potential. People are much more likely to put up with something that does not meet their expectations if they feel that it is means to an end, a stepping stone on the path of progress. Frustration sets in where these prospects are not present or not apparent.

■ Stresses and strains

Stresses and strains become apparent where the problems caused by ambiguity, uncertainty, overload and underload become irreconcilable (see Figure 6.2). The symptoms are:

- poor communications, in terms of both volume and quality; lack of accessibility and visibility;
- overattention to trivia and detail at the expense of the broader picture, aims and objectives;
- overattention to and overuse of procedures and rules at the expense of issue resolution and problem-solving;
- polarisation of approach: everything is either very good or very bad;
- poor interpersonal relationships, the presence of tension, friction and irritability;
- withdrawal, including absenteeism and sickness;
- the presence of blame, the search for scapegoats;
- loss of volume and quality of performance.

If allowed to go unchecked, the effects of stress and strain invariably include loss of general performance, motivation and morale, and the decline of general working relationships. Individuals within the department withdraw themselves, seeking to ensure that they carry out their tasks satisfactorily; at the same time, they will tend to seek opportunities elsewhere to remove themselves from the current situation. They pursue their own objectives at the expense of, rather than in harmony with, those of the organisation.

☐ *Situations leading to stress and strain*

The following organisation situations are likely to create stresses and strains for individuals.

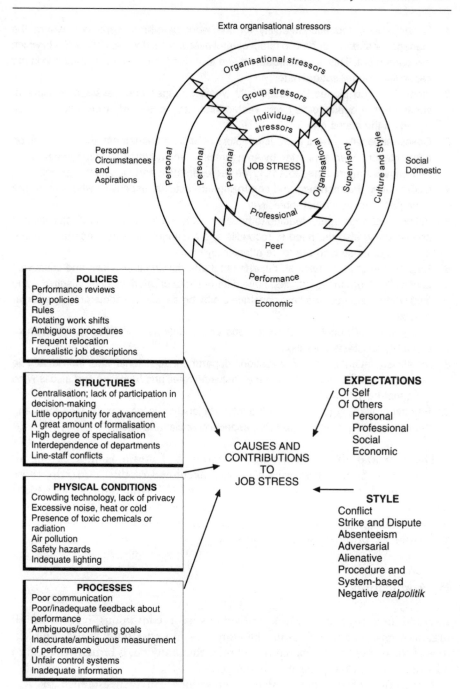

Figure 6.2   Stress: sources, causes, symptoms

1. Responsibility and accountability for the work of others, especially where the manager or supervisor has no direct control over what is done and the ways in which it is carried out. This is exacerbated if she also does not have full confidence in the capabilities of her subordinates.
2. Innovation and pioneering, especially where changes and developments are at variance or in direct conflict with vested interests, centres of power and influence based on the status quo.
3. Crises, especially where there is a history of crisis management and emphasis on confrontation, often supported by an aggressive and adversarial management style and negative approaches to employee representation and industrial relations.
4. Coordinating, harmonising and controlling interactions, especially where there are strong and conflicting sub-objectives.
5. Acting as change agent, leading to becoming a focus for anger and dissatisfaction; and including also the need to reconcile and assuage the fears, uncertainties and anxieties of those who are to be affected by change.
6. Engaging in cross-functional, departmental and divisional activities and initiatives, especially where those affected have different sets of priorities and objectives, and also where resource and time constraints may be an issue in some of the particular groups.
7. The placing of people in stressful jobs and situations who have no strength or capability for stress toleration.
8. Insufficient attention to organisation, department, divisional and individual role design, creating uncertain boundaries between roles and functions and also leaving gaps that have to be filled.
9. Refusal or inability to recognise the interrelationship between workplace roles and the others that individuals perform, especially social and family.

The potential for the existence of stress and strain is inherent in all organisations. Some roles carry a greater likelihood of this, especially those with too much responsibility or too few prospects for the future. The issue is therefore for organisations for recognise and understand the harmful potential of role dysfunction and produce structures, cultures and jobs that recognise this and avoid the problems as far as possible.

■ Application

Interaction with and between individuals is a continuous feature of all organisations. The main lesson, therefore, lies in understanding the complexities of the perception, personality and roles that individuals bring with them to all situations and the pressures that arise.

Recognition of this means that organisations can then establish the key characteristics and traits that are required, rather than trying (and invariably failing) to cope with the whole individual. For this to be successful, information must be gathered systematically to ensure that as wide and complete a picture is built up about and around the individual in relation to the organisation's requirements. This is also the context for effective work design and division; creation of structures and cultures; and organisational progress, development and change.

In turn, the effectiveness of all of this is dependent upon the nature of individuals brought into the organisation in the first place. The onus is therefore placed on making the recruitment and selection activities as accurate and informative as possible. This is to ensure as effective and harmonious a match as possible between individual and organisation. This is the context in which all recruitment and selection activities should be seen. The purpose is to find someone who can do the job, who will fit into the organisation (both the particular niche and the wider internal environment) and who brings potential for the future. This is the basis of an effective, continuous and harmonious working relationship.

■ Recruitment and selection

■ Testing

The main purpose of selection is therefore to be as clear as possible about the individual's main characteristics, aptitudes and capabilities. The best way to do this is to isolate those required by the organisation and then set up a series of tests that indicate the extent of their presence in the particular individuals. The tests themselves have to be tested for:

- validity: the extent to which they do the job required, that they test what is to be tested;
- reliability: the extent to which this is done on all occasions and in all situations.

BOX 6.7   Forms of test

These each have their place in particular situations.

Physical	To indicate strength, fitness, physical durability, robustness, ability to stand extremes of heat and cold.
Intelligence	To indicate mental agility, mental dexterity, mental awareness.
Verbal reasoning	To indicate how arguments are presented and developed, how an individual may present or develop a case, sales pitch, negotiating position and so on.
Presentation	To indicate self-presentation, awareness of audience, use of time, structure and a logical order of material, aims and objectives of a situation.

Numeracy	To indicate level of understanding and application or numerical forms, skills in adding, subtracting, multiplying and dividing, use of numeracy technology.
Literacy	To indicate levels of language usage and application, and also particular skills such as spelling and articulation.
Skills	To indicate levels and quality of skills in, for example, typing, shorthand, engineering, presentation.
Aptitude	To indicate the relationship between what the individual can do now as a prediction of what he may be able to achieve in the future.
Attainment	To indicate the depth of knowledge or skill achieved to date in terms of the organisation's current and future requirements.
Pressure	To indicate how the individual copes, prioritises and carries out work when put under some form of pressure (for example, time, interruptions); they may also be developed to indicate how the individual might cope with stress.
Work sampling	To indicate the range and quality of past activities as an indication of current level of competence.
Personality	To indicate the personality traits of the individual (they are normally carried out through use of multiple choice question-naires).

None of these is to be seen in isolation from other selection activities (see Table 6.1).

For each of these the word 'indicate' is used. None proves a certainty of performance. A typing test which an individual completes successfully proves that she *can* do it; it does not prove that she *will* do it in the work situation; and this applies to each form of testing indicated. Those that are less precise in output – intelligence, aptitude, personality – have to be structured further to provide a correlation between:

(a) the traits and qualities identified;
(b) those that are required;
(c) why they are required;
(d) the extent to which past successful holders of the particular job exhibited these;
(e) the extent to which these were key elements of that success.

They also do not predict or guarantee performance.

Tests are therefore used in combination with other forms of assessment for best effect (see Table 6.1). A small part of the personality and other properties of the individual is opened up by each. The greater the number of openings found, the greater the likelihood of effective assessment.

Table 6.1 Selection methods: summary

Method	Advantages	Disadvantages
Interview	• Opens up human relationships and contact • Enables discussion and questioning • May indicate key strengths/weaknesses	• Halo effects • Stereotyping • Self-fulfilling prophecy • Time constraints • Personal bias
Panel interview	• As above • Brings the views of several to bear	• As above • Different perceptions by panel members • Lack of cohesion • Defending preferred candidates
Handwriting	• None	• Unscientific
References	• A view and perception from independent sources	• May be corrupted • Personal bias • Incomplete • Dwells on past • Useless as predictor of future performance
Supervisory evaluation	• A view and perception from an interested and related party	• Personal bias • Dwells on past
Work sample	• First-hand indication of the achievements and output of the individual to date	• Based on past and current performance
Personal history, CV, application form	• Gives standard and standardised data	• Subject to perception and bias • Dwells on past achievements rather than shortcomings
Testing	• Indicates skills, knowledge, attitude, behaviour and traits • Meets precise aims and objectives	• Needs to be related to future required performance • Aims and objectives of the tests need to be precisely drawn up
Use of agencies	• Cuts down on time spent • Use of agencies' access to candidate fields	• Needs clear understanding of brief
Use of specialist agencies (head hunters)	• Cut down on time spent • Use of specialist knowledge and agencies access to specialist candidates	• Needs clear understanding of brief

Note: There are time and resource implications (and expense) in pursuing each and all of these effectively. This has to be weighed against the fact that making wrong or ineffective appointments is extremely expensive.

BOX 6.8   The Barnum Effect

Why are people so enthusiastic about personality tests? One view is that the tests are used to help the interviewer structure the interview and that they are not used in a predictive sense at all. This may be all very well, but one wonders what candidates would make of the idea that they are being interviewed on the basis of information that has no demonstrated relevance to their likely job performance.

More sinister is a trick used by salesmen to peddle inferior testing to the unwary and unsophisticated. Would-be clients are invited to take the test free of charge and the salesman offers an interpretation. Clients are intended to be impressed by the uncanny accuracy with which the interpretation reveals aspects of their character.

This is a confidence trick. It was revealed as such 40 years ago when it was shown that most people considered that a fixed personality profile fitted them rather well. The phenomenon came to be known as the fallacy of personal .validation – or the 'Barnum Effect' – because it shows that there's a sucker born every minute.

If you spend 20 minutes or so answering a whole host of questions about yourself, you ought to recognise yourself in the way your answers are read back to you.

From: Steve Blinkhorn, 'The Hazards of Occupational Testing', *The Listener*, 14 January 1988, quoted in Huczynski and Buchanan (1993).

■ Job descriptions

Job descriptions are collections of activities and tasks parcelled up into forms suitable for being carried out by individuals, either in isolation or else in cooperation with others. The best job descriptions indicate the nature and range of work to be carried out while leaving a degree of flexibility to enable organisations to maximise/optimise staff usage, and individuals to progress and develop. Scientific management took the operational approach and drew up highly specific job descriptions for the simplest and most specialised of tasks. The approach was developed and used for a long time for all kinds of activities, including those related to highly skilled, professional and managerial functions.

The simple approach gets around this in two ways. It removes the need for the physical and administrative effort necessary to draw up such job descriptions in large and complex organisations, and this releases resources for other purposes. The view is taken that the job title is in many ways itself a job description: doctor, secretary and sweep all carry with them clear indications of the likely work content. Moreover, it is clearly bad practice (and in some cases may be illegal) to give false and misleading job titles; it is damaging and demotivating to the staff concerned and ultimately inefficient and resource-consumptive to the organisation. In addition, the more specialised and complex approach often leads to demarcation and restrictive practice disputes and the guarding of key and high profile tasks by particular individuals and groups.

■ Person specifications

These are statements of the skills, knowledge, attitudes, behaviour and experience required by the organisation of its staff and potential staff. In general, the fitting the work to the person/fitting the person to the work (FWP-FPW) process indicated in Figure 6.3 matches these qualities with job requirements. The best use of the personnel specification also includes wider indications of qualities and attributes, potential for development, and professional and related interests so that there is an awareness of the general pool of talent which may become valuable at a later date.

Accurate person specifications represent best practice in the selection of effective staff. They are also increasingly important for legal reasons. People have the right to know that they have been accepted or rejected for appointments or promotions on the basis of capability alone, and to make a complaint if they feel that this has not been the case. This is especially important in relation to the application of equal opportunities laws and regulations.

Qualities required are normally listed and prioritised and weighted, and indicate the selection and assessment methods to be used for the particular position.

■ Measuring attitudes and values

The problems of measuring and assessing the intangible aspects – attitudes, values, commitment and enthusiasm – have never been fully resolved. Each may be observed or inferred over periods of time and in certain situations. Conclusions may be drawn from demeanour, expression and the amount of energy shown. They may be perceived in the approach to tasks and interrelationships with others and interactions with superiors and subordinates.

All of this is, however, subject to interpretation and perception and therefore coloured by the feelings and pressures of the interactee.

This is conquered to an extent by adequate induction and orientation programmes in which the required attitudes, values and levels of commitment and enthusiasm are directly addressed and instilled into those beginning with the organisation or commencing new jobs within it. The object is therefore to make sure that the required attitudes and values are adopted, rather than worrying about those that individuals bring with them.

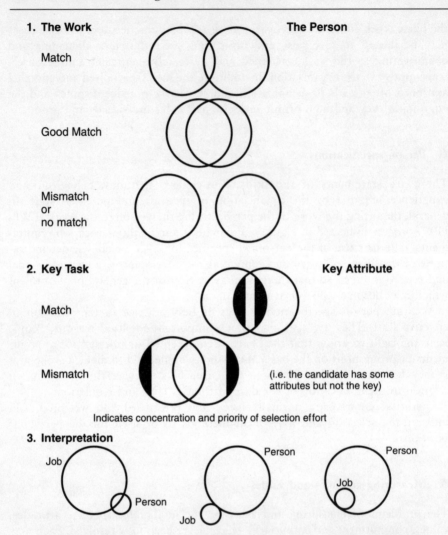

1. The Work   **The Person**

Match

Good Match

Mismatch
or
no match

2. Key Task   **Key Attribute**

Match

Mismatch   (i.e. the candidate has some
                                      attributes but not the key)

Indicates concentration and priority of selection effort

3. Interpretation

Job — Person

Person — Job

Person — Job

Job is too large for
person, leading to
stress and dysfunction

Person is too large
for job, but has no
attribute for it

Person is too large for
job, has attribute for it
but will soon get bored

Purpose: indicates requirement to define personal attributes in relation to the job

In all organisations, the process must be validated, that is, the relationship between key tasks and key attributes must be related to effective job performance. It must also be reliable, that is, any test used to predict performance from the process must demonstrate the quality concerned, and relate it to job performance, in all circumstances

Figure 6.3   Fitting the work to the person: fitting the person to the work

■ **Interviewing**

The best approach to interviewing lies in preparing a structure based on the qualities and attributes demanded by the job description and around which the person or specification has been drawn up. Each individual is interviewed to the same format so that a form of comparison can be made.

A proper framework such as this goes a long way to ensuring that matters of equality of opportunity and other legal constraints are addressed. It also allows for a certain amount of flexibility. It enables the interviewer to ensure that everything of relevance is covered. It also enables time and space to pursue points of contention, points which have not been covered to their satisfaction and to probe on particular matters.

Interviews are most useful for opening up a personal relationship between individual and organisation that may in turn become that of employer–employee in the future. They elicit a certain amount of information according to the structure and matters for discussion chosen by the interviewer. They can be used to begin to assess the candidates powers of logic and reasoning. They give an indication of the candidates general verbal and debating skills. They also give an indication of the basis and standpoint from which the candidate's presentation of his past performance and achievements has been delivered.

■ **Interview panels**

A one-to-one interview is clearly less daunting for the candidate than a panel of several. The main advantage to the organisation of constructing interview panels is that it enables a wider form of assessment to be made. Panellists can concentrate on their own areas of specialism, whereas a single interviewer may have to take on trust any answers covering areas with which she is not familiar or knowledgeable.

The panel system goes wrong when the members pursue their own ends and defend their own points of view. They may also defend their own preferred candidate and this may include refusing to accept someone else's first choice. In these circumstances it is usual either not to make an appointment and to incur the expense of re-advertising and reconstituting the panel; or to choose a candidate that nobody opposed.

■ **Work and aptitude sampling**

This is where a candidate is asked to submit a portfolio of work carried out in the recent past or on which he is currently working. This enables the selector to make a first-hand judgement of the standard and quality of work, areas of interest (and possibly also breadth) of expertise, and the type of approach taken.

Where required skills are easily tested, a work simulation can also be set up. For example, school teachers may be required to conduct a class under the eye of the assessors. Sales persons may be asked to make a presentation to a customer (either real or simulated).

BOX 6.9   Work and Aptitude Sampling: Situational Interviews

Some selectors try to get over problems in this area (for example, when they do not have the time, space or resources to set up a more real situation) by asking the candidate to read a particular scenario (or to describe one to them) and then asking her how she would respond. For example:

> One of your colleagues comes up to you and says some money has been taken from her purse. One of the other members of the department is known to have a conviction some time ago for theft.

> What would you do?

The problem with this approach lies in the different perceptions of both interviewer and interviewee. If the interviewer is looking for a preferred answer, will tend not to listen to that which is given once it becomes apparent that the 'right' reply is not forthcoming. The interviewee may attempt to counter this by giving a measured response and unfolding it according to the cues and signals received from the interviewer.

More generally, it is impossible to know what anyone *would* do until they were faced with the actual situation. The answer can only be hypothetical. Above all, the answer required or sought by the interviewer might be wrong.

BOX 6.10   A Note on References

References are useless for predicting future attitudes, behaviour and performance. They normally take the form of a short note or telephone conversation centred on impressions, aptitudes and qualities of the candidate. The usual participants are the current and future employer. The current employer will normally not have a full understanding of the future job; the future employer will not normally have a full knowledge of the current job. The result is that any impression formed is then left to the perception of the potential new employer who has only the selection information available on which to match up the reference and to make an informed judgement. References given are nearly always couched in bland tones. This is to avoid giving false and misleading impressions. Any negative element must in any case be supported by specific information. The whole is limited either to a single sheet of paper or brief conversation.

Some useful general points should also be made.

1. Excellence of past performance does not prove excellence of future performance.
2. Excellence of past relationships does not prove excellence of future relationships.
3. Unsatisfactory past performance does not prove unsatisfactory future performance.
4. Unsatisfactory current relationships do not prove unsatisfactory future relationships.
5. Personal dislike of the candidate by the current supervisor does not prove personal dislike of the candidate by the future supervisor.
6. Personal liking of the candidate by the current supervisor does not prove personal liking of the candidate by the future supervisor.
7. Current strengths and weaknesses of attitude and commitment do not prove future strengths and weaknesses of attitude and commitment.
8. Current position in an organisation does not prove adequacy for a future position in a future organisation.

When viewed in this way, most references are little more than a convention. In the UK the only legal requirement is to confirm the dates on which an employee commenced and left employment with a particular organisation. In particular, references taken up about middle-aged employees concerning occupations in the dim and distant past are normally completely worthless.

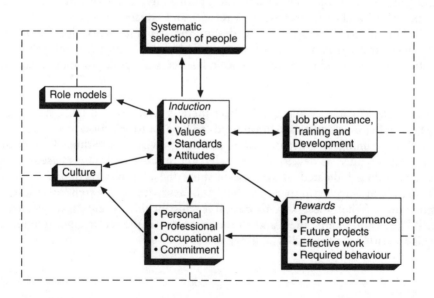

Figure 6.4   Effective individual and role development

■ **Assessment centres**

Effective selection and the basis for the successful role and occupational development is likely to be based on a combination of each of these needs. Tests, questionnaires, interviews and activities are structured:

- to bring out the skills and qualities required, indicating their presence or absence;
- to identify the required traits and characteristics;
- to provide consistency of assessment.

Initially expensive and time-consuming, the returns are found in the selection of successful and effective staff. Assessment centres are based on sound personnel specifications and the establishment and use of the best means of pinpointing, identifying and, where necessary, observing and inferring the required characteristics.

■ **Conclusions**

The importance for organisations lies in understanding and recognising the concepts of the whole person. This includes the complexities and contradictions of perceptions, roles, attitudes, values, drives and motivations. It includes the pressures of the environment, society, profession and occupation; and also the need to conform and cooperate. It requires attention to specific achievements and learning, development, variety and opportunity. The individual also needs to be valued and to be treated with respect and esteem.

Organisations therefore need to design and structure work, jobs and roles that meet and satisfy as much of this as possible. They must recognise that this is the basis of productive, effective and successful work, of individual and mutual satisfaction in both occupational and personal terms. They must also recognise the fact that problems are likely to arise and the nature of these when insufficient attention is paid and where there is a lack of full understanding.

Especially, much more attention needs to be paid to selection processes, both for those coming into organisations and for movements within. This means targeting as much as developing the selection process; and this is based on the understanding indicated above, establishing the true nature of the qualities required for successful performance and assessing the extent of these in individuals. Where necessary or desirable, this includes attention to particular attitudes, values and beliefs and to the pressures of the wider environment, as well as distinctive capability and expertise.

■ Questions

1. How does the study of personality and role help an understanding of organisation behaviour?
2. To what extent do role signs and status symbols (a) help and (b) hinder effective organisational processes?
3. What are the advantages and disadvantages of giving (a) highly specific and (b) very general job descriptions?
4. Briefly outline the use and misuse of each of the testing methods indicated in Box 6.7. Under what circumstances and for what jobs should each be used? What other information would also be required in each of the examples you have used?

CHAPTER 7
Communication

■ Introduction

The issue of communication is vital for the successful functioning of any organisation. All organisations normally establish formal mechanisms and processes of vertical and lateral lines or channels of communication to provide the means by which information – facts, ideas, proposals, emotions, feelings, opinions and problems – can be exchanged. They also normally create integrating activities such as groups, committees and other meetings, and the means of consultation or participation to improve the all-round quality and understanding of this information.

Effective communication is based on information:

(a) the volume available;
(b) its quality;
(c) the means and media by which it is transmitted and received;
(d) the use to which it is put;
(e) its integrity;
(f) the level of integrity of the wider situation.

Communications and information feed the quality of all human relations in organisations. Good communications underline good relations and enhance the general quality of working life, motivation and morale. Bad and inadequate communications lead to frustration, and enhance feelings of alienation and lack of identity and unity.

It is therefore necessary to consider each aspect of the communication process in turn. This is followed by a discussion of the elements that contribute to their quality and effective usage.

■ One-way communication

This is where edicts are issued by organisations to their employees, usually without any regard for their effect. This is invariably due to ignorance, and the effect is always dysfunctional. It occurs only in the worst of organisations with the most alienated workforce and the most insular management and directorates.

It also occurs, rarely, where the workforce or its representatives issue ultimatums to a particular organisation in regard, for example, to an impending strike; the effect is always to stoke up the fires of conflict.

In practice, communication is never purely one way; anyone issuing a communication normally has a general understanding of its effects upon the recipients. Communication of emergency procedures, for example, is directive and prescriptive and those to whom they apply fully understand the reasons for this.

■ Two-way communication

This is the dialogue process, the engaging in a communication-and-response process, the results of which are understanding, enlightenment, effective action and progress. It takes place in written and non-verbal, as well as oral, formats and constitutes the relationship between any sender and recipient of a communication.

■ Upward and downward communication

■ Downward

This is the use of communication hierarchies and structures for communication purposes. Information is cascaded down from directors to senior managers, from senior managers to junior managers and then to supervisors and their staff. This is also the means of promulgation of policies and directives, instructions, employee handbooks, rules and regulations, reports, memoranda, newsletters; and the focus of electronic information systems. use is made of committees, structures and methods. A version of this also takes place during managerial briefing sessions, presidential addresses from the Chief Executive Officer (CEO) or local person in charge and other mass meetings and general forums.

■ Upward

The nature, content and volume of upward communication arises from management style. At the extreme, where management is absent or inaccessible, this is limited to formalised channels such as joint consultative committees and joint negotiating committees and the raising of disputes and grievances. At the opposite end of the scale, where managers and supervisors walk the job and have regular continuous contact with their staff, a greater, regular and more accurate use for volume and quality of information is gained. It is especially useful to gather general views, attitudes, hopes and fears, aspirations, suggestions, proposals, difficulties and problems, both as background organisational knowledge, and also to maximise opportunities that become apparent. It is essential, above all, in heading off crises before they occur.

■ Lateral

It is useful to note at this point that many organisations do recognise the problems and constraints inherent in upward and downward regimented communications. They take steps to create for example, cross-boundary channels, cross-functional communications and interdisciplinary groups with a view to getting over this.

■ Formal and informal communication

These are the channels of communication, the ducts through which information is passed or fed.

■ Formal

These are the hierarchies, systems, procedures and committee structures referred to above. This also includes the use and operation of written procedures and policies, and the use of electronic systems.

■ Informal

These are the *ad hoc* gatherings that take place between people all the time at every place of work. This includes scribbled notes, post-its, canteen and tea room gatherings. Above all, it includes the organisational grapevine: the things that people gossip and chat about and other general discussion sessions.

■ Institutionalisation

These are informal gatherings that nevertheless have a validity or recognition within the organisation. They include professional and managerial cluster groups and also (in some organisations) work improvement groups and quality circles. They come therefore somewhere between the two extremes. There is a general measure of voluntarism in regard to participation in them (and thus a measure in some places of coercion also). At the same time the organisation will normally resource them, at least in terms of facilities, meeting rooms and basic equipment.

It is useful to view the components of organisational communication in this way. It is the traditional way of doing so and it is expected. It is a traditional framework for assessing the nature of organisational communications.

Most valuable of all, it identifies the problem areas, the limitations and potential for barriers in the field.

☐ *Consultation*

Consultative means of communication are used in the implementation of decisions and policies. The purpose is to ensure that those being consulted understand what is required of them and why, and the opportunities and threats of a particular situation. It is also a reflection of the requirement that people have for confidence in those in charge and in the directions that they propose. Effective consultation and the associated processes normally reflect the fact that what is proposed has been well thought out and tested.

Genuine consultation is also the means by which any flaws in decision-making processes or the implementation of particular proposals may nevertheless be raised. However well or thoroughly an issue has been thought through, it must be capable of wide general scrutiny and examination.

All those involved must be fully briefed and all information made available if the process is to be effective. Those being consulted must have this presented to them in ways that they can understand and assimilate (see Figure 7.1).

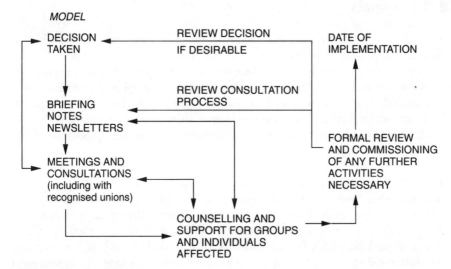

Figure 7.1 Consultation

☐ *Participation*

Participation is where all those involved take part (participate) in the decision-making process itself as well as its implementation. In order to do this, full information has to be made available to all involved. Again, the language and formats used must support this. Participation is not an end in itself. It is a means to effective organisation behaviour and work activity. If this is to be achieved, the information background must be as complete as possible.

Genuine participation requires effective and clear decision-making processes that have to satisfy the openness and cooperation indicated, but without discussing, stifling and analysing everything to the point of inertia. Effective participation must meet the criteria of both effective communication and effective decision-making.

Both consultation and participation require a fundamental organisation belief in their value and effectiveness if they are to be successful. Processes instigated in their pursuit must therefore be believed in, valued and, above all, used. Participation and consultation are reflections of culture and integrity. They bring with them instruments and institutions – discussion groups, committees, briefings, quality circles and so on – and also a fundamental openness of attitude and approach. Organisations which pursue these paths do so as the result of having decided that they are the correct suitable way of conducting their affairs.

■ Committees

Committees are constituted for a variety of reasons. From the point of view of communication, the important point is that they should enhance both quality and value rather than act as a blockage. If this is to happen, the purpose, scheduling of meetings, size, composition, agenda, control and recording must be managed. The ultimate test of the value of any committee is in its output. If this is either not forthcoming or not effective, then alternative means should be found of tackling the issues that the committee (or committee system of the organisation) is supposed to be facing.

Committees are heavily favoured by the *modus operandi* of sophisticated organisations. They are used to render inert something that is threatening to a particular vested interest. They are used to filter and edit information. They are used to draw the teeth of lobbies or pressure groups (consultative committees and advisory committees are particularly insidious forms of this). There is always a pecking order for committees that is understood, if not explicit. Committee membership is subject to patronage and the means of advancement and retarding. Membership of certain committees is often the mark of status or achievement.

Committee structures are often also heavily institutionalised. They constitute a major contribution to 'the way that things are done here'. Any assessment for operational effectiveness has therefore to be considered from this point of view. However overtly ineffective, any changes mooted must be capable of being accommodated within the existing establishment as well as improving the effectiveness of performance.

Finally, for all the criticism and imperfection indicated, committees are universally accepted and have acknowledged ways of doing things. They satisfy human needs of association and belonging and, more generally, of participating and contributing (whether real or illusory). Any move to change committee structures and operations must therefore recognise that these human needs must be satisfied in other ways if disaster and dissatisfaction is not to occur.

■ Elements necessary for effective communication

Factors that must be present if high-quality and effective communications are to be achieved are now considered. Distortion and misunderstanding are always potentially present, as are the general issues. They are subject to all the pressures of perception indicated in Chapter 3. The message sent is never entirely that which is received. Steps must be taken to minimise the potential for misunderstanding and misinterpretation.

■ Clarity of purpose on the part of the sender or initiator

This means addressing the questions of what the message is, and why it is being sent; the receivers and their likely reactions and responses; the possible range of reactions and responses; what is to be achieved as a result and what the barriers to this achievement might be. This is the basis of 'saying what is meant and meaning what is said'.

■ Integrity of purpose

This is the relationship between what is said and what is meant. This means using clear, concise and unambiguous terms so that there is no doubt about the impact on the receiver. The message is honest and straightforward, subject to as little interpretation and uncertainty as can be achieved by the sender.

Integrity (or lack of it) in communications tends to reinforce the general ways of working of the organisation and also the wider state of mutual trust, respect and esteem held by all concerned for each other.

Problems with communication integrity arise when:

- there is a lack of understanding of its fundamental importance leading to the issuing of communications in a state of ignorance of their full effects and impact;
- there are systems and traditions of organisation operation which lead to the issuing of unclear and distorted (and corrupted) communications on the basis, for example, that if people are not definite about anything, they cannot be called to account for it; or where people will avoid making commitments or promises that they cannot subsequently fulfil.

■ **Integrity of parties and relationships involved**

The basis of this is in the roles, personalities, working relations and context of communication involved; it is bounded by the standards of the organisation as a whole. At the core is the mutual trust and honesty of the particular relationship. In organisation behaviour terms, this is underpinned by the practices and processes of the organisation and its reactions to those who breach this integrity (whether this is indifferent, whether it punishes or whether it rewards those who do this).

■ **Use of language and media**

Much is made of these elements in this chapter. The general rule is that, while the message should be that of the sender (and sent on the basis of clarity indicated above), the language and media should be those most suited to the receivers. Acceptance of this rule tends to reinforce the need to think things through prior to issuing them and also helps to indicate those areas where problems might arise.

Moreover, the simpler and more direct the language used, the greater the initial level of familiarity or information gained on the part of the receiver, and the quicker things can be moved on.

The selection of the correct media is essential and many communications go wrong because the wrong choice is made. Again, the basic rule is simple:

Say what needs to be said; write what needs to be written; make best uses of all the senses of those affected.

This latter should be universally and creatively applied. Nissan UK for example, flew (and continues to fly) its employees to Japan to *show* them the organisation and head office of the company for whom they actually work. Richard Branson and Anita Roddick regularly visit their work locations – factories, shops, offices, airliners, Third World countries – to *show* their people that they care and are visible and accessible. The return for each is in the reinforcement of the mutuality of interest and respect and the integrity of the working relationship.

Otherwise, the main hard and fast rule is to ensure that if people need to retain information they are given (or have open access to) a written copy or summary, whatever the media used to put it across. Everyone then has the same point of reference and it can be used as the basis for further discussions if other points subsequently occur to anyone involved.

BOX 7.1   Communication Format

The principles indicated in the text are to be applied to all organisation means and methods of communication, especially letters, memoranda, reports, briefing papers and documents. They are to be applied also to advertising, promotion, brochures, literature, newsletters, prospectuses, forms and manuals (though this clearly also depends on the desired and wider presentation adopted).

It is also important in the approach to trade fairs and stands, demonstrations, catalogues, direct mailing, news media coverage and other public relations activities. As indicated in the main text, these should apply also to organisational rules, regulations and procedures.

Volume

The onus is to be placed firmly on quality, not volume. There is a balance to be struck between limiting the volume of information and ensuring the quality. In general, the greater the volume, the lower the likelihood that it will all be read or understood. The need is therefore to ensure that what is produced is as direct and concise as possible.

This is not always possible: in complex and sophisticated structures and bureaucracies, pressure is often placed on people to produce weighty papers as 'proof' of the fact that they have done a lot of hard work. Finally, whatever is produced is invariably retained in the organisation as a point of reference. Storage space, like all organisation facilities is expensive if unproductive, and the volume and quality of communications have to be seen in this light also. Too great a volume may not only be unproductive and ineffective as a method of communication, but it is also likely to constitute an ever-increasing burden to the unwary organisation.

■ **Volume and quality of communications**

The onus here is to balance the volume (to ensure that people get everything that they need and want) with delivering it in acceptable and usable formats. The purpose is not to limit access to information, but rather to ensure that everything received is of value and capable of being understood. In this lies the basis of a genuine openness of approach and integrity of relationships.

■ **Visibility**

People respond much more positively if they know who is issuing things. This is better still if they have a general and continuous face-to-face relationship based on mutual respect and understanding. This is much more likely where the particular manager or supervisor manages by walking around and demonstrates an active and positive interest in staff and activities.

■ Clarity and unity of overall purpose and direction

The greater the commitment to this, the greater the likelihood of effective communications. In contrast, where this is not present and where people tend to pursue their own interests, the more likely it is that the nature and quality of communications will reflect this. This leads to the issuing of material for the glorification of particular departments, self-promotion and also sometimes the denigration of others.

Clear communications therefore tend to reinforce clarity of both overall purposes and sub-aims and objectives, and also to concentrate the minds of those responsible for the ordering and direction of the organisation on the fact that the overall purposes and sub-aims and objectives should be clear at the outset.

■ Being positive

A positive approach to communications reinforces general positive attitudes, values and feelings on the part of all concerned. Language and messages should therefore reflect all the associated elements of encouragement, enhancement, enrichment, satisfaction, achievement, fulfilment, potential, creativity, innovation, progress and improvement.

Positive approaches and attitudes also enhance the motivation and commitment of the staff. It is much more likely than a harmonious and productive –

BOX 7.2   Being Positive

As stated in the text, this should be endemic. It should extend to problems and crises along the lines, for example, of 'We are in trouble *and* we are going to get out of it this way' (rather than for example, 'We are in trouble but we don't know what to do about it, but we will let you know as soon as we have thought of something').

The former reinforces the feelings of confidence and directness and clarity of purpose that the staff of any organisation expect, and it is much more likely to engage their positive attention and commitment. The latter simply provides fertile ground for rumour, stress and anxiety. It leads to loss of confidence, along the lines of 'If those at the top do not know what they are doing, how an earth should we? And why should we have any confidence in them?'

The positive approach to communications is again a reflection of clarity, integrity and commitment to purpose. It also feeds and reinforces this clarity and commitment.

and therefore profitable and effective – environment will be created. More generally, it is also certain that people will look forward to coming to work and that the whole experience of the organisation will be enjoyable as well as productive.

■ Rules, regulations and procedures

The purpose of these is to emphasise the standards of behaviour and the limitations placed upon people when they carry out their work. It is therefore essential that these are capable of being understood by all concerned. There should be as few as possible. They should apply equally to everyone, at whatever level of the organisation. They should be regularly updated (and the old thrown away). They should be simple, clear and easy to follow. Their main purpose is as a support rather than as a cause of behaviour.

■ General factors

These are matters of common courtesy, manners, the extent of genuine and general friendliness of approach between members of an organisation. The extent to which these prevail is a reflection of the prevailing mutuality of interest and common purpose. They also contribute to the avoidance of problems and disputes and, when these do arise, to their early settlement to the satisfaction of all involved. They also help to engender positive attitudes and values and mutual concern and respect.

■ Negotiation

Negotiation is the interactive form of communication that exists between two or more parties with a view at arriving at a situation that is acceptable to everybody concerned. It takes place at a variety of levels and for a variety of reasons within organisations. At departmental and individual levels, negotiations occur in the pursuit of the resolution of disputes and grievances. At the customer interface they occur in the resolution of complaints and clarifying the relationship. In relation to the wider community, negotiations exist to resolve differences over such things as planning, access, noise and other forms of pollution, expansion and extension (the reconciliation of the organisation's place in its environment).

A distinction is made between these forms of negotiation (which are essentially operational) and those concerned with the institutionalisation, containment and management of workplace conflict. The fundamental difference is in approach.

In the former case, the view in the vast majority of cases is: how can we resolve this issue to the general satisfaction of all concerned?

In the latter case, the broad approach is: this is a fight we must not lose. A 'them and us' becomes apparent. The issue becomes personalised. The wider context is lost in the pursuit of the specific issue. Above all, it becomes competitive: there are winners and losers, and for the latter, the injuries to pride and status and loss of face that goes with losing.

Ricardo Semler (1992) itemises this as follows.

1. Take a stand. Show the flag. Don't back down.
2. Guarantee that anyone who wants to work can, even if that means calling in the police.
3. Protect company property, with force if necessary.
4. Make it hard for the workers by closing the plant and suspending benefits.
5. Try to divide and conquer the strikers.
6. After it's over, fire the instigators and anyone else you want to get rid of, intimidating others in the process.

This is wrong. The wider position has been lost; the particular fight has become everything. Whatever is negotiated must be acceptable to *all* concerned, and the basis for effective future working relationships.

BOX 7.3   Bad Negotiations

Bad negotiations ruin communications. They destabilise effective methods of working. Energies and efforts are used up on the process and outcome of such negotiations rather than as part of the means of ensuring effective organisation performance. Both the organisation and its staff lose focus, lose sight of what they are supposed to be achieving and what is supposed to be happening at the place of work. Above all, they are extremely unprofitable: they use up organisation resources, often creating posts and occupations that could otherwise be used profitably. A couple of examples illustrate the point.

Student: I think that this piece of work is worth an 'A'.
Tutor: I think that this piece of work is worth an 'F'.
Student: Alright, we'll settle on a 'C'.

Employee: I want to come in at 12 o'clock.
Manager: You must be here at 8 o'clock.
Employee: Alright – I'll be here at 10 o'clock.

The point is that neither situation should be the subject of negotiation. The particular standard should be set by the person in charge of the situation, the person who is responsible for it. It is situations precisely such as these that allow the context for negotiations to become blurred and ineffective and that allow the negotiating process to get out of hand.

■ Non-verbal communication

Non-verbal communication gives an impression of people to others without saying or writing anything. It also reinforces what is being said or written. It also tends to give the real message – the non-verbal message is usually much stronger. The main components that must be understood are as follows.

Appearance This includes age, gender, hair, face, body shape and size, height, bearing, national and racial characteristics, clothing and accessories. Each of these items and their combined effect has great implications for: interviewing, public images, creating impressions, advertising, public relations, salesmanship, presentation, design brand, marque, lay-out, comfort and familiarity.

Manner Indicating behaviour, emotion, stress, comfort formality/informality, acceptability/unacceptability, respect/disrespect.

Expression Expression, especially facial expression, becomes the focus of attention and that is where people concentrate most of their attention.

Eye contact Regular eye contact demonstrates interest, trust concern, affection and sympathy. The depth of expression in the eyes generates deeper perception of feelings (anger, sorrow, love, hatred, joy).

Pose This is either static or active, relaxed, calm, agitated, nervous or stressful. It reinforces the overall impression conveyed. Different parts of the body (especially arms and legs) are used for expression, emphasis, protection and shield.

Clothing Especially in work situations, clothing provides an instant summary of people. Technicians are instantly recognised by their overalls, the police and traffic wardens by their distinctive uniforms; and so on. Many organisations whose staff deal regularly and consistently with the public insist either on a dress code or the wearing of a uniform as it helps to reinforce organisational image and the trust and confidence of the public.

Touch This reinforces a wide range of perceptions. Consider the difference between different people's handshakes and the impressions that these convey. Touching also reinforces role and sex stereotypes: the chairwoman banging her fist on the desk; the girl meticulously arranging her clothes.

Body movement This may be purely functional and fulfil certain requirements (for example, cleaning the car). Movements may be exaggerated, conveying anger or high emotions; languid, conveying comfort, ease or indolence; or sharp and staccato, conveying forcefulness and emphasis.

Position	This reinforces formality/informality; dominance/ dependency; superiority/subordination. People use position to enhance feelings of control and influence. For example, people may face each other across a large desk: this conveys a sense of security and defence to the person whose desk it is and a barrier to be crossed by the other. Chat show hosts sit without tables and ensure that their guests to not have recourse to this prop either. This puts the professional at an advantage and ensures that the guest is sufficiently alien to the environment to be subservient to the host.
Props and settings	Props and settings are used to reinforce impressions of luxury and formality. They are designed to ensure that whatever happens does so to the greatest possible advantage of the instigator. They either reinforce or complement perceptions and expectations, or else they contrast perceptions and expectations, so that the person coming into the situation is impressed for whatever reason.
Discrepancy	This occurs where the body conveys one message, while the spoken or written message conveys others.
Social factors	People are conditioned into having preconceived ideas and general expectations of particular situations. For example, people do not generally attend promotion panels or job interviews unshaven or dressed informally. There is no rationale for this other than the expectations of society and the general requirement to conform.
The other senses	Other aspects of non-verbal communication include: the use of scent and fragrance; the use of colour and coordination of colours; matters of social and ethical importance and expectation; design and use of materials.
Listening	Listening is both active and passive. Passive listening may be no more than awareness of background noise; it may also be limited to a general awareness of what is going on. Active listening requires taking a dynamic interest in what is being received. While the message is received through the ears, it is reinforced through eye contact, body movement, pose and through the reception of any non-verbal signals that are given by the speaker.
Reinforcement	Non-verbal communication tends to reinforce relative and absolute measures of status, value, importance and achievement; relative and absolute measures of authority, power and influence; confidence and well-being; and psychological barriers.

■ Language

This refers to the use of simple, direct and appropriate language, which is normally the language of the intended receiver. Communication is ineffective when the receiver does not understand what is said or written; in an organisational context, people also normally draw the additional conclusion that they are not supposed to understand what is being said, that there is a hidden message or agenda or that they are being deliberately misled.

■ Conciseness

Conciseness is the art of saying simply and directly everything that needs to be said. This is not to be confused with skimping or sketching: in each of these cases the attention of the receiver is again invariably drawn to that which is left out or not fully covered.

There is, on the other hand, a perception in some organisations that important material can be hidden away in long and sophisticated reports, or that such papers have critical material hidden away in them.

■ Presentation

This is the decision to choose the best means of putting the message across. The use of the right media for the particular message is critical. In simple terms this can be summarised as 'Say what needs to be said; write what needs to be written; show people what needs to be shown' and so on.

This is not as trite as it may first appear. Messages get lost or misunderstood precisely because of this (see Box 7.5). It is much more effective to show people a coca cola logo, a minutes format or a rule book rather than try to describe them. Communication is more direct, better thought out and better targeted. It remains longer with the recipient.

Closely related to this is the need to recognise which of the senses it is most appropriate to use in regard to the receiver. Taste, touch and scent are equally as effective and appropriate in the right circumstances. Again, if used correctly the message is both received and retained for longer.

■ Barriers and blockages

Barriers and blockages arise either by accident, negligence or design.

■ Accident

This is where the choice of language, timing or method of communication is wrong with the best of intentions. In such cases, those involved will simply step back from the situation and rectify it as quickly as possible. This is the only sure remedy. The worst thing that can and does happen is that the organisation takes on a defensive position and so a simple misunderstanding quickly becomes a major dispute or dysfunction.

■ Negligence

This is where barriers and blockages are allowed to arise by default. The organisation and its managers perceive that things are at least 'not too bad' or 'going along pretty well'. In such cases communication dysfunctions are seen as 'one of those things'. Specific problems are ignored or treated with a corporate shrug of the shoulders. From the staff point of view, however, these are the first signs of corporate mélees and neglect. If allowed to develop, the overwhelming perception on the part of the staff is that the organisation does not care for them or what happens to them.

■ Design

This is where the barriers and blockages are both created and also used by those within the organisation to further their own ends. They are used to bar the progress of others. In these cases above all, information becomes a commodity to be bought and sold, to be corrupted, skewed and filtered in the pursuit of the sectoral interest in question. This is endemic throughout the mid to upper echelons of the military, civil and public service institutions, multi-national companies and other multi-site organisations with large and complex head office institutions where an active and negative form of *realpolitik* exists.

BOX 7.4   Errol Flynn

'Errol Flynns' are so called because they exhibit all the characteristics of the great film star. In organisational terms they are glamorous: blue-eyed persons, clearly favoured, on upward career paths, with histories and track records of successes. They attract followers and courtiers. They have a series of triumphs (real and – overwhelmingly – imaginary) which gain organisational recognition. They are their own best publicists.

Above all, their greatest characteristic is to be, in organisational terms, just the right side of the drawbridge as it comes up; to escape their own disasters by the skin of their teeth.

Within this context the following barriers are identified.

1. The department, divisional, hierarchical and functional boundaries indicated above. In the context given, the propensity for distortion and corruption of communications between functions and through hierarchies is extremely high. This is enhanced by the inevitable presence or activities of those pursuing their own aims and objectives.
2. Language: again, this is discussed at length above. The point here is to emphasise that there is quite enough to go wrong in the process without the use of cloudy or

obscure language. This also applies to the wrong use of media and to the use of the wrong media.

BOX 7.5   Language Barriers

Forms of words and phraseology are used extensively to give off coded messages and to reinforce the real agenda that is being followed. Examples are as follows.

1. *With greatest respect, I respect your views, I am sure that you are a person of great integrity* = you are wrong, you are talking rubbish, I don't value you at all.
2. *We will take all steps, we are doing everything possible, we are complying with the law, we are complying with specific regulations* = we are doing as little as possible in the circumstances, we are doing the least we can get away with in the circumstances, you cannot tough us.
3. *We do not have the resources/money/staff/equipment* = we do not want to do it, we are not going to do it.

■ Distance

Distance in this context is both physical and psychological. The physical barrier also carries psychological overtones. For example, when one is operating at a physical distance from the organisational headquarters, there is a psychological feeling of autonomy also. This is compounded by the presence of overmighty subjects. The institution therefore generates its own identity. All of this acts as a barrier to effective cross-organisation communications.

At a more localised level, the psychological distance is compounded or reduced by the presence (or absence) of trappings such as offices, secretaries, forms of address and titles.

■ Trappings

Some trappings exude fear. For example, the person who has a car parking space, two personal assistants, a personal washroom, a personal fax and an office suite puts up barriers to communication with the more junior staff. The junior in turn, therefore, is both physically and psychologically discouraged from approaching that individual.

These trappings then become marks of success and achievement. The junior strives for the position and, when this is achieved, the trappings are retained as the ex-junior's own outward manifestations and symbols of success. The barriers become perpetuated rather than broken.

■ **Chains of communication**

The more filters through which a message must pass, the longer the chain of communication (see Figure 7.2), the greater the chance of distortion. This is the weakness inherent in the cascade effect illustrated in Boxes 7.6 and 7.7. It is attractive to the top managers of sophisticated organisations because it is simple and visual and therefore easily understood. It is almost universally inappropriate as a means of communication without substantial reinforcement through other means and channels.

BOX 7.6   The Cascade Effect

As stated in the text, this is attractive to hierarchies. Those at the top delude themselves that it works as an effective communication mechanism. It takes its name from the cascade appearance caused by pouring champagne into the top glass of a pyramid of glasses. The pouring is continued until the wine overflows and eventually fills all the glasses of the pyramid. The effect of this – both for champagne and for communication – is the same. The quality of both is lost and there is a good measure of wastage by the time the bottom of the pyramid is reached.

BOX 7.7   British Telecom

The introduction of a change programme at a telecomms corporation in 1989 in the UK was designed with the cascade effect in mind and was also a great example of it in action.

The original briefing for top managers and divisional directors was given at a three-day seminar at a four-star hotel. Middle managers were gathered together for two days at two-star hotels. Engineers and functional staff were briefed at half day meetings in village halls, and on some occasions were not provided with refreshments.

■ **Culture**

This a further manifestation of the issuing of communications from the point of view of the giver rather than the receiver. The barrier is caused by a combination of ignorance and disregard on the part of the particular issuer.

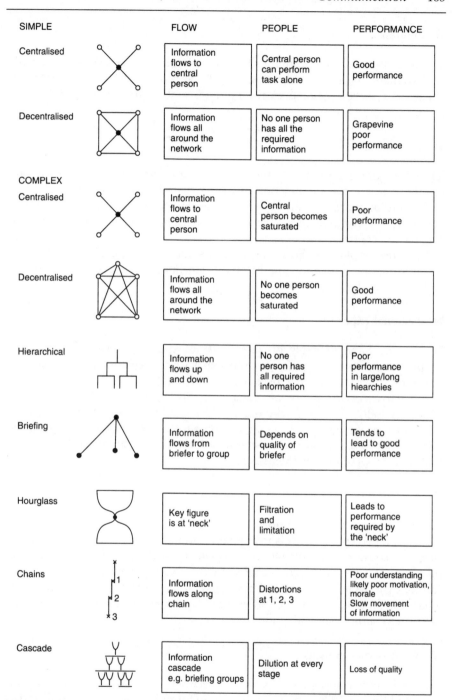

SIMPLE		FLOW	PEOPLE	PERFORMANCE
Centralised		Information flows to central person	Central person can perform task alone	Good performance
Decentralised		Information flows all around the network	No one person has all the required information	Grapevine poor performance
COMPLEX				
Centralised		Information flows to central person	Central person becomes saturated	Poor performance
Decentralised		Information flows all around the network	No one person becomes saturated	Good performance
Hierarchical		Information flows up and down	No one person has all required information	Poor performance in large/long hiearchies
Briefing		Information flows from briefer to group	Depends on quality of briefer	Tends to lead to good performance
Hourglass		Key figure is at 'neck'	Filtration and limitation	Leads to performance required by the 'neck'
Chains		Information flows along chain	Distortions at 1, 2, 3	Poor understanding likely poor motivation, morale Slow movement of information
Cascade		Information cascade e.g. briefing groups	Dilution at every stage	Loss of quality

Figure 7.2   Chains of communication

■ Interest

Whatever is issued must contain something of value to the receiver, either real or imaginary. There must therefore clearly be positive steps in the process to engage this interest, quite apart from questions of clarity, language, media and timing.

■ Institutions

These are the organisation's policies and procedures, and committees and groups. The greatest malfunction of these occurs where they outlive their use and value and are not abolished. When this happens procedures become complex and contradictory, and committees and groups seek reasons and excuses for continuing to exist.

The same applies to the appropriateness and value of control mechanisms and information systems and in the establishment of a general clarity of purpose and function of each.

■ Personal expertise

Persons are hired precisely because of their expertise! Nevertheless effective means have to be found whereby this expertise is used for the organisation's purposes and the experience of it retained in suitable ways.

The barrier occurs where individuals use this expertise as a bargaining chip. More generally, they may take organisational information when they change jobs (for example, where they join a competitor). They may also keep parallel sets of files and information systems, one for the organisation and another (often more accurate) for themselves.

■ Perceptions

The whole subject of perception is dealt with extensively elsewhere. However, the general perceptual barriers to communication may usefully be identified and summarised here. They include the misreading of the message; misreading or mistaking the cues and signals that go with it; seeing what one expects to see (rather than what is written) and hearing what one expects to hear (rather than what is said); a secondary and hidden agenda (see below) and misinterpretation of the non-verbal aspects.

■ Control mechanisms

This is where requests for specific information – usually output figures and costs and financial aspects – are requested in forms that are either inappropriate or which again may be taken and used for purposes other than those for which they were originally produced. This is exacerbated if they are perceived to show the manager or department in question in a poor light (either in absolute or comparative terms).

■ The need to know

This barrier occurs where organisations decide that information is to be issued in different ways, or different information is to be issued to different groups and individuals. It is a process of limiting the availability of information. On the face of it there is some sense in this: most organisations have far too much information to issue for any one person to understand, analyse and internalise.

The barrier arises from the reasoning behind 'the need to know'. As long as this is for operational reasons, it is sound. Otherwise, the message given is one of:

- a lack of capability to understand what is being said and especially that the organisation (or an individual superior) does not think or believe that the subordinate has this capability;
- lack of value or different levels of value placed on different groups of staff, especially those who are excluded from the 'need to know' list;
- access: in order to be privy to certain information it is necessary to have reached a particular level of the organisation. so communication becomes a trapping of personal status and importance;
- general disrespect: the operation of this form of approach to the giving of information gives off an overall view of lack of respect to those affected;
- psychological distance: again, this emphasises the differences and divisions that exist in organisations and between its functions, departments, divisions and individuals.

Operating a 'need to know' approach also leads to distortions in the presentational style and use of information media. What is issued is for the purposes of the issuer rather than the receiver, emphasising their distance and supremacy rather than imparting valuable and useful information.

More generally, any restriction on information leads to reductions in the capabilities of those who need to take decisions and make judgements. Even if operated from the highest, most positive and most moral standpoint this approach is restricting in this way.

■ Confidentiality

This becomes a barrier when it used as a means of attracting or acquiring status rather than for operational effectiveness. Clearly some matters are commercially and operationally sensitive and must be kept so; to enable free access to people's personnel files, technological advances, marketing initiatives or research and development inventions would be entirely counter-productive. In general, however, this is the main boundary. Others tend to reinforce feelings of disregard and lack of value indicated above.

■ Invisibility

Lack of visibility on the part of those issuing communications reinforces any feelings of 'one-wayness' in communications that may already exist. It also acts as a psychological barrier in its own right because there is no opportunity for debate, discussion or argument since the issuer is not present.

The value and quality of communications is therefore enhanced by visibility because it enables these misunderstandings to be cleared up quickly rather than being allowed to fester. Problem areas arise because staff debate the points among themselves rather than with those in the know and who carry influence. Imagination runs wild. All sorts of constructs are placed and rumours start to fly around. Effort has therefore to be expended at a later date to quell these rumours and get the organisation back on an even keel.

■ Information systems

Information systems are a combination of communications people and technology. Each has imperfections and therefore the potential to be a blockage or barrier. Information technology especially acts as a barrier where there is a lack of training for the staff, or a lack of full understanding of the system's capabilities, or where there are different and incompatible systems and formats present. This is often symptomatic of a wider malaise: a lack of foresight or planning (or wider knowledge) on the part of those responsible for their design, introduction and operation.

■ Rules and regulations

Rules and regulations are a barrier in all situations because they order and restrict people's activities. The problem arises when these are as set out below.

1. Long, drawn-out and complex, consisting of volumes of procedures that are designed to cover every possible eventuality or foible. This increases perceptions of restriction and negativity. It also indicates a more general negative view of the people (if they need this amount of regulation, they are regarded as potentially lazy or dishonest).
2. Written in language that is not simple and direct. The impression of restriction is compounded by the use of particular phraseology that seems to leave those in superior positions free to impose any restriction or interpret the rules as they see fit. While recourse to grievance procedures is always available to staff affected in this way, this requires energy and commitment from the staff. It is also in itself very negative and consumptive of resources that could be better used elsewhere.
3. Operated unevenly, where standards vary between different managers, supervisors, departments, divisions and functions. Some of this will be the fault of the individuals concerned; much always arises because of the nature and complexity of the rules themselves and the ways in which they have been written and applied.

4. Contradiction: the more complex the set of rules, the more likely contradictions are to exist. In these cases again, time and energy is spent on resolving individual issues when they do arise and in working out which of the contradictions is to be applied in the circumstances.

■ Personal demeanour

Personal demeanour is also a potential barrier in all situations. On particular occasions it becomes serious when enhanced by strong emotions, personality and professional clashes, or when the matter in hand is known to be contentious.

Matters of courtesy, forms of address and general means of human interaction have also to be considered here. Again, communications are likely to be worse where these are either not present at all, or else not valued.

■ The nature of work

The greater the intrinsic interest in the work, the greater the volume of reasons that the staff have for being there, the greater the likelihood that effective communications will exist. The reverse – where work is boring and alienating – normally takes place against a background of general lack of respect and trust. Most communications tend to reinforce this in these situations.

Workers (and they are often called workers, or at least referred to as such behind the doors of the corridors of power) make demands and threaten strikes and disruption if these are not met. Management devise approaches couched in forms of words that leave both room for manoeuvre and also a hard and coercive edge to 'the workers'.

■ Reinforcement

Reinforcement acts as a barrier where it and the given message are at variance. In these situations, the reinforcement is always that which is received and believed. It is damaging in each of the following ways.

1. Where what is said is positive, but where the reinforcement is negative. The most common form of this is in the use of positive language, but without underpinning the communication with absolute commitments or objectives. This lack is the reinforcement and is that which is believed, acted upon and reacted to, and which becomes the focus for analysis.
2. Where what is said is negative, but where the reinforcement is positive. This works well when, for example, the message is that 'We are in a crisis and we have to get out of it, and this is how we are going to go about it.'

It is a barrier when the organisation takes time and trouble to over-emphasise the positive or to set it in the wrong context. For example, the production of sectoral league tables indicating that a particular organisation is:

- 10th in a field of 70 in terms of profit/losses/costs/charges;
- 3rd most productive in the same field (in whatever terms that is measured);
- 23rd largest in the same field;
- no worse than anyone else;

can and do lead to feelings of complacency and introversion on the part of the organisation at large and individual members of staff.

■ Media used

This is a barrier when the format and language used are not appropriate. This applies to the spoken and written word and to any visual or pictorial information. It depends on recognising the needs of the receiver as well as the objectives of the presentation. Distortion occurs when one or the other is not met. It is especially prevalent in presentations:

- of statistics and trends, where figures and performance are taken in isolation or used out of context;
- where strong, visual and pictorial images are used to project a narrow view that is at variance with the wider picture;
- where discussion and debate are not genuine but conducted from the point of view or vested interest of the protagonist.

BOX 7.8   Use of Media

This is especially true of political debate. For example, one party persists with the view that 'Not enough resources or priority is being given to a particular area (for example, roads, education, health, social services and social security).' The other party counters this by saying that 'More resources are being spent in the given area than ever before.'

This is reinforced by the production of statistics for the end of being pursued. On the question of health, for example, one party will say that 'Waiting lists for treatment are longer than ever.' The other counters with 'We are treating more patients than ever before.' Each produces statistics to back up its point of view.

The result is a stalemate. It is compounded by the overwhelming impression given that:

(a)   there are only two possible points of view to hold, either one or other of those indicated;

(b)   the alignment of others to the point of view depends upon their own vested interest, personal and political preference and conviction;

(c)   'evidence' will subsequently be produced to 'prove' that waiting lists have got longer/shorter; or that resources have gone up/down.

Equivalent distorted forms of debate and discussion potentially exist in all organisation situations. The protagonists either take refuge in their own vested interest, seeking statistics to underpin their view; or else produce counter-arguments to the opposing point of view. No productive debate and discussion takes place. This dissipates any feelings of shared commitment and involvement, reinforcing the differences between various departments, divisions, functions, groups and individuals. It is compounded where one view is seen to be that of the organisation as a whole, or where the protagonist gains advantage or favour as the result of holding or presenting a particular point of view.

- where the delivery – especially written and oral – is accidentally or deliberately unclear (it also applies to the visual, when the pictures used are at variance with the overall message or else are not seen or recognised as reinforcing it);
- where one of the protagonists has to put on some form of show for the benefit of someone else who is assessing him, and where this assessment is based on reasons other than organisational effectiveness, (the organisation may require a particular manager to present something in ways that are deliberately unclear and may reward her for this, or a more junior member of staff may respond to something in a strident or controversial manner in order to gain a reputation among his peers, or to bring himself to the attention of those in authority for his own future advancement.
- where there is a party line to be followed and where the presentation needs do not match with this easily. (A trade union, for example, may have great sympathy with an organisation's need to restructure. It may have to reconcile this with its own need to be seen to be representing the interests of its members. This is compounded if the restructuring has effects and implications for their long term future, especially redundancy, retraining or redeployment. The union may therefore be forced into a position of opposition in spite of its own careful analysis of the situation.)

■ Lack of support

This is always a barrier, at whatever organisational level it occurs. If the marketing director does not have the support of the Chief Executive (CE) for the next marketing initiative or campaign, it diminishes the effectiveness of the work and presents a communication barrier because no absolute commitment was generated at the outset. This is a potential barrier in all superior–

subordinate relationships. It causes information to be withheld, distorted or presented in ways that are thought or perceived to be acceptable rather than what the organisation actually requires. It also tends to lead to issue avoidance based on the fact that the last time it was raised no support was forthcoming. At its most extreme it leads to scapegoating, bullying and the public humiliation of particular individuals. People always require public support. It is good for general morale for this to be seen to be forthcoming. If there are problems to resolve, any discussions should always be carried out in private; and the knowledge that this does indeed occur reinforces feelings of support.

■ Arrogance

People who are treated with arrogance by others always feel slighted. In many cases these feelings are much deeper and include lack of respect, even contempt. Arrogance in communications is to be found in forms of words that include 'Do this because I say so', 'Do this because I know best', 'Do this because I know what I am doing and you do not.'

The reinforcement that occurs here is usually that the arrogant person cannot be bothered to spend any more time and trouble on the matter or on those affected. What is reinforced, therefore, is the feeling of contempt.

■ Negativity

Use of negative language is always destructive. The balance of negative and positive language and messages is critical to effective communication (see Box 7.9). Where the balance is overwhelmingly positive, people tend to react quickly and positively to the negative, with a view to putting it right as soon as possible. Where the balance is overwhelmingly negative, the positive gets lost. The constant reception of negatives also chips away at the morale and esteem of the receivers.

Jargon is a barrier where the message receivers are not a natural party to the phrases or acronyms used. Both parties to the communication may quite happily conspire with this, the one to show off his superior knowledge, the other to give the impression that she knows more than she does. The general feeling, however, on the part of the receiver, is that she is being shown up as having gaps in her knowledge; and again, this is a further knock to her self-esteem.

Lack of sincerity – 'damning with faint phrase' – is also a barrier. People need to receive acknowledgement of genuine achievement rather than for steady-state activities. The volume and content of the latter should be recognised in review processes and meetings with the staff. Praise should be for results, completion, achievement and overachievement.

BOX 7.9   Negative Language and Messages

The use of words such as *but, only, never*.

Negative	Positive
It is excellent but it is very expensive	It is excellent and it is very expensive
He/she is only a secretary	He/she is a secretary
You will never get to the top unless . . .	You will get to the top if or by . . .

Acronyms

Two people engaged in a construction industry research project in March 1995 conducted a positive, happy and ostensibly productive conversation around the acronym WIRS. Only when one party wrote up a note at the meeting did it become apparent that at the core of the conversation was the construction sector's 'whole industry research strategy'. The other party had thought that it was about the workplace industrial relations survey.

Overpraising

Overpraising always gives a negative message because it reflects either a lack of sincerity or a lack of understanding on the part of the praiser. The only exception to this is where the subordinate has resolved a crisis or problem for the supervisor which could not otherwise have been achieved.

Ambiguity

This often occurs because of the simple human failing to order the thoughts before speaking or writing (for example, school teacher to class: Watch the board while I go through it').
   There may also be punctuation errors:

She said 'she didn't mind what I did'
She said, she didn't mind what I did
She,' said she, 'didn't mind what I did'

or errors of emphasis:

Long may you run
Long *may* you run
Long may *you* run

More insidiously phrases such as 'There are no redundancies planned at present' and 'There are no plans for reorganisation at present' give off a dual meaning; what is not said is whether there are future plans, and how long the present actually lasts. Reinforcement in these cases centres around 'at present'.

> More generally, the usual justification offered by managers and supervisors for over-emphasis on negativity to the exclusion of all forms of positive language is to the effect that 'If my staff do not hear from me, they know they are doing a good job.'

■ Realpolitik

In this context this is where the way of working of the organisation is defensive. It follows from this that information becomes a commodity to be guarded, filtered and fed into systems, including the grapevine, for managerial or departmental advantage as well as (or rather than) in the organisation's best interests. In these circumstances cluster groups and networks become the places where real messages get around the organisation. Managers are also known to make informal contacts in other parts of the organisation or departments other than their own (the equivalent of having their own spy network).

Managers also tend to attract information just in case they might miss something that could be to their advantage.

Very few organisations also take the view of openness of information and responsibility of the individual to do her filtering and editing. Invariably the approach taken is based on a perceived (usually spurious) conception of 'need to know' (as discussed above). Other than trade secrets and genuine inventions there is very little that is truly confidential.

BOX 7.10   Confidential Information

Yachting

Success of the Australian challenge for the Americas Cup in 1982 was put down to the revolutionary keel of the winning yacht. After the event the keel was photographed by the world's press. Dennis Conner, the losing American captain, had known about the keel from an early stage and had mock-ups and models of it available to him during the build-up of the campaign and the running of the races.

Yes Prime Minister

A scene from this BBC television series concerns a discussion between the Prime Minister and his senior adviser on widespread spying in general and on the fact that the (then) USSR received copies of Cabinet papers and minutes of meetings. At the end of the scene the Prime Minister asks the adviser 'So why don't we just send a copy of these papers direct to the Kremlin?' The reply is, 'This way we save the postage.'

■ **Trust and respect**

Lack of trust and respect on the part of any party to the transaction means that the message is studied for hidden meanings, get-outs and non-binding statements (such as 'We will do everything possible', a normal bureaucratic phrase that binds nobody to anything). Institutionalised lack of respect leads to the creation of myriads of complex (and invariably contradictory) processes and procedures for the management of the organisation in general and what is often described as industrial relations in particular.

■ **Timing**

The timing of communications is critical to their understanding and acceptance. Governments, for example, often slip out contentious issues while another is still a news story. They may wait until specific points in time (for example, Friday afternoon's governmental recess). They float ideas some weeks or months before the reality is to take effect in order to get those affected used to them and to get over any initial adverse response.

At organisational levels, the same rules still apply. Beyond that, and because of the more immediate personal relationships and responses to particular issues, great care will be taken in respect of holiday periods (including public holidays).

BOX 7.11   Timing

CoSteel Plc of Sheerness, Kent, UK gave notice of instant de-recognition of their trade union and radical changes to the way of working of industrial relations late one Friday afternoon. The staff were briefed on the Friday afternoon and given notes and leaflets to take home with them to be read and digested over the weekend. The union was told to clear its offices immediately. The staff had all weekend to get used to the idea. By the time they returned to work on the following Monday, the idea had familiarity and credence – and acceptance.

Again, use of language is critical. Phrases such as 'a matter of importance', 'with all due speed', 'as soon as possible', or 'as a matter of urgency' are normally disregarded by the receivers in sophisticated and bureaucratic organisations. Matters are only truly urgent and important until the next matter of urgency or importance comes along.

It is therefore clearly better to use precise days, dates and timings, such as by Friday, by 31 July, by 5 pm. Everyone then understands the precise position.

There is a point of immediacy also. Something that is proposed to come to pass in five years has no sense of focus (quite apart from the vagaries of both organisational and global turbulence). The other extreme is not giving people enough time to consider detailed proposals and plans: the reality of requiring a month's work in a day, for example.

■ Continuity

Whatever is issued must be seen in the widest context of the organisation in question and its activities. If the organisation is forever issuing important and urgent communications that have no subsequent consequence or results, the receivers will soon cease to take any notice of them. Lack of continuity also emphasises any perceptions of disorganisation or lack of competence on the part of those charged with the responsibility for the organisation in question.

■ Overt and covert

Whatever is issued must say what it means and mean what it says. The use of hidden and secondary agenda is a mark of the general state of the organisation's honesty and integrity. The state of the history of trustworthiness of organisation communications is critical to the ways in which they are received.

■ Conclusions

The main lesson to be learned is in the recognition of the existence of these barriers and of their effects. In each case the problem is compounded by repetition and continuity and by the fact that each compounds the effects of the others.

Part of the problem is also to be seen from the establishment of the organisation's clarity of purpose and activities. Clear and effective communications are much more likely to exist where this clarity has first been established.

The barriers indicated are also overwhelmingly negative in approach, attitude and outlook. One of the most effective steps that can be taken on behalf of any organisation is therefore to put everything in positive terms and avoid the negative.

This all contributes to an assessment that the general state of effectiveness of organisation communications, the successful and effective identification of these barriers, is a major contribution to this. Above all, they indicate areas where continuous observation and appraisal is necessary and where particular interventions are required when problems do arise.

Messages also lose their effect if and when nothing is seen to happen as the result of their being issued. This is, above all, where action is promised but not forthcoming; when promises are made but not kept; when people's opinions and views are asked for but then ignored. In each of these cases, if there is no intention of doing any of these things it is better to give a clear and unambiguous statement of what is to occur rather than engage in spurious consultative and participative efforts (these will in any case be construed as such at the time and will also colour the opinions of any such activities in the future).

Other forms of dishonesty and duplicity should also be recognised. The first is where information is sought from members of staff for one purpose which is then used against them for others. A common version of this is to ask people during selection and appraisal interviews what they think their weaknesses are and then to use these as excuses not to appoint or to develop or to give pay rises. This also occurs in forms of organisation-speak, whereby messages that are delivered are couched in terms such as 'There are no plans at present to close/make redundant/sell off', and 'We are considering a range of options', and 'Training and development and excellent prospects are available to the right person.' Such phrases are always subject to sceptical scrutiny.

The volume of information issued may also itself be a barrier. This is where one is told more than one wishes to know about a particular subject; or where one receives huge swathes of written information that is both incomprehensible and unusable in the form in which it is presented.

■ Communication agenda

This is the frame of reference for the communication in question. This is either direct and precise with the result that the message is clearly and unambiguously understood and received by those concerned or, conversely, it is indirect and imprecise with exactly the same result, except that in this case those involved assess the other negative and dishonest features of the communication in coming to their conclusions and understanding of it.

■ Stated or primary agenda

This is the way in which the communication in question is presented. The extent to which this is the real message depends upon the nature and clarity of the message and of the language used in support of it; and the extent to which the organisation then gives life and substance to it through the use of resources, of its placing in the system of priorities, and the behavioural encouragements and sanctions with which it is underpinned.

The reverse also exists. If the words used are empty and if there is no support for what is stated, the primary agenda will be disregarded and those concerned will look for the secondary and hidden agenda that always exists in such cases.

The problem also arises if the organisation changes and the initiative in question requires resurrection or rejuvenation. New forms of presentation and language must invariably be found when this occurs.

■ Secondary agenda

Secondary (and indeed multiple) agenda exist where the primary has no substance. There are many forms to look for and of which to be aware. Individuals put particular items out for a variety of purposes: for example self-aggrandisement, to be seen to be doing something, to prove that they have done something, because they know that the subject is close to the heart of the patron. Organisations put out messages that appear frothy and insubstantial, but which will contain something, somewhere, which is the item or concept that has the genuine purpose. Whilst most of the offering gets ignored, the one item does therefore gain a foothold and familiarity.

■ Hidden agenda

This is the extreme form of the above. It usually takes on some form of intra-organisational collusion or conspiracy. It is often a cause-and-effect type approach: for example, whereby a low pay rise is offered in the knowledge that the staff will strike, and that they can therefore be dismissed. This form also occurs in the field of new technology and new market introduction. New technology is introduced so that the old technology and those working on it can be divested. New markets are proposed in the knowledge that the sales team will not be able cope and so they too can be dismissed.

A variation occurs when a department takes on a highly prestigious or critical project. Once this is up and running and cannot be cancelled without great losses (including prestige), the particular department pleads for more resources.

This also occurs where a department or some individuals are given a particular task that cannot possibly be completed in the full knowledge and for the express purpose of exposing them as failures. They again become a target for corporate cuts.

Illustrated in this way the phrase 'hidden agenda' is a contradiction in terms. Watchers of organisational *realpolitik* felt that those directly involved and also (where appropriate) the organisational analysts all recognise the hidden agenda at an early stage. Hidden agenda are key indicators of organisational and managerial melée and of organisational toxicity.

■ Organisational toxicity

Organisational toxicity and toxic communications exist in organisations that have acquired malady or disease. The concept is akin to the presence of toxins in the human body, or to a toxic or poisonous substance.

Toxic communications are those that demotivate and demoralise staff, and dissipate the volume and quality of organisational effort and effectiveness. Their outward manifestation is to be found in clusters of staff conversing endlessly on the general state of the organisation, high levels of discipline and grievance, complicated and duplicated rules and procedures, and remoteness of managers from their staff.

This arises from negative views held and promulgated by the organisation and its managers about the staff, the situation and the activities (rather than the recognition that each negative should be the springboard for positive actions). Specific communications that are to be found in toxic situations are as follows.

Blame and scapegoat	The organisation finds individuals to carry the can for its corporate failings. Sales departments get the blame for falling profits. Personnel get the blame for disputes and grievances. Individuals are blamed for specific failures (for example, the failure of a particular promotion campaign; the failure of work restructuring). They are often also named in this respect and their failure publicised around the organisation.
	A more insidious version exists whereby the scapegoat is not official but names are allowed to get around the grapevine and where the organisation does nothing to deny the rumours or rehabilitate any individuals that are so named.
Accusation and back-stabbing	This is a development of blame and scapegoat. It exists where it is allowed to exist: that is, where the organisation either actively encourages, or at least acquiesces in, departments and individuals making accusations and allegations about each other. This is an integral feature of any blame culture.
Departmental feuding	This is where forms of internecine warfare exist between individuals, departments and functions. This is a derivation of both blame and accusation, where both become institutionalised. Again, some organisations either actively encourage this or at least acquiesce. An outcome of this is where individuals and departments gain favoured status, power and influence based on their ability to do others down. This is one of the prerequisites to gaining status of an overmighty subject or an overmighty department.
Meddling	This is where persons meddle outside their legitimate areas of activity. One of the most extreme forms of this is where top and powerful individuals promise favoured customers that special activities and deals can be done on their behalf and where, as the result, production, sales, marketing, finance and human resource functions are seriously disrupted. Meddling also includes the promotion and appointment of family and friends by the same individuals on the basis of kinship and friendship rather than capability. This also includes other forms of favouritism and patronage and the use of organisation resources for personal gain and benefit.
Secrets	In a toxic situation, information (as we have seen) becomes a commodity to be used as a source of influence and as a bargaining chip. Control, editing, filtering and presentation of information then becomes a departmental and managerial priority. Information becomes graded and classified. There emerges a culture of need to know on the one hand, and an overactive and destructive grapevine on the other.

Corporate self-deception

The other major feature of a toxic situation is where the organisation creates its own view of the world and its place within it. This usually occurs in two ways. The first is where an elite is created (or where a group is encouraged or comes to see itself as such). Securing its unassailable excellence, it produces plans, proposals and outputs that must necessarily also be correct and excellent. Where, for example, this is the output of a corporate policy unit, overwhelming pressure is put on the rest of the organisation to follow and conform to this. The group becomes unassailable; indeed, anybody who does question its excellence, legitimacy and output may themselves be marginalised or scapegoated. The blame for the failures of initiatives and policies derived by such groups is inevitably placed on functional departments and not the policy unit.

The other form of this is where the organisation is in decline. Rather than addressing the decline, it lives on past glories. It retreats into itself and creates its own view of the world. This has come to be known as the 'bunker mentality'. The expression comes from the last days of the Third Reich in 1944–5. The Nazi leadership created its own triumphal view of the world within its operations bunker in Berlin rather than facing the reality of defeat and invasion that was going on outside.

Negative labelling

We have referred elsewhere to negative connotations that are associated to particular jobs and occupations, especially those that are deemed to be of lower grades (for example, clerk or operative). The negative aspects of these differentials are always exaggerated and exacerbated in toxic situations.

Toxic communicators

Related to all of this is the toxic individual. This person, for a variety of reasons, issues toxic communications. These may be general and may be no worse than putting a negative or pessimistic construct on any form of information which he is required to transmit.

A more insidious version occurs where, for example, the person concerned has to communicate contentious organisation policy or courses of action. He does so with the rider that 'It's not my fault' or 'It's nothing to do with me' or 'I didn't want it.'

The worst version is clearly the individual who introduces toxicity however. This occurs where information is disseminated in particular ways, knowing the effect that this presentation will have or with a particular effect clearly in mind. Major examples of this are the use by organisations of trade union representatives and over-mighty subjects as the channels of information in particular situations.

Toxic communications	These are the outputs of toxic organisations and toxic communicators. The key features are bland and undirected offerings, hidden agenda and mismatch between message and media use. They take place in the context indicated above.

■ Transactional analysis

Transactional analysis (TA) is a system for the analysis of personal and interpersonal communication and behaviour. It was defined and evolved by Dr Erik Berne, whose thesis was that there existed in everyone three quite clearly distinguishable sets of attitudes and behaviours. He called these ego states. These are readily recognisable by the things that we say, the ways in which we say them and the support that we give them by way of body language, gestures and mannerisms. For example, the question

'Where is my pen?'

has a range of possible responses depending on the way in which the question is asked: for example,

'I don't know'
'It's on the table'
'I haven't had it'
'Where you left it'
'Am I to always be running round after you'

and so on. The tone of voice gives the clue as whether or not the pen is to be found, or whether an argument is to follow.

■ Ego states

TA involves using knowledge and skills to recognise ego states; and, from this, to adopt an ego state whether the transaction is to be effective or ineffective, business-like or crossed, leading to misunderstanding and argument.

The ego states defined by Berne are parent, adult and child. The parent is further modified into parent nurturing and parent critical. The child is further modified into free child and adapted child. Their importance lies in the fact that there is nothing in human communication that cannot be attributed to one of these. People talk and write from different states, and it is possible to identify this in most cases. From this a method of choice of response and an appropriate ego state can be adopted so that the transaction proceeds in an orderly and effective way.

■ Transactions

Transactions may be:

- complimentary – from adult to adult, parent to child, or child to parent;
- crossed – any other variation, such as parent to parent, child to child, child to adult, adult to child, adult to parent, parent to adult;
- ulterior – where the message that is stated is not the one that is implied. When this is the case, the ulterior transaction is inevitably that which is acted upon (indeed, the initiator will probably have devised it); or the ulterior is that which is intended to be received: for example, when one person says to another, 'I respect your views', what they actually mean is 'I do not respect your views.'

See Figure 7.3 for an illustration.

■ Games

Berne (1984) also identified a number of games that arose principally from ulterior transactions. He suggests that people spend a large proportion of their time and energy in these games, and that the main reason for this is to gain recognition or 'strokes' (units of recognition). Examples of these are as follows.

□ *Why don't you – Yes but*

The initiator states a problem and seeks the advice of others. They offer solutions based on the 'Why don't you', which the initiator then rejects with 'Yes but'. The initiator ends up feeling self-righteous and thinking that she knows best; the real message that comes from 'Yes but' is that the responder is not going to do anything.

□ *Now I've got you*

The initiator of this game contrives a situation whereby somebody makes a mistake. At the appropriate moment the initiator steps in and confronts the offender to make him feel bad while the initiator enjoys feelings of superiority and dominance.

□ *Kick me*

In this game, the initiator constantly does things which provoke criticism or punishment in order to get negative recognition, which is more important than getting no recognition at all.

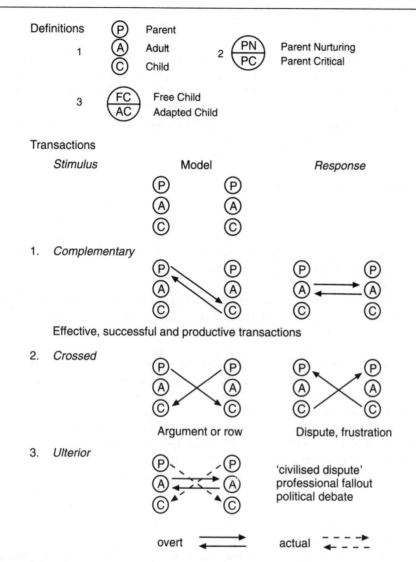

Figure 7.3   Transaction analysis: configurations

Source: Berne (1984)

☐ *I'm only trying to help*

This is where advice or aid, usually unsolicited, is constantly being offered. When it is eventually rejected the initiator can say 'But I'm only trying to help you.'

■ Scripts

Scripts are developments of games. They are created by individuals to form work scripts, social scripts or life scripts. They represent a form or summary of the way in which individuals choose to lead their lives. They make their plans around these in response to the range of messages – critical, prohibitive and negative, and also nurturing and supportive that are received from both the workplace and the wider environment.

■ Assertiveness

Another approach that has the purpose of producing effective communications has come to be known as assertiveness. It takes the point of view that any communication can only be effective if it is well thought out, its effect is understood in advance, and the message is delivered clearly and directly to the recipient.

The following forms of behaviour and demeanour are identified as the background to this. Each of these has negative effects on communication quality.

1. Aggressive, characterised by shouting, swearing, table thumping, arguments (cross-transaction). The matter in hand is lost as the aggressor strives to impose her point of view. Winning the argument becomes everything.
2. Hostile, where the main emphasis is on the personalisation of the matters in hand. Often also characterised by shouting and table thumping, the outcome is normally a personal attack (sometimes in public) on an individual or group.
3. Submissive, characterised by saying or doing anything that the other party wants so that he will finish the argument or transaction and remove himself.
4. Inconsistent, characterised by according people different levels of quality and value, and using different standards for different individuals and groups. This also extends to treating the same individual or group in different ways according to mood or the environment, for example.
5. Non-assertive, characterised by the inability of the individual to put her message across. This is either because she is not sure what to put across, or else she has not used the correct words or media.

In order to resolve the problems caused by these forms of approach an absolute standard of behaviour demeanour and language is used. This is called assertiveness.

Assertive behaviour, demeanour and communications consist of the following.

1. Language – clear, simple and direct; easy to understand and respond to on the part of the hearer or receiver; the words used are unambiguous and straightforward;

request and demands are made in a clear and precise manner and with sound reasons.

2. Aims and objectives – precise and clear; considered in advance; recognising the effect that the message is likely to have on the recipient.
3. Delivery – in a clear and steady tone of voice, or (where written) in a well presented and easy to read format. The use of voice is always even, neither too loud nor too soft, and does not involve shouting, threatening or abuse.
4. Persistence and determination – where problems or issues are raised by the recipient, the sender sticks to his message, aims and objectives; he does not become sidetracked; he answers any problems that are raised without diverting from the main purpose.
5. Positive and negative – the general thrust of the message is always clear and apparent; this does not vary, whether the overall tone is positive or negative. This approach is especially important in handling general staff problems, especially matters concerning grievances and discipline.
6. Face and eyes – the head is held up. There is plenty of eye contact and steadiness of gaze. The delivery is reinforced with positive movements that relate to what is being said (for example, smiles, laughter, nodding, encouragement; or a straight face when something has gone wrong).
7. Other non-verbal aspects – the body is upright; hands and arms are open (in order to encourage positive response and productive transaction); there is no fidgeting or shuffling; there are no threatening gestures or table thumping; or other displays of other forms of behaviour.

■ Situational factors

Assertive delivery is based on an inherent confidence, belief in and knowledge of the situation, and confidence in the people. Openness, clarity, credibility and personal and professional confidence all spring from this.

Any clarity of purpose or delivery is always spoilt through having to operate from a weak position or one which is not fully known or understood. This weakness or lack of clarity leads to other forms of behaviour and communications, as indicated above.

■ Conclusions

This chapter has concentrated on:

- the importance of communications as a critical factors of effective organisations;
- the extent and prevalence of barriers to effective communication;
- means by which the processes of communication may be understood.

The result of this is the ability to produce effective communications capable of being received, accepted and acted upon (or responded to). This is an organisational group and individual issue requiring recognition at all levels and remedial action where communications are poor or ineffective. It reinforces the need for clarity of purpose and language to which constant reference has been made. As many channels as possible or necessary should be used, giving the same message through each so that the message received is complete and not subject to editing, interpretation or distortion. Where communications are not direct, they are indirect and people will search for hidden agenda and meanings.

Organisations are therefore responsible for creating the conditions in which effective communications can exist. Managers and supervisors must be trained in both the content and processes. All staff must be made to understand the importance and value of their contribution and how this is best made. This only happens when there is a high-quality working environment and a suitable general management style is adopted. Effective communications are an integral part of this. More generally, this is the foundation of all effective interpersonal, professional and occupational relationships and relations between departments, divisions, functions and levels in hierarchies and throughout organisations.

■ Questions

1. Of all the barriers to effective communication, which in your view are the hardest to overcome, and why?
2. For an organisation with which you are familiar produce a communication strategy which addresses the problems that you know to exist, and which takes positive steps to conquer them. How will you know whether your strategy has been successful or not?
3. Discuss the view that because of the nature of organisational hierarchies and the differing aims and objectives of those within them, effective communications are not possible within organisations.
4. Identify the main strengths and weaknesses of television, radio and newspaper news and current affairs coverage. What lessons may be learned from this by organisations and their managers?

Influence, power and authority

■ Introduction

Influence, power and authority are present in all organisations and these stem from a variety of sources. It is first necessary to distinguish between them.

1. Influence is where a person, group or organisation changes the attitudes, values, behaviour, priorities and activities of others.
2. Power is the capability to exercise influence in these ways.
3. Authority is the legitimisation of the capability to exercise influence and the relationship by which this is exercised.

Authority is based on recognition and acceptance of the right and ability to restrict the freedom to act, to set boundaries and to encourage or order sets of activities for given reasons. Responsibility and accountability normally come with authority, especially in relation to the results achieved by the given activities and the ways in which these are ordered and conducted. Authority also refers to the establishment and enforcement of rules, regulations and norms.

Authority therefore legitimises the use of power and influence in organisations. If subordinates believe and accept that they are in junior positions, they legitimise the power and authority of the superiors. Chains of command, reporting relationships, spans of control and organisation structures all tend to reinforce the existence and legitimisation of authority and hierarchy. Legitimate power is a feature of many organisation roles. This may be supported and reinforced through the use of other power sources.

Authority is therefore a relationship which is recognised by those concerned, involving both exertion on the part of the superior and acceptance by the subordinate.

Power and influence arise from a variety of sources and these are indicated below. Power and influence may be legitimised, as indicated above, or illegitimate, such as the use by bullies of threats of physical violence in order to get their own way. Power and influence may be formalised, (again, closely related to the structure of authority), or informal, requiring the exercise of the resource outside the normal ways of working (see Box 8.1). For example, there may be present in a group a highly charismatic individual to whom people turn to have her problems resolved, whether within the normal frame of authority or not. The person concerned therefore builds up a much wider base of influence than their formal position warrants. In certain circumstances organisations have to recognise this in their own formal dealings with the particular group and individuals.

BOX 8.1   Informal Power and Influence: Overmighty Subjects

In sixteenth-century England the Tudor kings and queens were burdened with what came to be known as their overmighty subjects. These were the land-owning nobility whose support the monarch required to keep the peace in outlying parts of the country and who, if support was not forthcoming, constituted a real threat to the monarch's position. This support was therefore generated by hiving off parcels of land, local ruling rights and general autonomy to these nobles in return for their continuing to support the Tudor Dynasty. The kings and queens went on regular progressions throughout the country to try to ensure that the bargains that had been struck were adhered to. In practice, however, great areas of the country were effectively the personal fiefdoms of these nobles.

The same situation exists in many organisations today. Effective control of large parts has often to be left in the hands of particular individuals. The relationship is normally based upon the organisation conceding large measures of autonomy and freedom to act to the individual in return for his addressing and pursuing the organisation's interests in the particular area. As well as location however, organisations often become dependent upon these individuals in key critical and functional divisions and areas.

BOX 8.2   Informal Power (from *The Day of the Jackal*)

'It is cold at 6.40 in the morning of a March day in Paris and seems even colder when a man is about to be executed by firing squad. At that hour on 11 March 1963, in the main courtyard of the Fort D'Ivry, a French Air Force Colonel stood before a stake driven into the chilly gravel as his hands were bound behind the post and stared with slowly diminishing disbelief at the squad of soldiers facing him 20 metres away. A foot scuffed at the grit, a tiny release from tension as the blindfold was wrapped around the eyes of Lieutenant Colonel Jean-Marie Bastien-Thiry, blotting out the light for the last time. The mumbling of the priest was a helpless counterpoint to the crackling of 20 rifle bolts as the soldiers charged and cocked their carbides.

On 4 March the Supreme Military Court had delivered its verdict on Jean-Marie Bastien-Thiry. He and two others were sentenced to death. On 8 March, General de Gaulle listened for 3 hours in silence to appeals for clemency by the lawyers of the condemned men. He commuted two of the death sentences to life imprisonment, but Bastien-Thiry's condemnation stood.

That night his lawyer told him of the decision.

"It is fixed for the 11th" he told his client and when the latter continued to smile disbelievingly, he blurted out "You are going to be shot".

Bastien-Thiry kept smiling and shook his head.

"You don't understand" he told the lawyer, "no squad of Frenchmen will raise their rifles against me".

He was wrong. The execution was reported on the 8.00 a.m. news of Radio Europe No. 1 in French.'

Bastien-Thiry was a rebel French officer who had become involved with the Secret Army Organisation, the purpose of which was to lead a revolution against the then President, Charles de Gaulle, and remove him from office. He assumed that because he had a high reputation as a soldier and because of widespread disaffection with de Gaulle's rule, when the order came to shoot him the French soldiers would simply refuse to do this, and would instead turn their guns on the establishment.

Source: *The Day of the Jackal*, by Frederick Forsyth (Corgi, 1971).

Similarly, someone who is an authority – a source of knowledge and expertise, and therefore power – on a given area is able to influence the acts of those who come to them for advice and guidance. The quality of this may lead also to the building of a wider and deeper relationship and reputation, and the authority figure thus extends their influence.

Power and influence are to be seen as positive and negative. The positive occurs where power and influence are used to energise, enhance and develop productive and profitable activities. The negative is where power and influence are used to block or diminish activities, to limit the ability of others to succeed through the capability to restrict resources, money or information, for example.

Influence, power and authority are all themselves limited by organisational structures and methods of behaviour. Authority is normally given out for a limited range of activities or people only, and the extent of influence and the ability to wield power are therefore also limited. Authority also normally impersonalises: that is, when people act with authority, they do so in the name of the organisation and not in a personal capacity. The need to exercise authority will be founded on both personal and professional judgement; the actions carried out are in ways prescribed by the organisation.

BOX 8.3   Authority and Impersonalisation: Nazi Concentration Camps 1935–45

The Nazi regime in Germany (1933–45) established these camps from 1935 onwards as an integral feature of the management of the German Empire – the Thousand Year Reich. Their purpose was:

- to house and re-educate dissidents and those who held views contrary to those of the establishment;
- to house and hold hostage the families and friends of dissidents;
- to remove undesirables (for example, homosexuals and the disabled) from society at large;
- to exterminate inferior races and populations (Poles, Slavs, Gypsies and, above all, Jews).

People were sent to camps for fixed periods or for life. A total of 300 camps were constructed and operated over the period. Most of the camp commandants and administrators were bureaucrats (civil servants working for ministries in certain locations and following career paths). The guards were either soldiers or members of the prison service. All involved had power and influence over the lives of the inmates. Above all, they all had authority to act in the name of the state, in the terms of the Nazi Empire.

This, in essence, is why the horrors lasted for so long and affected so many. It was because the camps were run by instruments of the state and acted with its authority.

There is a range of sources of power and influence that in turn affect the authority relationship, as set out below.

1. Physical power: the power exerted by individuals by reasons of their bodily shape, size and strength in relation to others. Large multi-nation and multi-location organisations exert their own equivalent of physical power in the pursuit of market or sector domination and in the ability to select their own preferred range of prices, to determine the ways in which markets will operate and in the ability to command staff and expertise resources.
2. Traditional power: whereby the ability to command influence derives from accepted customs and norms. For example, traditional power is present in the hereditary principle whereby the office or position is handed down from parent to child. This happens with kings and queens and the aristocracy. The same thing happens in family businesses and those who work in them are likely to find themselves receiving direction from the next of kin at particular points in time. Other social offices and positions carry varying degrees of power and influence based on tradition (examples include priests and town mayors).

3. 'Divine Right' and 'The Natural Order' should also be considered here. Both have been used in the past to reinforce the position and influence of those in power. Divine right was ascribed to European monarchs during the Middle Ages and beyond; it attributed their position to the will of God so that anybody who rebelled against them was also attacking God. The natural order was – and is – a more general view in support of the status quo. It is usually propounded by those who are currently benefiting from this and in their own support.

4. Expert power: based on the expertise held by an individual or group and the demand for this from other parts of society. The power and influence that stems from highly prized expertise is dependent upon the volume and nature of demand, the location of the expert and her willingness to use her skill. Expertise comes as professional and technical skills, knowledge, aptitudes, attributes and behaviour. It also includes situational and social knowledge.

    It normally carries an economic value. This is dependent upon the nature of the expertise, on the value placed on it by those requiring it, and overall levels of demand.

    All expertise may be offered for sale, rent or hire.

5. Referent power: this is based on the degree of attractiveness of the person in the position of power. For example, someone with a high level of desired expertise may not be hired because of other undesired characteristics (for example, he may be scruffy, a bad time keeper or hold extreme political views) while, on the other hand, someone with a lower level of expertise may be hired because her wider characteristics or points of reference are considered more suitable. Referent power is also based on the personal relationships and friendships that are found in working situations.

6. Charismatic power: charisma is the effect of one personality on others, the ability to exert influence based on force of personality. (Charisma in leaders is dealt with in Chapter 9.) It is also the ability to inspire high levels of confidence and identity among other people. It is to be found in all parts of society. On a global scale Hitler, Napoleon and John F. Kennedy are all known to have had this. From the world of business, it is found for example, in Richard Branson and Anita Roddick. It is also present in people in all groups, clubs, organisations and teams.

7. Resource power: this is the ability to influence others based on the command of resources. This may be beneficial and positive, such as the giving and allocating of resources to enable someone else to succeed, the result of which is a feeling of well-being towards the resource giver.

    It may also be negative, threatening or coercive, based on the ability to limit or cut off particular resources if the receiver does not behave in certain ways.

8. Reward power: this is the ability to influence behaviour and activities by holding out and offering rewards for compliance and acceptance. The extent of influence exerted in this way is dependent upon the nature and volume of rewards and the extent to which these meet the needs of those over whom influence is sought.

9. The negative of this is the power to punish. Again, the extent of the influence exerted depends upon the nature of the punishment being threatened and whether this is felt to be important by those affected.

10. Reputation and confidence: organisations and individuals are able in some circumstances to exert influence based on their achievements to date and the respect and esteem in which these are held. Past reputation and influence, or past triumphs and successes are used as the basis for securing future work, for example.

11. Coercive power: this is the ability to bribe, bully or threaten people into doing something that they would not otherwise do. It is usually based on physical or economic strength and reinforced by negative and threatening attitudes and behaviour. It also normally carries dire consequences if the focus of effort does not do that which is required of them.

12. Conformity: this is where organisations and leaders set distinctive norms, attitudes, values and behaviour standards which those who wish to be a part of the situation are required to accept. This may be imposed formally by the organisation in the setting of rules and standards of behaviour and activity, or informally by groups exerting their own autonomous and informal pressures and norms. Pressure to conform may be positive: again, holding out rewards and success for those who choose (and are chosen) to follow the given path; or negative, coercive and threatening.

13. Position power: this is where someone is given power and influence according to the position or role held. Military and organisational ranks carry different forms and extents of this depending upon their position in relation to others. The nature of power also varies according to the positions involved. For example, a production supervisor has a direct influence on the daily activities of his work group; the production controller is likely to be responsible for the overall activities of the supervisor's group and directly for the activities of the supervisor; however, she is likely to exert little direct influence on the daily activities, in spite of the fact that she is in a superior position.

14. Legal/rational power: this is the limitation, ordering and direction of power and influence in the name of organisations. It is based on the setting of rules, procedures, regulations and norms for each job, role, department, division and sector, and for the individuals who carry out the work. It is based on certain principles:

    (a) the right and duty of organisations to establish what they consider to be the best ways of working;

    (b) the managerial prerogative (the establishment of persons in positions of command, responsibility and accountability to ensure that these are put into practice);

    (c) the willingness of subordinates to accept direction and the right of superiors to expect this;

    (d) duties of care placed on organisations by legal, social and ethical pressures which means that they will seek to operate in efficient, effective and profitable ways without being punitive or coercive.

BOX 8.4   Rational/Legal Power and Authority

In the UK there are three tests of this in the common law (which is that which has grown up through custom and practice, precedent and tradition). These are:

1. **The master-servant relationship**, in which it is held that all working relations are based upon the ability of one – the master – to direct and order the work of others – the servants – as they see fit. This is often currently called the managerial prerogative. Masters are required to take good care of their servants. Work and workplaces must be safe and not detrimental to personal health. The work may be hard but not punishing. Servants are expected to work hard and to the best of their capabilities. They may not be worked to death, disease or illness. Masters may exert discipline and servants are required to accept it, provided that this is positive and not punitive.

2. **The wage–work bargain**. Once people are hired by an organisation they must be paid (whether or not they actually carry out any work) according to the terms offered. The work carried out must also reflect expectations. For example, a secretary who has been told that she is to receive a salary of £12 000 per annum, payable in instalments of £1 000 per month, must receive this and may expect to be asked to carry out secretarial duties (as distinct from carpentry for example) in return.

   Both salary and duties may be varied by mutual agreement. Training may be necessary or desirable, and may be requested by either or both parties. If no agreement is forthcoming then the relationship may be changed and alternative work offered or sought within the organisation. If the original work has ceased or diminished and no alternative is available, the organisation and the employee may sever the relationship in accordance with the law and the organisation's own procedures.

3. **Fairness and reasonableness**. Organisations and their employees are required to act fairly and reasonably at all times. This especially is the test that is placed by courts and tribunals when adjudicating on employment law cases brought before them. This is because required standards of behaviour and demeanour vary between organisations. For example, attitudes and relationships between staff are different on a building site from those at a high fashion and exclusive clothes shop; the forms of dress required to work in the fields in winter are different from those in a public relations company. The question of fairness and reasonableness is always considered from this point of view.

These factors constitute the absolute boundaries of legal/rational power and authority in UK organisations.

Commercial power and influence is based on the ability to command and dominate market sectors, the habits and consumption patterns of customers and other factors related to commercial life, such as the ability to attract financial resources, technology and expertise; and the ability to gain access to sources of components and raw materials, market outlets and means of distribution. This influence is based on combination of reputation, esteem and confidence, and also economic size and strength. In many cases there are dominance–dependency issues to be considered (see below). Commercial power also sometimes leads to the ability to command or dominate the use of particular technology and expertise in ways that restrict its usage and availability to others, and which force other organisations in similar activities to seek alternative means of operating.

Much power and influence therefore stems from the ability to recognise, combine and use these resources effectively. For example, a highly charismatic personality may also have his position reinforced by a formalised position that enables conformity to be imposed on a given group. It is used in the energising of work, in the operation and enforcement of rules and procedures, in the

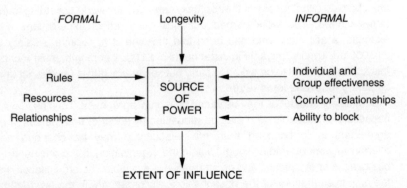

Longevity: people, groups and institutions become behaviourally both strong and influential when they have been in place for a long while. This has implications for needs and demands for change, reorganisation and restructuring.

Blocking: this is the power to prevent things from being done. It exists in most situations and is a combination of resource and reward restriction and work prioritisation. It is also the ability to call upon other resources and influences to ensure that the blocking process is effective.

Corridor diplomacy: this occurs as a route to be considered around problems when the formal procedures of the organisation have been exhausted. Power and influence are used between the parties concerned on an informal basis to try to explore other means of resolving the issue.

Success and failure: a run of successes may lead to an individual or group becoming acknowledged as expert, enabling their influence to grow. Conversely, a series of failures is likely to lead to loss of influence, whatever the absolute standard of the expertise present.

Group energy: this is the ability of the group as a whole to influence things, both positively and negatively. Groups can become very effective in dissipating the energies of those who come to them, especially negative energy. For example, those dealing with bureaucracies and who are constantly handed on from one person to the next expend a great deal of energy in this and may well give up altogether if the goal is not important, or if some other way of achieving it can be found.

Figure 8.1   Factors relating to the sources of power

creation, maintenance and development of working relationships and in the organisation, direction and management of people. An understanding of the nature, extent and sources of power is also essential when changes are being considered (see Figure 8.1).

Each of the factors indicated in Figure 8.1 constitutes a building block in the power base of the particular individual or group. The nature, prevalence and mixture of these varies both between and within organisations.

■ Centres of power in organisations

Each department, division, function and group always has its own power base to a greater or lesser extent. Their position is further influenced by the following factors:

1. The nature of their own function in relation to all the others present, and the nature and extent of the influence that they are able to exert.
2. The nature and volume of resources that they command and use, the ways in which resources are allocated, and the wider question of availability of resources.
3. The nature of intergroup and interdepartmental relations, and the extent to which these are positive and cooperative or negative, dysfunctional and divisive.
4. The physical size of certain groups and departments, the numbers of people involved and the scale and nature of resources and technology commanded.
5. Relations between operating departments and functions, and the organisation's top management (invariably the supreme centre of power).
6. Elements of group hierarchies. These are often found in sophisticated and diverse decentralised organisations where, for example, the head office and its functions have greater proximity to senior managers and directors, and therefore the physical capability and location to bid for resources, establish priorities, establish personal relationships and get ahead of the more distant activities.
7. The extent and nature of the authority vested in given officials; ranks, departments, divisions, groups and individuals; and the extent of autonomy and devolution that goes with this.
8. The capabilities of managers and group leaders, both in absolute terms – the extent of their managerial expertise – and also in relation to each other.
9. Critical factors such as the ability to command, limit, edit and filter information; the command of critical technology or expertise; and the influence of this upon the ways of working of other functions and groups, and on the organisation as a whole.
10. The structure of the organisation and the extent to which certain functions are accorded higher status, importance, influence and authority than others in the formal structuring.
11. The priorities of the organisation in its dealings with its customers, clients and markets, and also internally in terms of its operational ways of working.
12. The culture of the organisation as a whole, and of its different functions and groups (and there is often a distinction between the two). This includes prevailing shared

values, attitudes and beliefs, and to general levels of motivation, morale, mutual trust and respect; ethical considerations; and any absolute standards of integrity and activity.

Other centres of power in organisations are also present. These influence their capabilities to act and the ways in which both operations and management are carried out. They include the following.

Pressure groups and lobbies, both internal and external, which bring their own point of view to bear on particular proposals and activities.

As examples, internally a workgroup may lobby for improved facilities for itself, citing as reasons for this that many people have already left the group, and that they are difficult to replace. Pressure is then exerted on the organisation to consider the request and, if necessary reallocate and reprioritise resources in order to comply.

Externally, organisations are subject to public pressure groups wherever they contemplate engaging in activities that are, or are perceived to be, detrimental to the environment (for example, construction, infrastructure projects and waste disposal always have to cope with this).

Pressure groups may also arise among shareholders and other stakeholders a result of, or in response to, proposed sets of activities; or, conversely, they may propose or attempt to influence these sets of activities themselves.

Cluster groups of managers, supervisors, technical and professional experts working in different departments and locations also exert influence when they find matters of common ground that they can take to the organisation for resolution; again, this may lead to the re-ordering of certain activities in order to accommodate their concerns.

Specialist groups also exert influence according to the nature of their specialism. For example, safety committees and representatives must be constituted by organisations with a remit to ensure the health and safety of the organisation and all of those with whom it comes into contact. In general, any recommendations for action and improvement that they may make carry substantial influence and normally require implementation as a result.

Trade unions and other methods of employee representation carry varying levels of influence according to the nature and constitution of the representative body. This is enhanced (or otherwise) by the volume and density of union membership, the expectations and aspirations of the members, the nature of action that they are prepared to take or the pressure that they are prepared to exert in order to satisfy these expectations and aspirations. Historically, unions in some sectors – transport, public services, heavy industry, printing – were very strong in the UK and acted as regulators of work and activities. Much of this influence has been lost, although unions still act as a monitoring mechanism on general ways of working and as consultees in matters of change. Their greatest influence now lies in the representation of individuals in disciplinary, grievance and dispute cases, and any court or tribunal actions that may arise as the result.

Overmighty subjects and overmighty departments wield great levels of influence and autonomy in certain conditions. These exist in locations physically removed from head office and the main directorate and where a large measure of independence of operation is granted (for the source of the term, see above). Overmighty departments occur where, for operational reasons they are required to act autonomously. Overmighty subjects arise where (again for operational reasons) they are required to act in the name of the organisation in all aspects of work. The issue is compounded when the overmighty subject or division is stationed overseas from the organisational head office and in particular situations where the nature and delivery of the service is given broad or general supervision only by the managing officials. This may again be influenced by organisation tradition, such as where a long-serving individual who is always allowed to air her views and have these taken into account by the organisation (such individuals then become the target of lobbyists).

Mutual interest groups and alliances occur between individuals, groups and functions to try to exert wider pressures on organisations. This occurs for example, where one of these has failed and where there is nevertheless a widely perceived need for particular changes or activities to be undertaken.

The extent and prevalence of other means of interaction, participation and involvement. This includes departmental and group staff meetings, work improvement groups, quality circles and project groups. It may also include pioneering activities or research and development functions, where those involved are drawn from across the organisation.

External agencies and statutory bodies may be cited or even called in, in support of the point of view of a particular group given the right circumstances. For example, changes to working practices may lead to the health and safety executive being called in on the safety aspects of the new style of operations. If redundancies are foreseen, a group that is likely to be affected may call in the Advisory, Conciliation and Arbitration Service (ACAS). In both cases, access to the statutory body itself becomes a source of influence, and the organisation may have to accept either its recommendations or, at the very least, its guidance.

Vested interests. Groups pursue their own agenda when they perceive that it is in their interests to do so. This is especially apparent at times of change. When the changes proposed threaten a loss of power, influence and prestige, those concerned defend the interests of the status quo. On the other hand, people become advocates and lobbyists for change if they feel that their position is to be enhanced as the result.

Examples of the former have included trade unions that have sought to protect traditional ways of working, partly at least because their position of influence has stemmed from representing those who worked in the old ways. In the UK this has occurred on the railways and in the shipyards, car, printing and engineering industries. In other cases where new patterns of work based on technological change are envisaged, the unions involved have sought to draw up 'technology agreements' in which they have attempted to secure the position of their members through retraining, job protection and security of employment schemes.

Examples of the latter include, paradoxically, those from the same sectors, but who have lost their jobs in the various shake-outs. They have become enthusiastic lobbies for inward investment activities undertaken, for example, by Japanese car and electrical goods companies because these have brought work to otherwise depressed areas. Trade unions have sought – and been offered – new approaches to representation (above all, the single union arrangement that is a key feature of Japanese management style) and part of the reason for this is to secure fresh sources of membership and new spheres of influence from which an enhanced reputation will be gained.

More generally, there is pressure placed on groups to show results to justify their continued existence. Research and development functions therefore seek to produce inventions which they then lobby to have brought into commercial production as soon as possible as an indication of their continued use and value. Work improvement groups and quality circles also seek positive results in this way. Continued existence and supplies of resources may depend upon positive results being achieved and apparent to the rest of the organisation. This becomes especially important if there is competition for resources, or if groups succeed in gaining these at the expense of others. It is also important for the general well-being, motivation and morale of the individuals involved in these groups.

■ Power and influence relationships

These exist within and between all groups, divisions, departments and functions, and also between the individuals involved. The main features are as explained below.

■ Orders of priority

This refers to the position of each individual group or department in relation to all the others involved. This is often called the pecking order. It is established as a result of a combination of factors: the respect and regard held for the group or individuals by the organisation's top management; demands for resources and ability to command these; the extent of its influence on organisation output; the extent of its influence on internal ways of working; the size of the group and the nature of the expertise that it wields; its physical location; and the nature and quality of its leadership, output and results, both in absolute terms and also in those required and valued by the organisation.

■ Dominance–dependency

This is the extent to which some groups are able to influence, direct and dominate the courses of action of others, and the benefits and consequences that arise as the result.

Ultimately, all those who work in an organisation are dependent upon it for rewards and continuity of employment. This involves at least acquiescence and normally also, acceptance and compliance with its given ways of working. Dominance and dependency are features of all organisational and interpersonal relationships. Dominance–dependency may be entirely one-way (though this happens very rarely in practice). It is much more likely to be more complex; even a slaveowner is dependent upon the slaves to actually carry out the work.

■ Dominance–dependency and responsibility

It is much more useful, therefore, to see dominance–dependency as a process in which mutual responsibilities exist. Where groups are dependent upon the continued confidence of top managers for continuity and allocation of resources, the top managers are dependent upon the groups to produce results. This therefore tends to become the basis on which resources are allocated. Problems arise where there are priorities, competition for resources and where there is not enough to go around to everyone's satisfaction. This then becomes a basis for the assessment of the priorities themselves and of the consequences of not doing something or not doing it fully.

This may be seen also in the internal workings of groups, especially where this is negative. Organisations, managers and supervisors who approach their staff along the lines of 'If you don't want this job, there are X million out there who do', eventually find that people will not come to work for them at all. In such situations, also, the work that is produced is invariably bad, while absenteeism and dispute levels are high.

The dominance–dependency relationship is therefore to be seen as one of ebb and flow, of give and take based on understanding and acceptance of the inherent responsibilities (for a comparison of two approaches see Boxes 8.6 and 8.7).

BOX 8.5   **Dominance and Dependency in Organisational Relationships**

It is useful to identify the following conception of this.

1. Acquiescence: where the people have no particular respect or liking for the organisation and its norms, rules, customs and practices, but go along with

them because it is in their current interest to do so or where there are no apparent alternatives.

2. Compliance: a more positive approach than acquiescence, but where the fundamental basis of the relationship remains the same. This normally involves however, at least adopting the required patterns of behaviour.

3. Acceptance: where people adopt the norms, values and standards positively and with some degree of enthusiasm and interest; but, again, we are likely to see that at least part of this is dependent upon their current interest.

4. Formalisation: where conditions are placed on the particular relationships between the organisation and its staff: for example, the need to use particular processes, channels of communication and approaches.

5. Institutionalisation: where people adopt the norms, values and standards absolutely and use them as a key factor in their life and work patterns. Such an approach is often very effective in both progression through the organisation, and also in giving a structure to wider aspects of life. Institutionalisation is also a key feature in the lives of school children; those in the full-time care of health and social services (and prisons); and those who work for long periods of time in large, sophisticated and highly structured organisations.

6. Internalisation: where people adopt the organisation's beliefs and where these affect their personal beliefs and value systems; eventually such people come to 'believe in' the organisation and all its works.

7. Rejection: where people reject the organisation and everything concerning it. This normally leads at the very least to those concerned having stresses, strains, disputes and grievances. People who reject in this way are sometimes neutralised: for example, given project work that removes both them and their negative feelings from the mainstream activities. This may drive them to change their feelings from negative to positive. If this does not happen, the organisation normally rejects them.

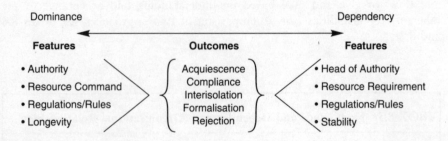

Figure 8.2   The power/relationship spectrum

BOX 8.6   Semco

'We simply do not believe our employees have an interest in coming in late, leaving early and doing as little as possible for as much money as their union can wheedle out of us. After all, these same people raise children, join the PTA [parent-teacher association], elect mayors, governors, senators and presidents. They are adults. At Semco we treat them as adults. We trust them. We don't make our employees ask permission to go to the toilet or have security guards search them as they leave for the day. We get out of the way and let them do their jobs'.

Source: Semler (1992).

BOX 8.7   Birds Eye: Skelmersdale, Liverpool, UK

The Birds Eye Factory at Skelmersdale, Liverpool was established in the 1950s. It produced frozen meat and vegetables for consumption by the UK domestic and wholesale sectors. It was part of a large international manufacturing company which had four other factories in the UK. The factory employed 1500 people. It was the largest single employer in the area. Being close to Liverpool there was high unemployment in the area following the demise of the dockyards. By the mid-1980s this was about 20 per cent. The factory was an integral part of the community and had been established there for about 40 years altogether.

The workforce was represented by several trade unions. Management–union relations were reasonably good at the informal level; however, at the formal level there was a long history of conflict. The unions were described as militant in their approach to negotiations and general dealings with the company.

In terms of productivity, this was the least efficient factory out of the five in the UK. Top management of the parent company blamed various groups: some blamed poor local management over the years; others the outdated policies of the unions; others still, the negative attitudes endemic in the local community culture.

The community was dependent upon the factory for employment and the prosperity that this brought. This in turn directly affected the numbers of shops and leisure facilities in the area; if anything were to happen to the factory then there would be a knock-on effect on these other activities.

The company that owned the factory closed it down in 1986. The effect was to remove the largest single employer from the locality. This greatly increased levels of unemployment. It also had the knock-on effects already mentioned on the rest of the area's commercial activities. The reasons quoted by the company for the closure were those indicated above (above all, the negative attitude which was endemic in the local community). There was a prevailing view at the time however, that the company's head office (in London) saw the situation only in terms of its own dominance, its ability to act in this way. Those affected perceived that at no stage did the company ever either acknowledge its dependency on the factory to produce a certain amount of production, or the responsibility that it carried for those who had given large portions of their lives to the company over the period for which it had been open.

■ Hierarchy

Organisational hierarchies are normally based on a combination of rank and function and this is reflected in job titles (marketing director; quality manager; production supervisor; personnel assistant). This is normally well understood by those in particular organisations. The process is clouded by job titles such as secretary, officer, executive and controller, and again these have to be understood by those involved.

The hierarchy is a feature of organisation design and is composed of structure, job and work allocation, and rules and procedures. It indicates where power and influence lie, and their extent and nature. It indicates spans of control, areas of responsibility and accountability, chains of command (the scalar chain) and reporting relationships. As well as a functional and divisional map of the organisation, the hierarchy is a representation of the nature and limits of power and influence (see Figures 8.3 and 8.4).

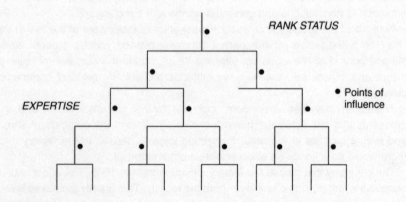

Figure 8.3   Hierarchies

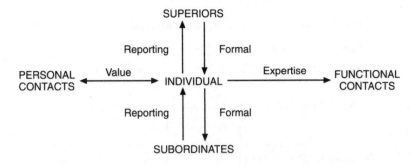

Figure 8.4 Influence relationships: the individual's position in the hierarchy

■ Status

Status influences the perceptions of power relationships in organisations. It is also a reflection of general perceptions of influence. Status is a reflection of the rank or position of someone (or something) in a particular group. Relative status is based on the interrelationship of each position. Status is based on the importance and value ascribed to the rank by the organisation and individuals concerned, and by the esteem and respect that accrue as the result of holding the given rank. Status is also based on the ambition, self-esteem and self-worth of the rank holder: the ability to say with pride, 'I hold job X' or 'I work for organisation Y.'

Status is therefore both given and taken. It is a feature of both individual and group perception. It is formalised largely by rank and capability. It also has informal features based on personality and integrity. Other individual capabilities, whether critical to group functioning and effectiveness or not, also influence status (see Figure 8.5).

Status is reinforced by the trappings that go with the rank held (such as personal office, expensive furniture, car, mobile phone, expense account), and by the volume and quality of items such as these.

It is also reinforced by the responsibilities of the rank held, such as the size of budget, numbers of staff or performance requirements. It is also often reinforced by the physical location of those concerned: for example, whether their office is in the 'corridors of power' (that is, the same as that of the top managers). In wider social circles it may also be reinforced by perceptions of glamour or excitement that are assumed to exist in certain occupations, such as show-business, publishing or travel.

The components of status may thus be represented.

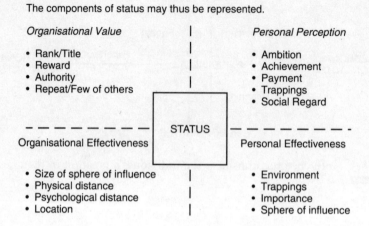

Organisational Value		*Personal Perception*
• Rank/Title		• Ambition
• Reward		• Achievement
• Authority		• Payment
• Repeat/Few of others		• Trappings
		• Social Regard

Organisational Effectiveness — STATUS — Personal Effectiveness

Organisational Effectiveness		Personal Effectiveness
• Size of sphere of influence		• Environment
• Physical distance		• Trappings
• Psychological distance		• Importance
• Location		• Sphere of influence

Figure 8.5   Status

■ Friendships

Friendship influences power relationships in organisations, where people who have positive feelings for each other also work together. A part of the way of working then becomes the desire to support friends to ensure that they derive some of the benefits which accrue from particular courses of action. The use of friendships or of personal contacts to resolve problems and address issues is a general feature of the informal organisation. It represents the ability to use personal influence (referent power) to the organisation's advantage.

■ Dislike

The converse is where antagonism exists between people. This is nearly always a barrier to effective organisational activities. It is used to block or hinder the progress of the other individual or group, and is compounded where operational reasons are given for the purpose of satisfying a personal grudge or grievance.

This is influenced by other personal emotions, such as envy, jealousy, hatred and resentment. It is also influenced by organisational and operational matters of expediency, especially where there is the need to find a scapegoat for a failure.

■ Organisational features

Some organisational features are easily seen as power relationships. For example, the supply chain, which is the process by which materials are drawn and combined together to produce finished goods and services. Influence can be exerted by groups that have key tasks to perform in this. By regulating their own output in pursuit of some other course, influence can be brought to bear for the stated purpose. Pressure is exerted to help ensure that the other purpose is satisfied (see Figure 8.6).

For example, a workforce unloading supplies from lorries may deliberately regulate their efforts in order to take a particular length of time. This may be: to prove or indicate that the reason that it took so long was because of a shortage of staff; to lobby for extra equipment (for example, cranes, forklift trucks); to seek more money ('We will work faster if you pay us more'); or to act in support of another group further down the chain that they know to be under pressure.

Resource bidding and allocation is also often a power/influence relationship. It occurs especially where there is the need on the part of the resource allocators to ensure that people are not seen to get everything for which they ask. This, it is considered, tends to lead to profligacy and inefficiency. Also, it may not be possible to satisfy everyone in this way.

Bidders for resources therefore prioritise their requests and arrive at proposals knowing that some things are going to be cancelled by the allocators. The result eventually arrived at is supposed to be something towards which everyone can work and with which everyone is at least satisfied. Both operational and behavioural actors are also satisfied in this way; a sound basis for effective operations is supposedly established, together with the knowledge that spreads around the rest of the organisation that the given department had to trim its sales to temper its proposals.

The process is also influenced by the organisation's own priority system, whereby resources are concentrated and directed towards that which is

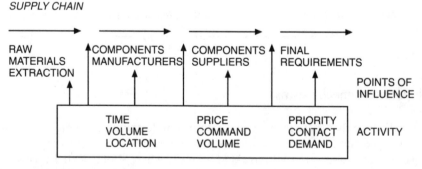

Figure 8.6   The supply chain and points of influence

important and away from lesser areas. The process is corrupted by lobbying and favouritism, expediency, the secondary agenda, and the need for triumphs and scapegoats. It is rendered operationally ineffective when resources are trimmed in ways which mean that nobody is able to do anything properly (see Figure 8.7).

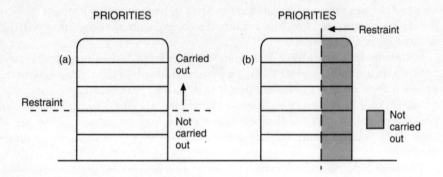

Figure 8.7   Resources and priorities

BOX 8.8   Strikes

Strikes are used as:

- enhancement of charisma, authority and influence by strike leaders;
- rites and rituals in pay bargaining processes;
- trials of strength between staff and managers;
- trials of strength between organisations and strike leaders;
- safety valves;
- additional holidays;
- catalysts for change.

In each case, an extension of influence and control is sought by the protagonists.

■ Control mechanisms

The influence that these provide also requires understanding. These exist in the following general forms, though their actual extent and nature varies between organisations (and often within them as well, where sophisticated forms and structures exist, and where operations and activities are diversified, decentralised and physically distant).

■ **Financial controls**

In these influence resides in the demands for financial information and the ways in which this is presented. It is also present in budgeting and resource allocation activities, and in checks on resource utilisation, timescales, progress chasing and checking, and the pressures exerted by those responsible.

■ **Staff controls**

This includes discipline, grievance and disputes mechanisms, the ways in which these are constituted, and the approaches taken by those responsible for their handling.

■ **Quality controls**

The standards of quality set, the means by which these are achieved, and the means by which problems of quality are identified and dealt with are all quality controls. This category is likely also to include attention to customer satisfaction (both internal and external) and systems of inquiry and complaints.

■ **Work allocation and job descriptions**

These are also sources of influence. This takes the form of requiring people to attend at set times, to produce set volumes (and quality) of output. It is also affected by flexibility of working arrangements and lines on job descriptions that state (usually at the end) 'Anything else that the organisation may require you to do.'

■ **Collective bargaining**

This is the means by which workplace conflicts are controlled and regularised. It is a combination of spheres of power and influence, brought together in particular situations; their strengths and weaknesses relative to each other; and in relation also to the organisation concerned.

BOX 8.9   Collective Bargaining, Power and Influence

The collective bargaining process was often influenced by the sheer number of unions involved. In the UK National Health Service (NHS), for example, there used to be up to 50 unions involved in some situations. The NHS needed to be able to deal with all of these on the basis of giving satisfaction to each in terms of their interrelationships with each other, as well as with the organisation as a whole.

Collective bargaining is normally highly regulated. Systems of rules and procedures are used to ensure that power and influence are used by each party concerned in ways that are capable of being managed, administered and controlled and to ensure that everyone receives fair treatment.

■ Factors that affect the health, safety and general well-being

Those factors, the means by which these are controlled and the extent and influence of health and safety committees, welfare offices and occupational health professionals, also influence the design of work environments and workstations. There are legal constraints affecting many aspects of work with which organisations must comply: extremes of heat and cold; the length of time worked without breaks; the length of time in front of computer screens. Influence therefore resides in the hands of those who must enforce these features.

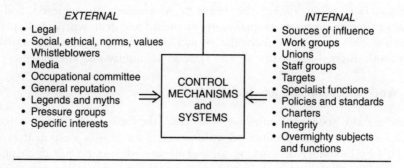

Figure 8.8   Behavioural influences on organisation control

■ Ethical controls

These are related to general standards of best practice and also to particular features such as equality of treatment. The driving force here (for good or ill) is likely to derive from the organisation's stated policy or point of view. Clear direction is given in the best cases. A form of direction emerges in the worst cases or where standards are not set by the approaches taken by individuals and groups to these matters, and the extent to which they are condoned and supported by the organisation.

■ Sanctions

Sanctions are sometimes taken against individuals and groups, and the ways in which these are applied can be a control mechanism. The power lies with those who carry out the sanctions and is also found in the relative ability of those affected to resist or combat them. This is in turn influenced by the general standpoint that is adopted by the organisation. It affects all aspects of organisational performance, either directly or indirectly: for example, general, individual and group behaviour, relationships between superiors and subordinates and the collective attitude and state of morale. It also affects perceptions of fairness and equality (or otherwise) of treatment.

■ Delegation

Delegation is the allocation of work to subordinates accompanied by the handing down of:

- authority in the given area to carry out the work and to make requests for equipment, materials and information, and to act in the name of the department, group or superior in the given area;
- control over the process by which the work is to be carried out. This normally involves. in turn, relaxing a part of the process of work supervision. Activities taken in pursuit of the task are normally left entirely to the subordinate.

There is an effect on the wider issues of responsibility and accountability. Overall responsibility, especially to the wider organisation, normally remains with the superior. Any problems arising, especially questions of failure or ineffectiveness, therefore remain a matter between the superior and the rest of the organisation. However, this is invariably accompanied by discussions between the superior and subordinate. Where such problems do arise, to apportion blame to the subordinate in dealings with the wider organisation will lead to loss of morale and accusations of scapegoating.

■ Effectiveness

For effective delegation to take place, strong mutual trust, respect and confidence must exist. On the part of the superior, this is based on respect for the capabilities, motivation and commitment of the subordinates and the fact that they are interested in the work and wish to pursue it to a successful conclusion. On the part of the subordinates, this is based on an understanding that they will receive support and backing in their efforts to get the work done, help with any problems and a proper assessment of the end results. This is always enhanced where a strong and effective reporting relationship is already established and mutual trust and confidence are already in place. This is in turn influenced by the relationship between the task to be delegated and the staff available to carry them out. The greater the control the superior has over this, the more likely that confidence and trust are present and the greater the willingness of the superior to cede the required measure of control.

For both, work is likely to be successful only if expectations are clearly set out at the commencement of work. This is reinforced wherever possible with the establishment of proper, measurable, deadlined objectives. The subordinates can then be given enough autonomy over the process to see that the work is done.

■ Rewards

The rewards of successful delegation are to be found in the freeing-up of the superior's time to pursue other things; and, for the subordinate, in the opportunities for job enhancement and enrichment. The expectations of both are raised and the nature of the working relationship is changed to reflect this.

Rewards should be forthcoming to subordinates in terms of more pay, kudos and recognition for jobs well done. The process is also likely to identify potential talent and capabilities, either for use in the department or elsewhere in the organisation. It also in some circumstances fosters and nurtures a new range of interests and raises the horizons for the subordinates.

The superior gains enhanced performance from the department stemming from raised morale and increased output. There is also often a 'Hawthorne effect': a positive change to the working relationship and environment that stems from taking an interest in the performance and progress of the subordinates.

■ Problems

The process is not to be trusted where it is used to impose unreasonable standards and workloads on subordinates. Those to whom work is delegated must be actually or potentially capable of carrying it out. If this is not apparent (or if potential that may have been assumed or identified is not fulfilled or realised), then the process should be stopped and another way of dealing with the work found. Its continued imposition on persons not capable of carrying it out leads to stress and strains, loss of morale and a reduction in the quality of the working relationship.

More sinisterly, delegation should never be used to prove a point. Even where this is positive, it may place to unacceptable strains on the subordinates. Where this is negative – for example, where a manager is setting out to 'prove' that something cannot be done – stress on the subordinate is again likely. If the manager then needs a scapegoat for the failure, this normally become that particular subordinate.

The key to effectiveness therefore lies in the integrity of the relationship between superior and subordinate and the honesty of the delegation process. As long as the work and the necessary authority and autonomy which are given and received on an open basis are of mutual interest, the process is likely to succeed and bring all the benefits and rewards indicated. Where this integrity does not exist, or where delegation is imposed rather than accepted, both performance and morale are likely to suffer and increases in stress become apparent.

BOX 8.10   Empowerment

Empowerment is a management buzzword of the 1990s. Empowerment may be summarised as the giving of measures of control and responsibility to employees over their work, work processes and working lives. The concept of empowerment is based on the view that people seek as much personal satisfaction and fulfilment as possible from all situations; that this includes work situations; and that responsibility and control lead to increased levels of satisfaction.

It is attractive to organisations because, by vesting these elements in front-line operative and other traditionally 'non-responsible' jobs, levels of supervision and management can be reduced. Expensive staff are no longer needed in current volumes. Complex and sophisticated supervisory practices, structures and controls can be simplified, thereby cutting down on overheads, non-productive processes and efforts, and the numbers of staff not actively engaged in primary output.

It is attractive to the staff (as long as the process is honest) because increased responsibilities are normally expected to lead to increased reward and benefit levels, and to increased prospects and opportunities. Potential may be identified that either the organisation or the individual may wish to develop. New levels and ranges of interest may become apparent.

Harvester

The following example illustrates the point.

Harvester, the UK restaurant chain, took steps to empower its restaurant and kitchen staff. The chefs decided what the menus for each week were to be and how often these were to be changed. They then became responsible for ordering the necessary levels and quality of stock, for ensuring that supplies were delivered, for ensuring their storage complied with legal and best professional standards and for chasing up any quality defects. They were responsible for setting ordering patterns, purchasing new kitchen equipment and ensuring that the place was clean. They dealt with the food and premises inspections and inspectors, and implemented any changes necessary as the result.

The restaurant staff (that is, waiters and waitresses) became responsible for all aspects of the eating area. They were required to clean and polish the tables, put flowers and candles out, and see that the restaurant was clean, tidy and welcoming to customers. They would greet customers, show them to their seats, take and process orders. At the end of the work period, they were to clean the restaurant area, check for security and close it down and lock up.

Both chefs and restaurant staff would handle any customer complaints directly, according to the nature of the complaint; rather than putting this through sophisticated managerial processes, these would be dealt with at the front line.

The company was therefore able to remove the differentiated, non-productive (or largely non-productive) jobs of head waiter, restaurant manager, work supervisor and general manager. Chefs and waiting staff were given large initial pay increases in return for accepting these ways of working.

The organisation adopted methods of supervision and control based on a roving and mobile area manager system (area managers would visit each of their sites at least once a week), a flexible but agreed budgeting system that enabled the staff to make a large range of decisions, and an emergency/problem-solving 24 hour hot line to the area management.

Empowerment is clearly very like delegation. It is useful to differentiate in this context, however, in order to make the point that a great deal of organisational potential lies down the delegation path. This is the case both in terms of the operational capability of the organisation and in the enhanced potential of and for the staff.

BOX 8.11   Misuses of Power and Influence

According to ACAS the extent to which power and influence is misused in the UK by people in organisations has never been greater. The main features are listed below.

1. **Favouritism**: the ability to influence an individual's career, prospects and advancement by virtue of a personal liking and at the expense of others.
2. **Victimisation**: (the converse of favouritism): the blocking or reduction of career prospects and advancement.
3. **Lack of manners**: calling out rudely to people, abusing and humiliating subordinates in public.
4. **Lack of respect**: treating subordinates with contempt, giving individuals dressing-downs in public; conducting discipline in public.
5. **Bullying and harassment**: overwhelmingly by superiors of subordinates. This is usually found in the following forms:

    (a) racial prejudice;
    (b) sexual harassment (especially of female staff by males);
    (c) bullying of the disabled by the able-bodied;
    (d) religious manias and persecutions (for example, where a Catholic company bullies the elements of its workforce that are of other religions);
    (e) personal likes and dislikes, especially where the dislike is based on a perceived threat to the security of the senior's position.

6. **Scapegoating**: the need to find someone to blame for the superior's errors.
7. **Inequality of opportunity**, the setting of a priority order for the advancement of staff based on gender, race or disability elements.

ACAS report that some cases are so acute that people are being driven to despair, nervous breakdown or even suicide by the activities of managers.

Curiously, managers and supervisors often do not see that they are bullying by the actions that they take. In many cases, they act this way because this is how they were treated and 'It made a man out of me.' They confuse being firm and assertive with bullying.

Some managers confirmed that they only acted in this way because they perceived that it would help to get the job done. Others openly acted this way because they saw the opportunity to wield and use power (in some cases knowing the effects that this was having, in other cases not).

Source: ACAS Annual Report 1994 (HMSO).

BOX 8.12   Power, Influence and Time

Time is the major driving force of vested interests. Where changes are proposed and whether the vested interest wishes to block or hurry these along, there is a time pressure to organise, to present the prevailing views in the best possible light and to gain support and dissipate opposition. People seek to achieve this as early as possible. Failure to do so is likely to allow competing groups and forces their opportunity. In many organisations, a failure to get organised quickly is perceived as a lack of interest in the outcome. Vested interests therefore seek resources, support and publicity, in order to influence key characters as quickly as possible. This also reinforces the perceptions of people that 'Something is being done' and 'We are making progress.'

■ Relationship structures and spheres of influence

It is clear thus far that a certain amount of power and the potential for exerting influence exist in all individuals and groups in organisations.

This must now be seen in context. The ability of an individual or group to bring influence to bear on others is dependent upon the following factors.

1. The nature of the relationship between all the parties, and whether this is cooperative, competitive or conflicting; based on mutual trust or antagonism; if more than two groups, whether there are alliances or other areas of mutuality between some of them; the personalities involved; whether the groups are permanent or *ad hoc*; the rules and boundaries within which the relationships take place.

2. The nature of the matters in hand and the extent of their importance to each individual and party concerned. For example, the organisation's tea person wields great influence over the Chief Executive if her desire for tea is overwhelming and if she cannot easily go elsewhere to get it.

3. The relationship between the overt, primary or stated agenda and any parallel, secondary or other hidden agenda, either on the part of the groups involved or some of the individual players.

   For example, trade union officials will often fight the cases that they know that they cannot win because it shows their concern and care for every member whatever their difficulties. Further, the trade union officials involved have their own career paths to follow and concern for all members is likely to be a key feature and requirement. The officials therefore gain a reputation for being prepared to fight any corner, and this in turn leads to both their own advancement and also increased membership brought on by feelings of confidence and goodwill generated by the approach.

4. Management style of the organisation and its tolerance of parallel, secondary and hidden agenda; the recognition of any dominance or dependency exerted in the steps that it takes to minimise and control this; the extent and presence of physical and psychological remoteness and distance.

5. The conduct of the relationships. This is likely to be based on:

   (a) conflict, a power struggle, the need for ascendancy in a particular situation;

   (b) cooperation (the establishment of areas of mutual interest) harmony (recognition of the need to resolve any issues for the greater good of all); openness (the extent to which each party involved is able, or feels able, to declare its own position completely); expediency (the need to gain a result quickly for some reason);

   (c) publicity, or what others are to make of the outcome of the matter in hand once this is known.

6. Structural factors such as divisionalisation, functionalisation and specialisation. The influences here are physical and psychological distance and the relative positions of expertise and their importance in the particular relationships. Demarcation and restrictive practice – tight description and compartmentalisation of jobs and work – is an extreme form of structural influence in this context. Based on the principles of scientific management it gave so much influence to some groups (especially the ability to block work) that alternative work structures have not been sought.

7. Information, information chains and the means by which information is disseminated and distributed. Power and influence exist in each aspect.

   For example, organisations that put information out on a 'need to know' basis have first decided what it is that each group and individual 'needs to know'.

   Information is further distorted by the cascade process (see Figure 8.8) and the means by which the cascade is achieved. Briefing groups, notes, memoranda, newsletters and staff meetings may all carry the same substantive message and agenda. However this is varied by the media used, the person conducting the briefing or meeting and the interpretation that is put by each group that is being briefed on what is being transmitted.

8. Command of information technology is a source of power and this is exaggerated where others have neither the ability nor willingness to use it or understand it. This also applies to summaries of information, whereby a large volume is presented in a shortened and ostensibly useful format. In this case the influence lies entirely with the editor.

Professional	*Hierarchical*
• Expertise	• Authority
• Direction	• Directional
• Usage	• Influential
• Audience	• Formal
• Content	• Accessability
• Context	• Hardware and Software
• Confidence	• Convenience
• Integrity	• Durability
Ethical	*Technological*

Figure 8.9 Influences on information flows and cascades

9. Technology and the expertise required to use it is also a source of power. This occurs in all activities. The influence that this brings to individuals and groups is dependent upon the nature of the technology and the operations involved, and again, the willingness or otherwise of others to use it and understand it. However, this can be illustrated at its simplest: staff on the switchboard have a great influence on the initial impressions formed by those who telephone a particular organisation: through the greeting given, the way in which this is delivered, the tone of voice and the transfer on. The technology itself also has influence, both in the numbers of calls that it can take and in how these are handled (for example, whether in a queuing system, engaged tone, pre-recorded voices, musical entertainment while the caller waits).

   This also applies to production technology, including the production controllers' knowledge of the capacity of equipment and their ability to optimise its use; and the knowledge of the staff involved, the extent of their training and their understanding of their own ability to slow down or speed up the processes.

10. Personal assistant syndrome. This occurs where people have influence in excess of their position in the hierarchy. The normal example of this is that of the personal assistant (PA) to the organisation's CE (or other top managers). The PA is used as the manager's personal resource, and as a sounding board and critic for possible and proposed courses of action. The PA therefore becomes an exerter of influence as the levels of mutual trust and confidence grow; and the relationship is reinforced if the judgement of the PA is shown to be sound.

PAs become the focus for lobbies and support from elsewhere in the organisation because they can (or are perceived to) provide a route to the sources of power. They have low status but high influence. They also become a source of quality information both to the manager for whom they work and also potentially for the rest of the organisation.

11. Cross-functional groups and committees influence the views of those who take part. They may also be used as sounding boards for ideas and proposals for action. They may therefore exert influence and again, this is likely to grow if their judgement is demonstrably sound. The same also applies to work improvement groups and quality circles.

12. Isolation. For whatever reason, isolation is a power relationship:

    (a) physical isolation brought on because of the remoteness of a group from the rest of the organisation (for example, an overseas subsidiary) leads on the one hand to the feelings of loss of control and involvement on the part of the main organisation; and, on the other, to feelings of autonomy and independence on the part of the subsidiary;

    (b) psychological isolation is brought on by matters such as resource starvation, denigration and general lack of respect and regard for the work of the group or for its members, which leads to the adoption of a siege mentality on the part of both the group affected as it defends itself from the pressures of the rest of the organisation, and also the organisation as it seeks to make fresh inroads into the already beleaguered group;

    (c) group-think is also a form of isolation. For example, top managers and directors may create their own view of the organisation in its environment without reference to reality, or based on an historic perception and reputation. Project groups and think tanks may also find themselves in this form of isolation if their relationship with the rest of the organisation is not carefully nurtured and managed.

■ Spheres of influence

These are created by a combination of formal and informal authority and power. They relate to the nature of activities and operations. They overlap and interact with each other (see Figure 8.10). Spheres of influence are less easy to define than areas of legitimate, expert and role/office power. They encompass especially areas of coercive/conformist referent and charismatic power. They also include specific areas of functional and legitimate power: for example, trade union officials have legitimate positions in any areas where they have members and the union is recognised; the human resource function has legitimate areas in any other function that requires its services, such as in recruitment selection and handling disciplinary hearings and grievances.

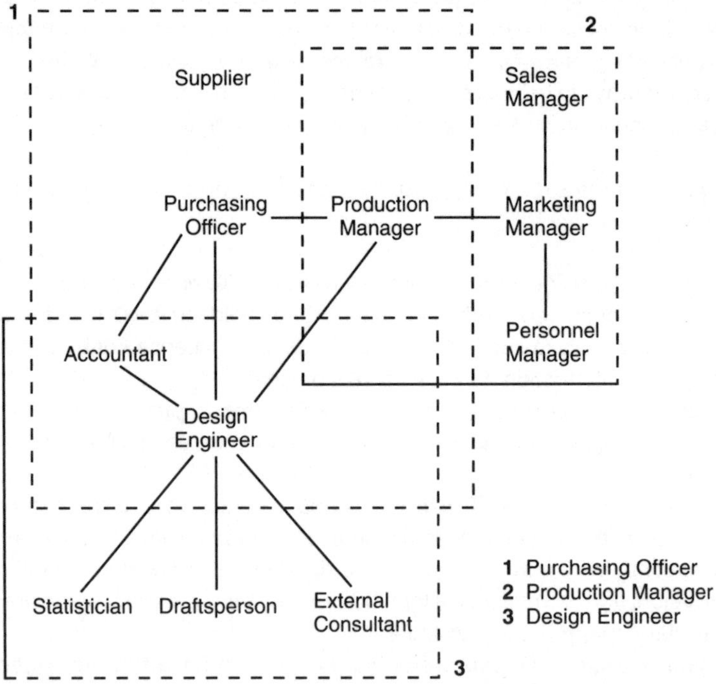

1. Purchasing Officer
2. Production Manager
3. Design Engineer

Figure 8.10 Spheres of influence

Source: from Luthans (1986)

Spheres of influence may be defined as 'the psychological territory of the individual or group'. Individuals and groups may have many spheres of influence in an organisation. Handy (1993) developed the idea as follows.

Ownership of territory is conferred partly by deeds and partly by precedent, squatting or staking a claim. The boundaries of the territory are set out in various ways; physically, with screens, offices, separate buildings; procedurally, through committee memberships and circulation list; socially, through dining groups, informal groupings, carpets and other status signs:

- territory is prized by its inhabitants; they will not willingly relinquish it, nor allow it to get overcrowded;
- some territories are more prized than others;
- trespassing is discouraged (you enter another territory by invitation only);
- one can seek to increase or improve one's own property even to the detriment of the neighbourhood as a whole;

- territory is not to be violated and if it is, there will be retaliation and conflict;
- territory is jealously guarded, especially in relationship to its own trappings and status (including office sizes, dining rooms, cars, PAs and secretaries);
- territory is always to be improved and enhanced, both in the interests of maintaining the current position and also in order that this may be improved.

Pressures to maintain and increase the sphere of influence depend on a variety of factors.

1. The confidence, respect and regard in which an individual or group is held. If it is high, those concerned seek to enhance and build on this. If it is low, those concerned are likely to seek other means of gaining influence (for example, through the control of information and functional triumphs).
2. Functional expertise, and the extent to which this is prized and valued by the organisation. Again, especially if this is low, other sources of influences will tend to be sought.
3. The rewards of influence. These are normally better work, increased resources, enhanced reputation, and moves up the pecking order. They also include (in some organisations) the ability to influence the direction, activities and operations of the organisation, and therefore transform (rather than merely enhance) the prospects of a particular department or individual.
4. Attaching oneself to an overmighty subject or department in the expectation of favours and enhancement.
5. Increased status and prestige for those involved. This often leads to increased benefits and pay and increased prospects (especially from within the organisation) for those concerned.
6. Favouritism on the part of the organisation's top managers, driven by real or perceived operational necessity, the top manager's own expertise and familiarity (for example, the director who cam up through the ranks of the marketing department is likely to continue to favour marketing), personal friendships, expediency, or the availability of a triumph.

The gaining and maintenance of influence in these ways is a continuous interactive and competitive process. The success of one group has effects on the others who, in turn, normally make counter-moves to nullify this and supplant them. This is both positive and negative. The positive seeks to offer something that is above what the others have; the negative is comprised of activities designed to discredit those who currently hold influence.

The other point to recognise is the need to extend the spheres of influence in these ways. Much depends on the ways of working of top managers and the extent to which they are influenced by these forms of activity (indeed, in some organisations these are condoned and encouraged); or conversely, recognising the inherently disruptive and destructive effects and taking steps to stamp them out.

■ Conclusions

The acquisition and use of power is a basic human as well as organisational need. The requirements and ability to control and influence the environment, and to make it comfortable and supportive, is a factor in all behaviour. It is necessary to understand the ways in which people seek to do this in organisations, and the effects of this on aims and objectives, performance, behaviour and resource utilisation.

How power is used and what type of power is used affects all aspects of performance, as does the means of dividing and allocating responsibility and authority. From this point of view, a key part of the creation, design and structuring of organisations consists of creating patterns of control and influence. This is formalised in hierarchies, reporting relationships, functional and expert activities and results areas. Space is also created for the operation of communication and information systems, and group and intergroup relationships, both formal and informal.

It is also necessary to pay constant attention to the ways in which power, influence and authority are used and wielded within organisations to ensure that this continues to be legitimate, and to ensure that conflict (see Chapter 11) and organisational politics (see Chapter 12), which might otherwise arise, are kept under control.

■ Questions

1. Taking one group of which you are member (social or work), identify the ways in which you influence the others and the ways in which they influence you. What conclusions and inferences can you draw from this?
2. Consider the Birds Eye example (Box 8.7). Why was the company ultimately unable to influence and persuade the staff to its point of view?
3. What steps should organisations take to limit and control the potential for undue influence of (a) managers and (b) experts?
4. On the basis of the evidence given in Box 8.6, where does the real power and influence in Semco lie? How is this wielded? What are the constraints and controls placed on those who work in the company; what are the strengths and weaknesses of these; and what potential problems might be foreseen?

CHAPTER 9

Leadership

■ Introduction

The need to study and understand leadership arises from the need for successful and effective direction of organisations together with the need to identify those characteristics required to be a successful and effective director, manager or supervisor: that is, a leader (whether of a total organisation or of a particular organisational sphere, function, department or division).

The leadership of groups and organisations has been studied using examples drawn from all eras of the past and from every part of the world. This has included attention to the conception, organisation and construction of the pyramids of ancient Egypt and South America and Stonehenge near Salisbury in the UK. The personalities and achievements of Julius Caesar and other Roman emperors, Charlemagne, the Black Prince, Machiavelli, Napoleon and Hitler have all been studied, as have the war campaigns of Rommel, Patten, Montgomery and others. The overriding purpose of all this has been to try to establish what makes a good leader and to distinguish the benefits and advantages that good leadership brings to organisations, groups and activities. Current management thinking and research generally concludes that leadership qualities are required of anyone who has any form of managerial or supervisory responsibility at any level of the organisation.

There is, furthermore, a more general move away from the use of administrative systems and hierarchies, and towards the empowerment of individuals, involving acceptance of responsibility and accountability for tasks and functions, in addition to simply carrying these out. These systems are often expensive and unwieldy, self-serving and ultimately stifling to organisational well-being. It follows from this that specific characteristics are required of those who take charge of (lead) these situations and that this extends to those empowered individuals who accept responsibility, authority and accountability. More generally it also indicates the continuing need to study, develop and enlarge the subject of leadership and management as a field of inquiry.

This must additionally be seen in the current context of the business world. This is turbulent, rapidly changing and global, and all organisations are influenced by this. There is no such thing as a stable sector or closed market. This is the backcloth against which all managerial activities take place. Sophisticated systems and procedures again tend to militate against effective operations. While an individual may be trained to be speedy, flexible and responsive, and to order the activities of his particular sphere of influence effectively, the systems and structures that have been created by organisations tend to act as barriers to progress.

Alongside this is the need for organisations to establish their own clarity of purpose, both overall and for each function, division and department. From this emerges the real nature of organisational leadership. Again, this tends to militate against the creation, value and usefulness of sophisticated administrative systems and procedures. It rather emphasises the leadership/directional expertise required.

■ Definition

A leader is someone who exercises influence over other people. (Huczynski and Buchanan, 1993)

Leadership is the lifting of people's vision to a higher sight, the raising of their performance to a higher standard, the building of their personality beyond its normal limitations. (P. F. Drucker, 1986b)

A leader is: 'cheerleader, enthusiast, nurturer of champions, hero finder, wanderer, dramatist, coach, facilitator and builder'. (Peters and Austin, 1985)

The leader must have infectious optimism. The final test of a leader is the feeling you have when you leave their presence after a conference. Have you a feeling of uplift and confidence? (Field Marshal Bernard Montgomery)

Leadership is creating a vision to which others can aspire and energising them to work towards this vision. (Anita Roddick)

There is a need in all organisations for individual linking pins who will bind groups together and, as members of other groups, represent their groups elsewhere in organisations. Leadership concerns the leader themselves, the subordinates, and the task in hand. (Handy, 1993)

From this range of definitions, certain initial key elements may be established.

- getting things done through people and all that entails, including the organisation of people into productive teams, groups, departments and functions;
- the creation of effective means of communication;
- the resolution of conflicts, both behavioural and operational;
- creating direction for the organisation, department, division or function;
- organising resources in support of all this;
- taking informed, effective and successful decisions;
- coping with change and uncertainty.

Some general priorities may also be established:

- getting optimum performance from those carrying out the work in whatever terms that is defined;
- ensuring continuity, development and improvement in those carrying out the work; monitoring and evaluating both the work and those involved; taking remedial action where necessary;
- relating the skills and capacities of those involved in the work to the work itself;
- seeking continuous improvement in all aspects of the work environment; and providing opportunities for continuous development and advancement for those in the organisation, department, division or function;
- motivating and encouraging the staff, and promoting positive, harmonious and productive working relations.

Leadership is therefore studied as an aspect of organisational behaviour for two major reasons. It is critical function in itself; and it is critical to organisation success.

Many organisations in the 1950s, 1960s and 1970s substituted bureaucracies, procedures and checks (such as industrial relations and quality control systems) for the direction, clarity of purpose and vision that comes from effective leadership. Part of this was because no clear universal understanding of effective organisation direction existed. These processes and procedures therefore became both instruments of progress and above all, restraints and checks: by proceeding slowly both order and understanding could be achieved. These are now understood to have been both costly and wrong. The qualities of effective leadership referred to above improve clarity of purpose and therefore also group and output performance (assuming that this clarity of purpose can be translated into action). Furthermore, it removes the burden of such systems from organisations.

More generally, there are cultural aspects of leadership which should be acknowledged. There are specific ways of doing things in different countries, regions or spheres of the world which must be recognised. In effect, these are the routes to the desired destination. In some cases (for example, Japan) failure to follow precisely the route indicated or required is likely to lead to business failure. Ultimate organisation responsibility lies with the person at the head. Whoever this is must be able to operate within their given sphere and within all the pressures that this may bring. Recognition and acceptance of this general point is the first prerequisite of success.

■ Critical nature

Ultimate responsibility for the organisation means accepting praise for success and blame for failure and assessing the chances of each occurring. Explicit in this is the need to assess the organisation and its place in its sectors and markets. It means giving direction to ensure that success is forthcoming and minimising the risk of failure. It means assessing resources, staff, technology, finance and marketing activities. It means drawing expertise into the organisation at all levels (at the lower levels this normally means ensuring that this is drawn in by others). It means ensuring that all structural, behavioural and organisational components are in place and suitable for their given purposes.

It invariably means also adopting strong moral and ethical stances. This is more extreme in some industries and sectors than others (for example, defence, tobacco). In general organisation behaviour terms this involves devising suitable standards of approach, attitude and activity towards staff, customers, clients and the wider community.

■ A note on the Chief Executive Officer

CEs and also those who occupy functional directorates are currently increasingly becoming the focus of studies. This is from two standpoints: the assessment of performance of top managers by academics; and the proliferation of autobiographies (for example, by John Harvey-Jones, the Roddicks, Victor Kiam and Akio Morita). This is indicative of the importance of the subject and the emphasis placed upon it.

Another standpoint is to emphasise the variety and complexity of a background for the study of leadership as an integral function of organisation behaviour. This background includes:

(a) the complexity and sophistication of the general managerial and top executive task;
(b) the complexity of the qualities required to carry it out;
(c) the ability of the person in question to bring to bear personal talents and attributes in order that this sophistication of purpose may be addressed;
(d) the ability to be flexible, responsive and resourceful in response to specific situations.

BOX 9.1 Chief Executive Officer Studies

Christensen *et al.* identify three roles of the CEO. These are: organisational leader; personal leader (that is, the focus of the organisation in relation to the staff); chief architect of organisational purpose.

Handy identifies: the helicopter factor (the ability to rise above the organisation and take an overview of it); the leader as organisational ambassador; and the leader as general practitioner.

Harvey-Jones identifies the overwhelming importance of the ability of any effective CEO to communicate in all forms and with all those with whom they may come into contact.

■ Identity

The CE gives a focal point for both staff and customers of the organisation. It is commonplace for customer complaints to be addressed to the top person in the organisation. It is also commonplace, for example, for employees of The Virgin Group to say (usually with considerable pride), 'I work for Richard Branson.' The same applies elsewhere. While it is most common in self-started businesses (that is, those where the founder-leader and CE are the same person), it is nevertheless quite usual for staff of British Airways to identify positively with Colin Marshall, or members of the Special Air Service (SAS) with Jan Carlzon.

In the USA this identity is generated from the reverse standpoint. Industry and commercial leaders of global organisations are major contributors to news and current affairs programmes. They become media figures in their own right and the employee is asked to identify with this as part of this process. This in turn becomes particularly important therefore in terms of staff motivation and also the organisation–market–community interface.

This identity is both positive and negative and occurs both as an active and passive process. That is to say, if an employee works for a CE who is subsequently revealed as a crook this hampers her opportunity of future employment elsewhere; this has happened to staff of the BCCI.

Passive identity usually means that there is a lack of identity with the organisation (and therefore commitment and motivation in relation to the organisation). It occurs where the CE is inept, an obfuscator or simply invisible.

■ Confidence

It is also necessary to recognise at the outset the importance of confidence in the CE. The range and source of confidence is important. It extends to staff, customers, clients and the community. It also extends to stock markets, backers, directors and governors. Once confidence on the part of any of these is lost it is unusual for the CE to remain in their job. This may occur very quickly and for a variety of reasons (see Box 9.2).

BOX 9.2   Chief Executives and the Loss of their Jobs

Margaret Thatcher, the UK's Prime Minister from 1979 to 1990, won a vote of confidence from her party in November 1990 but not by a large enough majority. She lost her job four days later.

John Akers resigned from his position of Chief Executive at IBM in January 1993. This was after the company had declared the then highest ever corporate loss of $5 billion. This was followed by a staff resizing (redundancy) policy for the first time ever.

Robert Stempel left his position as CE of General Motors following disastrous results worldwide in November 1992.

Gerald Ratner destroyed a whole business empire with one throw-away line. He made a disparaging remark about one of company's product lines at a conference in November 1991. The remark was widely reported and people turned away from his organisation and stopped buying all of its products. Not only did he lose his job but the company was required to go through both a name and an image change as well as a radical reorganisation.

In all cases the person indicated left the job before they had intended to do so and as a consequence of the circumstances noted.

■ Respect

As well as confidence CEs must enjoy the respect of everyone concerned – staff, customers, backers and the community. Above all, this must extend to the staff who should be able to trust the integrity, the judgement and the personality of the particular CE.

This has led some authorities to impose strictures on the private lives of top managers. It is essential that complete integrity at the workplace is maintained in all dealings, with all staff, always. While it is not good to impose moral and value judgements (which in any case will vary in importance between places and organisations and even within organisations), the acid test must be in any loss of respect. Again, any such loss, especially in regard to the relationship with the staff, makes for a very difficult working environment.

Each of these points clearly applies in lesser measures to those in more junior managerial and supervisory positions. For example, the typing pool supervisor becomes a focal point for those working in the typing pool, and the person concerned is critical to its successful operation. That person concerned must enjoy the confidence, identity and respect of those who work there if productive and professional work is to be achieved.

■ Leadership and management

From this, certain features begin to emerge.

Results   These are measured in terms of what they set out to achieve and what they actually achieved; how and why these were achieved; how they were viewed at the time and subsequently by posterity; and whether this represented a good, bad or indifferent return on the resources and energy expended in their pursuit.

Inspiration   In order to achieve success, leaders must have their own clear understanding of what this is, at least in their own terms. In order that people follow, and resources are attracted to their cause, this is normally translated into a simple, direct and positive statement of where the leader is going, how and why this is to be achieved and the benefits that this is to bring to others as a result. They must be capable of inspiring others: it is no use having a good idea if people do not recognise it as such.

Hard work   For all this to occur leaders must have great stores of energy, enthusiasm, dedication, zeal and commitment. They have to inspire and energise people and resources in pursuit of the desired ends. They also set the standards for their followers: in normal circumstances, hard work cannot be expected of others if the leader is not also prepared to put this in.

Honesty   People follow leaders, either because they believe in them or because it is in their interest to do so (or for a combination of the two). Leaders who fail to deliver are normally rejected or supplanted. Leaders who say one thing and mean another will not be trusted and people will continue to work for them only until they can find something else.

Responsibility   They accept their own part in both triumphs and successes, and also disasters and failures. This extends to rewards and consequences.

These features may be compared with the standard general list of 'the roles and functions of management'.

1. Establishing overall purpose, direction and policy aims and objectives.
2. Forecasting, planning, coordinating, harmonising and controlling the work and resources required.
3. Getting things achieved through people, giving orders and instructions; seeing that these are carried out; monitoring and evaluating the results.
4. The 'hand on the tiller' role of adjusting the operations of the group before these go seriously off course.

Also, as stated above, the words leader and manager are not interchangeable. The basic difference is in the terms used. 'Manager' is normally assumed to refer to a person in an organisation; 'leader' is a much wider definition, extending to kings and queens, religious denominations and social and political activities, as well as formally constituted organisations and their divisions.

However, a large measure of similarity is apparent. Given this parallel range of qualities and activities, it is reasonable to assert that there is a large measure of leadership present in the managerial job, and that there is a large measure of leadership required in such jobs.

BOX 9.3 Leadership

Peters and Austin (1985) identified a long and comprehensive list of factors present in a 'leader'; and they contrasted this with the mirror attributes of the 'non-leader'.

Leader	*Non-leader*
• Carries water for people	• Presides over the mess
• Open door problem solver, advice giver, cheerleader	• Invisible, gives orders to staff, expects them to be carried out
• Comfortable with people in their workplaces	• Uncomfortable with people
• No reserved parking place, dining room or lift	• Reserved parking place & dining table
• Manages by Walking About	• Invisible
• Arrives early, stays late	• In late, usually leaves on time
• Common touch	• Strained with 'inferior' groups of staff
• Good listener	• Good talker
• Available	• Hard to reach
• Fair	• Unfair
• Decisive	• Uses committees
• Humble	• Arrogant
• Tough, confronts nasty problems	• Elusive, the 'artful dodger'
• Persistent	• Vacillates
• Simplifies	• Complicates
• Tolerant	• Intolerant
• Knows people's names	• Doesn't know people's names
• Has strong convictions	• Sways with the wind
• Trusts people	• Trusts only words and numbers on paper
• Delegates whole important jobs	• Keeps all final decisions
• Spends as little time as possible with outside directors	• Spends a lot of time massaging outside directors
• Wants anonymity for himself, publicity for the company	• Wants publicity for himself
• Often takes the blame	• Looks for scapegoats
• Gives credit to others	• Takes credit
• Gives honest, frequent feedback	• Amasses information
• Knows when and how to discipline people	• Ducks unpleasant tasks
• Has respect for all people	• Has contempt for all people
• Knows the business and the kind of people who make it tick	• Knows the business only in terms of what it can do for him/her

Leader	Non-leader
• Honest under pressure	• Equivocation
• Looks for controls to abolish	• Looks for new controls and procedures
• Prefers discussion rather than written reports	• Prefers long reports
• Straightforward	• Tricky, manipulative
• Openness	• Secrecy
• As little paperwork as possible	• As much paperwork as possible
• Promotes from within	• Looks outside the organisation
• Keeps his promises	• Doesn't keep his promises
• Plain office and facilities	• Lavish office, expensive facilities and furnishings
• Organisation is top of the agenda	• Self is top of the agenda
• Sees mistakes as learning opportunities and the opportunity to develop	• Sees mistakes as punishable offences and the means of scapegoating

Peters and Austin add the following two riders to their version of these columns.

'You now know more about leaders and leadership than all the combined graduate business schools in America.

You also know whether you have a leader or a non-leader in your manager's office.'

Source: from Peters and Austin (1985).

■ Traits and characteristics

There have been a great many studies of leaders, directors and managers from all walks of life and all parts of history. By studying a range of leaders and managers from a variety of situations and background – for example, sport, politics, the military, exploration, religion and business – it is possible to infer and draw conclusions as to what the basis for their success or otherwise was and what the reasons and causes of this were. Their contribution can be assessed and analysed together with the other elements and factors present.

The main constraint on the approach relates to the ability to see these contributions, elements and factors in the given situation only, without being able to translate these into a wider context. Any conclusions thus arrived at have first to be related to current situations if the lessons present are to be fully learned.

Attempts to identify the traits and characteristics present in successful leaders are largely inconclusive, in that none identify all the attributes necessary to lead, direct or manage in all situations. However, the following characteristics are found to be applicable to most situations.

1. **Communication** – the ability to communicate with all people with whom the leader comes into contact regularly, continuously and in ways and language in which those on the receiving end will both be able to understand and to respond to.
2. **Decision-making** – the ability to take the right decisions in given situations, to take responsibility and be accountable for them, and to understand the consequences of particular courses of action. Part of this involves being able to take an overview or strategic view of particular situations, to see the longer term and to take a wider general perspective. This is sometimes called 'the helicopter view'.
3. **Commitment** – to both matters in hand and also the wider aspects of the organisation as a whole. This includes an inherent willingness to draw on personal, as well as professional, energies and to bring qualities of enthusiasm, drive and ambition to the particular situation.
4. **Concern for staff** – respecting, trusting and committing oneself to them; developing them, understanding them and their aspirations and reconciling these with the matters in hand. Staff should be treated on a basis of equality and confidence.
5. **Quality** – a commitment to the quality of product or service such that, whatever the matter in hand, customers receive high value and high satisfaction, and the staff involved receive recognition for their effort.
6. A given **set of values** with which others will identify, and to which they will commit themselves. There are few examples of leaders, directors or managers who succeed by being all things to all people in all situations.
7. **Personal integrity** – this includes vision, enthusiasm, strength of character, commitment, energy and interest; it also includes the setting and establishment of high absolute standards of moral and ethical probity.
8. **Positive attitudes** – held by the leader and transmitted to staff and customers.
9. **Mutuality and dependency** of the leader with their staff; successful leaders know their own weaknesses, and the importance and value of the people that go with them; above all, they know what they cannot do and where and when to go for help and support in these areas.

Rosemary Stewart quotes from an American study in which organisation executives were asked to identify what they thought were the main desirable qualities of managers. They came up with the following list.

judgement	dependability	initiative	emotional stability
integrity	fairness	foresight	ambition
human relations skill	dedication	drive	objectivity
	cooperation	decisiveness	

The problem with this approach is that it is very difficult to pin down those qualities and to measure the true extent of their prevalence. They are simply widely perceived to be held or to have been held by those characters who were studied. It also takes little account of the negative attributes that may be present, such as stubbornness, vanity, self-centredness, arrogance and conceit. In the particular context of situations where conflict existed – for example, those centred around kings and queens or around military operations – the nature and extent of technology owned by each side must be taken into account. In general, it is quite possible for a bad leader in those situations to succeed at the expense of someone who was better but who simply did not have access to, or command of, sufficient levels of resource technology or equipment.

BOX 9.4   The Leadership Functions Model

This model was developed by John Adair, working at the University of Surrey during the 1960s and 1970s. It recognises that certain traits, qualities, capabilities and aptitudes must be present in leaders; that these must be translated into action. It then reconciles this with emphasis on the work and the group that are the main features of the style approach to leadership.

The leader addresses the key tasks of achieving the task, building the team and paying attention to the individual members. Again, a balance of the three is required. The leader who concentrates only on the task by going all out for production schedules, while neglecting the training, encouragement and motivation of the group will always have problems of dissonance and dysfunction.

The leader who concentrates only on creating team spirit, while neglecting the job or individuals, will not get the maximum involvement and commitment which only comes from an environment that is both harmonious and genuinely productive. Staff members would therefore lack any true feelings of achievement or success.

Figure 9.1   Leadership functions model

The key leadership functions required are:

Direction,	Planning,	Communication,
communication,	appraisal,	decision-making,
coordination,	control	creativity,
assessment	development	resourcefulness

Adair developed training courses based around the concept of leadership functions, which he called 'action centred leadership'. The courses were structured around a series of practical tasks: for example, the organisation of given sets of materials by leaders and groups into productive activities (getting across an open space without touching the floor; organisating the carrying of loads from one place to another). Classroom exercises were centred around the study of war films, including *A Bridge Too Far, Twelve O'Clock High, Attack Alarm, The Longest Day*. Students on these courses assessed the general performance of the leaders. They assessed in particular the attention paid by the leaders in the films to achievement of task, motivation and development of the group, and attention to the individuals. From these activities, a body of first-hand experience would be generated by participants on which a discussion and evaluation of the effectiveness of particular approaches could be based. This could then be related to group performance; individual performance; the extent to which the task was achieved and the reasons for this; and the contribution that the leader made towards this. It also enabled the relationship between the total purpose and sub-objectives to be assessed; for example, in some cases individuals made very strong and effective contributions to groups which nevertheless ultimately failed. The study of the films *A Bridge Too Far* and *Twelve O'Clock High* in particular illustrates the need for coordination of effort between groups as well as within groups.

Source: Adair (1975).

■ Types of leader

The following different types of leader may be distinguished.

1. The traditional leader, whose position is assured by birth and heredity. Examples of this are kings and queens. It may also be found in family businesses, whereby child succeeds parent as CE or Chair when the latter retires.
2. The known leader, whose position is secured by the fact that everybody understands this, at least in general. Kings and queens are examples again. Priests are known to be leaders of their congregations. Aristocrats are known to be masters and mistresses of their own domains. It is known also that they will be succeeded by one from their own estate when they die or move on.

3. The appointed leader, whose position is legitimised by virtue of the fact that she has gone through a selection, assessment and appointment process in accordance with the wishes and demands of the organisation and the expectations of those who will now be working for them. This invariably carries a defined and formalised managerial role in organisations.

4. The bureaucratic leader, whose position is legitimised by the rank held. This is especially true of military structures and is reinforced by the job titles used and their known position in the hierarchy (corporal, captain, major, general). It is also to be found in more complex and sophisticated commercial and public organisation structures. This also normally implies managerial responsibilities.

5. The functional or expert leader, whose position is secured by virtue of his expertise. This form of leadership is likely to be related to particular issues: for example, the industrial relations officer may be a junior functionary who, however, becomes the acknowledged leader, director and problem solver wherever industrial relations problems arise, and whatever the rank or status of other people involved.

6. The charismatic leader, whose position is secured by the sheer force of her personality. Many great world leaders (good or evil) have (or had) this: Napoleon, Adolf Hitler, Winston Churchill, Margaret Thatcher, John F. Kennedy.

7. The informal leader, whose position is carried out by virtue of his personality, charisma, expertise, command of resources, but whose position is not formally legitimised by rank, appointment or tradition. This position may also be arrived at by virtue of some other activity for which he is particularly responsible (for example, local trade union representative).

■ Leadership and status

There also remains a view in the West that leadership is a function of promotion and status rather than capability. Yet one of the most enduring lessons of the post-war period is that excellent leaders do not always come from among the ranks of functional and technical experts: the best nurses do not make the best hospital managers, the best builders do not make the best building directors. There is clearly no rationale either for rewarding individuals and organisations by 'promoting' those with great expertise away from what they can do well and into that which they might not be able to do at all.

The problem of this form of reward and expectation must be addressed however. There is a prevailing culture across much of the Western world that part of this is to be paid in job titles which include the words 'supervisor', 'manager', 'director' or equivalent expressions. This is reinforced by the fact that in the same places such positions carry with them high social esteem, and reward status with commensurate levels of general influence and regard within their own communities. Effective organisations have clearly therefore to seek alternative means of satisfying these status and esteem needs of their people or at least of reconciling these with those of organisational performance. (The subject of status is fully discussed in Chapter 8).

■ Charisma and personality in leadership

Charisma may be defined as the 'distinctive element (or elements) of personality with which others identify'. It is enhanced by other aspects: job title, the organisation worked for, numbers of persons and other resources controlled, successes and failures, media image, stories, myths and legends. It is also a reflection of the degree of personal influence that is brought to bear on the situation (often in spite of the position held). This is the degree and the extent to which the individual remains influential when removed from the high office in question.

BOX 9.5   Charisma (1)

It is very easy for people to identify with someone who holds a position of influence and who has a strong, dominant or forceful personality.

Arthur Scargill generated overwhelming support for himself both when elected as President of the National Union of Mineworkers in 1979, and again in pursuit of the national mineworkers' strike of 1984/85.

John F. Kennedy conducted both his election campaign and the years of his Presidency based on his personality – his charm, his freshness, his vitality, his appearance and looks – rather than his expertise and potential for running the country.

Adolf Hitler had great personal presence with which he generated both pride and identity among the German nation of the 1920s and 1930s.

Margaret Thatcher fought the 1979 General Election in the UK, not on the basis of detailed and well analysed policies, but rather on the slogan 'I will make Britain great again.'

Charisma and the force of strength and personality both attracts and repels (this gives full meaning to the phrase 'magical personality'). Strong personalities are not 'all things to all people'. Examples indicated in each of the Boxes in this section have attracted fierce condemnation and criticism and strong feelings of rejection, as well as great loyalty and identity.

Charisma is also very brittle. Once the personality is breached – once illusions of strength, confidence and capability are shattered, strong negative feelings invariably come to the fore. The leader who fails to deliver what she promised or who fails to save the organisation that she was brought into lead is thus rejected in this way.

BOX 9.6   Charisma (2): Rejection

Examples again abound.

Arthur Scargill is still held in high regard by a majority of his Union members. When he became President of the National Union of Mineworkers in 1979 he had over 300 000 members. In 1996 the Union had 11 000 members. For most of those lost along the way extreme disillusion has set in.

The USA has had great cultural and national problems reconciling the glamour and the martyrdom of John F. Kennedy with subsequent revelations about his private life, the activities of the rest of the Kennedy family, and possible Mafia connections.

The entire civilised world has turned on Hitler and everything that he built following the brutality of the way in which his armies fought the Second World War and also the great evil perpetrated in the concentration camps.

The validity and extent of Margaret Thatcher's political legacy to the UK is coming under increasingly heavy scrutiny. In 1996, and within her Party, she still remains an influential figure.

■ Trait theories

This approach is taken to identify the traits, attributes and characteristics that are present in effective and successful leaders. The problem with this is immediate; identifying those attributes present in all leaders.

Handy identifies three only: above-average intelligence; a good measure of initiative; and a high level of self-assurance. He is also the first to point out that possession of these three do not in themselves make one a good leader.

On the other hand, to try to identify all those qualities necessary to carry out the complex and sophisticated range of tasks and activities indicated above (and emphasised in the note on CEs) is so broad as to be meaningless.

Other studies bring different angles to bear on this. Peters and Austin entitled their book *A Passion for Excellence; The Leadership Difference.* They identify (Box 9.3) a long list of attributes present in leaders which they compare and contrast with converses that are not to be found in genuine leaders but which may well be found in administrative and bureaucratic functionaries who have acted as substitutes for genuine leadership over the post-war period.

P. F. Drucker identified high principles of conduct and responsibility; high standards of performance (in whatever sphere and in whatever ways that was measured); and respect for staff both as people and as workers.

Glass identified characteristics of confidence; appreciation of people (again in both personal and operational terms); personal and professional tenacity; excellence in communication and listening; approachability; and resilience.

The great value in identifying such characteristics and attributes is that if it can be done successfully the following great benefits accrue:

- if they are attitudes, values, beliefs and personality traits then potential leaders and managers can be tested for these at the selection stage;
- if they are skill, knowledge and behaviour-related they can be taught to those who exhibit 'potential' and who have other organisational and operational attributes that may be required by the organisation in question.

More generally, it is plainly essential to have some means of identification of the attributes required by those who are to direct organisations.

Trait approaches provide a useful starting point. This is their great strength and attraction. The weakness is where these attributes become cast in stone and become immovable or an organisational nostrum ('all our leaders/managers/supervisors have quality x'). Organisations that take such an approach at least acknowledge that there is a fundamental difference between carrying out a job and organising, leading and directing others in the carrying out of it.

■ Style theories

The rationale for studying management styles is that employees will work better for managers who use particular styles of leadership than they will for others who employ different styles (see Table 9.1).

It is usual to classify leadership styles on an authoritarian–democratic continuum (see Figure 9.2). There is a body of evidence also that relates high levels of success of business and work, job satisfaction and employees, and fewer disputes and grievances to the participative and consultative end of the continuum.

Much of the basis for this is to be found in the Theory Y concept of McGregor (see Box). Other studies that tend towards this view include those of Blake and Mouton (the managerial grid) and Likert (System 4). From a different standpoint this is also supported by the view that effective working methods and participative styles of management feed off each other: that each improves the other. There is also a measure of support for this view in the Excellence Studies (both UK and USA).

There are caveats, however. Any management style must be supported by mutual trust, respect and confidence existing between manager and subordinates. If these qualities are not present then no style is effective. There must be a clarity of purpose and direction in the first place, and this must come from the organisation. Participation can only genuinely exist if this clarity exists also; it cannot exist in a void.

The factors are interrelated. Account must also be taken of the fact that where leadership style is to be truly democratic, the decisions and wishes of the group must be accommodated, whatever is decided and whether this is

Table 9.1   Leadership and management styles

Autocratic (benevolent or tyrannical)	Consultative/participative	Democratic/participative
1. Leader makes all final decisions for the group.	1. Leader makes decisions after consultation with group.	1. Decisions made by the group – by consultation or vote. Voting based on the principle of one person one vote; majority rules.
2. Close supervision.	2. Total communication between leader and members.	2. All members bound by the group decision and support it.
3. Individual member's interests subordinate to those of the organisation.	3. Leader is supportive and developmental.	3. All members may contribute to discussion.
4. Subordinates treated without regard for their views.	4. Leader is accessible and discursive.	4. Development of coalitions and cliques.
5. Great demands placed on staff.	5. Questioning approach encouraged.	5. Leadership role is assumed by Chair.
6. Questioning discouraged.	6. Ways of working largely unspecified.	
7. Conformist/coercive environment.	7. Leader retains responsibility and accountability for results.	

'right' or 'wrong' in terms of the demands of the work and the pressures of the wider environment.

The relationship between the leader, the work, the group and the environment may also be represented as:

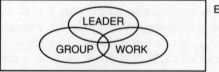

The factors also conflict with each other. The end result is the identification and adoption of a leadership style that is considered suitable for the matters in hand, taking into account the range of elements that each factor brings with it to the given situation.

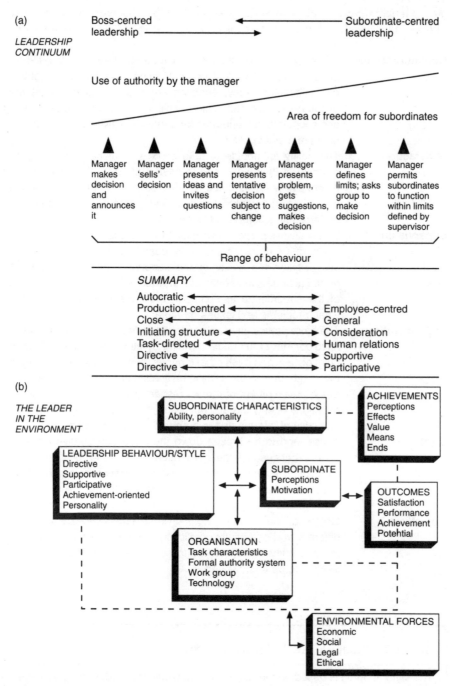

(a)

LEADERSHIP CONTINUUM

Boss-centred leadership — Subordinate-centred leadership

Use of authority by the manager

Area of freedom for subordinates

| Manager makes decision and announces it | Manager 'sells' decision | Manager presents ideas and invites questions | Manager presents tentative decision subject to change | Manager presents problem, gets suggestions, makes decision | Manager defines limits; asks group to make decision | Manager permits subordinates to function within limits defined by supervisor |

Range of behaviour

SUMMARY

Autocratic ↔
Production-centred ← → Employee-centred
Close ← → General
Initiating structure ← → Consideration
Task-directed ← → Human relations
Directive ← → Supportive
Directive ← → Participative

(b)

THE LEADER IN THE ENVIRONMENT

SUBORDINATE CHARACTERISTICS
Ability, personality

ACHIEVEMENTS
Perceptions
Effects
Value
Means
Ends

LEADERSHIP BEHAVIOUR/STYLE
Directive
Supportive
Participative
Achievement-oriented
Personality

SUBORDINATE
Perceptions
Motivation

OUTCOMES
Satisfaction
Performance
Achievement
Potehtial

ORGANISATION
Task characteristics
Formal authority system
Work group
Technology

ENVIRONMENTAL FORCES
Economic
Social
Legal
Ethical

Figure 9.2   Leadership spectrum

The participative/consultative style is supported by the work of Likert (see above). The benefits that are held to accrue from this are set out below.

Communication   Two-way communication is a key feature. There therefore exists a general basis of mutual understanding. This leads to problems being identified early, enabling steps to be taken before they become dramas and crises. This also enables understanding and support to be generated for particular activities and a mutuality of interest established.

Satisfaction   The ability for people to take some part in the structuring and ordering of their work, and to have a measurable autonomy and responsibility for its outcome enables them to push and develop their jobs to greater limits and to identify potential for the future and preferred directions and choices.

Supervision   This is always present. In participative situations this is not close or coercive or domineering. It is based on mutual interest and accessibility: the ability of the supervisor to identify and take remedial or developmental action where necessary; and the ability of the subordinate to approach the supervisor with confidence when problems and issues do arise.

Understanding   The more participative and open the style adopted, the greater the development of full understanding by all involved of each other's point of view and each other's hopes, aims and aspirations. Again, this contributes to the early identification of problems. It also leads to the development of mutual respect and trust, the ability to ask questions openly of each other and the development of a general mutuality of interest that is both positive and productive.

Barriers   These tend to be broken down the more participative the style. This is because of the generation of mutuality of interest and direction. It is related to the volume and quality of communications. It also constitutes much of the groundwork that enables a general fairness and quality of interest for all involved to be generated.

Objectives   Organisational, group and individual objectives are invariably different and potentially conflicting. Participative styles are more likely to bring these out into the open, enabling the mutuality of interest to be emphasised.

BOX 9.7   Leadership and Management Style

The style adopted is based on the relationship between the leader, the group, the task and the work to be carried out, and the nature and pressures of the wider environment.

The Leader

1. Preferred position on the autocratic–consultative–participative–democratic continuum. This is partly related to the personal comfort of the leader, partly to the nature of the task and partly to the desired relationship with the group. There may also be environmental pressures: for example, the organisation may have a general preferred leadership style that leads to pressures to conform on those responsible for particular groups. Groups may also seek to influence the nature of the style.
2. Personal and professional relationships between the leader, the group and individual members.
3. Personal, professional and operational confidence related to the need to gain results from the group involved. For example, a highly experienced group may be left largely to its own devices once the broad nature of the work is understood. A new and inexperienced group may need strong and regular direction, work structuring and individual (as well as overall) schedules and targets.
4. Mutual confidence, trust and respect based on the effectiveness of the general relationship between the leader and the group, and the leader's confidence in the capabilities of the group to get the work done.
5. The leader's own expertise and the extent to which this is valued by the rest of the group. Related to this is the nature of the leader's contribution to the group's effectiveness and whether he participates in the task or remain responsible purely for its coordination and control.
6. Visibility and accessibility, both in relation to the leader's own preferred autocratic–consultative–participative–democratic position and also in terms of the needs and wants of the group.
7. Psychological distance. To an extent psychological distance exists between leader and group in all situations because of the fact of the leadership position. In terms of style, this refers to outward manifestations and trappings such as the use of first names the creation of ranks and the nature of accessibility. This may be reinforced by the presence of physical barriers such as the leader having his own office, whether this is near to or far from the rest of the group, the presence of a secretary as a filter or barrier, the use of appointment systems and trappings such as expensive furnishings only available to the leader.
8. The leader's moral and ethical position and his set of personal and professional values.

The Group

The influence of the group on the preferred or desired leadership style derives from the following.

1. The extent of their need to participate. This may be professional, psychological or both. There is a general need for some measure of

psychological involvement by all people, in all situations. The greater the level of the technical or professional expertise present within the group, the greater the need to influence the shaping and direction of the work in hand.

2. Their confidence in each other. A greater level of structure, order and direction is required the more disparate the group elements. Trust, harmony and confidence, on the other hand, tends to lead to mutually supportive relationships and pressure on the leadership to concentrate on other things.

3. Their confidence, expectations and identity with the leader.

4. Familiarity with the given ways of working. If people are used to working in particular ways, they will expect this to continue unless a new approach is demonstrated to bring additional benefits. Groups used to a high level of autonomy, would have to be persuaded of the additional benefits that a highly visible and involved leader may bring before accepting this as the preferred way of working.

5. The size of the group involved.

6. Past experiences. The extent to which the group has been successful operationally, and a behaviourally satisfactory place in which to work.

7. Current and historic reputation. For example, a group with a bad reputation requires a form of leadership to lift morale and to raise its reputation in the wider organisation.

8. The mixture of expertise brought to the group and the need for cohesion in pursuit of the task.

9. The personal agenda of group members and the need for these to be harmonised with the overall purpose.

10. The values, moral and ethical positions adopted by the group and its members.

11. The need for support and contact with the leader and the nature of the support and contact required.

No group operates effectively in a void. All require some form of direction, support and a point of authority, wherever in the autocratic–consultative–participative–democratic continuum the leadership style is to be placed.

The Task

The features of the task that affect leadership style are as follows.

1. The nature and complexity of the work, and the mixture of expertise that this brings to the group. Leadership style is also affected by factors such as whether the work is routinised or pioneering, predictable or unpredictable, open-ended or closed, and has easily identified measures of success and failure.

2. Timescales and time pressures. In particular, short-term pressures lead to autocratic and structured approaches to work.

3. Routinised elements of work. Those elements of work that are routinised have to be structured and dealt with quickly. There are thus likely to be structured and directed elements in any situation.
4. The technology used and the effects that this brings to the ordering and structure of the work. This includes time pressures, operational structures and work organisation. The more dominant the technology, the greater the likelihood that the work will be highly structured.
5. Task priorities, the demands for work and the sources of those demands, both inside and outside the group.

Environmental Pressures

These are:

1. The structures and systems of the organisations, its overall culture, values and attitudes, reporting relationships, *realpolitik* and overall leadership style. The style adopted by managers in relation to particular groups and activities has to be capable of harmony with the rest of the organisation.
2. Wider legal, social and ethical pressures, the values of the community and environment in which activities are conducted.
3. Pressure for results in terms of volume, quality and time. These have to be reconciled in turn with budget and resource constraints and the agenda of other individuals and groups.

BOX 9.8   Group and Task Management

Features of leadership style related to the particular demands of group and task management may be identified.

The Group

Effective attention to the group is based on:

- interest in, and support of, subordinates;
- high-quality communications, listening to group members, being easy to approach, being understandable, keeping people constantly informed of group and individual progress, making people feel at ease, building confidence;
- identifying areas for remedial action and taking this based on an approach and attitude of development and improvement rather than punishment;
- creating an atmosphere of trust, honesty, openness, warmth and rapport;
- creating high morale and taking steps to motivate and encourage;
- valuing the contribution of everyone on a basis of equality;
- the role of leader as the group's servant and facilitator, responding to requests from members, and being the group's lobbyist and advocate;

- expressing appreciation, giving praise where it is due;
- the development of positive group relations, both personal and professional;
- consultation on changes and participation in change processes.

Ineffective attention to the group is based on:

- ruling with an iron hand;
- punitive approach to problems, apportioning individual blame;
- criticising others in public;
- seeking scapegoats from among the group;
- insisting that everything is done the leader's way, refusal to explain actions, refusal to consider other points of view;
- lack of general consideration and empathy;
- negative approach to relationships.

The Task

Effective attention to the task is based on:

- understanding of the requirements and nature of the work, and the application of expertise and equipment to get it done;
- planning ahead and scheduling, dividing and allocating the work;
- making expectations clear and understood;
- stimulating enthusiasm for the work, encouraging and helping people to get it done;
- giving clear direction on volume, quality and deadlines;
- setting priorities;
- ensuring that people harness their capabilities and work to their limits;
- managing the work pressures, identifying the required levels of effort, assessing points of stress and strain;
- monitoring and evaluating task performance and group output;

Ineffective attention to the work is based on:

- lack of clear purpose, aims and objectives;
- lack of clear planning and scheduling, letting the work drift;
- lack of appropriate technology, equipment and expertise;
- letting people do work in ways that they think best without monitoring and evaluating performance;
- the allowance of interruptions and diversions.

The clear requirement for a complete and effective style of management is attention to both group and task.

Overemphasis on the group – employee-centred leadership – is likely to lead to general feelings of comfort but a lack of attention to the work. It may also lead to group-think and lack of consideration of its relationship with the wider environment.

Overemphasis on the task – job-centred leadership – invariably leads to feelings of dissatisfaction among the staff. This is brought on by general perceptions that they are unvalued and that they are merely instruments in the pursuit of output. Expertise and attention is therefore required in both aspects, and this has then to be integrated with the nature of the style adopted.

BOX 9.9   Leadership Style: A Military Example

'You cannot expect a soldier to be a proud soldier if you humiliate him. You cannot expect him to be brave if you abuse him. You cannot expect him to be strong if you break him. You cannot ask for respect and obedience and willingness to assault hot landing zones, destroy dug-in emplacements if your soldier has not been treated with respect and dignity which fosters unit and personal pride. The line between firmness and harshness, between strong leadership and bullying is a fine line. It is difficult to define, but those in authority who have accepted a career as a leader of men must find that line. 'It is because judgement and concern for people and human relations are involved in leadership, that only people can lead and not machines. I entreat you to be ever-alert to the pitfalls of too much authority. Beware that you do not fall into the category of a little man, with a little job, with a big head. In essence, be considerate, treat you subordinates right and they will literally die for you.'

Source: General Melvin Zais: quoted in Peters and Austin (1985).

■ **Summary**

The fact that the group in Box 9.9 is highly structured and ordered does not alter the fact that a basic integrity of style is required. Whatever the nature of leadership style adopted, and whatever the distinctive features of the group and situation in which leadership is to be exercised, the following features must be present.

1. Value: behaviour that enhances subordinates, feelings of personal worth and esteem.
2. Interaction: behaviour that encourages members of the group to develop mutually satisfying relationships, respect, regard and confidence.
3. Task emphasis: behaviour that encourages the desire for high-quality performance and demonstrable success in the work that is to be done.
4. Work organisation: scheduling, planning, coordinating and controlling the work and the resources necessary to ensure that it is done.
5. Representation: acting as the group's advocate in the wider environment and ensuring that the achievements of the group are well understood and that the work conducted is in accordance with the overall demands of the organisation.

BOX 9.10   Blake and Mouton: The Managerial Grid

The managerial grid is a configuration of management styles based on the matching of two dimensions of managerial concern: those of 'concern for people' and 'concern for production/output'. Each of these dimensions is plotted on a 9 point graph scale and an assessment made of the managerial style according to where they come out on each. Thus, a low score (1–1) on each axis reflects poverty in managerial style; a high score (9–9) on each reflects a high degree of balance, concern and commitment in each area. The implication from this is that an adequate, effective and successful managerial style is in place.

Other styles identified are:

```
        9 |  Country                  Production
          |  Club 9:1                    Team
        8 |                               9:9
  C     7 |
  O       |
  N     6 |
  C       |
  E     5 |                  Balance
  R       |                    5:5
  N     4 |
          |
  F     3 |
  O       |
  R     2 |
          |
  P     1 |  Poverty 1:1              Task 9:1
  E       |
  O       +--------------------------------------
  P          1  2  3  4  5  6  7  8  9
  L
  E
(CONCERN FOR PEOPLE)
```

1. 9–1: the country club – production is incidental; concern for the staff and people is everything; the group exists largely to support itself.
2. 1–9: task orientation – production is everything; concern for the staff is subordinated to production and effectiveness. Staff management mainly takes the form of planning and control activities in support of production and output. Organisational activity and priority is concerned only with output.
3. 5–5: balance – a medium degree of expertise, commitment and concern in both areas; this is likely to produce adequate or satisfactory performance from groups that are reasonably well satisfied with working relations.

The 9–9 score is indicated as the best by Blake and Mouton. This illustrates the targets to be striven for and the organisation's current position in relation to each axis.

It also implies that the best fit is along the diagonal line: concern for the task and concern for the people should be grown alongside each other, rather than the one emphasised at the expense of the other.

The information on which the position on the grid is based is drawn from structured questionnaires that are issued to all managers and supervisors in the organisation section, unit or department to be assessed, and also to all their staff.

Source: Blake and Mouton (1986).

BOX 9.11   'Where Do You Want to Go for Your Holiday?'

A Swiss family of mother, father, son and daughter sit down in the spring to plan their family summer holiday. The father wishes to go to England. The mother wishes to go to Spain. The son wishes to go to Hungary. The daughter wishes to go to Southern Italy.

In the end they agree to go to Denmark. The result is therefore that nobody is going where they wish to go; the best that can be said for it is that it is a solution that nobody objected to. This form of participation carefully avoids addressing real issues, and genuine solutions to problems are not found.

There are also specific situations where a greater measure of direction is required. These include: emergencies; extreme conditions of hardship; and activities where there are prescribed and defined right and wrong ways of doing things. There is no scope for debate in these areas and the benefits to be accrued from participation have to be sought in other ways.

It should also be noted that many of the most currently successful organisations have adopted the consultative (rather than participative) approach. Again the benefits indicated in the participative or supportive style are to be drawn from elsewhere, and there is evidence (as we have seen and will see) that they are. The management style of McDonald's, Body Shop and Virgin Atlantic is prescriptive and directive. So also is that of Sanyo, Sony and Nissan. Many more traditional and older organisations, in both public and private sectors, are seeking to learn lessons from these model organisations and transform their management styles in pursuit of comparable results.

■ Vision and direction

Every leader and everyone who aspires to be in charge of anything and anyone must understand what they are leading or in charge of, where it is going and why and how it is to get there. This is built on a combination of situational knowledge and understanding, a view in the mind's eye of the direction to be taken for the future and a commitment to the matters in hand. This in turn gives life to the organisation that is created in its pursuit. This includes also all of the behavioural elements indicated in these pages.

The position of the leader in this regard is therefore critical. The vision and direction must translate into clarity of organisational purpose and from that into something which is capable of transformation into effective and profitable work. Such vision and direction is therefore to be seen as giving life to what is both possible and profitable in a given set of circumstances.

It is also essential to recognise the limiting factors in each case. This includes environmental elements, events that the leader/manager can control and those that are outside this control.

This vision and direction must also be articulated in different ways so that people – employees and customers, and also the community at large, backers, markets and all the other stakeholders and potential stakeholders – can identify with it and ascribe to it and follow it.

■ Are leaders special people?

The question is asked by Huczynski and Buchanan in the form 'Are leaders special men?' By this stage the answer must be an unconditional yes. There is nothing special in this answer; the question could just as easily be varied to 'Are clerics special people?' or 'Are engineers special people?' or 'Are cooks special people?', and the answer in context would still again be an unconditional yes.

The specialisms of a leader cover the areas indicated: traits and characteristics; levels and nature of understanding; qualities of mental toughness and resilience; clarity of purpose; precise and well developed style; and skills. It is then necessary that these are able to be translated into operational qualities. This is the basis upon which contingency approaches to leadership are developed.

■ Contingency approaches

Contingency theories of leadership take account of the interaction and inter-relation between the organisation and its environment. This includes the recognition, and accommodating of, those elements that cannot be controlled. It also includes recognising that those elements which can be controlled and influenced must be addressed in ways that vary in different situations; the correct approach in one case is not a prescription to be applied to others. In each case, therefore, there is a constant interaction between the leader's job and the work to be done, and between this and the general operations of the organisation in question.

The concept of contingency approaches to leadership was first developed by F. E. Fiedler in the 1960s. Above all, his work identified situations where both directive and participative styles of management worked effectively. The directive style was found to work well at the extremes, where the situation was either very favourable to the leader or very unfavourable.

'Favourable' was defined as a combination of circumstances where: the leader was liked and trusted by the group; the task was clearly understood, easy to follow and well defined; the leader had a high degree of respect within the group; the leader had a high degree of influence over the group members in terms of reward and punishment; the leader enjoyed unqualified backing from the organisation.

'Unfavourable' was defined as the converse of this; and also where the task was not clearly defined, or where the work was to be carried out in an extreme environment (discomfort, working away from home).

In either extreme the structured, prescriptive or directive approach was found to work well. In the former, the group would accept it because of the high general level of regard; in the latter, it brought at least a measure of order and clarity. Indeed, to be too participative in the latter extreme may be regarded as compounding the uncertainty and therefore as a sign of weakness and ineffectiveness on the part of the leader.

Adair identified three variables in any working situation. These are: the task; the team or group; and the individuals that make up the team. They are defined as unique; as having dual relationships; and as being fully interactive. The job of the manager is to harmonise the three in productive activity. This is therefore concerned with the reconciliation of differences, attending to personal goals and ambitions, team maintenance and production and output scheduling. This has all to be carried out in an organisational setting that is infinitely variable and developing and above all unique.

Each may be:

Effective }
Ineffective } dependent upon their application and appropriateness to given situations

This was developed into a three-dimensional (3D) model, as on p. 268, by W. Reddin.

Appropriate, effective

Bureaucrat Low concern for both task and relationships; appropriate in situations where rules and procedures are important.

Benevolent autocrat High concern for task, low concern for relationships; appropriate in task cultures.

Developer High concern for relationships and low concern for tasks; appropriate where the acquiescence cooperation and commitment of the people is paramount.

Executive High concern for task, high concern for relationships; appropriate where the achievement of high standards is dependent on high levels of motivation and commitment.

Inappropriate, ineffective

Deserter Low concern for both task and relationships; the manager lacks involvement and is either passive or negative.

Autocrat High concern for task, low concern for relationships; the manager is coercive, confrontational, adversarial, lacking confidence in others.

Missionary High concern for relationships, low concern for task; the manager's position is dependent on preserving harmony and there is often a high potential for conflict.

Compromiser High concern for both tasks and relationships; manager is a poor decision maker, expedient, concerned only with the short term.

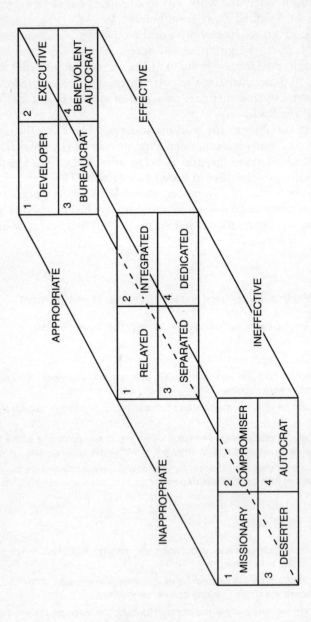

Purpose: The middle set of boxes identifies the four archetype leaders of Reddin's theory. These archetypes may then be translated into APPROPRIATE EFFECTIVE or INAPPROPRIATE INEFFECTIVE personal types.

Figure 9.3 W. Reddin: style of management behaviour

■ Best Fit

This is a summary view: that is, that all leadership theories have a contribution but that none by itself is the right or complete answer.

The Handy model of best fit relates the leader, the subordinates, the task in hand and the environment. These elements are both interactive and mobile.

This must be developed further. For example, if the group is ineffective it becomes easy to state 'best fit was not achieved' without necessarily carrying out any further investigation – which is very superficial.

Handy describes this as consisting of:

- support-behaviour that enhances group members' feelings of personal worth;
- interaction facilitation which encourages members to develop mutually satisfying and supportive relationships;
- goal emphasis which is behaviour that stimulates desire and drives for excellent operational performance;
- work facilitation, which is the classical management activities of scheduling, co-ordination and planning.

Peters states that to this may be added the need to nurture qualities of flexibility, commitment, responsiveness and drive. This is achieved by a combination of direction and support on the part of the leader, and is the responsibility of anybody who conducts any form of leadership or supervision.

Furthermore, in many parts of the Western world there has emerged a consensus culture. In its widest terms this means that people need and want and are entitled to know where they stand – so that they may consent to work and understand the basis on which this consent is requested or demanded.

Best fit is therefore a form of 'the organisation in its environment' approach to leadership: a super-contingency approach. It recognises the need to translate qualities and attributes into situational applications; and that each approach to leadership has a contribution to make.

■ The complexities of leadership

When the position of leader/manager/supervisor is taken on, certain assumptions are made and certain roles are adopted.

■ Assumptions

Leaders act in the name of the particular organisation, department or function. They therefore have a degree of power, influence, authority, responsibility and accountability. This is to be used in the pursuit of effective leadership performance. These may be enhanced, diminished or withdrawn by the organisation at any time (in Western organisations, this is usually, but not always, as the result of some form of consultation or appraisal of performance).

Leaders must be acceptable to all those with whom they come into contact. This applies both inside and outside the organisation. The range and complexity of relationships that they must develop are dependent on this.

Leaders have certain clearly defined tasks, activities and directions. They also have a sphere in which their personal judgement and initiative are to be exercised. This includes the qualities of flexibility, dynamism and responsiveness. It also includes characteristics of honesty, trustworthiness and integrity.

Leaders must have a working knowledge and understanding of the tasks being carried out by those in their sphere of influence. This does not mean being a technical expert. For example, managers who have secretaries cannot always type, but they must understand what typing is, how long typing takes, what is an acceptable level of performance, what is an acceptable level of presentation, what is the best and most suitable machinery on which typing is to take place, and so on; this extends to all spheres of activity. Where there is no such understanding dysfunction always occurs.

■ Functions of leaders in organisations

This is a general list of these functions. They may be found in all directorial, managerial and supervisory roles to a greater or lesser extent:

- setting, agreeing and communicating objectives;
- providing suitable equipment, resources and environment to enable people to meet their objectives;
- monitoring, evaluating and reviewing performance, appraisal of groups and individuals;
- giving feedback;
- setting standards of attitude, behaviour and performance;
- solving problems, both operational and human; administering rewards and punishments wherever necessary; dealing with grievances and discipline;
- organising and harmonising resources;
- ensuring inward flows of materials;
- ensuring that deadlines for outputs are met;
- taking effective decisions;
- developing the capabilities and performance of the group and its members;
- developing the efficiency and effectiveness of the group and its output;
- figurehead and representative roles inside and outside the department;
- parenting role.

It is clear from such a list that much of the leadership function of managers and supervisors is behavioural. Those aspects which are not overtly so still require attention to the behavioural aspects. For example, creation of an effective working environment requires consideration of such matters as personal proximity; organising work requires an understanding of the best ways to organise people to ensure that output is as good and as high as possible over long periods of time. From this, a further range of leadership qualities required in managers may be developed.

Empathy	Understanding the reactions of people to particular requests, situations and problems; understanding and sympathising with their point of view; the ability to identify with the likes, dislikes, aspirations hopes and fears of the group and its members.
Communication	In clear and straightforward terms, and in the language of the receivers.
Equality, evenness and fairness	Arising especially from the performance, monitoring, problem-solving, rewarding and punishment elements.
Creativity and resourcefulness	In developing the work and the staff involved; and in developing effective and positive relations with those from outside the group or department.
Attention	The active participation and involvement of all aspects of the direction of the work, of the functioning and interest of those carrying it out and in those external factors that affect it.

The following is a useful summary of the relationship between leadership and management.

■ **Roles**

□ *Figurehead*

The leader is the organisational figurehead: its human presentation to the rest of the world. This may be purely ceremonial involving the individual concerned in pleasantries, photo calls and general relationships with backers at gatherings such as the Annual General Meeting, or it may be a full-scale media role involving regular press, television and radio appearances, both as organisational advocate and professional expert. It may include public relations duties, walkabouts, attendance at fêtes and parties. It may include attendance at sectoral conferences, think-tanks, committees and working parties. In all cases both the presence and the authority of the leader in question is enhanced and given substance by the organisation that she represents. She turn adds substance, credibility and confidence to the organisation by the way in which she represents it.

□ *Ambassador*

Closely allied to the figurehead role is that of being the organisation's ambassador. Representing the organisation in many of the situations described above is often fully ceremonial. Representation at trade fairs, taking part in tendering processes, developing networks of other powerful and influential people (especially in government departments and, for global and multi-national companies, this means the world over) is all part of the leader's function. At lower levels of the organisation and within organisations this role involves looking after the department's interests, developing networks and clusters, taking steps to ensure harmony of working arrangements with other departments and within the organisation at large.

□ *Advocate*

This is where both the above are developed into a subjective, unbiased approach. At the macro level this is in the advocacy of the organisation, often at someone else's expense. Internally this may involve competing for resources, or defending a member of staff against attack from elsewhere within the organisation.

□ *Cheerleader*

This is where the leader boasts of the organisation (or department), achievements, expertise, capabilities and results. This is for any reason whatsoever. It covers the complete spectrum. It may be a part of the operational process of gaining resources for the department. At the other extreme, it may be the celebration of a particular success either by an individual or the department at large. As well as personal appearances this includes such things as appearances in organisational newsletters, giving presentations, trade press features and other photo opportunities.

□ *Defender*

Reference has been made to the defender role above. This comes into full being where there is some form of crisis or problem to resolve. It happens, for example, where there is a dispute between a member of staff and someone from another department; or a serious customer complaint. In this case the leader must balance the enduring and absolute obligations to the member of staff with the need to resolve the issue to the satisfaction of all concerned. This is dealt with elsewhere in the book; from the leadership point of view, two absolutes exist. The first is that under no circumstances does the leader abdicate responsibility; the other is that under no circumstances is a sacrificial lamb to be offered up for the purposes of appeasing a powerful or cantankerous member of the organisation, or customer.

□ *Prioritiser*

This role occurs on both the operational and behavioural fronts. It is a combination of assessing and judging both workload and *modus operandi* in ways that reconcile demands of the organisation, customers, clients and community with the internal factors of team and individual maintenance, development and growth. This involves, above all, a high level of development of the helicopter role, the overview of the organisation/division/department in its wider context. It also requires a level of 'prevoyance', anticipating issues that are likely to arise and having approaches in place to deal with them when necessary.

☐ *Maintenance*

Handy calls this the General Practitioner (GP) role. The following strands may be distinguished. There is the daily maintenance, which is the equivalent of dealing with odd aches, pains and sprains. There is the preventative maintenance, such as the continuous improvement of the work, working environment and procedures and practices that in turn continuously enhance the working life of all concerned. There is the breakdown maintenance which concerns the handling of crises, blow-ups and storms in a quick and effective manner. There is the consultative and check-up function which is an integral part of performance appraisal, development planning and constant improvement, and a part also of the generation of both a personal and professional relationship between the leader and his people.

☐ *Managing by walking about*

The output of this role is visibility, almost tangibility. The reality behind it is above all concern for the staff, both general and specific. The converse – not walking about – enhances and reinforces any feeling that may already exist of alienation, isolation, distance and lack of direction. Lack of visibility also generates doubts even where they were not hitherto present.

This occurs, for example, when a visible manager is replaced by one who is invisible. Again, the converse is true: the general morale of department/division/organisation in question always rises when an invisible manager is replaced by one who does walk about.

☐ *Model*

Leaders set models of role, style, standards, attitudes and behaviour for those who work for them. If the leader shows qualities of commitment, enthusiasm, energy and honesty these may be expected and are likely to arise in subordinates.

This extends to all aspects of leadership. The German people and institutions adopted the characteristics and attitudes of militarism and mastery that were preached by Hitler and the Nazi leadership in the 1930s and 1940s.

It also extends to general organisational behaviour and the reactions and responses of individuals. This is often graphically illustrated when human error is found to have been the cause of a major disaster (see Box 9.12). In these situations, the individuals concerned have invariably reacted as they perceive their superiors would have done. They may also have allowed the conditions to build up, thus creating the potential for disaster on the basis that nobody in authority seemed to think it important enough to consider.

Attitudes and values are also reinforced by the leader as model, whether these are established and nurtured by the leader or allowed to emerge among the group undirected.

BOX 9.12   Disasters and the Model of Leadership

In 1987 the *Herald of Free Enterprise*, a car and passenger ferry, operating between the ports of Dover, Calais and Zeebrugge, sank outside Zeebrugge Harbour, Belgium, with the loss of 200 lives. The cause of the disaster was water rushing in through the bow doors which had been jammed open. The ship had put to sea before the doors had been closed. The inquiry into the tragedy described the ship's owners, Townsend Thoresen, as a company 'riddled with the disease of sloppiness'. Nobody had thought it important enough to check or ensure that the doors were closed before the ship set sail. A key finding of the inquiry report was that the staff had behaved in ways that they perceived that they were required and expected by the organisation's top managers.

In 1988 there was a serious fire at the underground station at King's Cross, London; 31 people died. During the inquiry it came out that the conditions and circumstances which caused the fire were known to present and had existed for a long while. They had constantly been reported by safety representatives and committees over a period of years. Particular attention had been drawn to the wooden escalators, the build-up of oil and rubbish underneath these and the fact that travellers were allowed to smoke on the underground system. Nothing was done about this. In the end the fire caused by a cigarette dropped on to the floor which set fire to the rubbish that had accumulated and which, in turn, set fire first to the escalator. This then spread to the rest of the station.

In each case, the way in which those directly concerned reacted reflected the model behaviour inferred that had been established by those at the top of the organisation and responsible for its direction and activities, and the standards by which these were to be conducted.

■ **Summary**

Thus is illustrated the complexity of the overall role of leaders. In their own particular sphere they are the ring masters. This is quite apart from any particular knowledge or aptitude for the task in hand (as we have repeatedly made clear). The role elements indicated here are essential to the successful and effective leadership and direction of whatever level. To be an effective leader there is an overwhelming responsibility placed upon the individual to adopt these roles and the responsibilities inherent within them. It is also incumbent upon the person concerned to develop any of the qualities required in which they are not proficient.

■ Measures of success and failure

When the performance of leaders is being assessed it is again necessary to look at both the simple and the complex. In simple terms the view is taken (as with anything else) of measuring performance against pre-set objectives and the extent to which these were achieved. In practice, measurement of the leadership task and function is more complex. There are hard and soft elements. The hard elements will normally indicate quantifiable targets (to produce a return of x per cent; to generate y pounds in income; to reduce costs to z pounds; and so on). The soft includes measures of confidence, respect, loyalty and identity.

■ Confidence

Thus, the Chair of a publicly quoted company must maintain the confidence of the world's stock markets. If he does not, the share price falls. If this continues and the share price continues to fall whatever the activities and directions proposed by the CE in question, he will normally leave. This may also occur as the result of a bad set of company figures, either for a particular period or on a more continuous and long-term basis.

Confidence may also be lost among other backers and stakeholders. The leader in question may lose the respect and regard of the staff (as the result of some dishonest, expedient or unjustifiably punitive action, for example).

He may lose the confidence of the markets in which business is conducted. This occurs, for example, if a product is launched during his tenure which subsequently fails commercially, has a bad image or which it becomes apparent is unsafe or dangerous.

The converse of this is 'leaving a void'. This is where the confidence and identity of the organisation with the leader are fully integrated. Any question of the leader departing is therefore viewed with great alarm. For example, commentaries on the Virgin Group always include questions of 'What happens to the organisation if anything happens to Richard Branson?'

Confidence is only maintained through honesty and integrity. Where the leader (of anything) is caught lying the clear, instant and unambiguous message given out is that 'She is a liar.' Any subsequent dealing or transaction with this particular individual is therefore invariably prefixed by questions of the extent to which they may be trusted. It is in turn exacerbated during briefings for those who are to be involved with her along the lines of 'Don't believe a word she says' and 'Get something in writing and get her signature'.

■ The complex view

Measures of success and failure will also address the question of what else was achieved during the particular period of office. The direction taken may have opened up a great range of subsequent opportunities and a part of this measurement will relate to the extent to which these were exploited.

This can also be seen in the complexity indicated. The hard targets may be achieved, for example, but only at the expense of the soft (the destruction of staff relations, motivation and morale). Conversely a superbly integrated and supportive group may be built which never actually produces anything of substance. The targets that were set may turn out to have been unmeasurable, hopelessly optimistic or, conversely, far too easy. In the latter case in particular it is both easy and dangerous to indulge in an entirely false sense of success.

The legitimacy of the objectives and performance targets must also be generally and constantly questioned. To return to the hard examples quoted above, increases in output, profit and cost effectiveness by x per cent should always be treated with scepticism. They assume that the basis on which the percentage is calculated is legitimate and valid. They assume that this constitutes the best use of organisation resources. They assume (this especially applies to public services) that adequate and effective activity levels can be maintained.

It should be clear from this that the setting of organisation performance targets is a process capable of rationalisation and founded on the understanding of general organisation requirements. In the particular context of leadership, it should be clear also that ultimate responsibility for the success/failure in achieving these targets rests with the leader.

■ Conclusions

When studied in this way it becomes clear that, for all its dependence upon quality, styles, roles and assumptions there is much in the concept and content of leadership that can be pinned down fairly precisely. We have said little about appearance, manner or bearing: that is, the extent to which individuals look the part, sound the part, act the part (anything, in fact, rather than being the part). Instead, it is clear that there is a substantial body of knowledge and expertise upon which to draw both in the assessment of what leadership is, and also in the identification of who is to make a good leader (and who is not). There are lessons here for those in charge of organisations and personnel and human resource professionals. It is possible to take positive, informed and enlightened steps towards the successful and effective identification, development and appointment of the right people for these positions.

It is also clear that leaders are made and not born. People can be trained in each of the qualities and elements indicated so that (as with anything else) they may first understand, then apply, then reinforce and finally become expert in these activities indicated. This is understood to be on the same basis as aptitude for anything else, however. Not everyone has the qualities or potential necessary in the first place. There is nothing contentious in this: not everyone has the qualities or potential to be a great chef, racing driver, nurse or labourer, and in this respect leadership is no different.

■ Questions

1. What are the key attributes of a good leader? Give examples that illustrate these. To what extent can effective leaders lead in any organisation or situation; and to what extent is their effectiveness limited by the constraints in which they find themselves?
2. To what extent may the last three UK Prime Ministers be considered successful? Identify the criteria and means by which they are judged, and state whether or not you think these are valid and reliable.
3. What is the role of organisational leadership in a crisis or disaster?
4. Devise a leadership training programme for junior managers and supervisors with aspirations to become more senior. This should be of 6–12 months' duration. It should indicate aims and objectives, content, learning methods and the means by which success/failure would be judged and evaluated.

CHAPTER 10

Teams and groups

■ Introduction

Teams and groups are gatherings of two or more people that either exist or are drawn together and constituted for a purpose. This purpose is understood and accepted by all those involved, and may be:

- largely social – sports and leisure clubs;
- work or task oriented – workplace groups, committees, task and project groups, other *ad hoc* but organised gatherings;
- based on the norms and expectations of society – above all the family (nuclear and extended);
- based on the beliefs and values of the members – churches and religious groups;
- based on the expertise of members – the professional bodies, legalised associations;
- mutual interest: trade unions; also hobbies and interests.

Joining organisations and their departments, divisions, functions, locations and activities also constitutes team and group membership.

In society, people become members of groups and teams from an early age and move into and out of these throughout their lives. Very young children often go to play groups. A child may belong to the cubs or brownies, and then move on to the guides and scouts because there is an age barrier to membership of each. More generally, belonging to a school class or school sports team constitutes group membership. The process of belonging to, and joining and changing, groups is established at an early age and is part of the wider and general socialisation process. By the time of joining a workplace this is well understood.

Additionally, groups may usefully be defined as one of the following.

Formal	Constituted for a precise purpose. Formal groups normally have rules, regulations and norms which support the pursuit of that purpose. Formal groups also normally have means and methods of preserving and enhancing their expertise. Moreover, there are likely to be means and methods that enable people to move in, contribute and move out of a given group.
Informal	Where the purpose is less precise but still clearly understood and accepted by all involved. A card school falls into this category, as does a Friday night gathering of friends and colleagues at the bar.

Psychological   Viewed from the point of view that membership is dependent upon people interacting with each other, being aware of each other, and perceiving themselves to belong.

Groups may be distinguished in these ways from general gatherings of people drawn together for a more general purpose: for example, queuing to pay at the supermarket or waiting for a bus or train. Even in these circumstances a group identity may start to form. If the queue takes a long while to clear or if the bus or train is late, people start to form an identity, at least for the moment, based around the particular set of circumstances. This may lead to the constitution of a more enduring group for the future (a travelling group on the train, for example).

From this, an initial general set of group characteristics may begin to be identified.

1. The ability of each member to communicate with every other member of the group.
2. A collective identity based on a combination of the circumstances and environment in which members find themselves.
3. Shared aims and objectives: in the examples indicated above, these are the ability to travel and arrive at the required destination; the expectation (hope) that eventually those present will be served by the cashier at the supermarket; and the need to pass the time involved productively and comfortably in the activities indicated (that is, waiting and travelling).
4. Roles and structure: again in the examples indicated these may be: a joker; the finder of a compartment in which to sit; the provider of newspapers and magazines; and so on. The leadership structure may begin to be based around one who makes suggestions: 'Why don't we move to another queue/call the supervisor?'; 'Why don't we bring sandwiches/tea/ beer/cards?'; and so on.
5. Norms and rules: personal behaviour starts to become modified as a result of membership of the group. Smokers may resist or curtail their habit when in the presence of group members; patterns of dress may start to emerge. This is the general basis on which organisational groups are structured and developed.

■ Purpose

Organisational groups are constituted for a purpose, to meet a set of aims and objectives. These purposes generally fall into one of the following categories:

*   distribution of work, by department, division, function, location, skill, aptitude, expertise and quality;
*   controlling work, through the placing of managers and supervisors at the head of teams and groups of people constituted for the purpose of conducting work;

- project work and problem-solving, often constituted on an *ad hoc* basis and for the life and duration of the specific matter in hand (though there are certain circumstances were this leads to future activities);
- creative activities, brainstorming, information pooling and gathering, the generation of bursts of energy and enlightenment in response to given issues;
- to conduct inquiries into past activities, both successful and unsuccessful;
- to investigate and resolve conflicts, grievances, disputes and arguments between individuals and groups;
- clusters: of persons of the same profession or occupation from different departments; of equivalent levels of expertise in different fields; of equivalent rank (for example managers and supervisors); for the purposes of exchanging and gathering general information and knowledge; and a far wider understanding of the total organisational and professional picture;
- to take responsibility for the direction and management of a particular organisation's activities and services;
- to coordinate and harmonise sets of activities often from different sources, functions, departments, divisions and expertise;
- to implement initiatives, directions, policies, strategies and decisions;
- for other specific organisational matters, especially health and safety, staff relations and consultation.

Whatever the purpose, more precise characteristics and factors are required if the group is to be successful and effective.

■ Work groups and the individual

Work groups serve organisational purposes and provide a useful and effective means of dividing and allocating tasks. Individuals have a high propensity to work in this way. As stated in the introduction movement into, around and out of groups is a pattern of general behaviour learned and instilled from a very early age. Belonging to work groups therefore, is a means of satisfying social and affiliation needs long since learned while present within the organisation.

Through membership of work groups individuals also seek the following:

- distinctive work roles within which they can be comfortable and happy, and which satisfy their feelings of self-esteem;
- to establish a self-summary and self-concept which can be presented both to others in the work group and also to the world at large;
- contribution to productive, positive, profitable and effective activities (this in itself leads to satisfaction and feelings of personal success and raised levels of self-esteem);
- the ability to fulfil personal aims and ambitions which normally have to harmonised and entwined with those of a particular organisation.

These reasons for belonging overlap and conflict. Group norms and processes may also create distinctive pressures on individuals to perform in given ways, at certain speeds and to adopt given patterns of behaviour. This creates conflict between the requirements of the organisation, the group and the individual.

■ Conformity

This also indicates the pressure to conform. In many cases the individual must either conform to the group norms or be expelled or rejected.

If individuals choose not to conform they may be ostracised. Others in the group may choose not to work with them, either out of choice or because of group pressure placed on them to conform. These individuals may themselves be threatened with rejection or expulsion.

Conformity is therefore a very powerful pressure. It is a critical part of the norming process (see below). It also affects both the nature and the effectiveness of the performance of the group. Conformity may lead to group-think and the bunker mentality (the strength and belief in the world according to the view held by group members).

■ Group responsibility

Handy states that: 'Groups take riskier decisions than the individuals that comprise them would have done if they had been acting independently.' They behave more adventurously.

Fear of non-conformity also contributes to this. When a newcomer joins a group he is normally willing and eager to accept its norms and rules. A range of research underlines this.

The Milgram experiments of 1974 were based on the question:

'Would you torture someone else simply because you were told to do so by a person in authority?'

The experiments involved volunteers acting as 'teachers' of those trying to learn word pairs. If the subject got the pairs wrong the 'teacher' administered an electric shock. The shocks increased in intensity the greater number of mistakes that were made.

In fact, no electric shocks were administered. However, the volunteer 'teachers' nevertheless pressed the switch that supposedly gave the shocks when directed to do so by someone 'in authority'.

Defiance only occurred when the subject was first encouraged to do so by 'rebellious elements' drawn from among the other group members. Little defiance was exhibited by volunteers working alone.

Philip Zimbardo (Zimbardo *et al.*, 1973) created a simulated prison to observe the impact that the adoption of roles had on individual and group behaviour.

The group of volunteers were divided into two sub-groups, prisoners and warders. Within a very short space of time each adopted the expected, desired or inferred behaviour of their role. Thus the warders became aggressive, domineering, even bullying and violent. The prisoners at first became cowed and submissive. Later they sought ways of escaping. After 36 hours one prisoner left the experiment suffering from a nervous breakdown and 3 more followed during the next three days. Others promised to forfeit their fees for taking part in the experiment if only they were released.

■ Groups and violence

Conclusions drawn from among others, the Sharon Tate murder by the Manson gang in Los Angeles in 1973, and the rape by a gang of middle-class youths of a female investment banker in New York City in 1989, reinforced this view of the pressure to conform. The pressure of social disapproval on anyone who objected to the activity was likely to extend to violence against themselves if they did not take part.

This also helps to explain the behaviour of Nazi SS guards in concentration camps during the Second World War. They were mostly not psychopaths, but rather members of regiments (groups) with roles and tasks assigned to them. They had both the need to belong and to do the job well. The work in hand was ordered from a higher authority and 'had to be carried out'.

Tasks, achievements and pressures to conform were present. So also was shared responsibility. It also underlined the Milgram and Handy views in this way: while this was not adventurous behaviour, people nevertheless would act as members of groups in ways in which they would never dream of as individuals.

■ The creation of effective groups

Tuckman (1965) identifies four elements.

Forming The coming together of the individuals concerned; beginning to learn about each other (personality, strengths, capabilities); assessment of the group purpose; introduction to the tasks, aims and objectives; initial thoughts about rules, norms, ways of working and achieving objectives; initial social and personal interaction; introduction to the group leader/leadership; acquiring and setting resources; constraints, drives and priorities.

Storming The first creative burst of the group; energising the activities; gaining initial markers about its capabilities and capacities and those of its members; creating the first output and results; mutual appraisal and assessment of expertise and process. Initial conflicts tend to become apparent at this stage, together with the need for means for their resolution. Opportunities and diversions may also become apparent. Conflicts between group and personal agenda start to emerge.

Norming
The establishment of norms, such as the behavioural boundaries within which members are to act and operate; the establishment of rules and codes of conduct that underline and reinforce the standards set by the norms. By doing this the group provides itself with means of control and the basis of acceptable and unacceptable conduct, performance and activities.

For rules and norms to be effective they must be clear, understood and accepted by all. They must be capable of doing what they set out to do. They must reinforce the mutuality, confidence and integrity necessary to effective group performance.

Performing
The addressing of matters in hand; attacking the tasks to be carried out; getting results; assessing performance. This includes attention to group effectiveness and cohesion, as well as absolute performance measures: the two are invariably entwined.

This has to be seen as a process rather than a linear progression, a series of steps and stages. For example, early successes in the life of the group may strictly belong under 'performing' but are nevertheless essential to the gaining of mutual confidence, trust and reliance which are integral to effective 'forming'. Regarding this as a process also underlines the need for attention to the behavioural as well as operational aspects (see Box 10.1) – especially group maintenance.

BOX 10.1 Foundation of Corporate Norms

A person seeks to belong to peer groups wherever they congregate; this includes in organisational and corporate surroundings.

The tendency towards exclusivity exists in open-ended and corporate situations where people come and go. The formation of groups is influenced by the fact that fellow workers have been thrown together from the start in overtly unnatural mixes. At a large cocktail party groups will drift together and apart without constraints, but in a company people with different backgrounds and views are forced to work together and form groups. The bigger the company and the wider the range in social attributes of individuals, the better the chances are that there will be numerous groups with tight-knit and defensive norms.

Where both formal and informal norms co-exist, as they do in companies, the informal norms transcend the formal. This leads to what has been called the 'shadow organisation', in which the apparent management structure is actually superseded in importance by the mesh of group-norm dictates.

Individuals will go to extreme lengths to live up to the expectations placed on them by others, even doing things that in other circumstances they recognise as going counter to their own best interests, their characteristics, their normal standards of ethics and behaviour. They can persevere in this behaviour however with the easy rationalisation that 'Everybody else is doing it.'

Norms-imposed habits are lasting. Even when the original members of a group have disappeared, and/or when the norms themselves have lost their original purpose, there will be strong norm remnants unthinkingly respected by new members.

Negative norms cannot be changed unless the norm follower is made aware of their existence because most people respect and go along with the norms quite unconsciously; this is reinforced by pressures to conform.

◼ Issues facing work groups

The following is an indication of the main issues facing work groups:

- atmosphere and relationships:
  the nature of relationships; closeness, friendliness, formality and informality;
- participation: the nature and extent to which participation is to be allowed;
- understanding and acceptance of aims and objectives, and the commitment required for this;
- availability, access and use of information;
- means for handling disagreements and conflict;
- means and methods of decision-making;
- evaluation and appraisal of member performance;
- evaluation and appraisal of group performance;
- expression of feelings: how this should be done, the consequences of this, whether penalties (formal or informal) are to be issued and, if so, by whom;
- leadership: relating both to the leadership of the total group and also to the individual tasks for which it has been constituted;
- maintenance activities: including the development of group members and the bringing in of new and fresh talents and expertise as and when required;
- achievement and success;
- coping with failure.

◼ Adjourning

It is usual to add a fifth element signifying the end of the group. This is where the group disbands because the task is completed and there is nothing else for it to do; or because it is told to do so; or because it is broken up on the orders of a higher authority (for example, a site or operational closure).

In any case, for all but the smallest of groups and the shortest of life times, people leave groups and others join. Part of the adjourning element therefore

Effective Groups	Ineffective Groups
• Informal relaxed atmosphere	• Bored or tense atmosphere
• Much discussion, high level of participation	• Discussion dominated by one or two people
• Tasks, aims and objectives clearly understood	• Discussion often irrelevant, unstructured and away from the point
• Commitment of members of the groups to each other	• No common aims, objectives and purposes
• Commitment of members of the group to the tasks, aims and objectives	• Members do not value each other's contribution nor do they listen to each other
• Members respect each other's views, listen to each other	• Conflict is allowed to develop into open warfare; it may also be suppressed
• Conflict is brought out into the open and dealt with constructively when it arises	• Majority voting is the norm; pressure is put on minorities to accept this
• Decisions are reached by consensus; voting is only used as a matter of last resort	• Consensus is neither sought nor achieved
• Ideas are expressed freely and openly; rejection of ideas is not a stigma	• Criticism is embarrassing and personal
• Leadership is shared as appropriate; is divided according to the nature of the tasks; ultimate responsibility, authority and accountability rests with the designated group leader	• Leadership is by diktat and is issued by the group leader only
• The group examines its own progress and behaviour	• The group avoids any discussion about its behaviour
	• Lack of pride
	• Lack of identity

Figure 10.1 Characteristics of effective and ineffective groups

From: D. McGregor (1961)

includes reformation, integrating new members. A part of this is also concerned with celebrating the achievements of those who leave.

The final curtain

Owen (1985) finds that it is better for the future of the individuals concerned if a celebration of the group's achievements is held when it finishes. This gives everyone a point of reference for the work that has been done and the personal and professional commitment that was made. This is the equivalent to a funeral or wake, both mourning and celebrating its passing. Those involved then go on into the future, knowing that the past is complete and behind them and that a successful job was done with good people.

Group factors and characteristics

The main factors that affect the cohesion, behaviour and effectiveness of groups are as follows.

■ Size

This concerns the numbers of people involved and the nature of that involvement. Some authorities have tried to identify the optimum size for work groups. This has to be seen in the context of the nature of the task to be carried out: if a particular process needs two or fifteen people then this is the optimum size in the circumstances.

BOX 10.2   Group Size

There is a range of factors to be taken into account here. There are some absolutes: the size of a tennis doubles team is two; of a rugby team fifteen. In work situations the technology used may determine that a group size is three, eight, 30 or whatever.

In general terms there is a balance involved between size, contribution and participation: the larger the group, the greater the range of expertise and quality is drawn in, but the lesser the chance of a full participation by individual members.

Larger groups also have a greater risk of splitting into sub-groups (either formal, based on the work, or informal, based on workstation location, friendship, or the establishment of common bonds and interests). Total group identity may then become diluted. The interaction between the sub-groups becomes a barrier to the progress and achievement of the full group. The sub-groups create their own barriers themselves, especially if these have become constituted around the distinctive expertise of members. If this is in high demand by the rest of the main group, the sub-group establishes its own filter and priority systems based on its preferences and criteria.

On the other hand, smaller groups tend to avoid the sub-grouping effect; they may, however, develop a group identity so strong that it tends to lead to belief in its own infallibility and indispensability.

The size of any group therefore has clear implications, both for their management and leadership and also for participants if these pitfalls are to be avoided.

■ The size and scale of the task

This is a prerequisite to the effective gathering and constitution of the group required for its completion. This will normally also include specific aims and objectives, timescales and deadlines.

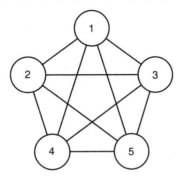

Figure 10.2   Simple sociogram of a 5-person group

■ **Nature of the task**

This affects group size as stated. If a task is complex, those required to do it may also bring a mixture of experience, expertise, approach and attitude which have to be harmonised in pursuit of the given purpose.

This includes the nature of the technology used and the degrees of expertise required to use it. It also includes the physical lay-out of the work and the environment created for this. Both have effects on the interaction of group members by virtue of the expertise brought in to use the equipment and the physical location and proximity of individuals.

■ **Individual roles**

Everyone brings a distinctive expertise and contribution to the work groups to which they belong. All contributions must be valued and this includes any intermittent or occasional involvement. Everybody involved should receive the same quality of respect and concern and be treated fairly and equally, whatever the nature of their contribution or expertise.

Distinctive and highly prized expertise is to be harmonised and integrated with the overall purpose.

■ **Individual ambitions and aspirations**

Everyone brings their own purposes to work groups to which they belong. Group memberships enhance and retard career paths, personal ambitions, pay and rewards and personal development. People are drawn towards those groups held in positive and high esteem, and away from those where the converse is true.

■ Group culture

This is the way in which group members think, believe, feel and act with and towards each other while they are members of the given group.

People have respect and admiration for the work of others in some cases, for example, but no social contact with them otherwise. This is especially true of (real or perceived) high-performing, task-oriented groups, whose whole energies are put into achievement, excellence and work quality. The culture is built on this, and anyone who does not perform to the required level (or is perceived not to do so) is likely to be rejected by the others.

This was also found to be the case in the 'Affluent Worker' studies. The groups studied were low- to medium-performing only. Both volume and quality of work was variable and loosely defined. There was however a strong work group identity founded on the alienative nature of the work. Again, this extended to the workplace only. Members did not mix at all away from work.

■ Group norms

These relate to the means by which the group regulates itself and its activities. Norms consist of sets of expectations, pressures, controls and rules by which group members interact and harmonise with each other, and by which they are regulated.

Some norms are established by group leadership, especially those concerning absolute standards of behaviour and integrity. Others are allowed to emerge (meeting patterns, work deadlines). Others may be imposed by the group on itself (the lay-out of the work environment; use of first names).

BOX 10.3   Group Culture

Some archetypal variations in individual behaviour include the mild, pleasant and kind individual:

- who is good to the family;
- who becomes an aggressive demon on the sports field on a Saturday afternoon;
- who in the work role of CE displays both vision and ruthlessness;
- who swears liberally in management meetings;
- whose mother has heard, but simply does not believe, the swearing or ·aggression stories.

All of these variations are brought out by the individual's membership of the different groups indicated: the family, the sports club, the work place, committees and the extended family.

■ Motivation of members

This is based on the perceptions, expectations and aspirations that individuals had on joining the group and the extent to which these are satisfied. Members may submerge some of these for some time if they have joined the group because it is (or is perceived to be) a point on their path of progress. Otherwise, high levels of motivation are not to be sustained if these expectations are not met.

■ Group identity and spirit

This is a summary of the strength of respect and identity held by members for each other and for the group to which they belong. It is based on establishing a common interest in task achievement, and confidence in, and dependence on, the group members. It is underlined and developed also through the other factors indicated here all of which feed off each other. It is enhanced by the pride, esteem, attitudes and behaviour that members have in relation to their membership of the group and in respect of each other.

■ Leadership

The particular responsibilities of leadership towards the organisation and direction of groups concern the need for attention to the factors indicated here. In group situations, leadership is especially concerned with:

- management of the task: setting work methods, timescales, resource gathering, problem-solving and maintenance functions;
- management of the process: the use of interpersonal skills and the interaction with the environment to gain the maximum contribution from everyone involved;
- managing communications: between different work groups and sub-groups and the disciplines and professions involved to harmonise potential conflicts and to ensure that inter-group relations are productive and not dysfunctionally competitive
- managing the individual: making constructive use of individual differences and ensuring that individual contributions are both valued and of value;
- management style: the creation and adoption of a style that is appropriate and suitable to the situation;
- maintenance management: ensuring that both the effectiveness of the work and of the group itself are supported, appraised and developed;
- establishing common aims and objectives that are understood, valued and adopted by all group members;
- establishing shared values and absolute standards of honesty and integrity (see above);
- creating an effective and positive group and team spirit.

■ **Maintenance**

All groups must be maintained, and this extends to all aspects of their functioning. Members leave and their contribution has to be acknowledged. New people are brought in and are inducted into the ways of working, attitudes, values, norms and expectations that exist. Group members undertake personal, professional and technological development activities, project and other *ad hoc* work to develop the knowledge, experience and expertise available to the whole group. Means and methods of solving problems exist to ensure that when issues do arise they are dealt with early and effectively and with the minimum disruption to the group and its activities. Means of methods of performance appraisal – both for the individuals involved, and for the whole group – must be created and established and their results acted on; effective group appraisal should identify reasons for success as well as for failure and where problems lie.

■ The determinants of group effectiveness

■ The group itself

This is the extent to which membership satisfies the social and psychological needs of belonging, identity, pride and esteem anticipated. It also concerns the professional and operational reasons for belonging (the extent to which membership has furthered the individual's ambition, professional or technical development).

■ The work and tasks

This is the successful output, production and productivity of the group. Effectiveness depends partly on the results achieved; partly on the members' perceptions of their own achievements; and partly on the wider organisation view of these achievements. High levels of productivity and output are themselves a source of psychological satisfaction. Under this heading should also be included the resources, technology and accommodation necessary to carry out the task effectively. The group normally understands the effects on output where these are inadequate and that therefore the work cannot be completed to the desired standards anyway.

■ Procedures and processes

This is the extent to which the ways in which the group works enhance the work in hand and the behavioural strength of the group. The wrong processes and procedures are likely to get in the way of effective activities and diminish the regard that members have for each other because they hold up progress, divert and dilute resources and reduce the time available for task completion and group maintenance.

■ Leadership, direction and management style

This is based on absolute standards of honesty and integrity. It is developed in relation to the differing nature of group members, the mixture of expertise present, the work that is to be carried out and the maintenance activities required in support.

■ The synergy principle

This is the principle by which the different qualities, elements and expertise present are moulded into a cohesive unit in order to produce results that could not be achieved by members working individually.

■ Morale and satisfaction

This is monitored through the study of absenteeism, accidents, member turn-over and the ability to attract, retain and develop new talent. It is established and developed through a basis of full understanding of the tasks and activities to be carried out and fulfilling the expectations of group members.

■ Group ideology

This is normally based around concepts of participation, involvement and recognition of the value of the contribution that each member makes. It is underpinned by norms and rules.

On the other hand, a measure of conformity is normally expected of individuals by the groups to which they belong. This works best where the individual aims and objectives are capable of being harmonised and integrated with those of the group.

Individuals may also choose to belong to a group (or seek to join it) because of the strong and distinctive ideology. Trade unions and religious institutions are clear examples of this. Some organisations – for example, Body Shop, Nissan – also attract people because of their strong commitment to the environment or product and service quality.

■ Power and influence

This is the position of the group in relation to others in the organisation. It is based on both behavioural and operational factors.

The behavioural factors mainly concern the matters of relative respect and regard in which the group in question is held by others in the organisation. There are questions of perception also related, for example, to the extent to which the given group is seen or believed to be high status, a stepping stone on the path to success, or a cul-de-sac from which no one ever emerges with credit.

The operational concerns include the nature of the work carried out and the value that this adds to the organisation's activities. It also concerns the ability to command and wield resources and information.

There are also elements of *realpolitik* involved: for example, the ability to block progress, to filter resources and information, to determine the speed, volume and quality of work.

■ Factors outside the group's control

These include environmental pressures and changes; changes of organisation direction and priorities; organisational and operational *realpolitik*; and changed/imposed group leadership. Any of these may raise, as well as lower, the profile and status of the group and the importance and value of its work. The raising of the profile may not always be good: it may place hitherto unfelt (and unacceptable) pressures on members. The lowering of the profile may not always be bad: in the short term it may enable members to produce results without constant checks on progress being made from outside the group.

■ Group cohesion

Cohesive groups are most likely to be achieved if attention is paid to the division, allocation and structuring of work, the creation of a behaviourally suitable working environment, and the installation of a leader or manager who is aware of the pressures and potential problems and acceptable to the rest of the group.

1. **Division of work**: this is to ensure that capabilities and expertise are used to greatest effect. It also includes enabling people, wherever possible, to follow their personal and professional preferences as long as this can be offered to everyone. Unpleasant, mundane and routine tasks are also to be shared out on a basis of equality.
2. **The creation of a suitable environment**: as well as general suitability and the availability of required technology and equipment, this must include proximity wherever possible. Difference of location is a physical barrier to group identity and therefore effectiveness. This difference may be a matter of yards, or thousands, or hundreds of miles. A suitable environment is created only if this is first recognised and then underpinned with adequate and effective methods and systems of communication. This is to ensure that the physical barrier is surmounted by activities expressly designed to get over it.

Again, therefore, there are implications and considerations for those responsible for the organisation, design and management of groups (see Figure 10.3).

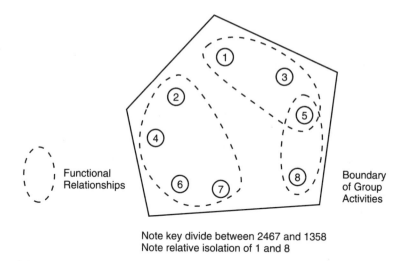

Note key divide between 2467 and 1358
Note relative isolation of 1 and 8

Figure 10.3 Group cohesion: sociogram of an 8-person group

BOX 10.4 Canteen Culture

This term is used to describe the non-formal, unofficial (and often unwanted) ways in which groups think, believe and act. It derives from unofficial meetings and interactions between members (for example, in the works or office canteen) where the real views, aspirations, attitudes – and prejudices – of those involved are nurtured and developed.

It is to be found in response also to the symbols and labels used: the managers' dining room, the officers' mess, the workers' cafeteria. These clearly differentiate between different grades and classes of staff. This reinforces group identity among those so labelled. It also provides exclusions and barriers to those who do not carry the particular label.

The canteen culture is often a very powerful organisational force, especially negative. Ways of working and patterns of behaviour are derived and developed according to the wants of the groups involved rather than the needs of the work groups of which they are also (invariably) members.

This culture is also used as a form of networking by people who wish to gain access to particular work groups, departments, projects and activities. They use these informal channels, rather than those devised by organisations if they perceive that these constitute the most certain routes of success and acceptance.

BOX 10.5　The Right Club

A variation on the idea of the canteen culture is that of 'belonging to the right club'. Those with aspirations to belong join the same sport, leisure and social clubs as those who hold influence in making appointments to particular groups. This also extends to membership of work interest and cluster groups within organisations and attending the local branch meetings of professional bodies.

Another derivation of this is 'the old school tie'. People who have received education at a particular school (especially public schools) or from a particular organisation (especially the army and armed forces) are deemed to 'have what it takes' to be a good and effective group member as the result.

Yet another variation is to be found in the stereotyping process: 'All Yorkshire people are dependable', 'All Lancashire people are strong', and so on.

In all cases the aspiring group members use these as the routes to entry rather than official channels.

BOX 10.6　Manchester City Football Club 1973

In late 1972, Manchester City Football Club had an excellent run of results. By early 1973 the Club was near the head of the football league and was widely expected to win the championship. The team was managed by Joe Mercer and coached by Malcolm Allison. There seemed no limit to the potential of the achievements of the team which had an excellent balance of star players (Francis Lee, Colin Bell, Mike Summerbee), journeymen and work horses (Glynn Pardoe, Wyn Davies, Willie Donachie, Tommy Booth, Ian Mellor) and long-serving and deeply loyal and committed members (especially Mike Doyle, the club captain).

The team did not win the championship that year. Reflecting on this, Joe Mercer said: 'The fact that we did not win was due to the purchase of Rodney Marsh [another star]. He came into the team in place of Ian Mellor. He was an incomparably better player than Mellor, but he upset the balance of the team.'

■ Groups

■ Creating an effective environment in which groups can operate

An understanding of this is critical to organisation success. The application of these principles will vary between organisations and situations and take account of the technology involved and the ways in which specific tasks are to be carried out. Within these boundaries, however, there is a range of issues that every organisation must address.

■ Principles

Standards of behaviour and regard must be established. These reflect the absolute and ethical standards to be established. They constitute the basis both of the professional working style that is to be adopted and of the nature of working relationships that are to be generated. It is also necessary to generate mutual personal regard between members. This covers the more general rights and wrongs and dos and don'ts of the particular situation.

■ Creativity and ideas

The key feature of the constitution of any group is its capacity for generating ideas. The means of doing this must be created. These include the constitution of regular meetings, brainstorming sessions and other forums for ideas. Anything that is creative and imaginative has to be encouraged. This is a reflection of the requirement for flexibility and control. Ideas have to be encouraged. Means by which these are to be assessed have also to be encouraged, but carrying neither penalty nor reward (this is a feature of implementation, not generation).

■ Control

This is essential as well. The requirement is to provide measures of progress, appraisal and performance and resource utilisation. It is also necessary to have means of performance rectification and sanction.

This must then be reconciled with the need for the total organisation to maintain its own control without creating huge administrative superstructures that lose sight of this purpose and create resource demands of their own.

Control is part of the group process. It is interactive and participative and only truly effective if everyone concerned is involved.

■ Consistency

This is required from two points of view. The first is in ensuring that all teams and groups within a given organisation receive the same equity and principle of treatment whatever their purpose or function. The other is in ensuring that all members of a particular group are treated with fairness and quality, the absolute standards indicated under the heading 'principles' above. A lack of fairness and consistency is one of the major causes of group malfunction.

■ **Support**

The relationship between an organisation and its groups is one of mutual support. The organisation needs its groups for effective, profitable and creative activity; the groups need the organisation for resources and a continuing base on which and from which to work.

This includes the establishment of appropriate communication and decision-making processes and reporting relationships. The outcome of the support for groups must be the elements of mutual trust, confidence and respect.

■ Group behaviour

The following forms of group behaviour may be identified.

■ **Conformity**

Conformity is the outward manifestation of a combination of behavioural, professional, organisational and operational activities. Its purpose is to ensure series and sets of standards and outputs, and to give the organisation in question and its groups their own distinctive identity and consistency.

Measures of conformity are plainly essential in certain regards. The universal use of organisational colour schemes, logos, slogans or staff uniforms is to give a strong distinctive and positive identity in regard to those who come into contact with the organisation. Organisational processes and procedures are devised to ensure that staff are treated with fairness and equity and that they receive equality of opportunity and treatment. They also ensure that customers receive clear and consistent messages.

In pursuit of this, standards of behaviour, address, attitude and performance are required and established. The organisation establishes norms, customs, modes of dress, modes of behaviour, attendance patterns, work manners, work organisation and performance measures of this work. The basis of all this is established at the induction stage and developed alongside other ways in which the organisation and its groups behave.

There is a clear relationship between the organisation and the individuals who work there. The individual has the basic choice of accepting these standards and norms, of complying with them or of rejecting them. Different measures and extents of conformity may therefore be established.

■ **Regimentation**

This is the coercive approach to conformity. This is imposed by the organisation or by parts of it on the staff concerned. It consists of requirements to adhere strictly to codes of practice, conduct, dress and address. It is most useful in dangerous and other extreme conditions where sets of series of behaviour can be devised in order to control the danger as far as possible and to provide step-by-step approaches as and when emergencies do arise. It is also used in more general organisation terms in military forces.

Moreover, it is to be found in those forms of organisation designed along strictly hierarchical lines where there are strict orders of progression from one position to the next, where promotion and advancement are based on loyalty and longevity of service, and where there are highly structured and restricted jobs, tasks and practices.

■ Internalisation

This is the receptive approach to conformity. In this, those working for the particular organisation adopt its attitudes, values and beliefs as their own. The interests of the organisation and its groups and those of the staff coincide exactly. There is an overwhelming responsibility placed on the organisation if this is what is required and/or if this is what happens in fact.

The attitudes, values and beliefs in question must be positive, beneficial, ethical and have a universal long-term interest. All of this is itself subject to interpretation by the wider society in question and by those in whose interest the attitudes, values and beliefs are engendered. The whole process is both subjective and highly corruptible. Examples of the extreme results of this include the Inquisition, Nazism, Pol Pot and the 'killing fields' of South-East Asia, and the ethnic cleansing of the new countries of the former Yugoslavia.

■ Compliance and acceptance

This is the recognition of the validity of the organisation's claim upon the talents and expertise of the person in question, and of the requirement to go along with this. It constitutes behavioural acceptance of the need to conform and a willingness to do this. It does not indicate anything deeper than this.

This is closely related to the discipline of the organisation. By accepting a job with the organisation, the individual accepts also any strictures and rule and regulations that may legitimately be devised and enforced in the pursuit of its purposes.

■ Eccentricity

This type of behaviour is not condoned nor encouraged, or rejected by organisations. Organisations are normally prepared and willing to accommodate eccentricity for its own purposes: for example, where particular individuals have rare or special skills that are required.

Forms of eccentric behaviour may be encouraged and nurtured by the organisation as part of its own creative processes. Research and development departments, for example, require creative and imaginative individuals, who defy and question conventions.

The main organisational behavioural problem is the extent to which such organisations are both prepared and willing to accommodate this behaviour. Eccentricity may be dysfunctional to the rest of the organisation. It may in itself create resentment among those in mainstream and steady-state mode departments and functions. It may create the perception (or indeed the reality) that eccentricity is tolerated in some parts of the organisation but not others.

■ Alienation

This is where an individual exhibits all the output forms required but works at the organisation without interest or identity in pursuit of his own aims and objectives. This form of industrial behaviour was widely acknowledged throughout the post-war boom of the 1950s. It was written up especially in the 'Affluent Worker' research of Goldthorpe *et al*. (1968). These studies demonstrated that those who worked in mass production and deskilled (and therefore boring) jobs would quite happily do so provided they received a standard of living which enabled them to live in some measure of comfort and to pursue interests away from the workplaces. There is a clear lesson here, therefore, for anyone who chooses these forms of work organisation in the provision of relatively high standards of wage.

BOX 10.7   Alienation

The classic form of this as indicated in the main text is that manifest in mass production situations. There is a wider context, however.

Inappropriate hospital management styles, for example, lead to the alienation of doctors, surgeons and nurses. The difference here is that those concerned fall back on their professions as their reason for being. They also use particular situations as the means to professional advancement, a stepping stone to the next post. They have no identity with their superiors in this situation.

■ Sources of potential group stresses and strains

These include the following factors:

1. The nature and mixture of the personalities involved and the nature of activities that are engaged in with the purpose of reconciling these.
2. The nature and mixture of the expertise and talent that is brought to the group by its different members. (This is especially important where some members of the group have expertise that is either rare or else of high price/high value).

3. Divergence of objectives between group members and between individual agenda and the objectives of the total group. This is inevitable; stress and strain comes about when these cannot be (or are not) reconciled.
4. The nature and mix of other and more general strengths and weaknesses that each of those involved brings with them to the group.
5. Means and methods of communication, consultation and participation; the availability of good quality information. Stress and strain is created when these are either inappropriate, inaccurate, dishonest or incomplete.
6. The changes in group composition and membership; changes in influence of particular members as the task unfolds; the bringing in of new members; the phasing out of those whose part of the task is done.
7. The clarity of purpose of the group.
8. Levels of confidence, trust, respect and regard held by each member of the group in regard to the others and of their position in the group.
9. The nature of the working environment, including ergonomic factors, technology, location and design of workstations and the physical distance/proximity that exists between group members. This also includes extremes of temperature, climate, discomfort, danger and location.
10. The form of management style adopted, its suitability to the situation and task in question and to the understanding of this on the part of all concerned. This includes means of communication and a nature of decision-making processes.
11. Levels of performance. Stress and strain is more likely to occur when the particular group is going through a bad patch or one that has no tangible result for a long period of time. It also occurs during levels of very high performance when individuals start trying to take credit for the team's total achievement.
12. Matters outside the group's control. To minimise the effect of these it is necessary to recognise what they are and the extent and frequency of their occurrence. Worrying about them is both unproductive and debilitating.
13. Team and group malfunction. Causes of team and group malfunction are as follows:

    (a) lack of clarity of purpose, direction, aims and objectives; and conflicting directions, aims and objectives;
    (b) lack of leadership and direction; inappropriate leadership style; extended and complex chains of command;
    (c) lack of resources; inadequate and inappropriate resources, including finance, expertise, premises and technology;
    (d) lack of mutual confidence, trust, respect and regard among group members;
    (e) lack of responsibility and autonomy (within the broadest context); lack of control; lack of ability to shape and influence its own destiny;
    (f) Inappropriate, convoluted, complicated administration, reporting relationships and procedures;
    (g) lack of balance of group maintenance and operational elements (what usually happens in this case is that the group spends all its time on its own development to the detriment and neglect of the work in hand);

(h) lack of wider regard and respect (on the part of the organisation and other groups) for what the group is trying to achieve, for its achievements, for its needs and wants;

(i) lack of recognition of progress and achievement; lack of measurement and assessment of progress and achievement;

(j) lack of ability to act as its own advocate, lobby, self-promoter;

(k) lack of interest in the work; lack of perceived respect and value of the work on the part of the wider organisation;

(l) lack of equality of treatment, value, regard and respect of group members; lack of equality of treatment of the group itself in regard to the rest of the organisation;

(m) lack of consultation, participation and involvement in the communication, decision-making and directorial processes;

(n) failure to play to the strengths and talents of group members; giving tasks to people who have no aptitude for them.

These elements may arise through neglect and indifference on the part of the organisation concerned. They may occur simply because the work of the group in question is a little way down the order of priorities (even though it is actually valued).

Dysfunction can also be engendered. This occurs in the worst forms of interdepartmental strife. It also happens where the organisation makes a point of moving its malcontents or failures to one particular location.

■ Team malfunction

Symptoms of group and team malfunction are as follows.

1. Poor performance in which deadlines are missed, output is sub-standard and customer complaints increase.

2. Decline: members decline or reject responsibility for their actions and for the group itself. They become involved in lobbying and seek to blame others for these shortcomings. The group breaks up into sub-groups and elites are created within the wider group. Individuals claim rewards and bonuses for team efforts. Scapegoating occurs, showing destructive criticism and dismissive behaviour towards others, both inside and outside the group.

3. Becoming involved in grievances with other group members; increases in the numbers of these; personality and personal clashes; overspill of professional and expert argument into personal relationships.

4. Increases in general levels of grievances, absenteeism and accidents; moves to leave the group.

5. Lack of interest in results, activities, plans and proposals of the group.

6. General attitude and demeanour that exists between group members; the general attitude and demeanour of individuals within the group; lack of pride and joy in the group; moves to leave the group again; difficulties in attracting new members to the group.

Some of these are clearly specific to group activities and functions, while others are more general symptoms that should be considered in the group context as part of the continuing monitoring of its effectiveness. Each gives an inlet for the person concerned with identifying and assessing trouble and potential problems with a view to tackling them.

Malfunction may also be caused as a result of the effects of an individual on the group.

■ Dominance and weakness

This sometimes occurs where one weak member is holding back the potential of the rest. It is much more commonly found where the group is dominated by one or two powerful individuals. This is an extreme form of the big fish in the small pond, akin to a shark in a goldfish bowl.

When this occurs malfunction is inevitable. The dominant individual either requires stronger support from the rest of the group or the broadening of horizons or to be replaced by another individual (often of lesser personality or talent but who is capable both of harmonising with the group and of excellent activity and a prosperous and harmonious existence within the given environment).

■ Personal issues

These cause malfunction when they are allowed to have an impact on the group. It occurs, for example, where two members have domestic, personal or social connections as well as a professional relationship. Problems occur when these affect the workings of the group.

This extends to the effects of personal problems and illnesses. These also affect performance and morale where they are allowed to dominate. There is a balance to be struck between clear obligations to support and care for one particular individual at the same time as maintaining group function and harmony.

■ Rejection

Malfunction is caused when individuals are rejected by the rest of the group. This occurs in two main ways. The first is where an individual is rejected because of an error that she has made and which is seen to be extremely costly or detrimental by the other members.

The other form occurs in relation to new members who are ostracised and given no chance to settle in and become effective. This happens for example where a much valued and respected (possibly also long-serving and popular) member has recently left and the replacement is forever being compared unfavourably with the previous incumbent.

■ Favouritism

This always arises as the result of bad leadership and management. The leader or manager in question identifies an individual whom they treat more favourably than the rest. The rest of the group find ways of coping with this. The most common form again is ostracism. The favoured individual may also be manipulated as a channel of expediency by the others (as a lobby for extra resources, for example).

■ Blame

This is where individuals blame the team or the group of which they are members for their own failure to progress.

■ Pecking order

One of the strategies for the management of variety of conflicts is giving everyone concerned the opportunity to do particular things (normally the most favoured or prestigious activities). When an individual does not get his turn he feels slighted and aggrieved.

■ Attitude and behaviour problems

This is where 'one bad apple affects the whole box'. The individual who takes no pride or joy in the work, no interest in the results and who is constantly critical or negative affects all the rest of the group. The manifestation of this is in absence, lateness, sloppiness of work, rudeness, negative criticism, grumbling and complaints.

■ Conclusions

The main lesson to be drawn from this is the need to recognise the range of things that affect group performance. They can arise at any time and very quickly. Those with responsibility for organising and managing groups will therefore constantly be on the look-out for these factors with a view to remedial action before they become problems or crises. This applies both to team performance and to team health, attitude and spirit. The task in this respect is both preventative and remedial. The preventative element is in the creation of an effective environment, procedures, practices and style that is suitable to the group and its activities. The remedial is based on the quick and effective diagnosis of problems when they do arise and on the generation of successful means of tackling these.

This is to be seen in the context stated at the outset of this chapter: teams and groups are to be seen as constantly devolving and developing, and dynamic. It is therefore impossible to have a range of prescribed approaches to be picked out in response to particular situations. Every situation will require treating on its own individual merits along the lines indicated, and identifying those elements, causes and symptoms of malfunction mentioned.

BOX 10.8   The 0.5% Rule

This is the rule that says that '99.5 per cent of people are penalised for the misdemeanours of the 0.5 per cent'. Rules and procedures are created with the stated purpose of standardisation of behaviour without reference to the fact that most people behave as they are required all of the time.

Thus, for example, when someone steals something, everyone on the premises is subject to searches and security checks. When someone is seen to be late arriving for work, sophisticated clocking-in and signing-in procedures are devised.

The certain result of this is the alienation of all those who do not steal and who do turn up on time. If there is a problem with an individual it is a problem that must be addressed as an individual issue.

There are also knock-on effects both ways. The more sophisticated the set of rules, the greater the length of time spent on them enjoying consultative, joint negotiating and other group management and industrial relations activities, and the greater the consequent waste of organisational resources. Conversely, if individual problems are dealt with on an individual basis by managers as and when they arise only, all the time energy and resources otherwise wasted is freed for other things. If the manager in question is doing her job properly misdemeanours happen only rarely and are dealt with quickly when they do arise.

Above all, either approach underlines the level of respect and regard in which the staff are held. The greater the level of this type of regulation and procedure, the lower the level of respect and regard. Above all, the converse is true: the fewer such rules and regulations, the greater the level of respect and regard in which the staff are held. In the latter case the staff are treated as adults and are much more likely to respond as such when required. The approach also requires that the general malcontent or criminal is dealt with on an individual basis. Rules are no substitute for judgement in any circumstances.

■ Problems with groups

Problems arise, above all, where the balance of attention to the group and to the task is wrong. In either case group output is affected. If the task is over-emphasised, effectiveness is nevertheless reduced because those involved become demotivated, pressurised, stressed and alienated. Group maintenance, which addresses each of the issues and ensures that they do not become problems is, therefore a key element in achieving successful operational output.

Overattention to the group itself leads to a reduction in importance of the task. It may also lead to group-think and the bunker mentality. The group begins to exist for the benefit of its members rather than the achievement of tasks. It may seek to redesign and reposition its aims and objectives and the work that it carries out to fulfil the objects and wishes of its members, rather than those of the organisation.

Other problem areas include the following:

1. Aims and objectives not being set and established clearly and accurately, leading to lack of understanding, clarity of purpose and direction.
2. Lack of common or mutual interest where it is clear that some members are present against their will; or where their own agenda and purposes are both overt and conflicting with those of the group.
3. Lack of recognition of the influence of constraints, especially related to resources and technology and the impact that these have on overall group effectiveness. As stated above, success in the task is a source of behavioural satisfaction. Where a highly committed group fails to achieve success because of a lack of resources, this leads to frustration and resentment.
4. Lack of clarity and consistency of direction, where what is expected of the group is constantly being changed and where these changes lead to many tasks being half completed or not completed at all. This is exacerbated where there is pressure put on the group by its customers and clients because of its inability to deliver its outputs successfully.
5. Lack of group identity or inappropriate group identity. This is found where an overstrong group identity emerges which leads to the concept of group-think indicated above.

Where there is no identity at all, a void exists in which members pursue their own agenda rather than the group's purposes. This is most likely to occur where there is no clarity of purpose or where this is inappropriate. It also happens where the leadership is not effective and where group members are subject to unequal or preferential treatment and where sub-groups are allowed to emerge.

Results achieved by the group also have a detrimental effect on identity and spirit. This is especially true where these are unvalued by the wider organisation or its influential members, or where these are for some reason impossible to achieve (for example, because of lack of resources or equipment).

BOX 10.9   Clarity and Consistency

A major demotivator of those working in education, health, social and other public services in the UK in the 1980s and 1990s concerned this. Reforms were introduced, amended, diluted and swept aside without any rational chance of success in the terms by which those concerned with the delivery of services would measure this. This led to both frustration and alienation on the part of persons with considerable professional expertise in the delivery of these public services.

For example, the UK Child Support Agency (CSA) was created in 1990 with the stated purpose of making recalcitrant parents pay a fairer measure towards the upkeep of their children. Rather than concentrating on those who did not pay, and could not be traced, however, the Agency first pursued those who could be traced and were paying, and often made them pay more than they were already (in some cases discounting and disallowing legal agreements and settlements previously made). The result of this was anger on the part of those members of the public affected, and frustration, resentment, stress and alienation on the part of those civil servants drawn in to work in the Agency.

Due to the lack of forethought and consequent failure to establish accurately the Agency's remit, it was certain not to succeed. Involvement with the Agency has also started to blight the careers of those in it, reducing their chances of progress and promotion in the civil service at large.

Much of this reflects the elements and characteristics of group effectiveness outlined above and the components of effective and ineffective groups (see Figure 10.1 above). It indicates key areas of both managerial attention and group members if things are not going well.

BOX 10.10   Committees

Committees are constituted for a variety of purposes. They are perceived to be representative and democratic and/or to bring together a range of expertise. All of this has then to be harmonised and directed at clarifying issues, managing and monitoring activities and solving problems.

Committees are generally very difficult to operate effectively. Their effectiveness is based on a clarity of purpose and agenda, leadership, size and mix of members, frequency of meetings and ability to deliver that which is determined by their deliberations. (For example, in many cases all committee members recognise the nature and extent of a problem, but stumble over proposals for its solution.) The committee may therefore be very effective at investigating an issue or clarifying a problem area, but have difficulty in getting any solutions that it proposes implemented. If the elements present on the committee are too disparate, there may also be problems with identifying the best way forward. Great care has therefore to be taken with their constitution if they are not to become sources of frustration for those people serving on them and who give up time, effort and resources to do so.

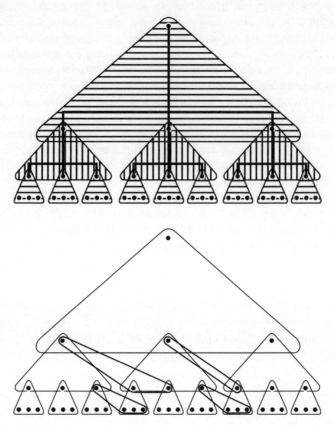

Figure 10.4   The linking pin model of Likert: the interrelationship of groups

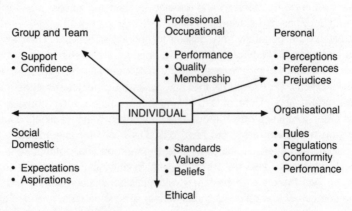

Figure 10.5   Divided loyalties

BOX 10.11   General Command Headquarters (GCHQ)

The UK GCHQ is at Cheltenham in Gloucestershire. It is part of the Ministry of Defence. It is used to monitor satellite communications passed all round the world; it was a key organisation in the gathering of intelligence and information during the Cold War. In 1983, following a spate of staff problems and industrial troubles, the government of the day issued a directive requiring all those working in the establishment to give up their trade union membership, which was considered in some quarters to be a feature and symbol of divided loyalties. A payment of £500 (later increased to £1000) would be made for this. Those not wishing to give up this membership would be offered transfers to other civil service activities if suitable moves could be found. If no appropriate transfer was available, staff members refusing to give up their union membership would be dismissed. In the event 14 members were dismissed. Appeals against the dismissal were rejected; their claims were also rejected by industrial tribunals and the UK Courts, though later upheld by the European Court of Justice.

The Group	The Task	The Environment
• Size	• Nature	• Norms
• Member characteristics	• Criteria for effectivess	• Expectations
• Individual objectives	• Salience of task	• Leader position
• Stage of development	• Clarity of task	• Intergroup relations
	• Choice of leadership	• External constraints
	• Choice of leadership style	• Pressures to perform
	• Choice of processes and procedures	
	• Motivation	
	• Productivity	
	• Member satisfaction	

Figure 10.6   The analysis of groups: the Handy model

BOX 10.12   The Trouble with Teams: Togetherness has its Perils

Peter Cook, a British satirist who died on 9 January 1995, loved to poke fun at British private schools and their cult of team spirit. But if you listen to management theorists you would think that these schools had unwittingly stumbled upon the magic secret of business success. With teams all the rage, management theorists are earning fat fees by proffering advice on how to build teams and how to inculcate team spirit.

   At first sight, the virtues of teamwork look obvious. Teams make workers happier by giving them the feeling that they are shaping their own jobs. They increase efficiency by eliminating layers of managers, whose job was once to pass orders downwards. They also enable companies to draw on the skills and imagination of the whole workforce instead of relying on specialists to watch out for mistakes and to suggest improvements.

Having started with corporate giants such as Toyota, Motorola and General Electric, the fashion for teams has spread rapidly. A recent survey suggested that cell manufacturing (in which small groups of workers make entire products) is being experimented with at more than half of America's manufacturing plants; and teams are growing more powerful as well as more numerous. Their task was at first to execute decisions under the supervision of managers, not to make decisions. The current fashion however, is for self-management.

Companies as different as Xerox (office equipment), Monsanto (chemicals) and Johnson & Johnsville Sausage (foodstuffs) are allowing teams to decide on everything from hiring and firing to organising the flow of work. At New United Motor Manufacturing (a joint venture run in Fremont, California, by General Motors and Toyota), teams of workers elect their own leaders and invent ways of improving quality and efficiency.

Hewlett-Packard, a computer maker, has gone even further in mixing the specialisms represented in single teams. Its teams bring together engineers, technical writers, marketing managers, lawyers, purchasing professionals and shop floor workers. At Corning's, a ceramics plant in Erwin, New York, teams are fed business information so that they can understand how their plant is faring in the market. Informed workers, it is assumed, are less likely to make unreasonable wage demands. Still it would not surprise every inmate of a British private school to learn that teams are not always flawless ways to motivate and inspire people. Like many management fads, the one for teams is beginning to produce its trickle of disappointments. A. T. Kearney, a consultancy that continues to favour teams, found in a survey that nearly 7 out of 10 teams failed to produce the desired results.

A common error, says A. T. Kearney, is to create teams instead of taking more radical decisions. In many businesses it is still more effective to automate work than to reorganise the workforce. Years ago, Sweden's Volvo was praised for introducing self-governing teams in its car factories at Kalmar and Uddevalla in order to make the work more interesting. More interesting it duly became, but also so expensive that the company was forced to close the experimental plants and concentrate production at Gothenburg on a traditional assembly line.

Even when creating teams really is the appropriate solution to a firm's problem, managers often make a hash of running them. A typical mistake is the failure to set clear objectives. Another is to introduce teams without changing the firm's patterns of appraisal and reward from an individual to a collective system. That can send the workforce fatally mixed signals: employees are expected on the one hand to pull together, but on the other to compete for individual rewards.

Teamwork, moreover, costs money, the biggest additional expense being training. Not unreasonably, members of supposedly self-managing teams start wondering how to manage. This gives birth to an epidemic of woolly courses on conflict management and stress resolution. Meetings swallow time as empowered workers break off from the tedium of making things and chat endlessly instead about process improvement or production imperfections.

Although many such courses are superfluous, advocates of team-based production can see that the best teams are made up of people with broad enough skills to step easily into each other's shoes. Providing such cross-training, as the theorists call it, is arduous. In some of the more complicated team structures such as those in chemical plants it can take team members 6–10 years to learn all the jobs they might be called upon to do.

However, the chief problem with teams is political. Almost invariably their creation undermines some existing distribution of power in a firm. Middle managers often see shop floor teams as a threat to their authority, and perhaps to their livelihoods. Many workers see teams as a source of division and a goad to overwork. On at least two occasions, American unions have used the National Labour Relations Act of 1935 which makes it unlawful for an employer to dominate or interfere with the formation or administration of a labour organisation to foil attempts to introduce teamwork.

Besides, although the cheery vocabulary of teamwork makes excitable use of words such as empowerment, teams usually replace top-down managerial control with peer pressure, a force that is sometimes no less coercive. 'People try to meet the team's expectations' says one worker at New United Motors in Fremont, 'and under peer pressure they end up pushing themselves too hard'.

Some workers may prefer being told what to do, shouldering the burden of decisions themselves. Those who welcome responsibility sometimes find it hard to discipline their wayward colleagues. And there is always the danger that teams will impose a deadly uniformity and stifle the special qualities of individuals. As many a graduate of Britain's private schools will tell you, such places have made little use of the brainy wimp who hated rugby and spent a childhood shivering on the sidelines. That, in a way, was Peter Cook's point, and one that management theorists have been slow to notice.

Source: The Economist, 14 January 1995.

■ Group development

The creation and formation of effective teams and groups is not an end in itself. To remain effective, cohesion, capabilities and potential must be maintained and developed. This takes the following forms.

1. Infusions of talent from outside, bringing in people with distinctive qualities and expertise to give emphasis and energy to particular priorities and directions.

2. Infusions of new skills, knowledge and qualities from within through the identification of potential from among existing members and giving them training and development, and targeted work that has the purpose of bringing out the retired expertise.

3. Attention to group processes when it is apparent that these are getting in the way of effective task performance; and attention to task performance when it is apparent that this is ineffective.

4. Attention to the relationship between team and task. This may involve using a good team to carry out a difficult or demanding task; or using the difficult and demanding task to build a good and effective team. From either standpoint, the results will only be fully effective if the task achievement is within the capabilities of the group. As long as this is so, the rewards of success are likely to contribute greatly to overall group performance, well-being and confidence among members.

5. Attention to team roles, both to build on strengths and also to eliminate weaknesses. This is likely to involve reassessing what the requirements and priorities are; reassessing the strengths and weaknesses of each individual; and possibly leading to reallocation or rotation of roles and infusions of new talent, either from within or without.

6. Attention to team roles and expertise from the point of view that different qualities, expertise and capability are likely to be more or less important at different phases of activity. This may lead to infusions again, or to the buying-in of expertise (for example, using consultants) on an 'as-required' basis. It may also involve the recognition that members of the group may need to be divested once they have made their particular contribution.

7. Recognising the concept of group life cycle. Akin to that of the product life cycle, it recognises points at which infusions and divestments may need to be made. It also recognises the more general requirements for re-energising, revitalising, rejuvenating – or even ending – again, along similar lines to products.

Other factors in group development include the following.

■ Starters

This refers to the extent to which new members are welcomed into the group and the steps taken to ensure that they settle in as quickly as possible, become comfortable and start to make a positive contribution to the work.

Insufficient attention to this – whether by accident, ignorance or design – is likely to cause dysfunction. It is certain to make the critical contribution of new starters less effective. This may in turn colour the perceptions of their capabilities by the rest of the group forever, making it certain that they will never be fully effective.

■ Leavers

This refers to the view taken of individuals when they leave the group. It includes the extent to which their contribution continues to be valued after they have left, and the prevailing attitudes towards both themselves as individuals, and their capabilities and achievements.

Some groups take a negative view of individuals who leave. This is likely to stem from feelings that the group itself is being rejected, which sometimes leading to a questioning of its value and worth among those who remain. It may arise also from envy on the part of those remaining where the individual is going on to demonstrably better things.

This negative view may also occur as a form of self-protection for those who remain behind. In order to help preserve the cohesion of those remaining, the leaver becomes 'the common enemy'.

■ Rejuvenation

This stems from a combination of realising that the group is under performing or under achieving, and the determination to do something about this. Successful rejuvenation normally comes about as the result of these factors.

1. General acceptance on the part of everyone concerned that this state of affairs exists.
2. Identity between members and within the group, together with a strong desire for it to succeed.
3. Universal acceptance of the way forward, whatever that may be. This is much more effective where it is agreed among the members than where it is imposed. If a particular course of action is clearly indicated, then effort must be spent in convincing everyone involved of its merits. A lesser course of action which has full support is often more effective.
4. Infusion of resources, such as skills, knowledge, qualities, finance and equipment, time and communications.

■ Reprocessing

This involves going through a version of the group cohesion process but with those already present. This can be seen as:

- reforming,
- re-storming,
- re-norming,
- re-performing.

It is most likely to be effective where the need for the group and its work is strong but where insufficient attention has been paid to group processes, so that identity is not strong and current levels of output are suffering as the result.

■ Recognition

This involves attention to the ways in which the work of the group is received. It is likely to be more of a problem where the organisation's style sets great store on recognition of achievement (rather than the fact of it), and also where there is a need on the part of group members for recognition.

Group development activities have their greatest effect when everyone is involved and where real problems and issues are addressed. The environment in which these take place is less of a problem than the content. If the content is artificial, then the effect may be counter-productive. In these situations members often feel that they are wasting their time. In the end, the binding element is the purpose for which the group has been created and this will ultimately be the measure of its net value, worth and achievements.

Team and group development and enhancement has the final purpose of increasing the potential for achievement and output, and of augmenting the existing levels of creativity, dynamism and performance in its pursuit. With this come development of the group itself, in terms of commitment, identity, involvement, ownership and participation.

■ High-performing teams and groups

The characteristics of high-performing teams and groups may be summarised as follows.

1. High levels of autonomy, the ability to self-manage and self-organise. This also includes team responsibility for self-regulation and self-discipline. It encourages the fast and effective resolution of problems and a commitment to dealing with issues before they become problems.
2. Clear and unambiguous performance targets, capable of achievement and related to overall organisation purpose; understood, accepted and committed to by all concerned.
3. Full responsibility for all aspects of production and output process, quality assurance, customer relations and complaints. Issues and problems are identified and addressed to the particular team so that improvements can be made directly without going through sub-processes and procedures.
4. Job titles do not include references to status, differentials or trappings, or other elements of psychological distance.
5. Team-based reward systems available and payable to everyone who contributed, based on percentages of salary rather than occupational differentials.
6. The open approach: to environment lay-out (no individual offices, trappings, barriers or other factors of physical and psychological distance); self-commitment for the whole team; open communication systems and high-quality communications; open approaches to problems and issues; open airing of grievances and

concerns (these are usually very few in such circumstances, so that when they do arise full attention is paid).

7. A federal relationship to the core organisation with reporting relationships based on monitoring, review and evaluation of production and output targets and other task-based indicators. General management style must be supportive rather than directive, bureaucratic or administrative.

8. Fast and easy access to maintenance and support staff to ensure that equipment breakdowns are repaired as soon as possible and that production levels can be kept as high as possible for as long as possible.

9. Full flexibility of work, multi-skilling and interchangeability between task roles. Group roles are assigned to people's behavioural strengths.

10. Continuous development of skills, knowledge, qualities, capabilities and expertise; continuous attention to performance quality and output; continuous attention to production, quality, volume and time; continuous attention to high levels of service and satisfaction.

11. High levels of involvement, confidence, respect and enthusiasm among group members, both towards each other and the work.

12. Attention to equipment and technology to ensure that this is suitable and capable of producing that which is required to the stated and expected standards of volume, quality and time.

13. Simple, clear and supportive policies and procedures covering organisational rules and regulations, human resource management and discipline, grievances and disputes.

14. Continuous monitoring and review to ensure that the intended focus and direction is pursued and that group activities are in accordance with this.

■ Conclusions

The characteristics and effectiveness of groups has been extensively researched and there is a measure of agreement around the critical elements and factors: clarity, conformity, harmony, achievement, spirit and maintenance.

The effective use of groups is a concern for all organisations because of the nature of work and the different skills, qualities, aptitudes and expertise that have to be harmonised. Some organisations have made this their central feature.

The Body Shop is created around a tribal culture, according to its founder Anita Roddick. The effectiveness of the company is dependent upon the adoption of this by all those who come to work for it. Those who do not share this vision do not stay.

Japanese employees introduce themselves by giving the name of their company first: 'I work for Honda', 'I work for Nissan.' The strength of team and group identity is with the company. This is distinct from the British, whose first identity is with their generic group or profession – 'I am a nurse', 'I am a bus driver' – rather than the company. This is sometimes perceived to lead to

Table 10.1   Archetype team members

Type	Symbol	Typical features	Positive qualities
Company Worker	CW	Conservative, dutiful, practicable	Organising ability, practical common-sense, hard-working
Chairman	CH	Calm, self-confident, controlled	A capacity for treating and welcoming all potential contributors on their merits and without prejudice A strong sense of objectives
Shaper	SH	Highly-strung, outgoing, dynamic	Drive and a readiness to challenge inertia, ineffectiveness, complacency or self-deception
Plant	PL	Individualistic, serious-minded, unorthodox	Genius, imagination, intellect, knowledge
Resource Investigator	RI	Extroverted, enthusiastic, curious, communicative	A capacity for contacting people and exploring anything new An ability to respond to challenge
Monitor–Evaluator	ME	Sober, unemotional, prudent	Judgement, discretion, hardheadedness
Team Worker	TW	Social oriented, rather mild, sensitive	An ability to respond to people and to situations and to promote team spirit
Completer–Finisher	CF	Painstaking, orderly, conscientious, anxious	A capacity to follow-through Perfection

Source: R. M. Berbin (1986)

divided loyalties (see Figure 10.5) especially where there is no clear set of priorities. By contrast, employees of both the Body Shop and Japanese companies place their organisations at the top of this list.

Japanese organisations reinforce this through the attention that they pay to the creation of work groups and the training of these once they are constituted, providing them with the best technology and equipment and in the selection of the right leader. Again, a contrast may be drawn: the leader of a Japanese work group must be acceptable to the group members. The leader of a Western group is likely to be externally appointed, based on his technological or professional expertise.

The creation of effective work groups increases the burdens placed on organisations and their managers in terms of attention to behavioural as well as operational factors. Successful groups come about as the result of a combination of the effectiveness of both of these elements. Both group members and group managers require the ability to think things through, develop and present arguments, make judgements and persuade others to their point of view. The reward to be gained by organisations are to be found in consistent and high levels of output delivered by committed people with a real concern for satisfaction and success. This is the rationale for constituting effective work teams.

■ Questions

1. What are the major disadvantages of committee work and how can these best be overcome?
2. What are the major symptoms of group-think or 'the bunker mentality'? What steps should organisations take (a) to ensure that these do not arise in the first place; and (b) to address them when they do arise?
3. Identify the main reasons why canteen cultures arise and the steps that organisations should take for dealing with them.
4. Identify the main roles and functions of group leaders. What are the best ways of (a) identifying these; and (b) training individuals to be effective group leaders?

CHAPTER 11

Conflict

■ Introduction

Conflict exists in all situations where individuals and groups are in disagreement with each other for whatever reason. This potential therefore exists everywhere, where two or more people are gathered together; a world without differences and disagreements is inconceivable! Much of the conflict in the world stems from the basic lack of recognition of this, and the inability to address it in ways designed to alleviate its effect or, better still, identify the positive and beneficial potential that is inherent in most situations.

Prima facie, therefore, the potential for conflict exists in all forms of organisation. It is essential that all those concerned with conception, direction and ordering of organisations understand its sources and causes, and are able to address these positively.

■ Levels of conflict

The following levels of conflict may be distinguished: argument; competition; and warfare. Argument and competition may be either positive, healthy and creative; or negative, unhealthy and destructive. Warfare is always destructive.

The nature, symptoms and causes must be understood and these then become a focus for management action in striving for productive and harmonious places of work.

It is useful, therefore, at the outset to establish the presence of conflict in organisations (as in all human situations). Conflict may be seen as positive and beneficial, a force capable of being harnessed for the greater good and contributing to organisation effectiveness. It is also clearly negative in many forms. Three distinctive variations on the theme are also apparent.

■ Argument, discussion and debate

This takes place between groups of two or more people and brings about (whether by accident or design) a better quality, more informed and better balanced view of the matter in hand. Provided that it is positive, the process of argument and debate leads to a better understanding also of the hopes, fears and aspirations of other group members. Furthermore, it can identify gaps in knowledge and expertise. This can then be remedied, either through training or the inclusion in the debate of persons with the required expertise. It helps in the

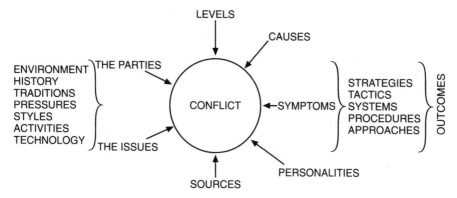

Figure 11.1 The nature of organisation conflict

process of building mutual confidence and respect. It also encourages individuals to dig into their own resources, expertise and experience and to use these for the benefit of all concerned. It helps to build group identity. It leads to a better quality of decision-making, and understanding and acceptance of the reasons why particular directions are chosen.

Argument, discussion and debate become unproductive if not structured. People must be clear what they are debating, otherwise they will inevitably argue about different things. At the very least this leads to group dysfunction and disharmony in the particular situation. The essence is therefore to be able to set out the desired aims and objectives of the discussion and to have available as far as possible all necessary information.

The form of argument must be capable of allowing people to express strongly-held views without sowing the seeds of potentially deeper and divisive differences. Attention is therefore paid to the behavioural as well as the structural side. An atmosphere of trust and confidence must be created if this is to be successful. People have to be supported in their views even if the group eventually decides to go in different directions.

Attention is required, therefore, to the outcome of the debate and the management of whatever is decided (this is always assuming that something is decided). Discussions and debates in committees for example, very often do not resolve anything or determine courses of action, but rather agree to review the situation at a later date or else to talk some more about the matter in hand. If this goes on for too long, the committee itself becomes the focus of resentment because it never achieves or decides anything. Assuming that decisions are taken, the implications and consequences of these are to be fully understood and accepted by all.

Failure of argument, debate and discussion processes does not necessarily lead to more serious strife, though this may (and does) happen from time to time. The relationship is neither linear nor one-way. For example, a serious conflict that has recently emerged into the open may be managed and made positive through a continuous airing of the matter in debate and discussion. Where voices are raised and feelings run high in debate, this is not a problem as long as the group situation can accommodate this effectively and where relationships then return to normal after the event.

BOX 11.1   Rules for productive and positive argument, discussion and debate

1. Mutual interest of all concerned in the resolution of the matter in hand.
2. Commitment to the debate itself and to the matters on the agenda.
3. Honesty and openness so that differing views may become public and be heard without prejudice or penalty to the holders.
4. A structure for the debate that addresses issues; facts; feelings; values; and which has a clearly understood purpose. This is true of all good discussions. Creative acts such as brainstorming have the clear intent of producing a wide range of ideas in as short a time as possible. The best committees work to an agenda, remit and terms of reference.
5. Mutual trust and confidence in the personalities and expertise of those involved.
6. Respect for all points of view.

There are therefore both positive and negative aspects of the argument, debate and discussion process. It is likely to indicate where more serious differences may lie, especially if these indicate persistent clashes between particular individuals; where alliances start to form in the debating chamber and carry on after the debate has finished; and where people adopt contrary positions based on countering the views of someone else in the group.

Argument itself is not going to resolve the problems and it is necessary to look more closely into the situation. Invariably, there will be deeper and underlying conflicts that need to be addressed if the group is to be made effective again.

■ Competition

Competition exists between individuals and groups and within organisations. It also exists between organisations. It is either positive or negative, healthy or unhealthy. At its best, competition sets standards for all to follow, whether within the organisation or within the entire sphere which it operates. On a global scale, the standards of production, quality and managerial practice of certain organisations are held up as models to which the rest of the world should aspire. Some sectors arrange their organisations into league tables, thus shining a competitive light on some aspects of the activities carried out.

□ *Setting standards*

Competition exists between organisations as they pursue, acquire and defend market share. Customers are attracted because of the price, quality or value mix of the products on offer. Competitive processes include increasing the attractiveness of the product mix to their customers. This normally means making developments that put the particular organisation ahead of its competitors. The competitors then respond in turn, and so the process goes on. It is compounded and complicated when an alternative range of products or services is brought out by one operator, extending customer choice still further. It is also compounded when a new player enters the field for the first time setting completely different standards of practice.

□ *Energy and creativity*

The process of setting standards for commercial competition generates energy and creativity among organisational staff. Qualities, skills and expertise are all brought to bear on the problems as they arise. The competitive process remains healthy (from an organisational behaviour point of view) so long as this energy is harnessed in the pursuit of activities that both satisfy the market and stimulate and enhance the qualities and talents of the staff leading to individual and group achievement.

□ *The nature of competition*

This may either be:

- closed or distributive, where one party wins at the expense of others;
- open or integrative, where there is scope for everyone to succeed;
- collaborative, where the boundaries of operations of each party can be set to ensure that everyone has a fair share of 'the cake' (that is, whatever is being competed for). The competitive environment may be dominated by one party or a few large parties who each take what they want from the situation and whatever is left over is disputed among the remaining players.

In organisational behaviour terms, competition is more likely to be fruitful and productive if it is open and if the rewards for competing effectively are available to all. Competition is likely to degenerate into conflicts where, for example, competition for resources or accommodation is closed and one party succeeds at the expense of the others.

□ *The purpose of competition*

Competition between groups is much more likely to degenerate into conflict or warfare if this form of relationship is simply encouraged without adequate structure and without due consideration of the purpose and of those involved. Competition between individuals within groups is also likely to become disruptive.

BOX 11.2   Competition: Examples

Privatisation

A stated intention of the various government privatisation programmes of the 1980s and 1990s was to improve the commercial performance of the organisations affected. Previously state monopolies (so the thinking went), they had no .standards of performance built on genuine customer regard, and neither did they have any particular need to address questions of inefficiency or effectiveness. As monopolies they would simply put their prices up whenever they needed more money. By exposing them to competitive and market pressures (again so the thinking went) much of this would be cured and standards would rise. This was felt to be especially appropriate for the hitherto state-run industries of the former USSR countries as they learned to compete on the global commercial markets.

Creativity

A Paris advertising agency that was asked to make housework attractive to men came up with a range of designer utensils. Some examples of the results are:

● a vacuum cleaner in red with speed lines and a distinctive sporty logo (akin to the Ford Escort RS 1600);
● washing machines and dishwashers in dark blue, again with a sporty and motor-car orientated logo;
● an ironing board that unfolded like a Black & Decker Workmate and with a maroon or blue crush velvet surface;
● housework gloves with lycra straps.

The utensils never went into commercial production.

In organisational behaviour terms, for competition to be positive and productive a number of conditions must exist. The rules of the competition must be fair (and be seen to be so) to all concerned. They must be understood and accepted by everyone. The rewards of competing must be available to all involved and given to those who succeed. The competitors' destiny must be in their own hands: they are to succeed or fail by their own efforts and not by the arbitrary decision of persons elsewhere.

The rules must be adhered to and groups who cheat – those who find themselves disadvantaged by the rules – are not to be rewarded for finding alternative means to the given end. Those in charge of the situation have considered all alternatives and have arrived at the conclusion that this form of approach is the best way of achieving the stated goal.

Competitive relationships exist best within organisations where attention is positively given to standards, creativity, the nature of the groups and the purpose of creating the situation. The aim is to bring out the best in everyone concerned, to improve performance and efficiency, to set absolute standards for activities and from this to form a base from which improvements can still be made. If these elements and rationale are not present, then organisations should consider alternative means of achieving their purpose. A negative competitive approach is likely to lead to interdepartmental strife, especially where the form of competition is closed.

■ Warfare

Warfare exists where intergroup relations have been allowed to get out of hand, where the main aims and objectives of activities have been lost and where great energies and resources are taken up with fighting one's corner, reserving one's position and denigrating other departments and functions.

☐ Causes

Resources

Internal organisation warfare is often centred around resource questions and issues. It emerges when departments and individuals perceive that those who have control over resources are susceptible to non-operational approaches. They are also perceived to have their own reasons for issuing resources to particular departments (for example, the availability or potential for triumphs; gaining favour and acceptance as the result).

Influence

Competition for power and influence is also apparent. A multiple agenda is normally pursued. Particular groups and individuals present their achievements in the best possible light. This takes various forms, and aims to ensure that:

- real achievements are recognised;
- achievements are presented in ways acceptable to the sources of power and influence (for example, CEO, top managers, particular shareholders and stake-holders, the community at large);
- the group is receptive to patronage and that there are rewards to be gained by both the patron and those who come within their ambit;

- they are presented as major achievements, the best possible return on resources and expertise put in;
- the department or individual is presented as having high value and expertise themselves, available for higher favours, good jobs; and that they can be relied upon to produce 'the right results';
- the results are attached (where possible or desirable) to questions of organisation success.

This is also re-presented as:

- showing other departments and individuals in an unfavourable light;
- denigrating the skills, expertise, qualities and achievements of others;
- stealing the achievements of others or attaching oneself to their coat-tails;
- identifying any slight disagreement as a major barrier to progress;
- apportioning blame for failure to others.

Divide and rule

Warfare is the normal outcome of management styles based on divide and rule. It is superficially attractive because it breaks a whole entity down into component parts along the lines that, for example, a tonne of bricks may not be lifted by one person, but each individual brick may be and so the tonne is eventually shifted.

The analogy is false and so is the premise on which it is based. Dividing the whole into small chunks in this way causes energy to be expended by the individuals and groups on fighting their own corner rather than bonding to the common cause. To finish the analogy, the individual brick becomes the centre of attention rather than the use to which they can all be put.

Organisations and their managers that practise divide and rule therefore create battlefields on which the wars for resources and prestige are to be fought. The rules of combat are normally simple: winning is everything; and the losers may expect to lose influence, prestige, resources and possibly also their jobs. The process is normally additionally complicated by the 'dividers and rulers': victories and triumphs are handed out in non-rational (more non-rational) ways, designed to ensure that everyone is 'kept on their toes' and 'takes nothing for granted'.

This is compounded again by clandestine meetings, denigrations and denouncements involving individuals and groups in relation to each other and the organisation's top managers in its dealings with some groups.

Struggles for supremacy

Individuals and groups follow paths very similar to those of nations at war as they strive to succeed in warfare situations.

Alliances are formed between different parties and so factions grow up. These may be overt or clandestine. Groups seek a fifth column: sources of influence in the departments that hold power, sources of information in the departments with which they are working. Promises of reward are made to be delivered when victory is achieved; this comes in the form of promotion, increased pay, prestige work or a prestige location for the next job.

Resources and expertise are gathered together. This especially includes information of a nature and quality that can be used to enhance the one cause and damage the others. Public relations, presentational and lobbying skills are also required to ensure that what is done and achieved is seen in the best possible light by those with influence.

BOX 11.3   Reigns of Terror

Reigns of terror have been used by rulers, emperors, kings and queens through-out the ages as a means of keeping their subjects in check. The idea on which this is based is that if subjects live in a constant state of fear, this will prevent them from taking up arms and rebellion against those with power and authority. Indeed, they would be too frightened to do anything lest it be construed as rebellion.

A direct parallel may be drawn with organisational behaviour and associated managerial practices. Reigns of terror are a form of divide and rule in which dissidents and non-conformists are marginalised (and sometimes sacked). Once these have been removed, however, the leadership looks for other marginal groups; if there are none apparent they will be created anyway. Everyone there-fore becomes at risk.

Again, the idea is superficially attractive along the 'keeping everyone on their toes' lines. The result is normally that indicated above: everyone is too scared to do anything and therefore production, output and morale all collapse.

Moreover, many reigns of terror were not notably successful. Caligula, Nero, Robespierre and Danton were all themselves assassinated during their own reigns of terror. Persecution of early Christians by the Romans went a long way towards ensuring the survival of the Catholic Church. In turn, the persecution of the Catholic Church of its own dissidents in the fifteenth, sixteenth and seventeenth Centuries helped to ensure the survival and success of the Christian Reformation. The Nazi Empire – the Thousand Year Reich – lasted 12 years only (1933–45) and it used every organ of state in its reign of terror.

There are therefore clearly lessons to be learned by managers who are tempted by the divide and rule approach, and by organisations which encourage it.

The effects of these forms of internal strife are entirely negative. They divert people from their main reasons for being in the organisation. They are extremely wasteful of resources, time and energy. Success is only possible in individual terms and in the very short term (for example, the individual uses a warfare triumph as the means for getting his next job; and, if this is outside the organisation, then it will need to be addressed in terms that are meaningful to the prospective employer.

From a wider perspective, the base from which organisation welfare and strife grows is founded on certain tenets that have an initial attractiveness to the unwary. The outcome is wholly disruptive and destructive. It destroys morale, careers, people, output, quality and value, and will destroy the entire organisation if either encouraged or allowed to go unchecked.

■ Sources of conflict in organisations

Most organisational conflicts can be traced back to one or more of the following.

1. Competition for resources and the basis on which this is conducted.
2. Lack of absolute standards of openness, honesty, trustworthiness and integrity in general organisational behaviour and in dealings between staff, departments, divisions and functions, between different grades of staff and between seniors and subordinates; lack of mutual respect.
3. Lack of shared values, commitment, enthusiasm, motivation and low morale.
4. Unfairness, unevenness and inequality of personal and professional treatment, often linked to perceptions (and realities) of favouritism and scapegoating.
5. Physical and psychological barriers, especially those between seniors and subordinates, and also those between departments, divisions and functions.
6. Inability to meet expectations and fulfil promises; this is always compounded by the use of bureaucratic (mealy-mouthed) words and phrases.
7. Expediency and short-termism that interferes with dilutes the results that would otherwise be achieved.
8. The nature of work and its professional, expert and technical context.
9. The structure of work, and the division and allocation of tasks and jobs.
10. People involved, their hopes and fears, aspirations, ambitions, beliefs, attitudes and values.
11. The presence of vested interests and pressure groups.

■ Right and wrong

Differences in attitudes, values and belief cause conflict. This occurs most often when the demands of the organisation and the standards, expertise and ethics of its staff are at variance.

For example, hospitals are required to work within management and administrative budgets and this often means that the medical work has to be prioritised and ordered to keep within these financial targets. On the other hand, doctors and nurses have an absolute professional commitment to treat all those who come to them to the best of their ability.

There is also the relative commitment to the profession and the organisation. Conflict occurs when the individual is required to choose between the demands of the profession and those of the organisation where these cannot be reconciled. Operational factors have also to be considered: the balance of professional with managerial and administrative work for example, and the willingness of the individual to accept this.

This is in turn compounded by the attitudes inherent in the wider working relationship between organisation and individual. If this is largely positive and supportive, there is likely to be a greater willingness to take on peripheral and extraneous duties. If this is negative, the individual is more likely to retreat from the organisation and into the profession to find comfort among other members.

A conflict in expectations can therefore be seen again. The individual who desires to be a professional and seeks the scope to practise her expertise to the full, experiences frustration when required to spend what she considers to be inordinate amounts of time on non-professional, non-expert activities.

Conflict is also caused where the attitudes, values and belief of the organisation in general are not the same as those of the individuals who carry out the work. People may, from time to time, be asked to do something that is counter to their own personal beliefs. For example, they may be asked to lie on behalf of the organisation (to give a false excuse for the failure of a delivery, for example), and then to sustain this, in public at least. They may be asked to dismiss or discipline someone else in ways again with which they have no sympathy. The outcome of each may be essential to the organisation's continuing integrity, but it is a question of reconciling the ends with the means.

This form of conflict also occurs where there are strong religious and political beliefs present. Ideology is a contributory cause of conflict (for example in relations between trade unions and organisation, and trade union representatives and managers). Each has a point of view to represent in ideological as well as situational terms, and these have to be reconciled. Religious beliefs become important when staff are asked to work on holy days by their organisation. Wider ethical questions may also become apparent among staff working in specific sectors – for example, armaments, tobacco, alcohol, medical research – and these all require addressing by the organisations involved.

More general questions of equality of treatment and opportunity also fall into this category. Some organisations treat people with different absolute standards according to their race, gender or disability (in spite of the law), and also according to their grade, job or location. This invariably causes resentment and a multi-tier system of worth and value.

There is also the extent to which prejudices, received wisdom and preconceived ideas are allowed to prevail. These are present in every individual, in every situation. They become important in this context when they present barriers to effective working relationships, equality of treatment, as drives for or against change and the offering and restriction of opportunities.

BOX 11.4   The Auditor

Robert Seton worked as an auditor for a UK county council in the early 1990s. He was invited to the wedding of a colleague in September 1994. He was very pleased for his colleague; he attended the church service and the reception and wished his colleague all the best for the future.

When he returned to work he was studying some papers that related to the colleague who had just got married. One of these concerned an invoice addressed to 'The Old Rectory' in the village where his colleague had just got married. Studying the papers closely, he found that the colleague had indeed hired the person who lived at 'The Old Rectory' to do some work for him shortly before he got married.

Robert brought this to the attention of the county council's CE. A full inquiry and investigation was launched. The accusation to his colleague was that he had presented the clergyman concerned with some work in return for conducting his marriage for free.

A month long investigation was held. The following transpired:

- the person who lived at 'The Old Rectory' was not the clergyman but a management consultant who had been hired legitimately to carry out the work, and who had been paid a fee of £400 for doing this;
- the clergyman's fee for conducting the marriage was £90;
- the county council spent £1500 on the investigation itself.

Robert wondered whether he should feel ashamed of himself as the result of instigating this investigation and the way in which it had arisen.

■ Symptoms of conflict

These are:

1. Poor communications between groups, individuals and the organisation and its components.
2. Poor intergroup relationships based on envy, jealousy and anger at the position of others, rather than mutual cooperation and respect. People turn inwards to the members of their own group and away from others.
3. Deterioration of personal and professional relationships, increases in personality clashes.
4. Increases in absenteeism, sickness, labour turnover, time-keeping problems and accidents.

5. Proliferation of non-productive, ineffective and untargeted papers and reports, the purpose of which is publicity and promotion of the individuals and the departments that issue them.
6. Proliferation of rules and regulations covering especially the most minor of areas of activities.
7. Proliferation of changes in job title, especially 'upwards'. Thus, for example, a supervisor may become a 'section controller' or a financial manager the 'director of corporate resources'.
8. Escalation of disputes and grievances arising out of frustration and anger (rather than antagonism at the outset), and leading to personality clashes and antagonism as well as operational decline.
9. Proliferation of control functions at the expense of front-line functions.
10. Taking sides and ganging up so that, when problems are identified, people join or support one side or the other. This happens with long-running disputes and grievances; in these cases the original cause has normally long since been forgotten.
11. Informal corridor and washroom gatherings that persistently discuss wrongs, situational and organisational decline.
12. The growth of myths and legends via the grapevine; minor events become major events, small problems become crises, a slight disagreement becomes a major row.
13. The growth of arbitration: that is, the handing up of organisational disagreements to higher (and sometimes external) authorities for resolution. The main cause of this is the need not to be seen to lose, especially as the result of personal efforts. At the point of decision, therefore, the matter is handed on to a different authority to remove the responsibility for the outcome from the parties in dispute.
14. The decline in organisational, departmental, group and individual performance. This is often mirrored by increases in customer complaints, relating either to particular individuals and departments or more seriously, to the organisation as a whole.
15. Disregard and disrespect for persons in other parts of the organisation. This is mostly directed at management, supervision and upper levels by those lower down. It is also to be found among those at higher levels when they speak of employees in disparaging tones ('the workers' and 'these people', for example).
16. Overattention to the activities of other departments, divisions and functions, together with spurious pseudo-analysis of the particular situation.
17. Non-productive meetings between persons from different departments, divisions and functions based on the needs of individuals to defend their own corner and protect what they have.

These are the outward manifestations of organisational conflict. It is necessary, however, to look more deeply for the causes of conflict rather than treating the symptoms. Otherwise, for example, ever-greater volumes of communication reports and paperwork are fed into systems that are already overloaded, and to people who treat the content with disdain and eventually contempt. In personal relationships and disputes, the temptation is for organisations to take a firm (even hard) line with the warring parties. The normal effect of this is to escalate rather than dampen down the conflict.

■ Causes of conflict

The main causes of conflict in organisations are as follows:

1. Differences between corporate, group and individual aims and objectives, and the inability of the organisation to devise systems, practices and environments in which these can be reconciled and harmonised.
2. Interdepartmental and intergroup wrangles overwhelmingly concerned with:
   (a) territory – where one group feels that another is treading in an area that is legitimately theirs;
   (b) prestige – where one group feels that another is gaining recognition for efforts and successes that are legitimately theirs;
   (c) agenda – where one group feels that it is being marginalised by the activities of the other;
   (d) poaching and theft – where one group attracts away the staff of the other and perhaps also, their technology, equipment, information and prestige.
3. The status awarded by the organisation to its different departments, divisions, functions, group and individuals. This is to be seen as:
   (a) formal relations, based on organisational structure and job definition;
   (b) informal relations, based on corridor influence and possibly also personal relationships;
   (c) favoured and unfavoured status, the means by which this is arrived at and what it means to those concerned;
   (d) the organisational pecking order and any other means by which prestige and influence are determined.
4. Conflict arises also both from the status quo, where people seek to alter their own position, and from changes that the organisation seeks to make. For example, when an individual or group suddenly loses power, a void is left which all the others rush to fill. Conversely, an individual or group may suddenly find itself in favour (for many reasons, operational necessity, expediency, the possibility of a triumph for the favour-giver), and the others rush to do it down.
5. Individual clashes – both professional and personal – lead to conflict if the basis of the relationship is not established and ordered. For example, one individual sees that a point of debate is a personal attack or a questioning of their professional judgement, and 'a lively discussion' may be regarded by one as the straightforward airing of a point of view, but by another as questioning his expertise and integrity. This is also often the cause of feelings of favouritism leading to clashes between

the recipients (perceived or actual) of preferential treatment, and the others around them. Bullying and scapegoating is also a form of individual clash, causing conflict between both bully and bullied. This again may lead to conflict based either on support for the victim by others, or by others following the leader and setting upon the victim themselves.

6. Personality clashes also fall into this category. They become seriously disruptive if allowed to proceed unchecked and if steps are not taken to ensure that there is a professional or operational basis on which relationships can be based.

7. Groups may be drawn into conflict as the result of a clash between their leaders or between particular individuals.

8. Role relationships have the potential to cause conflict. This is based on the nature of the given roles. For example, trade union officials are certain to come into conflict with organisations in the course of their duties: they are often representing the interest of members who have some kind of trouble or dispute. Other role relationships that should be considered are:

   (a) senior–subordinates – conflicts of judgement, conflicts based on work output, attitudes, style;

   (b) appraiser/appraisee – where there are differences (often fundamental) over the nature and quality of the appraisee's performance and the action that this may cause to be taken;

   (c) functional roles – conflicts between production and sales over quality, volume and availability of output; between purchaser (concerned with cost and quality) and producer (concerned with output); between personnel (concerned with absolute legal and ethical standards) and the departments which call on their services (concerned with solving problems, speed, expediency); between finance (efficiency) and other functions (effectiveness);

   (d) internal–external – the priorities and requirements of external roles (shareholder, stakeholder, bank manager, lobbyist, public interest group, community), and reconciling these with the organisation's aims and objectives and those of their staff and activities;

   (e) parallel roles – clashes occur, for example, where two or more people are competing for one promotion place; or where two or more people ostensibly carrying out the same job have (or are perceived to have) work of varying degrees of interest, quality, status and prestige.

9. Effects on third parties: this is another way of looking at secretarial and personal assistant syndrome (see Chapter 8). It occurs because of the nature of the position held. The secretary/PA to a top executive or senior manager is a low-status/high-influence role. This causes particular forms of approach to be taken when dealing with secretaries and PAs, and may lead to the editing of information or lobbying for support by those from other functions.

10. Wider effects: for example, where a policy clash between sales and production leads to personal and professional clashes between individual members of the department involved. This arises out of loyalty, personal and professional commitment to the department and the given policy.

11. Internal customer/client or channel breakdown: clashes occur between people in any position or function when channels of communication, reporting relationships and hierarchical structures malfunction. If information or other output required elsewhere in the organisation is not forthcoming, attention focuses on the department or individual responsible in the search for an explanation.

12. Conflict with the job held also occurs. This comes in the following forms.

   (a) **Conflicts between job and job holder** – this is largely related in the cases of expert and professional staff, to frustration in terms of the ability to use expertise to the full; the lack of scope for professional development and advancement; or ability to progress. In the case of the less expert, semi- and unskilled staff this is normally related to routine patterns of work and the alienation and loss of self-worth that occurs as a result.

   (b) **Conflict between job and organisation** – this concerns the relationship that exists between the two; the availability of opportunities; the extent to which these are offered; and the expectations that were placed at the outset on, and by, each, and the extent to which these have been fulfilled (see Box 11.5).

   (c) **Conflict between job holder and organisation** – this is the extent to which pay, supervision, management style and the work environment are suitable and effective. Low pay leads to low feelings of self-worth, especially if there is little prospect of real increases in the future. Inappropriate supervision and management style cause diversions away from effective work leading to feelings of frustration, and this is compounded if the style is confrontational or abrasive. Frustration also occurs if, for example, the right equipment is not (or not always) available. It also occurs if the general ambience of the environment is tatty or unkempt, and this again leads also to feelings of reduced self-worth. It is seen as a reflection of the value placed on those who work by the organisation.

BOX 11.5   Karen Wells

Karen Wells joined a large hospital in the south-east of England as a personnel assistant straight from college. She was impressed by the welcome that she received. She went through an extensive induction course and looked forward to starting work in earnest.

After a few weeks, however, frustration began to set in. The job advertisement to which she had responded promised 'a lively working environment, hands-on personnel experience, the opportunity to become involved in all aspects of human resource management work. Professional training and development [were] to be available to the right person.'

As the weeks and months went by, she found her frustration greatly increasing. She was employed on clerical and filing duties. Because she could type, this quickly became a secretarial post. She regularly provided tea and coffee for meetings. She sometimes sat in on these and occasionally took minutes, but was not allowed to participate.

After six months, she confronted her supervisor with her concerns. She was told: 'After the induction course we did not know what to do with you. All the personnel work is covered and so there is no opportunity for you there. We are pleased that we have found you a clerical job.' On the specific point about training and development she was told bluntly: 'You are not the right person and so training and development is not available to you.'

After this meeting, she reviewed her situation; she looked again at the job advertisement which had said also 'starting salary up to £14 000'. She had started on £9 500. When she had mildly questioned this at the time, she had been told that it was normal practice and not to worry.

Karen Wells left the hospital after ten miserable months and now works for a major clearing bank.

13. Lack of clarity of reporting relationships causes conflict. This is likely to occur when different functions want the same information or results but published or delivered in different ways. The nature of the relationship may also be unclear. This occurs where information published could conceivably be used against the issuing department. For example, a department may issue a statement of performance indicating a set of factors to the organisation's financial controller based on the nature of its own operations. This may be taken out of context and used as a comparative measure of performance in relation to other departments within the organisation.

The same may occur on an individual basis. During performance appraisal, an individual may be asked to make a statement of the area of future development that she thinks she requires. This is then turned around by the recipient to indicate areas of weakness or incompetence. In the worst cases it is used to block rewards, pay rises and the opportunity to progress.

14. Conflict also occurs where somebody works for two superiors. Again, the most common form is where each superior wants the same work done but the results produced in different fors or to different deadline. In this situation, conflict also occurs where there is no agreement between the two superiors involved as to the nature of the subordinate relationship, especially in terms of commitment, time, energy and location.

BOX 11.6 Causes of Conflict: Forms of Language

A symptom of the existence of some of these causes is to be found in language forms. These proliferate as levels of conflict inherent arise. Some examples are given below.

1. 'A plan exists' – means that something has once or twice been discussed; it is perhaps required; no decision has been taken; and do not be surprised if it does or does not happen.
2. 'With the greatest respect' or 'I respect your views' – normally means that the other person is thought to be talking or producing rubbish.
3. 'I work too hard', 'I cannot leave things', 'I find it impossible to go home at night' – become the normal statement of weaknesses at appraisal interviews if the individual perceives that he will otherwise be penalised.
4. 'You move in exulted circles' – normally means that the person being addressed has influence and prestige far beyond that which their level of perceived competence deserves.
5. 'We did all we could' – usually indicates that one individual or group is going to make it absolutely clear that they were let down by others in a situation where some form of failure has occurred.

15. Giving credence, status and importance to the views of vested interests causes conflict. It especially causes resentment among those who do not lobby for their points of view and therefore lose out (or perceive themselves to do so) as the result. Conflicts normally come out into the open and may also escalate into warfare as everyone forms themselves into vested interest groups or attaches themselves to particular lobbies.

16. Hidden, secondary and parallel agenda cause conflict. These proliferate where overall aims are not well or tightly drawn; where they do not, or are not able to accommodate those of the individuals involved; and where people feel that, even if they do well with the work, they are not likely to receive due recognition. The parallel agenda therefore addresses these points: the need for individuals to progress; the need for recognition and the status and kudos that accrues as the result. At the very least, the organisation's purpose is diluted.

    In pursuit of this, other activities start to emerge. The department or group concerned is likely to start to engage in other means of achieving its objectives, such as using any negative or blocking power that it has available; restricting and prioritising its own output; choosing deadlines to its own greatest advantage.

    Those involved may also come to see or feel that the real issue is to fight for resources and/or prestige and reposition their activities accordingly. This is especially true where lobbies are seen or perceived to succeed at the expense of others.

17. The issuing of differentials causes conflict. Difficulties here include company cars, company parking spaces, personal computers and fax machines, mobile phones and other executive technology, the flexibility to work from home, personal secretaries and assistants, differentiated office furniture. Conflict is caused when the allocation of these elements is done (or seen to be done) from a point of view of patronage, prestige and status rather than operational necessity.

    This also enhances conflict and resentment where:

(a) people receive differentials who do not (overtly) need them, while those who do need them do not receive them;

(b) some people on a given grade receive them, while others on the same grade do not;

(c) people on a given grade in one department or division receive them, while others on the same or higher grades in other departments and divisions do not;

(d) some people receive them (or some of them) because of operational necessity, while others on higher grades do not receive them either for operational necessity or for reasons of prestige.

BOX 11.7   Ford Sierras

In 1984 a UK building society decided to change all the company cars of their managers and sales staff. They were to be equipped with the latest model, the Ford Sierra, which had come out in the previous year to replace the Cortina.

In the London region there was a delay in this and those affected had to wait for their new cars. The reason was that every car issued over the period by the London Ford dealerships came with a free sunroof. The building society took the view that it would cause less trouble to wait a while for the cars without the sunroofs than to have some of the cars with sunroofs, but not all.

Some common factors begin to emerge:

Honesty   The greater the integrity of the situation, the relations between groups and individuals and the relationship between the organisation and its staff, the greater the likelihood of the effective management of conflict. This includes hierarchical and reporting relations.

Expectations   Conflict emerges when expectations are not understood and where they are not met.

Understanding   Much of this concerns empathy, a recognition of how people are expected and anticipated to behave in given situations and sets of circumstances. Human emotions, especially those of envy, jealousy, anger and greed, are brought into being when people are confronted with a situation in which they perceive themselves to be losing out.

Fear and resentment flourish if the nature of the situation is such that those involved feel threatened by the success and prestige of others relative to their own position.

Groups and individuals all seek to improve their position in all circumstances. They seek the capability to do this through any means, channels and resources available. Organisations either leave these open, remove them or close them down. If own group or individual pursues one channel successfully, others will follow. If this is not successful they will try other methods. Groups and individuals are attracted to where the rewards that come from the improved position are forthcoming.

As well as a summary of the factors present in the causes, this indicates the main behavioural components of the conflict itself. Recognition of these therefore greatly contributes to an understanding of conflict itself and of some of the issues that have to be addressed if it is to be managed and contained, and if relations between groups and individuals are to be made positive and productive.

A complex picture of the potential for conflict, its emergence and strength begins to take shape. This involves:

- the level of conflict, and whether positive or negative;
- the nature of conflict, whether positive or negative;
- the source (or sources) of conflict;
- the causes of conflict;
- its symptoms.

To this may be added the following factors.

1. The parties to the conflict. The simplest form of conflict involves two parties only. Much organisation conflict is more complex, however.
2. The issues in dispute; the strength of feeling that the parties involved have concerning them; the interests and agenda of those involved; the extent to which there is a hierarchy of contentious issues.
3. The dynamics of the conflict: its causes; its sources of energy (see Figure 11.2), the extent to which it is formalised; the extent to which it is personalised; the length of time it has been going on and is allowed to run on; the extent to which the eventual outcome is predictable; the range of possible outcomes.

At this point, therefore, a basic conceptual framework exists for the understanding of conflict. It is important to know also that conflict, once it has been generated, is likely to feed off itself, gathering a life of its own (see Box 11.8) if it is allowed to proceed unchecked.

BOX 11.8   The Start of the First World War

At first glance, there is no apparent relationship between the assassination of a minor nobleman in Sarajevo, Bosnia, and the death of 15 million French, German, Russian, British and Commonwealth soldiers in northern and eastern Europe. However, the two are indeed cause and effect.

The Archduke Franz Ferdinand of Austria was assassinated by a Serb in Sarajevo on 1 August 1914. Austria immediately took this as an act of war and mobilised itself to invade Serbia.

At this point the domino effect of alliances became energised. Russia declared that any attack on its ally, Serbia, would constitute an act of war against itself. Because of a treaty signed between Russia, France and Great Britain (the Triple Alliance) the others were drawn in as well. Also quickly involved were the countries of the British Empire who rushed to the defence and support of the motherland.

Austria sought help from its ally, Germany, which sent a huge army across the Rhine to invade northern France and Belgium. The Triple Alliance responded, and battle lines were drawn across northern Europe for most of the next four years.

The war took less than a fortnight to start. The cause was quickly forgotten. What mattered was winning.

- The personalities involved
- The departments and functions involved
- The agenda of those involved
- The organisational point of view
- The interests of those involved
- The presence and influence of third parties (for example, the CE, trade unions)
- Any absolute organisation standards, rules, regulations and practices involved

- Expediency
- Need for triumphs, scapegoats and favours
- Relative necessity and compulsion to win
- Wider perceptions of the dispute
- Wider perceptions of the outcome
- Alliances: the ability to call on outside support

Figure 11.2   Sources of energy in conflict

It may deepen also if allowed to continue: professional disagreements and disputes may become personalised or degenerate into interdepartmental warfare.

BOX 11.9   The Outcomes of Conflict

Win:Win

The integrative relationship in which everyone is content.

Win:Lose

The distributive relationship in which one side wins at the expense of the other (or others).

Lose:Win

Lose:Lose

The ultimate outcome of the distributive process that occurs when the dispute escalates. In industrial relations terms this normally means recourse to strike, lock-outs or arbitration. This is the result of both sides becoming entrenched. In these cases a rational solution found between the two parties is unlikely.

A result may eventually be gained internally if a dominant–dependency relationship can be called into play. From a workforce point of view this occurs mostly where the staff have control of output (for example, as used to happen with newspapers). The organisation's normal standpoint in these cases is the economic: the necessity for staff members to be paid.

Arbitration may also be called upon to resolve disputes between individuals, especially those involving the superior subordinate relationship. Many such cases lead to job loss, accusations of victimisation and prejudice, and are resolved only through the courts and industrial tribunals.

Note: in all but integrative cases, the behavioural outcome is as important as the substantive. People do not like to be defeated. Neither do they like to have been seen by others to have been defeated. A large part of the distributive process therefore covers the need to find suitable forms of words to address questions of wounded pride and loss of face that would otherwise occur. The great benefit of going to arbitration in these cases is the ability to present the outcome as an independent or outsider's view and therefore acceptable.

Operational	Behavioural
• Dysfunctional	• Loss of face
• Inefficiency	• Wounded pride
• Squandering of resources	• Triumphalism
• Loss of productive effort	• Scapegoating
• Customer complaints	• Humiliation
• Customer loss	• Loss of faith
• Loss of confidence	• Loss of integrity
• Loss of trust	• Loss of morale
• Loss of morale	• Loss of confidence
• Loss of performance	• Loss of trust

Several of these items occur in each column. The purpose is to draw the relationship in terms of business performance as well as organisation behaviour.

Figure 11.3   Operational and behavioural outputs of conflict

■ Strategies for the management of conflict

Thus far it is established that the potential for conflict is present in every human situation (families, social groups, guides, scouts etc.) and organisations are no exception. Many of these issues, present throughout society, are emphasised and concentrated by the fact of their being in work organisations and are compounded by the ways, structures, rules and regulations in which these are constituted.

The first lesson, therefore, lies in the understanding of this. The second lesson is to recognise that, if attention is paid only to the symptoms, overload is placed on the existing systems of the organisation as indicated above.

From this, in turn, there derives the need to adopt strategic approaches (rather than operational) to the management and resolution of conflict. This is based on a framework designed at the outset that should:

- recognise the symptoms of the conflict;
- recognise the nature and level (or levels) of conflict;
- recognise and understand the sources of conflict;
- investigate the root causes of the conflict;
- establish the range of outcomes possible;
- establish the desired outcome;
- establish the outcome that is the very least that is acceptable.

On to this framework can then be built strategies designed to ensure that the desired outcome is to be achieved.

It is clear from this that the symptoms are nothing more than the outward manifestation that something is wrong; and that it is what has brought these to the surface that needs to be addressed. For example, it is no use sending sales and reception staff on customer care courses because of an increase in complaints if the causes of the problems lie within production functions. It is equally useless to train managers and supervisors in the use of disciplinary and grievance procedures without also giving an understanding of what discipline and grievance handling means in terms of a particular organisation.

The desired outcome therefore removes the symptoms of the conflict by addressing the causes, rather than vice versa.

This is the starting point for effective conflict management.

Effective strategies for the management of conflict clearly vary in content between organisations and situations. In this context the main lines of approach are as follows.

1. Attention to standards of honesty and integrity to ensure that people have a sound understanding of the basis on which the relationship between themselves, their department, division or group and the organisation as a whole is established. This is brought about by absolute commitment on the part of the organisation and those responsible for its direction and its top managers, and translated into the required management staff by those responsible for the direction and supervision of the rest of the staff.

2. Attention to communications to ensure that these meet the needs of receivers, and that what is said or written is simple and direct, capable of being understood, honest and straightforward.

3. Attention to the hopes, fears, aspirations and expectations of all those who work in the organisation. Much of this is based on empathy and mutual identity and commitment, and dissipated by compartmentalising and differentiating between staff groups.

4. Attention to the systems, procedures and practices of the organisation and the ways in which these are structured and drawn up and the ways in which they are operated. This especially means attention to equality and fairness of treatment and opportunity; the language and tone of the procedures themselves; and the training and briefing of managers and supervisors in their purposes, emphases and operation. This also normally means the presence of sanctions for those who do not operate these systems with integrity.

5. The establishment of organisational purposes common to all those present in the organisation, with which they can all identify and which transcend the inherent conflicts of objectives. This is the approach most favoured, for example, by Japanese companies in their operations in Western Europe and North America.

6. The establishment of a universal identity and commitment to purpose. In organisation behaviour terms, this involves attention to the outputs of the stated purpose and the benefits and advantages that are to accrue as the result of their achievement. This is the starting point for the establishment of:

   (a) performance-related and profit-related pay schemes, and the generation of the identity, commitment and interest that are the key elements of the best of these;
   (b) briefing groups, work improvement groups and quality circles that reinforce the mutual confidence, commitment and respect of those involved.

7. The removal of the barriers that exist between departments and divisions. This involves attention to matters of confidence and respect and to the level, quality and style of communications that affect operational relationships.

8. The establishment of organisation conformism, based on creation of desired means and methods of participation and consultation, and fused with absolute standards of honesty and integrity. Attention is required here to:

   (a) the representation of employees and the means by which this is to be achieved;
   (b) their scope and structure;
   (c) the agenda to be followed;
   (d) the rules of engagement (the means by which these are to be operated).

These are the main organisational behaviour approaches required to address and tackle the sources and causes of conflict. They are based on the recognition of its universal potential to exist; the approach in particular organisations clearly varies. They arise from an understanding of the nature of conflict and of the need to recognise rather than attack the symptoms. Energy devoted to dealing with conflict represents energy not spent on more productive activities; time and resources used in understanding and assessing the causes and dealing with these therefore bring their own payback in terms of reduced time, stresses and strains caused by the reality of problems and disputes.

BOX 11.10   Operational Approaches to the Management of Conflict

---

The operational approaches used by organisations normally take the following forms.

1. Developing rules, procedures and precedents to minimise the emergence of conflict and then, when it does occur, to minimise its undesirable effects.
2. Ensuring that communications are effective in minimising conflict; bad communications may cause conflict or magnify minor disputes to dangerous proportions.
3. Separation of sources of potential conflict which may be done geographically, structurally or psychologically (for example, through the creation of psychological distance between functions and ranks).
4. Arbitration machinery may be made available as a strategy of last resort.
5. Confrontation may be used to try to bring all participants together in an attempt to face them with the consequences of their action.
6. Benign neglect: this is the application of the dictum that 'A problem deferred is a problem half-solved.' This can normally only be used as a temporary measure while more information is being gathered or a more structured approach is being formulated.
7. The use of industrial relations operations for the containment and management of conflict, including consultation, participation, collective bargaining and negotiating structures.

■   Conflicts and industrial relations

From an organisational behaviour point of view, the source of what is usually called industrial relations arises from the reality of conflict in places of work. People bring their own aims and objectives to work and pursue these as well as, and often in place of, those of the organisation:

Individual objectives
- money;
- prospects;
- advancement;
- progress;
- perks;
- status;
- esteem;
- respect;
- regard;
- development.

Organisational objectives
- success;
- profits;
- effectiveness;
- reputation;
- confidence;
- development;
- progress.

Historically, these divisions were enhanced by adversarial views taken by organisations and their managers about the nature of work and workers, especially, McGregor's Theory X view that people are lazy and uncommitted and will only work if bullied, bribed or threatened. This was in turn compounded by the environment created as the result: confrontational styles of management and supervision, lack of continuity or protection of employment, and differentiated wages for the same (or similar) types of work.

The basis on which industrial relations – the relationship between organisations, their managers, their staff at places of work – was developed was therefore often that of mutual mistrust and antagonism. This would from time to time break out into open warfare. Staff (workers) would sabotage machinery, spoil products, block factory gates or come out on strike. The employers would lock the workers out, forbid unions and combinations, dismiss the workforce and hire others to take its place.

This is a simplified and generalised representation of the bad and worst practices and relations rather than the best (and there were, and are, plenty of much better examples of industrial relations practice). However, it illustrates the general foundation of industrial attitudes:

- the pressure on workers to combine and to seek employment protection, to try to influence wage levels, to seek mutual support among themselves rather than from the employer and to build defensive walls around themselves in the form of demarcation lines and restrictive practices;
- the pressure on employers to get work out of people who were by now well entrenched in this mentality, the development of systems and styles of supervision to try to ensure that levels of satisfactory performance at least were achieved, the need for short-term as well as long-term results, conformism to prevailing attitudes and ways of working, and the belief that the wage was the sole driving force behind the workers.

In summary, a siege mentality is created and perpetuated. Relations between the parties take on the forms of wars of attrition. Every interaction is studied for double meaning, hidden agenda, the potential for deceit and duplicity. Every issue is argued from all possible points of view. Progressing and developing the relationship between parties in this kind of situation is extremely arduous. Given the slightest opportunity, people retreat to their familiar entrenched.

■ Perspectives on industrial relations

A more rigorous approach to understanding the nature of industrial relations and workplace conflict is to identify the different standpoints that may be adopted and the consequences of each. Three distinctive perspectives may clearly be identified.

☐ *Unitary*

This assumes that the objectives of all involved are the same or at least compatible and concerned only with the well-being of the organisation and its activities. People who come to work in such organisations, therefore, either subsume or entwine their objectives with those of the organisation; organisation and individual success and effectiveness are inextricably linked. The most successful of unitary organisations (for example, McDonalds, Virgin, Marks & Spencer) set very distinctive work performance and personal standards to which anyone working in the company must conform. This is also a key feature of the Japanese approach to the management of the human resource.

☐ *Pluralism*

Pluralism admits a variety of objectives, not all of them compatible among those working in organisations. Recognising that conflict is therefore present, rules, procedures and systems are established to manage this and limit its influence as far as possible. The legitimacy of these interests is also understood, and much of the management of organisations that accept the pluralist view is concerned with reconciling these differences.

☐ *Radical*

This is the view that commercial and industrial harmony is impossible until the staff control the means of production and benefit from the generation of wealth. Until recently, this was a cornerstone of the philosophy of many trade unions and socialist activists in industry, commerce and public services in the UK.

BOX 11.11 Traditional Tales of Industrial Relations

An understanding of the background to current industrial relations activities and practices may be gained from the following.

Dark Satanic Mills

The traditional view of industrial relations during the early to mid-nineteenth century in the UK is founded on the work queuing system. Each day three queues would gather outside the gates of factories and mills: children, women and men. The owner would take in children first, then women and finally men. This was because the pay rates for children were the lowest, followed by women, while men were the most expensive. The people who worked one day were not certain of employment the next.

The result was that workers, especially men, formed themselves into combinations and self-protection groups. These were based on group rules and standards that none of them would work anywhere where others had been disbarred or undercut by the use of women and children, or for less than the daily rate agreed among the members. These groups were formed around the sector of the work (these came to be known as industrial unions); or around the nature and occupation of the work (craft and expertise unions); or around the locality (these came to be known as local and regional unions and later merged and amalgamated to become national unions). This took place alongside legislation that barred or restricted the working hours and places of work of women and children.

Down and Out in Paris and London

George Orwell worked as a kitchen hand at the Ritz Hotel, Paris, in the 1920s. Under French law the staff would receive a day's pay once they had worked up to lunchtime. Orwell recounts the story of one kitchen hand, Jean Louis, who would work hard up until lunchtime and then, once the money was guaranteed, would become obstructive and angry, and refuse to do things.

Affluent Workers

The factories of Luton formed the basis of the affluent workers studies of the 1950s and 1960s. Industrial relations was a form of co-operative alliance between organisation and workers that enabled satisfactory production to be achieved. From time to time strikes would take place. These would be well signalled by the unions in advance and the companies (especially Vauxhall) would be given plenty of warning, either to resolve the potential conflict or to feed it. In the latter case a strike of between one and three weeks would normally occur. This was considered by management to be the equivalent of a safety valve. It was therefore an acceptable form of regulating the behaviour of the staff and containing the boredom and alienation inherent in the work. It effectively became part of the fixed costs involved in making the factory work.

Triumph and Disaster

In March 1984 the National Union of Mineworkers' Vice-President, Mick McGahey, told the National Coal Board Chair, Ian MacGregor, that there was shortly going to be a major miners' strike.

MacGregor did not believe him. He pointed out that there had been a mild winter; coal stocks were at record levels; coal-fired power stations had themselves stockpiled; oil and nuclear electricity generation were also at record levels. The men had had good pay rises in previous years and were now near the top of the industrial earnings league.

McGahey replied that all of this counted for nothing. The new President, Arthur Scargill, was determined to have a triumph. The strike would be called to protest at the closure of pits.

The strike was called and went ahead in all areas except for Nottinghamshire. The National Union of Mineworkers broke in two and a new body, the Union of Democratic Mineworkers, was created in Nottinghamshire.

The dispute lasted a year and a day. At the end, the men marched back to work behind their bands and their banners.

At the start of the strike there were 250 000 miners. In 1995 there were 14 500.

The lesson from each is that nobody ultimately benefits from adversarial and alienative approaches to industrial relations. Eventually each employer has used up time, energy and resources in coercive and punitive staff management that could, and would, have been better used elsewhere. From an organisational behaviour point of view, each approach illustrated is very destructive to relationships, respect, confidence, mutuality, trust and esteem.

■ Industrial relations strategies

Devising an effective strategy for the management of industrial relations is as critical to the organisation as anything else. It sets the whole tone by which the employer will deal with the staff and workforce. The stance taken will ultimately depend on the industrial or commercial sector concerned (or whether it is a public or government service). In general, one of the following positions will exist.

Conflict The basis on which the staff are to be dealt with is one of mistrust, divergence and the admission of conflicting aims and objectives; disparity of location; divergence and complexity of patterns of employment and occupations; and a recognition of the fact that these aims and objectives will not always be compatible with those of the organisation. In these cases, the industrial relations strategy will be devised to contain the conflicts and reconcile the differences and to promote levels of harmony as far as possible.

Conformity The diversity of staff and technology may be as great as in the above scenario, but the industrial relations strategy rather sets standards of behavioural and operational aims and objectives that in turn require the different groups to rise above their inherent differences.

Whichever is adopted there are common threads. Organisations must understand the nature and strengths of the types of staff that they employ. They must recognise that there are divergences of aims and different priorities that must be resolved if effective and profitable work is to take place. The nature of industrial relations and the related staff management activities will therefore vary accordingly. At the outset all staff, whatever their occupation, are required to form an identity with the organisation that is both positive and complementary to its purposes. Boundaries of performance and behaviour requirements are to be established in order that these purposes are achieved effectively and successfully. Issues to do with the nature and style of workplace regulations and staff representation must also be resolved. Above all, industrial relations and staff management are to be seen as continuous processes and areas for constant improvement.

Whichever approach is adopted must therefore be supportive of the wider aims and objectives of the organisation. This will extend to the capabilities and qualities of the workforce; the extent to which they are highly trained or professionalised; and the conflicting demands placed on them by their expertise and the organisation. It is also necessary to recognise that in certain circumstances staff have very strong group and traditional identities, perhaps because of their profession or because of sectoral traditions or a long history of unionisation, for example.

The organisation must then go on to set standards of performance; standards of ethics, behaviour and attitude; boundaries of industrial relations activities; procedures for the management of disputes, grievances, discipline and dismissal; consultative, participative and communication structures. The precise forms of workforce representation, including the recognition of trade unions and professional associations, will be decided. From this emerges the desired aura of workplace staff relations. This is the backdrop or general impression that is created alongside the actual practices. Whichever strategy is adopted also, it is important that both managers and staff know which it is, where they stand and what their mutual expectations are. Needless disputes can therefore be kept to a minimum. Finally, the approach taken is supported by staff hand books and rule books, the nature and content and usage of procedures and formal structures.

A strategic approach to specific industrial relations matters will also be adopted. As well as briefings for staff and training for managers in industrial relations skills and knowledge, organisations will take an approach to the management of workplace conflict based on answers to the following questions.

1. What is the likelihood of a dispute occurring? If it does, how long might it last? What are the wider consequences to ourselves and to our staff?
2. If it does occur, can we win it? What are the consequences of winning? What are the consequences of losing?
3. If it does occur, what costs are we going to incur? As well as financial costs, there are questions of public relations, media coverage and local feelings to be considered.
4. What happens when it all settles down? How will we interact and work with the staff into the future? How long is bad feeling likely to last?
5. What other ways are there around the matter or dispute in hand? Is it possible to use these? What are the pros and cons of each?
6. What are the behavioural and psychological aspects that surround the issue? If the organisation wins, what will be the effect on the workforce?
7. What are the implications for managers? Do they need a triumph?

8. What is the likely effect on morale?
9. If a question of win:lose is to arise, what are the likely effects of each: for example, if the organisation is to lose, would loss of face be important? How could face be saved if that were to arise? What would be the response of the workforce and its representatives?

From consideration of the matter in hand in this way, and by using these questions as a framework for discussion and analysis of the dispute, two critical questions emerge.

1. Why are we seeking, entering or preparing to enter into this dispute?
2. What is the price to be paid, and is this worth paying?

The answer to these questions is integral to the success of any strategic approach to specific industrial relations matters.

■ Collective bargaining

Collective bargaining is the traditional process by which agreements between employers and employees or their respective representatives are made. These agreements may be made at national, regional, local sectoral or plant and unit level. It may involve very senior and highly trained personnel at sectoral or national levels, and elected lay representative at the other extreme.

Two separate strands of collective bargaining can be identified. These are: the substantive, concerning the matters in hand; and the procedural, concerning the means by which the matters in hand are to be addressed.

The process of collective bargaining is based on mistrust and conflict: a fundamental divergence of interests between employers and employees. At stake initially therefore is a basis on which the two can agree to cooperate together at all. It is made more difficult where there exists a long history and tradition of workplace conflict. Collective bargaining is a framework for the management of this conflict. Much of the process is stylised and ritualised. Anyone who wishes to operate it effectively must understand its importance. Only if this is achieved can the instruments of collective bargaining and the language be used effectively.

□ *The bargaining framework*

The first offer or claim is always made on the basis that it will be rejected (if for any reason it is accepted straight away, this generally causes resentment rather than instant satisfaction).

There then follows a process of counter-offer and counter-claim, with each party working its way gradually towards the other.

The content of the final agreement is usually clearly signalled before it is made. The basis of what is genuinely acceptable to each party is signalled also.

Serious disputes occur either when one side is determined not to settle, or when there is a genuine misreading of the signals from the other party.

Settlements are normally couched in positive terms in relation to all concerned to avoid the use of words such as loss, loser, climb-down and defeat. These have negative connotations for anyone involved and tend to store up resentment for the future and to polarise attitudes for the next round of bargaining.

Bargaining may take any of the following forms.

1. Distributive – it may be necessary to settle with one group or part of the workforce at the expense of others; it may not be possible to satisfy everyone.
2. Integrative – it may be possible to resolve problems to the satisfaction of all concerned.
3. Attitudinal structuring – this is the part of the process by which each side influences the attitudes of the participants towards the other. Attitudes are formed and modified by the nature of the orientation that each party has towards the other and towards the matters in hand. This may be competitive, whereby the parties are motivated to defeat or win the other over to their point of view; individualistic, in which the parties concerned pursue their own self-interest without any regard for the position of the other; or cooperative, whereby each party is concerned about the other, as well as its own position. Part of this process also seeks to ensure that people understand the true nature of their own position and that of the other party; to ensure that people's expectations are met as far as possible in such situations; and to ensure as far as possible that the two are compatible.
4. It may be necessary to take a hard or extreme initial stance to try to persuade the other party to revise its expectations. This occurs for example, where a group of workers have unreasonable or unreal expectations of a level of pay rise.

The collective bargaining process is also concerned with structuring the attitudes of those concerned towards each other. They seek to try and build impressions of honesty, trust, openness, firmness, reasonableness and fairness. They also seek to generate the fundamental credibility and integrity in the position that they have adopted. For example, it is no use taking a hard or extreme initial stance if this is then instantly changed.

■ Conformism

Conformist industrial relations requires the subordination of divergent and conflicting interests at the workplace in the pursuit of common and understood aims. These are set by the organisation in advance of any staff agreements. The stance normally taken is that the organisation must be successful, effective and profitable, and that the purpose of industrial relations, as with all other workplace activities, is to contribute to this.

For the approach to be truly effective, overwhelming obligations rest with the organisation and its managers. Standards are present and prescribed and are not the subject of negotiation. Managers must therefore seek to resolve problems and promote harmony. Conflict of interests between groups must be kept to a minimum. Fundamental causes of dispute (especially those to do with pay and conditions) must be resolved to set deadlines and not be allowed to drag on. Any pay rise must meet the expectations of the staff, or else the reasons for not meeting expectations must be clearly articulated. Grievances and disputes must also be speedily resolved, rather than being allowed to fester.

A further prerequisite to the success of this approach is that the staff identity with the organisation must be strong and must be gained at the outset of employment. Organisations that adopt conformist approaches in this way tend to invest heavily in induction and orientation programmes for all staff to ensure that they adopt the values and attitudes required. This leads to rejection as well as acceptance: the organisation does not seek to be all things to all people. Conformist organisations do not normally accommodate values other than their own.

The position of trade unions and other staff representative bodies is clearly defined and limited at the outset of any agreement. The basis of agreement is set by the organisation. The union or representative body is invited to work within it; and, if it feels unable to do this, it will not be recognised but rather alternative staff representation methods will be sought.

■ Other means of reconciling workplace conflict

■ Conciliation

This is a means whereby employers and employees seek to reach mutually acceptable settlements of their disputes, usually by placing the matter in the hands of a neutral and independent third party. Conciliators examine all sides of the case. They analyse areas of agreement and areas of dispute, and present these back to the parties involved. They identify areas where agreement can be made in order to try and effect a reconciliation between the parties.

■ Mediation

If, for example, conciliation fails the two sides may seek a third party to mediate in the dispute. The mediator will put forward hisown positive proposals aimed at resolving the matter in hand. The mediator may produce this in the form of a report outlining recommendations for a satisfactory settlement.

The benefit of the mediation and conciliation approach lies in the ability of the third party involved to see the dispute from a detached point of view and to find ways around the behavioural and operational blockages that inevitably exist.

■ Arbitration

Arbitration differs from conciliation and mediation in that the arbitrator determines the outcome of the dispute by proposing a settlement; in cases that go to arbitration it is normal for both parties to agree to be bound by the findings of the arbitrator at the outset. The usual form of arbitration is **open** arbitration in which the arbitrator has complete discretion to award whatever she sees fit within the given terms of reference and which will provide an effective solution to the problem. The arbitrator also has regard to behavioural matters and the forms of words in which agreements are couched; this is to accommodate the perceptual and behavioural niceties required as indicated above.

Pendulum arbitration is a closed form of arbitration. Again, the arbitrator hears both sides of the dispute. She will then, however, decide wholly in favour of one party or the other. Someone therefore always wins (and is seen to win), and someone always loses (and is seen to lose). The concept of pendulum arbitration is based on the idea that faced with the prospect or possibility of losing a dispute, each party will wish to resort to resolving the differences without getting into this situation. The approach is widely used by Japanese companies operating in the West. In these companies there are strong cultural pressure on managers not to get into disputes, and not to lose them if they do. Again, therefore, there is a pressure to resolve problems rather than to institutionalise them.

Pendulum arbitration normally represents the final solution to any dispute in organisations that use it. There is normally no appeal against the arbitrator's findings. This is clearly stated in the staff handbooks and agreements of the organisations concerned. Those entering into pendulum arbitration agree to be bound by the outcome before the arbitrator hears the case.

■ Conclusions

Understanding the sources and causes of conflict draws away from the hitherto accepted view that organisational strife is caused by troublemakers, trade unions, whistle blowers and other prima donnas or overmighty subjects or groups. Strategies and systems for the handling and management of conflict clearly institutionalise rather than resolve conflict. They also tend to reinforce (rather than dissolve) more deeply held negative attitudes of mistrust, dishonesty and duplicity.

The current view therefore, is that conflict is inevitable and that it is potentially present in all human relations and activities; this includes work. In organisations it is determined by physical lay-out, physical and psychological distance, intergroup relationships, hierarchies, technology, expertise and by the interaction of individual group and organisational aims and objectives.

Rather than the use of channels, procedures, institutions and forms, the desired approach is to give everyone a common set of values, goals and purposes for being in the organisation, whihc both recognise and transcend the presence of conflict and reconcile the differing aims and objectives. Destructive conflict is minimised and resources otherwise used in the operation of staff management and industrial relations systems are released to be put to more positive and productive effect.

■ Questions

1. Outline and discuss the benefits and drawbacks of referring every single dispute or argument to arbitration.
2. What are the advantages and disadvantages of the collective bargaining approach to the management and resolution of conflict?
3. Consider the Karen Wells example (Box 11.5). What actions were necessary (a) by Karen Wells and (b) by the hospital to ensure that the relationship was productive and harmonious from the outset?
4. Check any organisation (or department within an organisation) with which you are familiar against the symptoms of conflict indicated above. What conclusions can you draw? On the basis of your analysis, what action should now be taken?

CHAPTER 12
Realpolitik

Realpolitik is the art of survival in the particular organisation and situation. This requires knowledge and understanding of the ways in which both organisation and situation operate, and of the different pressures and influences that are brought to bear. It also requires knowledge and understanding of the likely outcome of particular approaches. It is further necessary to adopt particular forms of approach to different individuals based on an understanding of what they are receptive to and what they are likely to reject.

All organisations have their own internal politics (the means by which influence and rewards are gained or lost). An understanding of this is essential from the following points of view.

1. The organisation itself, and those responsible for its governance, direction and performance need to recognise the nature and prevalence of the different forms of political activity. This includes the effects on operations, effectiveness and success. Much of the infighting and competition at different levels and among functions may not be apparent to those at the top. Further, they may not perceive that their activities, those achievements for which they issue rewards and punishments, or the basis on which resources are allocated create strife and dissension elsewhere. They may also hide behind 'the need to consider the wider picture' and the equivalent as reasons and excuses for encouraging and rewarding the activities of lobbies and pressure groups, or of being seen to favour particular departments at the expense of others.

2. Organisation politics are also often encouraged and used as forms of control by those at the top. They observe the effects of encouraging this form of behaviour in terms of giving some form of direction and focus to the different groups and individuals. They may also observe this behaviour as some kind of 'rite of passage' (the opportunity for an individual or group to prove themselves). In absolute terms, however, this only has any form of validity where it is clearly linked to organisational purpose and effectiveness. Success and failure should never be seen merely in terms of the ability to operate and compete within the system.

3. Teams and groups that depend on particular forms, resources and support for their continued well-being and existence need to establish relationships with those who hand these out. As well as performance effectiveness, the basis of this is likely to include other matters such as support for the backers in other initiatives, sharing of the profits and merits of success, and distance from any apparent failure.

4. Individuals need to be able to create physical and psychological space in order to be able to pursue their own aims, and practise and develop their expertise. Ideally, this will all accord with the organisation's overall direction; even where this is so, a

certain amount of politicking and lobbying is normally required (for example, for new and improved equipment the opportunity to attend training and development). Where this is less apparent, the individual will in any case seek to ensure that his own aims and objectives are met to a greater or lesser extent, whether or not these comply with those of the organisation. Where the situation is very bad, individuals will pursue their own goals to the exclusion of those of the organisation.

5. Departments, divisions and functions become involved in organisation politics, overwhelmingly because of the need to compete for resources and to maintain their own reputation and standing. Again, this is invariably present to some extent even in the best of organisations. In other cases, competition for both resources and reputation is often based on the distributive principle whereby one succeeds at the expense of others, and this becomes the driving force behind departmental success.

6. Understanding, surviving and operating in the political systems of organisations stem from this. It is very short term and anyone who tries to take a more rational, long-term and operational view is likely to lose out at the expense of those who know how the political system works and how to succeed within it. Otherwise, the major output of these forms of activity is interdepartmental and interindividual conflict (see Chapter 11), together with the prioritisation and use of resources in the pursuit of political advantage at the expense of operational effectiveness.

■ Survival

Individuals and groups have to survive long enough to become successful and effective operators. They have therefore to be able to make use of systems, procedures, practices and support mechanisms. With the best will in the world, there is no point in taking an enlightened or ethical view of this if the organisation's ways of working will not support it. People therefore develop their own format for the niches that they occupy and the roles and functions that they carry out, in order to maximise their chances of being effective and successful operators (as distinct from expert in the performance of their expertise or function). In each case this consists of the following.

1. Developing approaches based on a combination of role, function and personality, adding a personal strand to the professional and operational. This means developing measures of trust, warmth and liking as a part of the professional and operational dealings.

2. Developing approaches based on individual influence. This involves recognising the nature of the influence of the individual and the ability to present it in ways useful to others within the organisation.

3. Developing networks of professional, personal and individual contacts and using these as means of gaining fresh insights and approaches to issues and problems.

4. Developing funds of bargaining chips – equipment, information, resources, expertise – which can be used in trade-offs and for mutual advantage and satisfaction when required.

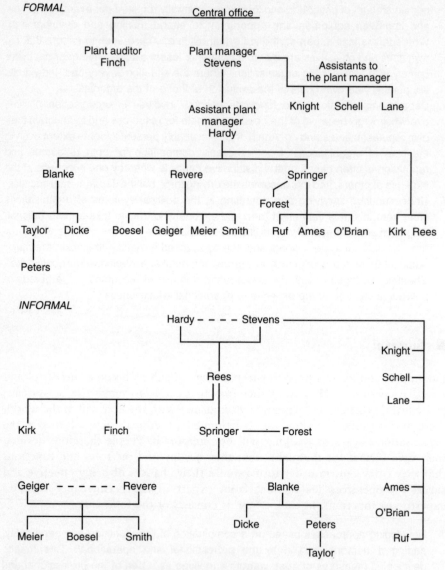

Figure 12.1   Formal and informal organisation relationships

Source: from Luthans (1990)

5.   Developing a clarity of thought around the entire aspects of organisation operations
     and activities. This is based, on the one hand, on what is important, urgent and of
     value, and to whom; and, on the other, on what facilitates progress, and what
     hinders or blocks it. This also involves recognition of where the true interests of the
     individual lie and how these can best be served in the situation.

Different forms of each approach are required for each role and function carried out. A different approach may also be required to the same individual or group where there is interaction on more than one basis. For example, a production supervisor may be able to request financial information from the accounts supervisor in one way; while the approach to the same supervisor would vary considerably if the supervisor were also the local union lay official representing a grievance on the part of the member of the production team.

■ Spheres of influence

These are discussed in Chapter 8. In this particular context, however, people construct their own spheres of influence in order to give themselves both space and time to be able to operate a stage further on from the capacity to survive. Around this are constructed personal networks and support systems that enable help and assistance to be sought for problem-solving, project work and general support. This includes the formation of pressure groups and special interest groups, professional and peer group clusters. Each comes to prominence when wider organisational matters demand it, requiring particular input, or threatening its territory or influence. People gravitate towards those that are deemed to be successful and effective, or those that are suitable and which can be made to work to their advantage; and they gravitate away from those that are deemed to be unsuccessful, ineffective or unsuitable.

■ Patronage

This is where the position, hopes for advancement and influence of an individual or group – the protégé – are placed at the disposal of another – the patron. The patron provides encouragement, resources and space so that the protégé may prosper and flourish. A form of effort–reward relationship is thus engaged. The protégé depends for success on performing the task, and acting and behaving in ways acceptable to the patron.

At its best, this is found in mentoring, nurturing and other positive and encouraging relationships, the output of which is both organisation and individual development. In other cases, it is at the core of organisation and intra-organisation power and influence struggles and consists of 'favours for favours': support and compliance in particular activities in return for rewards and favours when the struggle is over and successfully concluded.

These forms of bonds and alliances may take place within a particular group or department, or between members of different functions. In either case, the overall effect is the subversion of organisation and group purposes in the pursuit of the agenda of the members of the bond or alliance.

It is invariably a dominant–dependent relationship, and as such is fraught with dangers for the protégé. If the prevailing organisation climate changes or the dominant partner loses interest, or adopts a different perspective on the work of the protégé, the latter is likely to find that she is cut adrift and isolated, or else that the rewards promised may simply not materialise (whether because expectations are unreal or because the patron changes his mind).

■ Succession

Grooming the successor is also a form a patronage. Overtly sound and logical in concept, it nevertheless raises more general questions of the honesty and integrity of the relationship between patron and protégé as well as that which may exist between the patron and other members of their staff. For those who appear to have been placed out of the running, the effects on morale are always negative. Again, however, the problem ultimately lies with the chosen successor: when the patron leaves, those in overall control may decide that the particular individual is not right to succeed to the job for whatever reason. The protégé may also no longer be acceptable to their peers once the patron has been removed.

More generally, succession planning of any sort is fraught with uncertainties brought about by constant change. Any guarantee that a particular job is certain to be available in 2–3 years' time is highly questionable in any situation. In most circumstances, promises of this nature cannot be made for periods of longer than between 3 and 6 months. This is quite apart from the fact that any protégé who seeks such a promise to be made or who receives one, or any patron who makes such a commitment, is almost certainly either unaware of the vagaries and uncertainties of any situation, or else is fully aware of them and seeking to generate a certainty of position within them. In summary, it is easy to see how this form of activity may become tainted and corrupted, and open to interpretation as such by all others involved and affected.

■ Favouritism and victimisation

Favouritism is an extreme form of patronage. It occurs where the patron gives advancement or rewards to the protégé as the result of some personal quality or attribute.

The converse is victimisation and occurs when the patron takes a dislike to the subordinate, again for some personal reason. He/she is then used as a scapegoat or victim when required. If this is allowed to get out of hand, it is stressful and demoralising to the individual affected and also to those around them. The worst excesses of this are bullying, harassment, persistent personal attacks (physical and verbal), the blocking of opportunities and prospects for advancement.

■ The ability to influence

Both patronage and also general political relationships within organisations depend on the extent to which one party may exert influence over others. The key features of this are set out below.

■ Dependence

The greater the dependence of a protégé on a patron, the greater that person's susceptibility to being influenced to go in particular directions or to pursue particular projects.

■ Uncertainty

Where people are unclear or uncertain about the correctness or otherwise of an action, they will nevertheless tend to carry it out if requested or directed to do so by someone in authority because *their* responsibility for it is thus removed. Also, where people are unclear about current activities and behaviour, there is a greater propensity to change to something that gives clear guidance or sets firm standards.

■ Expectations

Where the expectations of those in organisations and their groups are well understood, anything that is presented to them in ways that are perceived to meet and satisfy them is more likely to be accepted and complied with. Where expectations are not well understood or where there is a lack of attention to the presentation, acceptance is less certain.

■ Authority

The greater the authority behind a particular drive or initiative, the more likely it is that it will be accepted. This is true whatever the form of authority, be it rational, legal, expert or charismatic.

■ Confidence

This is the key element, the one which binds all the others together in patron–protégé relationships (indeed, in any superior–subordinate relationship). It is the confidence on the part of the patron that the protégé will deliver the matter in hand effectively and in ways beneficial to both; and the confidence on the part of the protégé that the patron is a reliable and adequate source of influence for her own purposes.

■ Position assessment

People assess their position in the wider organisational scheme of things and also in the influence stakes, pecking order and respect and esteem in which they are held. They will do this for themselves, their occupational profession and their department division and function. They assess their strengths and weaknesses, the opportunities and threats that prevail and from this take steps to ensure that their future is secured as far as possible.

They will assess where intergroup and interpersonal frictions and hostilities lie, and the reasons for these. From this battle plans (by any other name) are constructed and drawn up, both to preserve the position (defensive) and also to develop and enhance the position, usually at the expense of others (offensive).

This also involves assessing where blockages to progress lie and taking steps to remedy these. It normally means opening up channels of communication and other relationships with the particular areas in question and establishing mutual interest and confidence. Where this is concerned with problems relating to sources of influence and resources, it often means a combination of self-promotion (of capabilities, qualities and successes) together with identifying the interests of the blockage (see Box 12.1). From this range of activities emerges a true clarity of position in the organisation's political scheme. As all departments, groups, divisions and individuals will do it on their own behalf, the potential for a system of lobbies, special interest groups and alliances starts to become apparent.

BOX 12.1   The Interests of the Blockage

The main reasons for refusing to deal with someone from elsewhere in the same organisation normally fall into one or more of the following categories.

1. Disdain – the people, department or activities are seen to have no value. This may be the result of general perceptions. It may also be the result of preconceived ideas and notions. It may have arisen as a matter of historic fact (for example, where previous results have been poor, or because previous cooperation between those affected was disastrous).
2. Lack of clarity – where one or both parties views the activities of the others with suspicion based on a lack of knowledge and understanding.
3. Benefits of associations may not be clear, especially where one party perceives the benefits but the other does not.
4. The wider picture – whereby associating with one group may cause the feelings of other groups to be influenced in turn. (For example, department X has a relationship with department Z; department X is approached by department Y to open up relationships. Department Y is the enemy of department Z. Department X therefore takes the whole picture into account before opening up relationships with department Y.)

---

5. Dominance–dependence – the extent and nature of the need for the relationship, and the position of the two parties on the dominance–dependence spectrum.
6. The potential relationship – the perceptions of the extent to which it can and might be developed to mutual advantage and, above all, in the interests of the blockage. In this case the onus is clearly on the approacher (see main text) to indicate the likely benefits to the blocker.
7. Lack of trust – the extent to which those involved say what they mean, and mean what they say; and the extent to which each can deliver what is promised.

■ Special relationships

The most important of these are those which exist between the CEO's department and other functions; and between the head office and outlying functions of those organisations that are so designed. Invariably, there is a draw of resources, prestige, status and influence towards the head office (and very often this occurs at the expense of those both physically and psychologically remote from the centre).

Right or wrong, it is a key relationship and those who seek to operate successfully must recognise its extent. Where necessary, this relationship must be nurtured and developed and the interests of the CE or head office engaged. Conversely, it is a key part of the CE and head office function to recognise the presence and prevalence of this, and to ensure that the relationships between themselves and their more distant functions remain productive, effective and harmonious.

This is also a problem between parallel functions that have little or no physical or personal contact. Some format is clearly desirable to ensure at least an adequate measure of understanding and communication. Where no responsibility is taken for this and where no direction is given, these functions will tend to form their own *ad hoc* alliances and special interest groups to ensure that when they need it they have a strong and united voice.

■ Confidence and trust

The key feature in the nature of organisation politics arises from the level of mutual confidence and trust held by those in particular relations. Where there is no confidence or trust the relationship is corrupted at the outset.

In terms of organisation politics, this may be a constraint within which the groups and individuals have to work. In the worst cases it tends to lead to blame scapegoating and negative presentation (the denigration of the efforts of others as well as the promotion of self).

Confidence and trust are destroyed where one party gives these freely and they are not reciprocated; and where information or resources are given over and then used against the giver. They are affected by the balance of truth – the extent to which communications and interactions take place on an overt or covert basis – and, above all, by the use of direct and indirect language, adherence to deadlines and orders of priority.

In organisations with highly developed political systems, confidence and trust start off at a low level, and both individuals and groups will make sure that they are very certain of the integrity of those with whom they are dealing before giving out hostages to fortune, departmental secrets and specific matters concerning their own expertise or trade.

■ Ideologies

From time to time individuals and groups are called upon to interact with those whose ideologies and values they find repugnant. While in absolute terms it is easy to encourage them not to have any association, in practice this is not always possible.

For example, it may be essential to deal with somebody who is known to be a bully to their staff (or their family) or with someone who is known to take all the glory and credit for success for themselves and to find scapegoats and others to blame for failures.

This may also apply to wider political, ethical and religious questions (for example, where it is essential to have dealings with an organisation that takes a particular view on something that is for similar reasons repugnant). As stated elsewhere, lying, cheating, stealing and bribery are always wrong. However, the current interests of the business may require that a bribe be offered to a particular individual in order to secure work in the immediate term. Elsewhere, during the apartheid period in South Africa, organisations were faced with either conducting their business under the constraints of that particular regime, or of not operating at all. The development of countries such as Poland, Hungary, Czechoslovakia and Vietnam was held up for decades because of the prevailing ideologies of the USSR and USA. Anyone who dealt with the USSR during the Communist regime had to do so by working within a system that repressed all forms of dissent and choice.

■ Territory

People defend their territory and view any encroachment upon it as a threat. One group given a remit that is at least partly normally that of another may therefore expect to receive protests from the other as the result (either to themselves directly, or else to the party that commissioned the work).

On the other hand, people seek to extend and expand their territory, both physically and psychologically. They seek extension of their influence. They seek both to preserve and enhance their total position within the organisation to make themselves as indispensable as possible and, from this, to gain additional resources, prestige and influence. This may be called territorialism. Fed by the twin needs of preservation and enhancement, it involves both seeking opportunities for expansion and also constant attention to the threats of those seeking to extend their influence.

Territorialism also feeds the processes by which departments, divisions and groups build their own defensive walls in the form of ordering and prioritising the work that they do for others and in editing and filtering information in and out. On the other hand, part of this also consists of recognising where the defensive walls, secrets, special interests and caches of information of other individuals and groups lie, and finding the means by which these may be accessed.

Jealousy is a key feature of territorialism. It exists as an extreme form of the need to guard and preserve whatever expertise, resources and information are held in the department or group. Where encroachment or pressure occurs, this leads:

- to uncertainty for the future, especially where the expertise, resource or information is no longer seen to be critical;
- to resentment because the fact of the exertion of pressure strongly indicates that the area in question is not (or is no longer) sacrosanct or stable;
- to loss of confidence and faith in the future which is damaging to morale;
- to those affected developing their own view of the uncertainty which often leads to their seeking opportunities and openings elsewhere (perhaps even 'crossing the floor' to work for the group currently exerting the pressure).

Moreover, there is nearly always resentment when groups and departments are merged. This is very difficult to manage without giving the overwhelming feeling that one has been taken over by the other (or, where more than two are involved, that the new group will not be founded on the basis of the domination of one of the old). This is often only partly addressed by the installation of new leaders and managers from outside, the provision of new facilities and equipment and the restructuring of work. It is greatly exaggerated where key appointments to the new group are from within one of the old, and especially where these constitute a direct transfer of function and authority. Those not part of the old 'key group' tend to feel themselves to have been taken over and their old work to have been invaded and swallowed up. This is also very damaging to individual feelings of esteem and worth: when a department or group is swallowed up in this way it puts a negative perception of importance and value on that which was carried out before and therefore on the value of those affected to the organisation overall.

■ Ambiguity

Problems arise when spheres of influence, roles and lines of activity are not clearly delineated. This especially occurs where everything else is overtly highly ordered and structured. It also occurs where aims and objectives are not clear and where people therefore tend to operate in a void. In this circumstance groups and individuals use this to extend their boundaries, build their own empires and pursue their own aims and objectives.

This is set to be a problem for organisations as they seek culture and attitude change, pursue programmes of continuous improvement and customer focus. Areas of concern arise where there are matters of role boundary on the one hand and the demands of customers and clients on the other. Interventions made by groups and individuals for the good of customers may lead to wrangles and squabbles if this requires exceeding normally or traditionally demarcated boundaries. Similarly, groups and individuals tend to resent matters of their concern being picked up by others and handed on to them for resolution (whether from the most positive of standpoints and with the best will in the world or not).

At stake for effective operations, therefore, is the requirement to find ways of working and an organisation political stance that attend to both overall effectiveness, and personal feelings. Given that hitherto accepted notions and norms of high levels of structure and order are passing away, those responsible for the management and design of organisations have to address the issues of ambiguity, uncertainty and tolerance to get over these problems and yet leave people with an overall clarity of purpose and distinctive format to which to work.

■ Communications

Organisation politics are reflected in the nature, style and content of communications. Any situation is improved or otherwise by the quality of communications. In particular, any negative is exacerbated by bad and inadequate communications poorly delivered. This is reinforced by any feelings and realities of physical and psychological distance from those who are pronouncing. In these situations the grapevine, the work of vested interests and special interest groups, and other bodies (trade unions, cluster groups, professional associations) flourish and lead to loss of direction, purpose and morale.

Invariably, this leads to increases in disciplinary problems, disputes and grievances, both between individuals and the organisation and between departments. It also leads to an increase in the operation of formal procedures in these areas, especially the number of disputes that go to arbitration. Because of the lack of understanding that stems from poor quality communications, both individuals and groups tend to feel that the only satisfactory outcome is one that is handed down by an independent referee or arbitrator. Where this is allowed to persist over long periods of time, complicated procedures, systems and structures are devised to try to accommodate these issues.

The result is that interdepartmental strife and wranglings become institutionalised. In turn, it becomes part of the organisation's remit to handle these. Indeed, it becomes in the interest of those parts of the organisation dealing with the construction of procedures and the management of strife that the problems should continue; for, if they did not, there would be no job for them.

All of this is traceable back to the lack of clarity that is brought on by bad and inadequate communications and communication systems and processes. Moreover, as these situations develop, information is fed into the systems in the interests of those who hold it. It therefore tends to become distorted, refined, edited and even falsified and corrupted.

■ Human interaction

The common thread running through all of these elements is human interaction. The worst examples occur when human interaction is allowed (or even encouraged) to go uncontrolled and undirected. The behavioural, operational and organisational effects are clearly recognisable as, in the worst cases, are specific issues concerning resource consumption and staff demoralisation.

Given that all organisations are bound to consist of human interactions the onus is therefore on those responsible for their design, ordering and direction to ensure that these are productive and effective, rather than dysfunctional and destructive. This applies to the overt and direct relationships that are generated when departments, divisions and groups are created, and also to the less tangible aspects of creating the conditions in which harmony, trust and confidence can exist.

Their outcome is therefore ideally that:

- factions, pressure groups, vested interests and other cliques and special interests will be drawn together on matters of prime importance to the organisation, its aims and objectives and in pursuit of their own goals as they see them in harmony with those of the organisation;
- bonds and alliances are formed to pursue the organisation's best interests rather than what they see as narrow self-interest within its confines;
- politicking is engaged in on the basis of drive for operational effectiveness rather than personal or group survival. It can be just as frustrating for those concerned when this form of lobby is turned down by the organisation on the basis that it does not find the proposals suitable in its own terms. However, this normally arises from a much higher level of general understanding and particular effectiveness and integrity of relationship, so the rejection is normally professional rather than personal.

The focus of organisational relationships is based on professional and technical expertise rather than personal relationship and patronage at all levels, and whatever the factors of distance and function may be.

■ Political activity

Political activity is that which is engaged in under each of these headings. Based on human interaction and grouped around vested interests, special interest groups, clusters and other gatherings, it consists in the main of meetings, the formulation of political strategies, lobbying and presentation.

■ Meetings

These may be formal or informal; clandestine or overt; targeted or general; proactive, reactive or responsive. They may be enmeshed in procedure, regularised, open or *ad hoc*. They may be targeted where action is taken as the result of the decision of the meeting. They may be influential, whereby action is supposed to arise as the result of the meeting being called (for example, a meeting called by members of a particular union or staff group concerning their pay may be enough to ensure that a pay offer is made by the organisation without further representation). They take place to create initiatives and interests from their own point of view and to respond to issues in which they have a direct involvement.

In each case there are common factors: consideration of their own best interests, devising strategies and tactics, assessment of the strengths and weaknesses of the position, and of the opportunities and threats that are present. The process is both time- and resource-consuming, even where the activity is legitimate and being pursued as a contribution to the best interests of everyone. In other cases these activities replace the organisation's aims and objectives as the main energy and driving force behind the work; in the worst cases, they constitute the work itself and everything else is set to one side.

BOX 12.2   Intra-Organisational Political Meetings

1. Staff meetings.
2. Open meetings.
3. Clusters (professional, technical, peer, *ad hoc*, or based on mutual interest or common cause).
4. Special interest groups.
5. Work improvement groups and quality circles, where these develop into a wider form of mutual interest.
6. Unions and staff representative, consultative, negotiating and participative groups.

■ Political strategies

These are normally based on one or more of the following.

1. Alliances with powerful people and groups: especially with those either in or close to the corridors of power and with others among the upper levels of the organisation. People may also seek out junior staff from the CE's Department and other highly influential functions – PAs and secretaries, for example – as informal friends, advocates and sources of information (secretaries and PAs at all levels have access to both volume and quality of information; for an indication, see Box 12.3).
2. Showing quick results: this is in any case excellent for group morale. It is also often politically necessary to be able to prove to backers that their backing was not misplaced.
3. IOUs: this is where a favour given brings with it the expectation of something in return, whether instant or deferred, and the expectation that the debtor will be expected to pay up when asked.
4. Information acquisition and manipulation: as referred to elsewhere, information is a resource. When viewed from this standpoint, it has to be filtered, edited and represented (even misrepresented and corrupted) to ensure that the given interest is best served. Information is also packaged under such headings as 'top secret', 'classified' or 'restricted': again, from the political point of view, this gives it exclusivity and desirability, and therefore value.

BOX 12.3   Stalin

The 1917 Bolshevik Revolution in Russia was led by Lenin, together with his supporters, Zinoviev, Kamenev, Trotsky and Stalin (who was Party Secretary). The coup was successful. The Communist regime was established and all the organs of state passed from the monarchy which had been overthrown into the control of the Bolsheviks.

In 1923 Lenin died. Everybody expected that Trotsky would succeed him.

However, as Party Secretary, Stalin effectively acted as the 'neck of the hourglass' through which all information – both incoming and outgoing – had to pass. During the period of Lenin's rule he was able to assess his own position of strength. When Lenin died, Stalin knew exactly who was supportive of him, who was compliant or acquiescent and who was hostile. He had also built up a body of more junior supporters who could be put into positions of power when the need arose.

On the death of Lenin, Stalin seized power and proclaimed himself to be the new leader of Bolshevik Russia. He exiled Trotsky and removed from office all of those who were hostile to him, replacing them with his own supporters. Later this extended into purges and reigns of terror in which all of those who had even vaguely considered alternatives to him were removed.

> The fact that Stalin could achieve all this was originally based entirely on his ability to gain, use, command and manipulate information to his advantage and thus secure his position.

5. Battlefields: in political terms, people tend to avoid pitched battles because they may lose (and, moreover, be seen to have lost). The more usual approach adopted is the gradual or incremental: chipping away at the target, rather than setting out to destroy it in one fell swoop (apart from anything else, the victor of an overt and decisive engagement may be seen as a bully, and the defeated as a victim). The gradualist approach is generally much less noticeable and is therefore not regarded as a threat.

   Guerilla war is also engaged in where one department or group seeks to denigrate the efforts and achievements of others. It consists of sniping, gaining adverse coverage and identifying the weaknesses of others and spotlighting them (one of the most powerful positions of all is that of spotlighter: the light is shone on the particular point desired and the spotlighter remains in the relative darkness and invisibility behind the light).

   The language used here is that of military engagement and this reflects accurately the organisational behaviour equivalent. Battles and wars are fought both to preserve and maintain position, and also to enhance it. Those involved store up memories of victories and defeats so that they may build on successes and take steps to avoid future failures.

☐ *Advice and guidance*

This is received, judged and evaluated. It must be accepted or rejected on its own merits. It has to be considered from the point of view of the giver as well as the receiver.

When advice and guidance are sought it should always to be borne in mind that the giver will have his own vested interest and point of view. Where counsel is given, its quality and emphasis is also invariably tainted by one's own particular interests.

☐ *For and against*

This is the standpoint that states that 'anyone who does not support us is against us'. Anthony Jay (*Management and Machiavelli*, 1967) states that:

> The guiding principle is that senior people in taken-over organisations should either be warmly welcomed or encouraged, or else sacked. If they are sacked, they are powerless. If they are down-graded or neutralised, they will remain united, resentful and determined to get their own back.

Elsewhere in organisations it becomes possible to establish who is friendly and sympathetic and who is not as the focus of political activities. Invariably, positions of friendship and support are reinforced by the IOUs and favours; and positions of antagonism by spotlighting and ensuring adverse coverage of activities.

☐ *Use of crises*

Crises can be manipulated and used to make critical, successful and high profile interventions. They also have the purpose of apportioning blame and identifying beneficiaries, winners and losers. If a threat comes from outside the organisation, it can be used as a lever for extra resources and influence. The overt response is to counter the threat, the covert is to gain extra resources at the same time, using the situation to full advantage to gain greater comfort and stability.

This also relates to the basis of engagement in disputes. People may become involved in a small affair because a successful outcome can be presented as a major triumph. Conversely, they may withdraw from major and important crises because they see little prospect of gaining any personal or group advantage for themselves whatever the outcome.

☐ *Personal position*

There are three archetypal forms:

The **godparent** builds up a fund of IOUs, favours, connections and influences based on the giving and receiving principle: for every favour carried out, a return is expected at some point in the future and will be requested when necessary. This derives from the book and film of *The Godfather* (Mario Puzo) in which the central character created an empire, originally based on a series of favours and IOUs.

The **scout master** builds up retinues and networks (both formal, based on reporting relationships, and informal, based on personality and influence) of junior staff, protégés and dependents. By taking on the overt mantle of mentor and guide, a position of personal influence is developed covertly. The result is that a position of influence is constructed among those at more junior levels. These in turn support their scout master in their current position. Any organisation development that takes place is also at least partly influenced along the lines required by the scout master.

The **overmighty subject** is the person who uses a position of relative functional authority and autonomy to build up her sphere of influence as her own personal fiefdom to generate indispensability and to distribute favours among her chosen people. The overmighty subject flourishes best when physically distant from the main organisation (for example, in charge of a remote or outlying branch) or when she has a distinctive expertise without which the organisation perceives that it cannot manage.

☐ *Indispensability*

This position is arrived at by individuals and groups, usually as the result of having produced a key result or series of positive achievements that coincide with the interests of someone more powerful or influential. This is then used by individuals or groups to their own advantage: they discover the continuing priorities of the key person and present their own capabilities and objectives in terms which meet these. The overt relationship is one of faithful servant; the covert can be stated as 'Now you have got me exactly where I want you.'

☐ *Use of the Peter Principle*

This involves giving a group or an individual a task that is known to be well beyond their capabilities. They are therefore certain to fail. This failure can then be used to remove any influence or prestige that the individual or group concerned have hitherto enjoyed.

■ Lobbying and presentation

The key to all successful internal political activity lies in the effectiveness of lobbying and presentation. Much of this is implicit and even stated as part of the forms of political strategy indicated above. The rest lies in the ability to recognise those emphases of particular initiatives and activities that are likely to gain a sympathetic hearing and those that are not. The problem then is to find the right channels and media to be used to best advantage, and to combine these to form an effective case that can be well presented. As with all communications, therefore, success comes about as the result of understanding the requirements of the receivers and choosing the right media, format and language. In political activities, and especially when dealing with senior figures, this invariably includes attention to:

- flattery, vanity and triumphs;
- timescales (often the lobby has only a limited time in which to put across their case);
- the combination of substance and presentation (a fair case well presented invariably succeeds at the expense of a brilliant case poorly presented);
- the merits and demerits of other lobbies and interest (part of any political process consists of denigrating opposing points of view, as well as the sound delivery of one's own case).

Lobbying also involves, first, the engagement of other vested interests and special interest groups who may be persuaded to a particular point of view, perhaps because it is related to their interests, or because they may see an advantage accruing as the result of support, or in return for favours previously given; and second, use of statistics and other information supports and emphasises the case, especially when these can be related to direct and positive statements (for example, 90 per cent of people are in favour of this; by doing this we will double our market share in 12 weeks). These can also be used in less rational and even overtly spurious ways (for example, next door had a 12 per cent pay rise, you're offering us 3 per cent, what is the certain affect of this on our morale?) but which nevertheless may be effective. National politicians engaged in public and media debates are expert at this, as are trade union representatives.

☐ *Negotiation*

Negotiation is a form of lobbying. However, rather than straightforward presentation, it takes the form of seeking to establish a position on a given issue with which everyone concerned can be at least contented. It can be used as a tool, technique or means of intervention as part of each of the political strategies indicated above.

For details of the content and process see Box 12.4. In general, each party has an opening position. This is presented to the opponent on the basis that it cannot possibly be accepted; it simply exists to put down a mark and also to draw out the opponents opening position. Indeed, where the opening position of one party is instantly accepted by the other, this leads to frustration on the part of the demander that they did not ask for more.

The rest of the negotiation consists of the following factors.

1. Attention to the absolute nature, strengths and weaknesses of the total position adopted.
2. Attention to the desired outcome.
3. Arrangement of demands and positions in orders of priority and importance so that trade-offs can be made by dropping or diluting lesser items in order to pursue and gain compliance on the core issues.
4. Empathy (understanding the other side's point of view, aims and objectives and priorities).
5. Attention to the progress of negotiation because people on all sides like and need to see positive movement rather than deadlock or inertia.
6. Attention to positive and negative power and influence, in particular the ability to block the other side's priorities if the need arises.
7. Attention to the behavioural aspects of negotiations. These fall into two categories. First, an agreement that is reached too quickly may lead the followers of either party to feel that they were not best served by their negotiator; this has to be balanced with the feelings of frustration, as indicated above, that are likely to arise if no progress is made (or perceived to be made). Second, there are the ritual and behavioural aspects to be considered. In many situations, these reflect what people expect to see on the part of their negotiators and how they expect them to behave. This includes the use of strong and confrontational language, media coverage, stories of late night and all night sittings; all of this proves that the negotiator is working extremely hard on behalf of his people and their interests.

8. Attention to the outcome. The ideal is to arrive at win:win (see Box 11.9). Where this is not possible, the presentation of the conclusion and outcome has to be considered from a variety of points of view.
9. The extent to which there is a need for one party to be seen to have won and the other to be seen to have lost.
10. The extent of the need for one party to be seen to have had a triumph and the other to be seen to have had a disaster.
11. Lingering feelings of resentment, jealousy, the desire for revenge or getting even.
12. General effects on motivation and morale.
13. The extent of the need to restore and conduct productive and harmonious relations in the future once the matter in hand is resolved.

For lobbies and negotiations the important thing from the point of view of organisation politics is to be successful and to be seen and perceived as such. Success draws support just as failure dilutes it and turns it away; and this applies even when it is known that success was achieved by accident or as the result of external forces, or where failure occurred in spite of the fact that the quality of the particular lobby, approach or negotiation was seen to be very high. For example, Margaret Thatcher is widely perceived to have won the UK general election of 1983 as the result of having fought and won the Falklands War in 1982; while Neil Kinnock was so widely perceived to have fought a brilliant campaign in the election of 1987 that even though he lost, he retained his position (although when he lost again in 1992 he was swiftly removed).

BOX 12.4   Content and Process of Negotiation and Lobbying

1. The parties or protagonists: their role and position, the extent of their legitimacy and validity, the extent of their influence, the other forces at their disposal, their reputation, their particular interests, other factors riding on their position (especially questions and consequences of success and failure).
2. The position: in terms of ideal outcomes, and the base line or absolute minimum requirements for a settlement. The win:win, win:lose, lose:win, lose:lose; and the content and consequences of each.
3. The opening gambit: to satisfy the twin concerns of putting down a marker and to ensure rejection (see text).
4. The range of processes available:

    (a) formal, including meetings, conventions, papers and documents;
    (b) informal, including meetings, personal contacts, favours, IOUs, off-the-record briefings and conversations.

5. The range of bargaining counters and chips available, also formal and informal.

6. The expectations, aims and objectives of all those involved; personal and hidden agenda as well as overt or stated purposes.

7. The range of possible outcomes; those which are supportable and those which are not; the potential and possibility for each of these to arise and the steps necessary to ensure that they do or do not; actions to be taken as a result.

8. The behavioural and ritual aspects that have to be satisfied; in many cases the ability to accommodate these is the key to success or failure (see main text).

9. Marketing and public relations: the presentation of the case with credibility and confidence; the drawing in and engagement of support and sympathy; continued attention to the publicity surrounding the case; the ability to present both the progression and the outcome in favourable ways.

10. Delivery: of that which was indicated or promised; translating agreement into practice and action.

■ Organisational health and well-being

Organisational politics are the barometer of its general state of health and well-being. The indicators of this are set out below.

1. Levels of absenteeism, sickness and turnover: the stated reasons why each of these occur and the attitude adopted towards them by the organisation at large as well as by individual managers and supervisors. The key features are: the nature and extent of procedures to deal with these and the ways in which these are used; the use to which any general and specific information thus gained is put; the volume of time and resource expended on these, including the creation of departments and functions for their purpose.

    Particular figures can indicate both general and specific causes for concern, excess absence or departures from particular areas, for example (see Box 12.5). These are always a general indication of states of morale, confidence and motivation.

BOX 12.5   Sickness and Absence

The determination of acceptable levels of each varies between organisations. Some general indicators can be given, however.

1. For each percentage point it effectively means that an additional member of staff per hundred is being employed who would not otherwise be necessary. For example, if absenteeism is 10 per cent across the organisation, an extra

10 members of staff per hundred employed are required; or it takes 110 people to do the work of 100. For a working year of 200 days, each percentage point represents 2 days off sick per member of staff.

2. The extent and prevalence of colds, coughs and general pains as stated reasons in self-certification schemes should always be a cause for concern. Where high and increasing, this is invariably symptomatic of declining or loss of morale. Where low it is an indication of satisfactory and acceptable states of these at least, and the organisation should continue to concentrate on what it is doing well.

3. Japanese companies (and increasing numbers of others that perform well) pay particular attention to sickness and absence and their example is copied by others who show the same concern. They pay specific attention both to morale and to standards of interpersonal relationships and treatment. Self-certificated absence levels are low to negligible and, when these occur, they are always followed up.

    Sanyo UK Ltd, at Lowestoft, always arranges for a home visit, and the company sends a get-well card together with either flowers or chocolates.

    Toshiba UK Ltd, at Plymouth, addresses sickness and absence during its induction courses that all new staff follow. It takes the view that 'If you are a person who has a lot of time off, you should seriously consider whether you wish to work here; we employ you because we value you and need you to work; absence puts pressure on those who do turn up.'

Stress is a cause for concern. In each case self-certificated absence is negligible. It may have its roots in job design and work patterns, or in interpersonal relations, or in levels of accident and injury (or a combination of all of these). Work design can be attended to at a functional level once the problem is identified. Stress caused by interpersonal relationships is normally symptomatic of behavioural malaise.

The number of accidents and injuries also tends to rise as morale declines. This is especially true where pressure is known to have been exerted on people to work in particular ways because of operational pressures, staff shortages and in response to the particular drives of managers and supervisors. Stress, worry and fear may also be by-products among other staff arising from accidents to others.

Each of these constitute a reflection of the state of organisational well-being, and of the attention that is paid to it. Each also reflects the wider general climate that currently prevails.

2. Levels, nature and purposes of meetings: the extent to which people are, in reality, employed to attend meetings (rather than for their substantive purpose) and the effects of this on the rest of the work. The purpose and agenda of meetings is a strong indication of this and is reinforced by the extent to which people need to be seen to be present as distinct from having any real contribution to make.

3. The nature of rewards and favours: the reasons for which they are issued. Here the remedy lies directly in the hands of those in overall control. By simply offering rewards for achievement of aims and objectives rather than because of presentation, lobbying, visibility or psycho-fancy a swathe of political battlegrounds may be removed.
4. The attitude to failures and mistakes: where this is negative and punitive it encourages those concerned to seek scapegoats and victims. It also develops fear and this in turn, leads to the construction of barriers and protectors by which people can insulate themselves from failure. Where mistakes are viewed as a learning experience, much of this is removed.

    Again, this should be seen from standpoint of both results and politics. Where the overall political system is positive and healthy, poor performance is likely to be seen as the starting point for learning and development.

    Where the overall system is unhealthy, this becomes more complicated. Excellent results may be unacceptable politically (for example, where somebody achieves something that nobody else had previously managed). The emphasis may be on presentation rather than achievement, and so excellent results which are poorly marketed or publicised may not carry sufficient weight (see Figure 12.2).

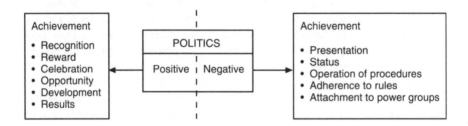

Figure 12.2   Politics and achievement

5. The extent to which departments, divisions, functions and groups continue to serve the purpose for which they were created; the extent to which they are allowed to outlive their usefulness; and what happens to them after they have served their purpose (whether they are destroyed, reconstituted, rejuvenated, made redundant, redeployed, given other projects, encouraged to seek work as a result of their own initiative, and so on). The key factors are the extent to which the organisation assumes responsibility for this, and the extent to which the group itself does so (for example, by making itself indispensable, and therefore indestructible); and the extent to which the skills, knowledge and qualities of those involved are transferable elsewhere. For more positive and enlightened organisations, this last is much less likely to be a problem than the other two.
6. The balance of core and peripheral activities; primary and support functions; and the emphasis put on each. Special attention is required for the extent of checking and control functions; the extent of the influence of these; and the extent to which the

interaction between these and other functions becomes a part of the ends (rather than the means or processes) of primary functions. Strong indicators of these are highly specialised job titles (for example, clock control supervisor, clock card clerk) or extremely vague job titles (for example, director of corporate affairs). They arise from the notion that 'something needs to be done' but without sufficient attention to what this might be, or why, or how. They may also arise as the result of having to find a niche (and therefore a job) for someone whose previous remit has expired and, again, this often occurs without sufficient attention to the what, why or how.

7. The treatment, priority and attention given to vested interests, pressure groups, lobbies, special interests and other pressures, and the reasons why these either succeed or fail (and the reasons why they are perceived or seen to do so). This especially concerns again, whether they succeed or fail because of the particular merits of the case that they put forward as distinct from their ability to energise powerful forces (for example, influential individuals and the media).

BOX 12.6   Pressures

In 1990 a district council in the south-east of England gave planning permission for a home for 32 mentally handicapped young people to be built in the middle of the suburban and middle-class residential area. Those living in the area did not want it. They appealed to the district council who turned down their appeal and upheld their original planning decision. They appealed to the county council who again upheld the planning decision. They then appealed to their Member of Parliament (MP). He wrote to both the district council and the county council voicing the concerns of the residents and asking for the reasons why planning permission was given and asking also for information on the outcome of the proposal so that he could at least allay some of the fears of those who were to be affected.

Overnight the proposal was dropped. The reason given was that the accommodation was no longer required.

The residents were delighted. The MP, however, was not. He angrily wrote again to the district council and the county council. He stated that their planning processes and regulations should be strong enough to be capable of withstanding a simple request for information from an MP, or indeed, from anyone else. He pointed out that he had not even asked for the proposal to be queried, let alone dropped.

---

8. The extent to which information gathered for one purpose is used for others. For example, at times of performance appraisal, individuals are often asked to state what their weaknesses are, wherein they think their performance could be improved and what needs for development they may have. In some cases such information may be used to block promotions, restrict openings and opportunities or, in the worst

cases, this may even lead to disciplinary action. This is also true of financial information: when a set of results is reported for one purpose, these may then be taken out of context and used to indicate particular general levels of performance.

BOX 12.7   Distinctive Features of Public Service Organisations

These are:

- the aim is to provide services for the well-being of the community and what this precisely constitutes is not always apparent or easily defined;
- the difficulty with setting clear and measurable aims and objectives, both for public service organisations as a whole and also for their departments, groups, teams and individuals;
- the scale, variety and complexity of their operations;
- the wider political environment, and the relationship between politicians and servants (including those between MPs, civil servants and local government officers and elected councillors);
- the level and nature of trade union involvement;
- problems with integrating the activities of different national and local government departments; problems of duplication of effort;
- problems of identifying areas of authority, responsibility and accountability;
- the demand for uniformity of treatment and public accountability, and for ever-increasing standards of service;
- problems of measuring standards of service performance, arising from the lack of clarity of aims and objectives;
- the divergent and conflicting pressures placed on politicians, service managers and service professionals;
- traditional career structures;
- the tendency towards rigid personnel policies, administration systems, boundaries of authority and responsibility and fixed salary gradings;
- the length of hierarchy and reporting relations;
- attitudes of resistance to change;
- division and compartmentalisation of activities leading to divisions, blockages and barriers between different levels in hierarchies and different professional and occupational expertise;
- lack of access to top management and others responsible for taking decisions;
- emphasis on systems and procedures rather than professional service outputs;
- emphasis on bureaucratic and cultural controls rather than those related to nature and quality of output.

■ Conclusions

The main lesson is to recognise that politics exists in all organisations and all organisations are political systems. Throughout the environment there are various agenda: departments and their managers have secondary and hidden agenda, promoting themselves and their advancement as well as undertaking particular courses of action.

The situation is always made worse by bad and inadequate communications and communication systems so that people find things out via the grapevine or through vested interests. In these situations, pressure groups, vested interests, overmighty subjects and trade union officials prosper and flourish. This usually leads to increases in the numbers of disputes and grievances concerning both individuals and also between departments; and an increase also in those disputes and grievances that go on to a formal basis and are either referred to arbitration, or elsewhere for resolution. Rules and regulations become the end itself, and not the means to an end. Where these situations are allowed to persist over long periods of time bureaucratic superstructures are devised and additional staff and procedures taken on and adopted; such interdepartmental and organisational wranglings then become institutionalised and part of the ways of working. They also create a tier or function of staff whose professional existence depends on continued high levels of grievances and disputes.

Those responsible for the design and structure of organisations must there-fore recognise these components and vagaries of the work environment. In the medium to long term the negative aspects outlined have extremely demoralising and debilitating effects on everyone concerned, and this ultimately includes customers and clients. There is therefore a direct relationship between the state of organisational politics and performance success and effectiveness. Organisa-tions must recognise these activities for what they are, and take remedial steps wherever necessary and desirable.

■ Questions

1. Why do relationships within organisations tend to become tainted and corrupted?
2. Outline and identify the means by which effective and successful succession planning may take place.
3. Outline and discuss the basis on which special rewards and favours should be issued by organisations to members of staff. How should these be promulgated to staff? How can the fairness of their operation be assured?
4. Consider Box 12.6. Why did the county and district councils prefer to change their mind about the planning position, and what in your view did they expect to gain and achieve by doing so?

CHAPTER 13
Ethics

■ Introduction

Ethics is that part of business which is related to absolute standards and moral principles. More generally, it is concerned with human character and conduct, the distinction between right and wrong and the absolute duties and obligations that exist in all situations.

Some views and perspectives on the relationship between ethics and business are now given.

- Business ethics applies ethical reasoning to business situations and activities. It is based on a combination of distributive justice – that is, the issuing of rewards for contribution to organisation goals and values; and ordinary common decency – an absolute judgement that is placed on all activities. (Elaine Sternberg, 1995)

- Ethical issues concerning business and public sector organisations exist at three levels.

  At the macro level there are issues about the role of the business in the national and international organisation of society. These are largely concerned with addressing the relative virtues of different political/social systems. There are also important issues of international relationships and the role of business on an international scale.

  At the corporate level the issue is often referred to as corporate social responsibility and is focused on the ethical issues facing individual and corporate entities (both private and public sector) when formulating and implementing strategies.

  At the individual level the issue concerns the behaviour and actions of individuals within organisations. (Johnson and Scholes, 1994)

In *Changing Corporate Values* (1990), Adams, Hamil and Carruthers identified a series of factors and elements as measures against which the performance of organisations could be measured in ethical terms. These factors are:

- the nature of business;
- the availability and use of information;
- participation, consultation, employment relationships, the recognition of trade unions, means and methods of representation;
- relationships with the Third World (where appropriate);

375

- the nature of particular products – especially where these included armaments, drugs, tobacco and alcohol – and the means by which these were produced, marketed and sold;
- connections with governments, especially where these were considered to be undesirable or where the regime in question was considered to be unethical itself;
- general approaches and attitudes to staff and customers;
- attitudes to the communities in which they operated;
- attitudes to environmental issues, especially waste disposal and recycling; replant-ing; the ways and means by which scarce resources were consumed;
- business relationships with suppliers and markets;
- product testing (again, especially where this involved the use of animals or parts of the environment).

Peter F. Drucker (1955) wrote:

The more successfully the manager does their work, the greater will be the integrity required. For under new technology the impact on the business of decisions, time span and risks will be so serious as to require that each manager put the common good of the enterprise above self-interest. Their impact on the people in the enterprise will be so decisive as to demand that the manager put genuine principles above expediency. And the impact on the economy will be so far reaching that society itself will hold managers responsible. Indeed, the new tasks demand that the manager of tomorrow root every action and decision in the bedrock of principles so that they lead, not only through knowledge, competence and skill, but also through vision, courage, responsibility and integrity.

Payne and Pugh identified the relationship between the absolute standards of the organisation and its 'climate'. They stated that 'Climate is a total concept applying to the organisation as a whole or some definable department or subsystem within it.' It is descriptive of the organisation. There are four main aspects of climate:

- the degree of autonomy is given;
- the degree of structure imposed on work positions;
- the reward orientation, either in terms of individual satisfaction or organisational achievement;
- the degree of consideration, warmth and support.

There is clearly therefore a variety of points of view from which the wider question may be addressed. At the core, however, lies a combination of:

- the long-term view (rather than the short or medium);
- absolute standards relating to organisational policies, aims and objectives;
- common standards of equity, equality, honesty and integrity;

- relationships between organisation standards and absolutes, the carrying out of performance and the distribution of rewards;
- relationships between means and ends, and actions and motives;
- reconciliation of conflicts of interest;
- the duty and capability to exist in the long term.

It is necessary to identify the nature of those legitimate interests. If the organisation is not profitable and/or effective it will close (or be closed down). The first duty to staff and customers, is to ensure long-term permanence. This only occurs where there exists a fundamental integrity of relationships and activities, and where this extends to all dealings with every stakeholder. From this arises the confidence and the ability to conduct activities over the long term. Ethics therefore pervades all aspects of organisation's activities and performance.

■ Survival

Survival is the main ethical duty of the organisation, to its staff, customers, communities and other stakeholders. For this to happen over the long-term, a long term view must be taken of all that this means. For business and companies, profits must be made – over the long term; for public services, this means effectiveness – over the long term. This is the basis on which confidence and an enduring and continuous positive relationship with customers (or service users) is built and developed. This is also the only ground on which an effective and satisfactory organisation for the staff is to be created.

Short-term views, expediency and the need for triumphs all detract from this. Especially, there is a serious problem in this area with some public services. For example, the output of education can take 15–20 years to become apparent. Health and social services have similar extreme long-term requirements and commitments. Yet those responsible for their direction (both service chiefs and cabinet ministers) need to be able to show instant results to be presented before the electorate or before the selection panel for their next job.

This is not wholly confined to services. For example, pressures from bankers and other financial backers in some sectors (especially loan makers) can lead to companies being forced or strongly encouraged to sell assets during lean periods in order to keep up repayments or show a superficial cash surplus over the immediate period. This happened with the UK construction industry over the early 1990s when there was a great decline in work brought on by recession and general loss of confidence. Short-term cash gain was made through the sale of assets (especially land banks). Long-term survival was threatened because these assets would not be present when any upturn in confidence and activity came about.

However, this again has to be balanced against matters of general confidence and expectation. If backers expect to see a series of short-term positive results then these have to be produced, especially if backing may be withdrawn if these are not forthcoming or do not meet expectations. This implies re-educating backers into the long-term view. It also means seeking out others who are disposed to take the long-term view.

■ Relationships with employees

This refers to the nature of participation and involvement, and the point of view from which this is approached. Basic integrity in employee relations stems from the view taken of the employees, their reasons for working in the organisation, their reasons for being hired to work in the organisation and the absolute levels of esteem in which they are held.

Confrontational or adversarial styles of employee relations are always founded on mistrust and reinforced by offensive and defensive positions adopted by the two sides concerning particular issues. Even the phrase 'the two sides' confirms and underlines this. Resources are consumed in this way to the detriment both of organisation performance and also of resource utilisation (those used in these ways cannot be put to better use elsewhere). This form of employee relations is therefore unethical. On the other hand, greater or full participation and involvement is only ethical if the point of view adopted is itself honest: if a genuine view of respect and identity is taken. This is apparent – or not – in the continuity and enduring nature of this relationship. It is underlined by the volume, quality and relevance of information made available to the staff, the means by which problems are addressed and resolved, the prevalence of equality of treatment and opportunity, and the development of staff.

It also refers to the attention to the standards set to which employees are to conform and the reasoning and logic behind this. It covers all aspects of the traditional personnel area: recruitment and selection, induction, performance appraisal, pay and reward, promotion and other opportunities for development and advancement. Above all, at its core lies equality of treatment for everyone.

■ Responsibilities and obligations to staff

The general responsibilities and obligations to staff consist of providing work, remaining in existence, equality and fairness of treatment, compliance with the law and the specific regulations of training and development. The basis on which this is established consists of the following.

1. Acknowledging the range of pressures and priorities that exist in the lives of everyone, including health, family, social, ethical and religious pressures, as well as those related to work. The outcome of this is understanding rather than interference

or imposition. It sets the relationship between work organisations and people in context. It indicates areas where stresses and strains are likely to arise. It indicates the relationship between organisation and individual priorities, where these coincide and where they diverge. It indicates areas for accommodation and for regulation.

2. Acknowledgement of extreme human concerns. This refers to personal crises: serious illness, death, bereavement, divorce, drink and drug problems. The concern is to ensure that the organisation gives every possible support to people facing these issues so that a productive and profitable relationship is maintained even through such times. Individuals can and should be referred to outside professional support services and agencies for these matters with the full backing of the organisation.

   As a last resort however, organisations do not have the right to pry into people's personal affairs. Individuals may be referred for counselling or other expert help and advice only if they give their consent unless the matter is adversely affecting their work performance beyond a fair and reasonable extent, or where they constitute a real or potential threat or danger to their colleagues or the activities of the organisation.

   Problems related to drug or alcohol use or addiction always fall into the latter category and are therefore always a matter of direct concern. Organisations set absolute standards of handling and using equipment, carrying out activities and dealing with the public. Addiction and abuse problems directly affect each of these. The individual has therefore to be removed from these situations and supported through rehabilitation.

3. Confidentiality and integrity in all dealings with staff. This is the cornerstone on which all effective staff relationships are built. Where confidences are not kept, or where sensitive personal and occupational information become public property, the relationship is tainted and often destroyed. Confidentiality also encourages people to be frank, open and honest themselves, and this leads to a genuine understanding of issues much more quickly. It also enables managers and supervisors to address their matters of concern – for example, declines in standards of performance and behaviour – directly and immediately they are observed.

   The following approaches may be adopted:

   (a) **ice-breaking** – using one issue as the means of breaking into a wider area to identify the real nature of problems and causes for concern;
   (b) **drawing out and understanding** – based on a general discussion, often conducted from the employee's point of view and leading to an understanding of her perspective;
   (c) **confrontation** – the direct presentation of the matters of concern.

   Whichever is used at first, the three interrelate. By using each approach in turn, a full understanding may eventually be achieved and effective proposals formulated (see Figure 13.1).

4. Support for individuals when either they or the workplace identify any problems. In most cases, this is to ensure that people are not penalised as the result of the pressures and strains indicated above. Support should only be withdrawn by the

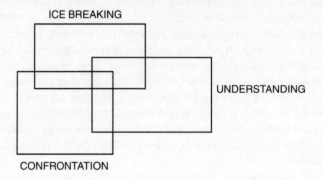

Figure 13.1   Causes for concern

organisation where the individual is compromising the total relationship or the quality of activities. When this happens, the organisation has to consider the integrity of the relationship between itself and all of the staff. Part of this support therefore means creating the conditions in which individuals are able to confront issues knowing that help is available and that they are not to be penalised, and neither will their concerns become matters of public knowledge.

5. Respect for individuals based on the value of their contribution to the organisation. If they bring no value, they should not be there in the first place. Ideally therefore, the fact of their employment (in whatever capacity) equates to high and distinctive value; where it does not, stress and conflict invariably occur.

    This respect extends to all aspects of the relationship. It includes attention to the current job, future prospects, continuity of working relations, creation of suitable working environments, creation and maintenance of effective occupational and personal relationships, and the creation and maintenance of effective management and supervisory styles.

The traditional or adversarial view of this approach to responsibilities and obligations was that it was soft and unproductive, and diverted attention away from production and output. Organisations could not afford to be 'nice' to their employees while there was a job to be done.

The reverse of this is much closer to the truth. The acknowledgement, recognition and understanding of the full nature and range of complexities and conflicting pressures on individuals is the first step towards effective and profitable activities. By engaging on a basis of honesty, confidentiality, trust, support and integrity – rather than coercion, confrontation, dishonesty and duplicity – a long-term positive relationship can be established. The interests of both organisation and individual are bound up with each other, especially over the long term. Ultimately, therefore, the interests coincide. A critical part of this approach is concerned with creating the basis on which this can be built.

■ Relationships with customers

This is the basis of the commercial or service provision: the respect and value in which the customers and clients are held. From this springs the drive for product quality, presentation and offering; for public relations and other customer management and service activities; and for handling complaints.

It also impinges on the staff. Where staff know that high standards of customer service and top quality products are being offered, the relationship between organisation and staff is also reinforced. The converse is also true: where these standards are low or falling, or where it is known that poor products and services are being offered, the integrity of the relationship between organisation and staff is also compromised.

This has an impact on all production, output and sales activities; especially in terms of attention to product quality, the terms under which it is offered, its uses and availability and recognition of the levels of satisfaction that are required by the customers. In the long term, if this is not present, confidence is lost. While it is possible to identify areas where short-term gain has been made without integrity (for example, in the sale of building products, home improvements, life assurance and pensions, poor quality Christmas presents), there is no (or a reduced) likelihood of repeat business occurring. This also fails to satisfy either the long-term criteria or the requirement of confidence on the part of the employees; above all, there is no integrity of relationship. This way of conducting business is therefore also unethical.

This also refers to attention to the marketing activities undertaken and the point of view adopted. Creative and imaginative presentation is highly desirable as long as this underlines (and does not misrepresent) the quality, desirability and image of the particular product or organisation. Again, where integrity is missing, the relationship is invariably short term and terminated by loss of confidence in the organisation and loss of regard for its products and services. This applies to all aspects of marketing: promotion and advertising, packaging and presentation, direct sales and distribution.

These are the main relationships upon which successful and effective organisational performance is built and developed. These are underpinned by the following.

■ Corporate governance and direction

This is the position adopted by the organisation that is apparent from its policies, aims and objectives and the means established by which these are to be achieved. In this context the extent of honesty and integrity are immediately apparent. This is reinforced by the clarity and realism of overall purpose, the basic approach taken to customers, markets and staff, and management style; and underlined by the rules, systems and procedures that are put in place to support all of this, and the ways in which these are presented, delivered and implemented.

■ **Stakeholders**

Attention to the relative position of stakeholders is based on the recognition that some – especially staff, customers and owners – are more critical than others (for example, the local community pressure groups and vested interests). Each has its own position and is worthy of being dealt with from the point of view of honesty and integrity, and is worthy also of respect and esteem. However, organisations will not normally accommodate a peripheral interest at the expense of the core purpose, although they will (or may) do this if it can be successfully integrated. The best organisations seek ways forward that are capable of integrating the peripheral interest with that of the core.

■ **Resources**

There are ethical implications for resource utilisation. Profligacy is wasteful and therefore wrong, even where constraints are not apparent. It is also unsatisfactory, normally leading to a general loss of care and consideration. It is also off-putting to customers: for example, those customers visiting luxurious offices may well come to the conclusion that a good part of the business that is being conducted is being used on expensive furnishings rather than business performance and effectiveness. In general therefore, it is bad business.

A useful equivalent in public service terms may also be drawn. This is the propensity – very often driven by managers and directors – to use up the year's budget in time for the year ending (usually February and March because of the end of the financial year on 1 April). Resources that have been managed and constrained for 9 or 10 months suddenly become expendable; this is reinforced if there is no prospect of carrying the resources forward to the following year. The result is that departments affected in this way engage in any activities or purchases that are guaranteed to use up the resources.

On the other hand, resource constraints lead to choices and priorities. This leads in turn to the consideration of who should receive resources and who should not, and why. An ethical assessment will look at organisational aims and objectives. Other elements include establishing whether everything is to be attempted in the knowledge that it will probably fall short of full success and effectiveness (common in public services); or whether resources will be concentrated on that which can be completed fully at the expense of that which cannot.

Resource constraints also lead to resource battles in many cases and this compounds the issue. Problems especially arise when resources are seen to be distributed on the basis of favour and expediency as distinct from operational necessity; or to head office functions at the expense of outlying and often frontline activities.

The ethical line is therefore to maximise and optimise resources in the pursuit of objectives. This is based on the judgement and integrity of those responsible, taking into consideration what is best for the organisation and its long-term future.

■ **Conduct**

This is the basis on which all relationships are founded. They key is the attitude adopted by staff to each other and by the organisation to all of its people. It is underlined by establishing standards of conduct and enforcing them, so that a clear distinction is made between what is acceptable and what is not. Everyone is held in confidence, respect and esteem. This is in turn underlined by the nature, emphasis and application of the rules and regulations.

■ **Professional standards**

This is attention to the quality of staff, the ways in which they apply their particular trades and expertise, and the expectations and requirements that are placed on them by the organisation. These standards are to apply to everyone. There is no reason why ostensibly unskilled or simple tasks and jobs are not to be carried out to the highest possible quality. This is supported by the organisation's commitment to provide the correct working environment, equipment and style of supervision; and by the standards of respect, trust and esteem referred to above. Absolute standards are present and upheld where each of these elements is present; and where one falls short, this may lead to the beginnings of questioning the integrity of the relationship. Where the shortfall is allowed to persist, professional standards inevitably fall in all areas. There is, moreover, a loss of self-worth all round and those with distinctive trades or professions retreat into being professional or expert practitioners (as distinct from an organisation practitioners) and may seek employment elsewhere where these standards are known (or perceived) to be higher.

■ **The law**

Compliance with the law may or may not be ethical; this again depends on the attitude and standpoint adopted. Organisations are known to hide behind the law in certain circumstances, especially where legal standards are lower than the absolutes that are known to be required.

BOX 13.1 Corporate Environmental Trade-off

In one case an organisation, a German chemical company, took this a stage further. It was situated at Basle on the banks of the river Rhine at the border between Germany, Switzerland and France. It had a large amount of liquid toxic waste to dispose of. It worked out the cost of having the waste treated and decontaminated properly. It then set this against the maximum fine that would be incurred if the waste was simply dumped into the river. To treat the waste properly would cost millions of dollars, while the maximum fine was $500 000. The company took the decision to dump the waste in the river. It floated downriver, killing everything in its path, and was only dispersed when it reached the North Sea.

The company was prosecuted. It pleaded guilty and paid up $500 000 for the fine. This it saw as the price of getting rid of this particular consignment of waste.

This applies especially to waste disposal and discharges and the relationship between the organisation and its environment (see Box 13.1). It occurs also in all dealings with staff: the right to disclosure of information, and rights to time off work, to breaks, to maternity leave, and to minimum levels of redundancy notice and pay. Organisations comply with the law because they have to and not because they know that this is the correct approach to take.

Organisations should nevertheless comply with the law. Not to do so questions and is likely to destroy the total integrity and honesty, and the standards which it has set itself. Condoning acts that are against the law (even encouraging them) also destroys integrity (see especially the Simmonds case (described in Box 13.2), where one of the perpetrators was promoted and received advancement as a direct result. In the Hargreaves case no other official involved was either named or identified; neither was any disciplinary action taken against them.

BOX 13.2   Employment Law

Jean Simmonds

Jean Simmonds was a school teacher in Lancashire, UK. In 1986 she put in for, and received, promotion to Head of Department. Two years later she put in for, and again received, promotion to Deputy Head. In 1992 and 1993, however, she received no further advancement in spite of the fact that each of her previous promotions had been based on merit and she was widely regarded as a potentially excellent and effective head teacher. Eventually she questioned this lack of advancement with the County Education Department and with her local County Councillor. She was told: 'Off the record this is a matter of sex discrimination. You will receive no further advancement because you are a woman.'

Suffering from stress and outrage, she took her case first to ACAS, and then to an industrial tribunal. The county council involved and the education department both paid her compensation because of this form of discrimination. A condition of the settlement was that the official who had decided that she should not be promoted on the grounds that she was a woman should not be named or identified. Since the case he has been promoted twice and is now Deputy Director of another education department elsewhere in the country.

John Hargreaves

Hargreaves worked for a large UK insurance and finance house. He was the senior manager, responsible for all of the organisation's taxation affairs. In 1985, while checking the company's year-end accounts, he found discrepancies in the taxation arrangements and the money that was due to be paid to the Inland Revenue. He reported this to the Board of Directors and was assured that this was to be put right and would not occur again. The following year he found the same discrepancies and uncertainties. When he again confronted the Board of Directors with this, he was dismissed. He took his case to an industrial tribunal, and subsequently sued the company for breach of contract and loss of his reputation. The eventual settlement was in the order of £300 000.

No other official lost their job as the result of this; it was also a condition of settlement that no other official should be named or identified.

■ Health and safety

Health and safety at work is covered by the law. It is also a distinctive element in its own right, simply because it is such a fundamental reflection of respect for people (and especially lack of respect for people: see Box 13.3). The problem lies in the organisation's acceptance of its responsibility to take an absolute view of its environment, technology and other equipment, its procedures and practices, its staff and any other persons who visit or use its premises; acknowledging the entirety of things that can go wrong; and designing each element so that nothing can go wrong.

This is a continuous responsibility and requires reaction as and when new knowledge becomes available.

For example, asbestos was used during the period 1930–60 as an effective fireproofing material in buildings and construction workers worked with it in the same way as any other material. When it became apparent that it caused skin disease and also that the dust which it produced was harmful to the lungs, protective clothing (including breathing protection) became obligatory. The best organisations went out and bought the correct equipment and insisted that their staff used it; and when the equipment was improved, went out and bought it again. Other organisations phased the equipment in, or they made it available to the staff to use if they wanted to, or simply rejected the evidence.

BOX 13.3   Health and Safety: Horror Stories

'We will safety ourselves out of business' (line from safety film *Intensive Care*, Ceramics Glass & Mineral Products Industry Training Board, 1980).

'Riddled with the disease of sloppiness': verdict of Lord Justice Sheen on the then Townsend Thoresen car ferry company following the inquiry into the *Herald of Free Enterprise* disaster in March 1987 at Zeebrugge.

'The men will be asking for nappies next': memorandum quoted by the Sheen Inquiry as above. The remark was attributed to the Townsend Thoresen Shipping Superintendent. It followed a request for a system of lights to show whether the doors to the ship's card decks were open or closed.

'The mechanics refused to fly in these planes': The CE of Vietnam Airlines, September 1994. He was referring to the company's inability to maintain its fleet of Ilyushyn and Tupolev airliners in an air-worthy condition; more generally, they also compared very unfavourably with the Airbus and Fokker airliners with which the company was beginning to be re-equipped.

No fewer than 116 Lockheed 111 star fighter military aircraft crashed due to mechanical failure before the plane was grounded. It was used during the 1960s and 1970s by the air forces of Western nations as the main offensive fighter and bomber aircraft during this period of the Cold War.

The ethical approach is not altruistic or charitable, but rather a key feature of effective long-term organisational and business performance. The commitment to the staff is absolutely positive. This does not mean any guarantee of lifetime employment, but it does mean recognising obligations and ensuring that staff recognise their obligations in turn. These obligations are to develop, participate and be involved; to be flexible, dynamic and responsive. The commitment of the staff to organisation, and of organisation to staff, is mutual. This also extends to problem areas – especially the handling of discipline, grievance and dismissal issues and redundancy and redeployment – and the continuity of this commitment when these matters have to be addressed.

Organisations are not families, friendly societies or clubs. By setting their own values and standards and relating these to long-term effectiveness they become distinctive. They are almost certain to be at variance from those which are and would be held by natural families and clubs. Problems that arise are clouded therefore, where the organisation does indeed perceive itself to be 'a big happy family': families are able to forgive prodigal children, and organisation may not be able to afford to do so if they are to maintain long-term standards or if substantial damage has been done to customer relations, for example. Organisations exist to provide effective products and services for customers, while families and clubs exist to provide comfort, society and warmth. These elements are by-products; they are not the core.

Organisations are not obliged to provide employment at all except insofar as they need the work carrying out. They will select and hire people for this on the basis of capabilities and qualities. They have no obligation to take staff from the ranks of the unemployed (though they may choose to do so). They have no obligation to locate for all eternity in particular areas (though, again, they may choose to do so).

Organisations that pursue high ethical standards are not religious institutions, and neither do they have any obligation to reflect any prevailing local traditions, values, customs, prejudices – or religion.

Japanese organisations setting up in the UK were, and remain, successful precisely because of this. Rather than trying to integrate their activities with the traditions of their locations, they brought very distinctive and positive values with which people who came to work for them were required to identify.

Organisations must distinguish between right and wrong. Lying, stealing, bribery and corruption are always wrong and can never be ethically justified.

This has to be set in the context of the ways in which business is conducted in certain sectors and parts of the world. If a contract is only to be secured by offering a bribe, the relationship is corrupted and based on contempt. If and when prevailing views change, the total relationship between organisation and customer is likely to be called into question and any scandal or adverse publicity that emerges invariably affects confidence. It is in any case extremely stressful for individuals to have to work in this way, or indeed to connive or conspire to any overt wrong-doing (though this may clearly be accommodated if the organisation institutionalises such matters, protects individuals who are caught or accepts responsibility for every outcome).

■ Means and ends

Crimes are not annulled by altruistic motives even though they may arouse human sympathy: for example, where a hungry person robs a rich person just so that they can eat. Robin Hood was a robber, whether or not he gave the proceeds of his robberies to the poor. The sale of cocaine on the urban streets of Europe and North America is wrong even if it provides the means of economic survival to the people of South America.

This applies to organisation practices also. If a manager dismisses an employee to make an example of him, and if the employee did not deserve dismissal, then a wrong act is committed even if it brings the remaining staff into line. If the organisation secures its long-term future through gaining a contract by offering a bribe to a major customer, then a wrong act is committed. In each of these cases, stated ends are very unlikely to be secured anyway because there is no integrity in the relationship. In the first case the staff will look for other ways of falling out of line (but without risking further dismissals); in the second case the corruption may come to light and the relationship be called into question or cancelled as a result.

Organisations must recognise and resolve conflicts of interest. The first step lies in acknowledging the legitimacy and certainty of these, and from this establishing the steps necessary for their resolution in ways which best benefit the long-term future. Conflicts of interest arise between individuals, within and between departments and divisions, and may be based on general professional and expertise disagreements as to the best interests of the organisation (as well as matters of infighting and operational and personality clashes).

The ethical approach consists of early recognition of problems; addressing these when they arise and before they are allowed to fester and become *causes célèbres*; and indicating clearly what is to happen as the result and why this is in the best interests of the organisation. This is then transmitted to all concerned.

BOX 13.4　Good Ethics is Good Business

Although ethical conduct is not sufficient to assure business success and business success is no guarantee of ethical conduct, distributive justice and ordinary decency do typically enhance long term owner value. They do so in many ways but chiefly by obviating the difficulties of operating without them. Stakeholders who doubt the good faith of the business or of their colleagues are more likely to spend time in protecting their backs than in performing their functions. Time resources and energy which could be spent more productively and rewardingly are consequently diverted to basic self-preservation with a direct opportunity cost to the business. Decent treatment, in contrast, permits and encourages stakeholders to get on with the job.

The costs of disregarding ordinary decency and distributive justice are far-reaching. In a business characterised by lying, cheating and stealing this illusion of low morale typically replaces initiative and enthusiasm; team work becomes difficult at best and long term commitments counter-productive. When exertions on behalf of a business are rejected or penalised rather than encouraged and rewarded they are unlikely to be repeated. Distributive justice and a modicum of decency are therefore essential for the business to operate; without them the business is unlikely to attract the best people or their best efforts. But when they are respected, the business will normally be characterised, not only by responsibility and integrity, but by maximum long term owner value.

From: Elaine Sternberg (1995).

This recognises the presence of each of the elements and factors discussed and indicates the need for these to be considered, analysed and evaluated during decision-making processes and problem-solving activities. It may also indicate the need for further investigations to take place; the need for additional sources and quality of information; and the nature and level of resistance to particular courses of action that may occur.

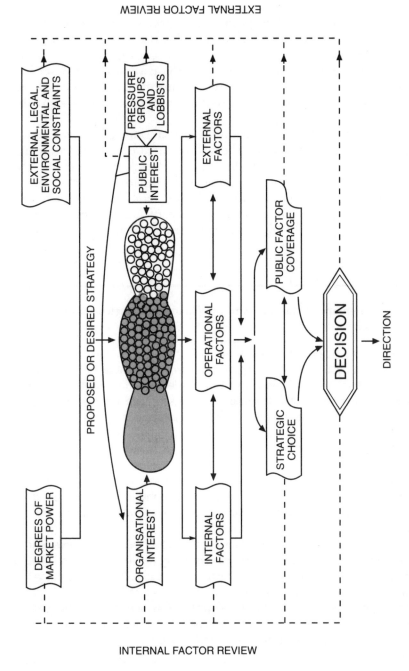

EXTERNAL FACTOR REVIEW

INTERNAL FACTOR REVIEW

Figure 13.2   Decision-making model including ethical considerations

■ Decision-making

Organisations must structure decision-making processes in ways that consider the range and legitimacy of ethical pressures. This also means understanding where the greater good and the true interests of the organisation lie, and adopting realistic steps in the pursuit of this. An ethical assessment will consider the position of staff, the nature and interrelationship of activities, product and service ranges, mixes and balances, relationships with the community and the environment.

Invariably the presence and activities of lobbies, pressure groups and vested interests will have to be considered. This will be based on an assessment and judgement of the validity and strength of their concerns and the means and methods which are being used by these groups in their pursuit. It also normally means taking steps that address these, either in terms meaningful to the particular groups or in presenting the benefits of particular initiatives in terms that outweigh the concerns or which reconcile them with organisation purpose (see Box 13.5).

BOX 13.5   High-Speed Rail Links to the Channel Tunnel: Contrasting Views

These links were proposed at the same time as the Channel Tunnel was commissioned in 1985. Their construction would provide a fast and effective rail link between London and the Tunnel in the UK; and between the Tunnel, Paris and Brussels on mainland Europe. It would also in each case provide additional general rail capacity to alleviate pressures on the systems that were already in place.

In France, the cities of the north of the country – Lille, Amiens, Arras – fought to have the link pass through their location because they perceived the benefits that would accrue to themselves and their regions as a result. These links were completed in 1993. Amiens and Arras missed out and this caused great resentment. The line runs on the French side between the Tunnel and Lille where it forks, turning south to Paris and north to Brussels.

In the UK, the towns and villages of Kent fought against having it anywhere near them because they perceived the construction blight that would occur while it was being built and the noise pollution once it was in operation. The link has not yet been commissioned and is not yet known which route will be taken.

This example illustrates the contrasting views that can be taken of anything. Its importance lies in recognising the reality and legitimacy of views and perceptions, and the barriers that have to be addressed and overcome.

■ Conclusions

The ethical approach to organisation and activities is adult and assertive. It is not soft, religious or moral. It takes the view that continuous and long-term existence is the main duty of organisations to their staff, customers, community and environment.

Above all, it requires a fundamental shift in corporate attitudes away from the short term or expedient, from the instant approach to returns, from the needs of influential figures and from wasteful and inefficient budgeting and control systems. This is to be replaced by active participation and involvement by all in the pursuit of effectiveness and success. It requires valuing everyone: staff, customers and the community. Organisations are only sustainable in the long term if adequate and continuous investment is made in technology, staff and staff development, research and development into new products and service and in constantly improving and updating (and where necessary, abolishing or divesting) products, services, processes, systems and practices.

There is a direct relationship between organisation success and the principles and standards adopted. High-profile current and recent failures – for example, BCCI and Maxwell – have demonstrated the consequences of this lack of basic integrity. The inefficiencies of some public services – for example, health, eduction and social services – arise from a combination of short-termism and the dominant pressures of key players. The results achieved by organisations that do adopt high and absolute standards – such as Body Shop, Virgin and Nissan – clearly indicate the levels of achievement possible whatever the sector.

■ Questions

1. Why do (a) private and (b) public service organisations have such difficulty adopting long-term views of their future? Identify the main issues to be addressed and reconciled and the difficulties involved in each sector indicated.
2. Under what circumstances (if any) may organisations legitimately be dishonest with their staff, customers, markets, community and environment? What are the short- and long-term benefits and consequences?
3. Outline the legitimate reasons for the existence of the armaments and tobacco industries. Of all their activities, which may be considered ethical, which may be considered unethical, and why?
4. Indicate the content of an 'ethics' staff training programme. To what extent, how and why would this vary between different groups of staff: administrative, professional, technical, clerical, management, supervisory and operational?

CHAPTER 14

Culture

■ Introduction

Organisation culture is an amalgam and summary of the ways in which activities are conducted and the standards and values adopted. It encompasses the climate or atmosphere surrounding the organisation, prevailing attitudes within it, standards, morale, strength of feelings towards it and the general levels of goodwill present.

It is an essential feature of effective organisation creation and performance. It arises from the following elements.

History and tradition	The origins of the organisation; the aims and objectives of the first owners and managers, and their philosophy and values; the regard in which these are currently held; the ways in which they have developed.
Nature of activities	Historical and traditional, and also current and envisaged; this includes reference to the general state of success and effectiveness and the balance of activities (steady-state, innovative, crisis).
Technology	The relationship between technology and the workforce, work design, organisation and structure; alienative factors and steps taken to get over these; levels of technological stability and change; levels of expertise, stability and change.
Past, present and future	The importance of the past in relation to current and proposed activities; special pressures (especially struggles and glories) of the past; the extent to which the organisation 'is living' in the past, present or future, and the pressures and constraints that are brought about as a result.
Purposes, priorities and attention	In relation to performance, staff, customers, the community and environment; and to progress and development.
Size	And also the degrees of formalisation and structure that this brings. Larger organisations are much more likely to have a proliferation of divisions, supervisory structures, reporting relationships, rules, processes and procedures tending to cause communication difficulties, interdepartmental rivalries and problems with coordination and control.
Location	Geographical location, the constraints and opportunities afforded through choosing to be, for example, in urban centres, at the edge

of town or in rural areas. This also includes recognising and considering prevailing local, national and sectoral traditions and values.

Management style The stance adopted by the organisation in managing and supervising its people; the stance required by the people of managers and supervisors; the general relationships between people and organisation and the nature of superior–subordinate relations.

This is the context of organisation culture. A simple way of defining organisation culture is:

'The ways in which things are done here.'

Culture is formed from the collection of traditions, values, policies, beliefs and attitudes that prevail throughout the organisation.

Specific pressures are also present.

BOX 14.1 Characteristics of Culture

Culture is:

- **learned** – rather than genetic or biological.
- **shared** – members of groups and organisation share culture;
- **continuous** – cumulative in its development and past on from one generation to the next;
- **symbolic** – based on the human capacity to symbolise, to use one thing to represent another;
- **integrated** – a change in one area will lead to a change in another;
- **adaptive** – based on human qualities of adaptability, creativity, innovation and imagination;
- **regular** – when participants interact with each other, they use common language terminology and recognised and accepted forms of behaviour;
- **norms** – distinctive standards of behaviour;
- **dominant values** – advocated by the organisation and expected by participants;
- **philosophy** – policies concerning beliefs and standards of performance, attitude, behaviour and conduct;
- **rules** – the formal rules that underline the constitution of the organisation; the informal rules that govern the interaction of individuals on a daily basis;
- **organisational climate** – conveyed by the environment, the physical lay-out, the ways in which participants interact and the relationships with the outside world.

■ Pressures on organisation culture

■ External pressures

The particular attitudes, values and ethics of the locality in which business is to be conducted and from where the organisation staff are to be drawn will create external pressures. In many parts of the world this includes religious pressures. Other forms of prejudice may also have to be taken into account: for example, some people do not readily accept direction from women or members of particular racial or ethnic groups.

Local working practices and customs, especially relating to hours of work and ways of working, have also to be considered. In some parts, activities close down for several hours in the middle of the day; in others, people start and finish early, for example.

In some cases also, strong pressure is placed on people to accept the invitation to dine out with colleagues and groups drawn from the rest of the organisation. While this may be presented as an invitation it may actually be an instruction, and rejection of this is likely to be detrimental to the career or prospects of the individual and the general respect in which she is held.

Physical distance affects culture. The inability to see and meet others – for example, when work is being carried out in a foreign location or one remote from the main organisation – has effects on the structuring and ordering of tasks and activities, relationships between the staff at the location, and relationships between the location and head office. It also affects decision-making processes, and the attitudes and approaches to local problems and issues. Those at the location, and especially the person with overall responsibility and control, are likely to experience feelings of isolation from time to time and may need to be supported if the overall effectiveness of that part of the organisation is to be sustained.

Psychological distance is also important here. It is likely to exist as a feature of physical distance even if there is a full range of electronic and telecommunications available. Psychological distance is also certain to be present to a greater or lesser extent between the organisation and the local community at least at the outset, and it is also likely that this will never quite be removed.

The organisation's own culture and the interaction of its prevailing attitudes, values and beliefs with those of the locality have also to be considered. Strong prevailing practices and standards may have to be reconciled and harmonised between organisation and community. This is best achieved if a high level of mutual understanding, respect and interest is developed quickly, and if high overall standards of probity and integrity are also established.

Standards of living and the wider expectations of the community should be considered from the point of view that there is no point in offering high levels of material reward if these are not valued by the people of the location. There is no point in offering promotion and advancement prospects if people do not want to move from the area.

The organisation's success in a particular location therefore involves understanding its expectations, and presenting and harmonising its own objectives and interests in ways compatible to all.

☐ *Reputation*

This must be seen from all points of view. The organisation may go into a given location for commercial advantage but with preconceived ideas or prejudices (which may either be positive or negative). The organisation may bring with it a particular reputation (again, positive or negative) and, again, either about itself or the sector which it represents and within which it operates. There may be wider questions of prejudice, fear and anxiety to be overcome as the organisation tries to live up to (or live down to) its reputation. Areas that have had bad experiences of multi-national activities in the past, for example, may be anxious about the next influx.

The activities of stock markets, and the price and values of shares all bring pressure from time to time. This becomes acute when questions of confidence, or possible takeovers and mergers – and therefore changes – are raised.

☐ *Legal*

All organisations have to work within the laws of their locations. These exert pressure on production methods, waste disposal, health and safety, marketing and selling, contractual arrangements, staff management, human resources, industrial relations and the equality (or otherwise) of opportunity and access, community relations, organisational and professional insurance, and the reporting of results.

Pressures are compounded when the organisation operates in many countries and under diverse legal codes. Balances have to be found in these cases to ensure that, as far as possible, everyone who works for the organisation does so on terms that transcend the varying legal constraints. Organisations are therefore obliged to set absolute standards which more than meet particular legal minima. Moreover, the phrase 'We comply with the law' invariably gives the message that 'The only reason that we set these standards is because we have to', and that the organisation has therefore been pressured into these standards rather than achieving them because it believes that they are right. It calls into question not just the organisation's attitude to the law, but also its wider general attitudes, values and standards.

BOX 14.2   Union Carbide: Bhopal

The worst ever industrial disaster occurred on 3 December 1984 at the chemical plant at Bhopal, India. The majority shareholder in this plant was the US Union

Carbide Company. Over 3000 died, either instantly or else as the result of injuries and illness sustained.

As the result of inadequate safety measures, water got into a tank of the chemical methylisocyanate, and this vapourised and escaped into the atmosphere. Because it was heavier than air it effectively flooded the ground level of the atmosphere with a lethal and suffocating gas. The people who died or were injured either suffocated or choked to death.

Management practices and procedures were found to be at fault. More important, however, was the corporate approach to both activities and the environment. The company was condemned for an attitude of complacency and disregard, and a clear implication that different and lesser standards were both acceptable and in place because of the location of the plant in India. The company set much higher standards for its activities elsewhere in the world, especially in the Western world where both public awareness and legal pressures were much stronger.

The effects of the disaster were far-reaching, however. Union Carbide lost both global and domestic reputation and confidence. The chemical industry as a whole came to be viewed as negative and dirty. Inquiries into the general standards of the industry at large revealed a great range of attitudes and approaches to the inherent operational problems and to waste disposal, and also to the likelihood and consequences of accidents and disasters.

The disaster caused a widespread loss of confidence on the part of the Indian people concerning all multi-national activities in their country. Bonds of trust were broken. Restoration of both the reputation of Union Carbide and also that of the chemical industry at large took 11 years (*The Economist*, 24 November 1994). More generally, it meant that any organisation wishing to set up activities in that part of the world was certain to be faced with 'The Bhopal Effect': the local reaction based on past experience to Westernised industrialised activities.

☐ *Ethical*

Ethical pressures arise from the nature of work carried out and from the standards and customs of the communities in which the organisation operates. There are also general ethical pressures on many activities concerned that are covered by the law; examples of these pressures are given in Box 14.3.

Again, the ideal response of any organisation is to put itself beyond reproach so that these pressures are accommodated and leave the way clear to developing productive and harmonious relationships with all concerned.

BOX 14.3   Examples of Ethical Pressures

1. Activities: most activities carry some form of commitment and others are imposed on their staff by organisations. For example, medical staff have commitments to their patients; community services staff have commitments to their customers; public servants have commitments to their clients.
2. Sectors: again, there is a universal commitment not to supply shoddy goods and service, but rather to provide products of integrity. Some sectors have additional problems with this (for example, tobacco, alcohol, armaments and medical research).
3. Waste disposal: the onus is clearly on organisations to make adequate arrangements to clear up any mess made by their processes. Some areas and countries have lower standards for this. Organisations assess the convenience of easier dumping of rubbish and balance this against absolute standards of right and wrong and any loss of reputation that might occur in the future if their waste leads to some form of contamination.
4. Equal opportunities, staff management, industrial relations and health and safety: high standards of practice in each of these areas are marks of respect and care towards staff, customers and communities. Their absence or variations in them lead, apart from anything else, to feelings of distrust and loss of confidence, and therefore to demotivation of the staff.
5. Results reporting: the pressure here is in the presentation. Ideally, this should be done in ways that can be understood by anyone who has an interest or stake in the organisation and, indeed, anyone else who would like to know how it is performing. Again, obfuscation tends to lead to those taking an interest to look for hidden meanings and agenda.

■ Internal pressures

1. The interaction between the desired culture and the organisation's structures and systems. Serious misfit between these leads to stress and frustration and also to customer dissatisfaction and staff demotivation.
2. The expectations and aspirations of staff, and the extent to which these are realistic and can be satisfied within the organisation. This becomes a serious issue when the nature of the organisation changes and prevailing expectations can no longer be accommodated. Problems also arise when the organisation makes promises that it cannot keep.
3. Management and supervisory style, and the extent to which this is supportive, suitable to the purpose and generally acceptable to the staff.
4. The qualities and expertise of the staff, and the extent to which this divides their loyalties. Many staff groups have professional or trade union memberships, continuous professional development requirements and career expectations, as

well as a requirement to hold down positions and carry out tasks within organisations. In many cases – and especially when general dissatisfaction is present – people tend to take refuge in their profession or occupation, or their trade union.

5. Technology and the extent to which it affects on the ways in which work is designed, structured and carried out.

6. Working customs, traditions and practices including restrictive practices, work divisions, specialisation and allocation, unionisation and other means of representation; and the attitudes and approaches adopted by both organisation and staff towards each other (flexible and cooperative, adversarial, degrees of openness).

7. The extent to which continuity of employment is feasible; or, conversely, to which uncertainties surround future prospects for work and employment. This includes degrees of flexibility, the extent and prevalence of employee and skills development, learning sub-cultures and the wider attitude of both staff and organisation to this. It also affects reward packages.

8. Internal approaches and attitudes to the legal and ethical issues indicated, the extent of genuine commitment to equality of opportunity and access for all staff; whether or not different grades have different values placed on them, standards of dealings with staff, customers, communities, suppliers and distributors.

9. The presence of pride and commitment in the organisation, its work and its reputation; standards of general well-being; the extent of mutual respect.

10. Communication methods and systems, the nature of language used, the presence/absence of hidden agenda.

11. Physical and psychological distance between functions, departments, divisions and positions in the organisation and its hierarchies.

■ The cultural web

The cultural web is an alternative way of looking at the internal pressures upon organisation culture. People draw heavily on points of reference which are built up over periods of time and which are especially important at internal organisational level. The beliefs and assumptions which comprise this fall within the following boundaries.

1. The routine ways that members of the organisation behave towards each other and that link different parts of the organisation which together comprise 'the way that things are done'. These, at their best, lubricate the working of the organisation and may provide distinctive and beneficial organisational competency. However, they can also represent a 'taken for granted' attitude about how things should happen which can be extremely difficult to change.

2. The rituals of organisational life, such as training programmes, promotion and assessment, point to what is important in the organisation, reinforce 'the way we do things around here' and signal what is actually valued.

3. The stories told by members of the organisation to each other, to outsiders and to new recruits, embed the present organisation in its history and flag up important events and personalities.
4. The more symbolic aspects of organisation, such as logos, offices, cars and titles, or the type of language and terminology commonly used.
5. The control systems, measures and reward systems emphasise what is actually important and focus attention and activity.
6. Power structures are also likely to be associated insofar as the most powerful groupings are likely to be the ones most associated with what is actually valued.
7. The formal organisation structure and the more informal ways in which the organisation works are likely to reflect these power structures and again, to delineate important relationships and emphasise required levels of performance (Johnson and Scholes, 1992).

■ Cultural influences

Geert Hofstede (1980) carried out studies that identified cultural similarities and difference among the 116 000 staff of IBM located in 40 countries. He identified basic dimensions of national cultural and the differences in their emphases and importance in the various countries. The four dimensions were, as set out below.

Power–Distance	The extent to which power and influence is distributed across the society; the extent to which this is acceptable to the members of the society; access to sources of power and influence; and the physical and psychological distance that exists between people and the sources of power and influence.
Uncertainty Avoidance	The extent to which people prefer order and certainty, or uncertainty and ambiguity; and the extent to which they feel comfortable or threatened by the presence or absence of each.
Individualism–Collectivism	The extent to which individuals are expected or expect to take care of themselves; the extent to which a common good is perceived and the tendency and willingness to work towards this.
Masculinity–Femininity	The distinction between masculine values (the acquisition of money, wealth, fortune, success, ambition, possessions) and the feminine (sensitivity, care, concern, attention to the needs of others, quality of life); and the value, importance, mix and prevalence of each.

■ Power–distance

The study looked at the extent to which managers and supervisors were encouraged or expected to exercise power and to take it upon themselves to provide order and discipline. In some cases – for example, Spain – this expectation was very high. Relationships between superior and subordinate were based on low levels of mutual trust and low levels of participation and involvement. Employees would accept orders and direction on the understanding that the superior carries full responsibility, authority and accountability. Elsewhere – for example, Australia and Holland – people expected to be consulted and to participate in decision-making. They expected to be kept regularly and fully informed of progress, and had much greater need for general equality and honesty of approach. They would feel free to question superiors about why particular courses of action were necessary rather than simply accepting that they were.

■ Uncertainty avoidance

People with a high propensity for uncertainty avoidance (that is, those that wished for high degrees of certainty) tended to require much greater volumes of rules, regulations and guidance for all aspects of work. They sought stability and conformity, and were intolerant of dissenters. Uncertainty caused stress, strain, conflicts and disputes. Stress could be avoided by working hard, following the company line, and adherence to and compliance with required ways of behaviour. Where uncertainty avoidance was lower, these forms of stress were less apparent; there was less attention paid to rules and less emphasis placed on conformity and adherence.

■ Individualism–collectivism

The concern here was to establish the relative position of individual achievement in terms of that of the organisation, and also the wider contribution to society and the community. For example, in the UK and USA overwhelming emphasis was placed on individual performance and achievement. This has implications for membership of teams and groups and the creation of effective teams and groups in such locations. It also indicates the extent of likelihood of divergence of purpose between the organisation and individuals. Where collectivism was higher, there was also a much greater emphasis on harmony, loyalty, support and productive interaction. There was also a much greater attention to organisational performance, as well as the position of the organisation and its wider environment, and its contribution to society, in addition to the achievement of its own desired results.

■ Masculinity–femininity

This considered the value placed on different achievements. Cultures with high degrees of masculinity set great store by the achievement of material possessions and rewards (see above). Those with high degrees of femininity saw success in terms of quality of life, general state of the community, individual and collective well-being, the provision of essential services, the ability to support the whole society and to provide means of social security.

The work emphasises the importance of cultural factors and differences in all areas and aspects of organisational behaviour. It indicates both the strength and interaction of cultural pressures. It indicates the source and nature of particular values, particular drives and barriers and blockages, and behavioural issues and problem areas that all organisations need to consider. Above all, it illustrates the relative strength of some of the main cultural and social pressures that are brought to bear on all organisations in all situations.

■ Summary

These pressures indicate the context in which organisation culture is founded. Culture is present in all organisations. It is either positive (which tends to attract people), or negative (tending to repel people), which people tend to reject; it may also be one of the following.

□ Designed

This means that the culture is shaped by those responsible for organisational direction and results, and created in the pursuit of this. This involves setting the standards of attitudes, values, behaviour and belief that everyone is required to subscribe to as a condition of joining the organisation. Policies are produced so that everyone knows where they stand, and these are underpinned by extensive induction and orientation programmes and training schemes. Procedures and sanctions are there to ensure that these standards continue to be met. Organisations with very specific cultures are not all things to all people: many, indeed, make a virtue of their particular approach of 'Many are called but few are chosen.' High levels of internalisation of shared values are required.

Other perceptions emerge from this. Feelings of confidence, trust and respect are created. Individual response to the level of organisation commitment that is evident in this approach tends to be high.

□ Emergent

This is where the culture is formed by the staff (and staff groups) rather than directed by the organisation. The result is that people think, believe and act according to the pressures and priorities of their peers and pursue their own agenda. This is clearly fraught with difficulties and dangers: organisations that allow this happen will succeed only if the aims and objectives of the staff coincide absolutely with their own.

It leads to the staff setting their own informal procedures and sanctions, or operating formally in ways that suit their own purposes rather than those of the organisation. Individuals and groups, again, are not all things to all people; they may and do reject those who refuse to abide by the norms and values that they have set for themselves.

☐ *Informal*

Sub-cultures exist in all organisations. They relate to membership of different groups and vary between these (for example, in the state of openness of dealings between members). Sub-cultures become more destructive when they operate contrary to absolute standards. Forms of this are as set out below.

1. The canteen culture, whereby the shared values adopted are those of groups that gather away from the work situations and in such places as the washroom or canteen.
2. Elites and cliques, whereby strength and primacy is present in some groups at the expense of others. This leads to overmightiness. It affects operations when the elites and cliques are able to command resources, carry out projects and gain prestige at the expense of others; to lobby effectively for resources at the expense of others; and to gain favour at the expense of others.
3. Work regulation, whereby the volume and quality of work is regulated by the group for its own ends rather than those of the organisation; when it sets and works to its own targets which are at variance with those of the organisation.
4. Informal norming, whereby individuals are pressurised to adopt the attitudes and values of those around them rather than those of the organisation. This occurs most when the organisation's own norms are not sufficiently strong or structured to remove the local or group pressure.

■ Archetype cultures

The following archetypes may be distinguished.

■ Power culture

This is where the key relationship exists between the person who wields power and influence, and those who work for them. It depends on the figure at the centre who is the source of power. Everyone else draws their strength, influence and confidence from this centre and requires its continued support to ensure prosperity and operational viability. The relationship is normally terminated when there is a loss of confidence on the part of the person at the centre of power with those who work for her. Individuals generate power cultures when they attract those who have faith in them and who wish to be involved with them.

The main problem which a power culture must face is that of size. As it grows and diversifies, it becomes difficult for the person at the centre to sustain continued high levels of influence. There is also the problem of permanence, of what happens when the person at the centre of power passes out of the organisation. In situations where she has generated the ideas, energy, identity and strength of the situation, a void is left when she leaves or dies.

The structural form of the power culture may be seen as like a spider's web, or wheel (see Figure 14.1). The main relationship between the subordinates is with the centre.

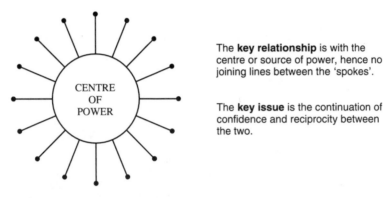

The **key relationship** is with the centre or source of power, hence no joining lines between the 'spokes'.

The **key issue** is the continuation of confidence and reciprocity between the two.

Figure 14.1   Power culture + structure: The Wheel

■ People/person culture

People/person culture exists for the people in it: for example, where a group has decided that it is in its own overriding interest to band or form together and produce an organisation for its own benefit. This may be found in certain research groups; university departments; family firms; and companies started by groups of friends where the first coming together is generated by the people involved rather than the matter in hand. The key relationship is therefore between people, and what binds them is their intrinsic common interest. Hierarchy and structure may evolve, but these too will be driven by this intrinsic common interest.

The **key relationship** is between the people; what binds them is their **intrinsic** common interest.
Hierarchy and structure may evolve incidentally; they too will be driven by this intrinsic common interest.

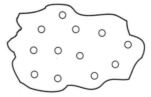

Figure 14.2   People/person culture + structure: The Mass

■ Task culture

Task cultures are to be found in project teams, marketing groups and marketing-oriented organisations. The emphases are on getting the job completed, keeping customers and clients satisfied, and responding to and identifying new market opportunities. Such cultures are flexible, adaptable and dynamic. They accommodate the movements of staff necessary to ensure effective project and development teams and continued innovation; and concurrent human activities such as secondments, project responsibility and short-term contracts. They are driven by customer satisfaction. They operate most effectively in prosperous, dynamic and confident environments and markets. They may also generate opportunities and niche activities in these and create new openings. Their success lies in their continued ability to operate in this way.

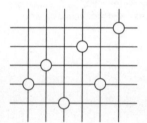

The **key relationship** here is with the task. The form of organisation is therefore fluid and elastic.
The **structure** is often also described as a MATRIX, or GRID; none of these gives a full configuration – the essence is the dynamics of the form, and the structure necessary to ensure this.

Figure 14.3　Task culture + structure: The Net

■ Role culture

Role cultures are found where organisations have gained a combination of size, permanence and departmentalisation, and where the ordering of activities and preservation of knowledge, experience and stability are both important and present.

The key relationship is based on authority and the superior–subordinate style of relationships. The key purposes are order, stability, permanence and efficiency.

Role cultures operate most effectively where the wider environment is steady and a degree of permanence is envisaged.

Other forms may also be identified.

■ Focal elements

This is where the organisation identifies one key element as its cultural base. These are to be found in such areas as safety and learning cultures, whereby the particular point – safety or learning, for example – is placed at the centre of the organisation's commitment to standards. Examples of safety cultures are

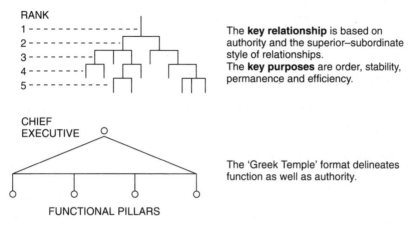

RANK

The **key relationship** is based on authority and the superior–subordinate style of relationships.
The **key purposes** are order, stability, permanence and efficiency.

CHIEF EXECUTIVE

The 'Greek Temple' format delineates function as well as authority.

FUNCTIONAL PILLARS

Figure 14.4 Role culture + structure: The Pyramid or Temple

Western airlines and the oil industry, whereby everything is designed, built, structured and organised so that accidents and disasters cannot happen. Examples of learning cultures are to be found across all sectors and are instigated by companies as integral to continuous change and improvement, drives for flexibility and dynamism, the development of potential, quality and organisation behaviour transformation.

■ Tribes

This is where organisations create a tribal concept. This is usually accompanied by a strong vision from the top. Its purpose is to unleash strong creative forces and generate high levels of enthusiasm, ethics, energy and fun. This is the stated position above all, of the Body Shop. It is also to be found in some people cultures. It may also be found as a feature of other creative and dynamic pockets of organisations. Regular brainstorming groups also produce this among themselves, especially where their activities are successful.

■ Pioneering culture

Pioneering cultures are the extension of the process of constant improvement and innovation into constantly questioning the ways in which things are done, continuously seeing new markets, projects and opportunities. It involves attention to processes and practices, technology, organisational form and structure, customers and staff.

The objective is the equivalent of 'getting the response in first': anticipating and responding to changes in customer needs, improving the organisation as a whole, developing and enhancing productive and staff quality. This is a part of the thrust of business process re-engineering and total quality management (see page X).

■ Entrepreneurial culture

This is where the thrust of the organisation is aimed directly at creating and fostering new initiatives, generating new business ideas and ventures, and then often selling them on, either in the form of franchises or as sales of assets to other organisations. An example of this is fast food – the sale of franchises by McDonalds, Kentucky Fried Chicken, Wimpy, Burger King – where the attraction to the customer is the consistency of the product, wherever and whenever it is bought. Other examples are the Next, Storehouse, Habitat, Mothercare, Tie Rack and Sock Shop retail chains; these grew up where opportunities were identified and acted upon by individuals who then either withdrew from the company that they had founded or else took on experts and managers in order to sustain the fledgeling business.

Other more general examples are to be found in computer software, games and entertainment; and also in the supply of components to manufacturers and assemblers.

Entrepreneurial cultures are based on the creativity, dynamism, vision, energy and enthusiasm of the entrepreneur, who may nevertheless lack the organisational and behavioural expertise necessary to sustain a permanent and continuing enterprise.

■ Intrapreneurial culture

Intrapreneurs – enterprising individuals who work within organisations rather than creating their own – are hired by organisations as change and development agents. They gravitate to those places that give the space and direction needed for their qualities of creativity, dynamism, vision and energy. They act as internal pioneers, constantly questioning the status quo, seeking ways of improving products, services, processes, quality and satisfaction, and enhancing the effectiveness of the organisation as a whole. The most successful intrapreneurial cultures are those that combine an overall clarity of vision and purpose with the ability to enable high-quality individuals to operate with the freedom and space that they need.

■ Summary

These archetypes are very seldom found in isolation. In practice, most organisations (except for the very small) have features of each. Some conclusions may be drawn, however. Whichever the dominant culture, the main concerns are:

- relationships between people, hierarchies, authority, reporting, attention to task and interaction during work;
- standards, of behaviour, attitudes and performance; of integrity, honesty and openness; of mutual respect and regard;
- values and shared values, the basis on which these are established, and the gaining and maintenance of commitment; the creation of a strength and identity of purpose;
- a management and organisation style that is suitable both to productive and effective work, and also to underpinning the standards and values that ensure this can take place;
- expectations and aspirations, ensuring that what the organisation offers is clearly understood at the outset by all who come to work in it and reconciling these with those of the people concerned;
- being positive and dynamic rather than negative, emergent and inert;
- working within the pressures and constraints present in particular situations, locations and types of work; and devising means by which these two can be reconciled with organisational purposes, aims and objectives;
- establishing universal interest in the success and future of the organisation; reconciling and harmonising the divergence of interests, personal and professional aims and objectives within the organisation's overall purposes;
- establishing a strength of identity between staff and organisation; a common bond; pride and positive feelings in belonging to the organisation; and a team, group and organisation spirit.

BOX 14.4   Identity

A telecommunication giant ran a series of culture change programmes for all its people in 1991 and 1992. The purpose was to generate a new feeling and high degree of identity and commitment among those working for the company in the wake of recent privatisation, restructuring, job losses and redundancies.

Senior staff were flown to locations in Spain, Portugal and the south of France for a week to be put through their programme. For the same purpose middle and junior management and supervisory staff attended two-day programmes at 2, 3 and 4–star hotels around the UK. Skilled, semi-skilled, unskilled, operative and clerical staff attended half- and one-day programmes at village halls, colleges and company training centres.

At the end of the programme each member was given sets of papers and handouts to take away with them and these were packaged in distinctive bags with the company's logo printed on them.

Consultants and trainers who carried out the work in the village halls and training centres reported that most people either left the bags behind or else turned them inside out before leaving the venue.

BOX 14.5   Joint Ventures

Organisations involved in joint ventures normally create a company or entity with its own distinctive identity for the duration of the project. This is to generate positive feelings of commitment towards the matter in hand and override the view that would otherwise be maintained by those involved that they continue to be a part of their old organisation. A fragmented and disordered – and negative – approach and identity would thus otherwise ensue. By creating the separate and new identity, the negative is overcome and a distinctive focal point for the work in hand is established.

■ Other aspects of organisational culture

Other features of organisational culture may be distinguished.

1. Relationships with the environment: including the ways in which the organisation copes with uncertainty and turbulence; the ways by which the organisation seeks to influence the environment; the extent to which it behaves proactively or reactively.
2. History and tradition: the extent to which the organisation's histories and traditions are barriers or facilitators of progress; the extent to which the organisation values and worships its past histories and traditions; key influences on current activities and beliefs; the position of key interest groups (for example, trade unions).
3. The internal relationship balance: the mixture and effectiveness of power, status, hierarchy, authority, responsibility, individualism, group cohesion; the general relationship mixture of task/social/development.
4. Rites and rituals: these are the punctuation marks of organisation operations. They include: pay negotiations; internal and external job application means and methods; disciplinary, grievance and dismissal procedures; rewards; individual, group, departmental and divisional publicity; training and development activities; parties and celebrations; key appointments and dismissals; socialisation and integration of people into new roles, activities and responsibilities.
5. Routines and habits: these are the formal, semi-formal and informal ways of working and interaction that people generate for themselves (or which the organisation generates for them) to make comfortable the non-operational aspects of working life. They develop around the absolutes – attendance times, work requirements, authority and reporting relationships – and include regular meetings, regular tasks, forms of address between members of the organisation and groups, pay days, holidays and some trainee development activities.
6. Badges and status symbols: these are the marks of esteem conferred by organisations on their people. They are a combination of location (near to or away from the corridors of power for example); possessions (cars, technology, personal

department)s; job titles (reflecting a combination of ability, influence and occupation); and position in the hierarchy pecking order.

The effects of rites, rituals, routines, habits, badges and status symbols all lie in the value that the organisation places on them and the regard in which they are held by the members of staff. There is no point in offering anything, or in undertaking any form of cultural activity if a negligible or negative response is received. In general therefore, these forms of culture development both anticipate people's expectations and seek to reinforce them and to meet them.

■ **Stories, myths and legends**

All organisations have their fund of stories, myths and legends. The nature and content of these represents and reflects the current state of organisational culture and well-being (see Box 14.5).

■ **The grapevine**

All organisations also have their own grapevine; this is the means by which stories, myths and legends become circulated and gain currency. In simple terms, the grapevine is the difference between what people want to know and what they do know: in particular, where communications are bad, a lot of personal time and energy is wasted on informal clusters, talking through particular scenarios and wondering what the future is to hold for them. In the worst cases, this is very destructive of motivation and morale (see Box ??).

■ **Power and influence bases**

In cultural terms, this refers particularly to the reasons why measures of influence are found in particular places. It also refers to matters of organisation politics: the means by which people interact in order to facilitate their own position.

■ **Ideal culture**

The ideal culture is one that serves the organisation effectively. It may be summarised as the shared patterns of attitudes, values, beliefs and behaviour, covering strategy, operations, decision-making, information flow and systems, managerial and supervisory behaviour, the nature of leadership and the general behaviour of the staff. It involves setting absolute standards of ensuring that these are achieved. It also requires reference to each of the elements and factors indicated above.

The relationship between the ideal and the actual culture should be a matter of constant concern because both develop. Specific attention is paid to those gaps in culture that cause problems where, for example, people follow the leads, values and norms of their work or professional group rather than those of the organisation. Technological advances and changes may mean that suddenly the ideal hitherto striven for has to be changed in order to accommodate new divisionalisation, patterns of work, retraining, regrouping, and so on.

Sub-cultures, parallel cultures and covert cultures are all bound to exist in organisations; the problem is to ensure that they do not damage or detract from total organisational performance. They must be capable of harmonisation within the overall standards, and any sub-cultures that do not conform to this should be broken up.

The purpose is to arrive at something which is dynamic and which adds value to operations and energises the people positively. It affects attitudes and values and the ways in which people regard themselves, each other and the organisation as a whole. It affects customer relations and relations with the wider community. It contributes to perceptions and images and wider feelings of general confidence.

BOX 14.6   Culture Development

The basic approach is not to allow culture to emerge to form itself at the whim of the staff, but rather to create that which is desired by means of predetermined and targeted interventions.

1. Strategy and direction, to ensure that everyone understands that their place is in the pursuit of the organisation's purpose whatever job they are carrying out. For example, a cleaner at NASA (North American Space Administration), interviewed on television in 1967, when asked what his job was, replied 'I am helping to put the first person on the moon.'
2. Reorganisation, to ensure that old ways, procedures and practices are confined to history. Anything may act as a lever for this: new technology, new premises, work and job redesign, training and development. For each new store that it opens at out-of-town sites, for example, the Tesco supermarket company provides extensive job training for all the staff who are to work there, whether or not they have worked for the company in the past. This is to ensure that they now know the new and absolute standards to which they are required to conform.
3. Induction, to ensure that the required attitudes, values, beliefs and standards are understood by all at the outset. Reinduction is required where the prevailing standards are no longer satisfactory.
4. Other human resource activities, targeted to give impetus to the new. This includes everything: rewriting job descriptions (and the retraining that is then required for new job holders); changing recruitment advertising; attention to qualities and capabilities of new and existing staff; repositioning and reorientation of performance appraisal, industrial relations and staff management activities.

5. Use of fashions and fads such as total quality management, customer service training and business process re-engineering as the means of doing that which is required. The main service of these to all organisations is to challenge existing thinking and to act as the means by which desired developments can be introduced.

6. Use of dramas and crises to get people to think. Where necessary this may involve overstating the case. For example, the entry of the Virgin Group into the cola market had business analysts and pundits wondering publicly if this was to be the beginning of the end for Pepsi and Coca Cola. This plainly was a vast exaggeration. However, the volume of attention given was quite sufficient to ensure that everyone at both Pepsi and Coca Cola continued to pay positive attention to their own activities.

7. Use of new language, which is ideally both more direct and also sufficiently different from the old. This drives and reinforces development. It also reinforces understanding and acceptance as long as the language is more direct. It is also a general underlining of the fact that there is a general new way in existence.

8. Use of project work and cross-functional teams to break down existing barriers and fiefdoms, as well as generating expertise and potential among employees, and also raising their sights and expectations. Furthermore, this enables positive relationships to be built between departments and individuals with different expertise and professions.

Adapted from Egan (1994).

■ Culture management and attention to culture

As stated above, both the actual culture and the perceived ideal are subject to constant development. With this in mind, the best organisations therefore pay this constant attention. There are some basic assumptions here.

1. Culture can be changed and developed. There are too many examples where this has happened to think otherwise. Nissan UK transformed a population of ex-miners, shipbuilders and steelworkers into the most productive and effective car company in the UK. Toyota at Derby is following suit with former railway staff. British Airways transformed a bureaucratic nationalised monopoly into a customer-orientated multi-national corporation. British Steel transformed itself from a loss-making national corporation, riddled with demarcation and restrictive practices, to a profitable, effective and flexible operator.

2. Culture should be changed and developed. The constant development of operations, technology, markets, customer bases and the capabilities of the human resource also make this inevitable. Current ways of working and equipment, and

current skills, knowledge and qualities serve current needs only. The future is based around the developments and innovations that are to take place in each of these areas. Therefore, the culture must itself develop in order that these can be accommodated.

3. Culture change is long and costly. It is certainly true that, where stability has existed for a long while, it is traumatic at first, and therefore costly in terms of people's feelings and possibly also in terms of current morale. It is made easier for the future if new qualities and attitudes of flexibility, dynamism and responsiveness are included in the new form and if this is reinforced through ensuring that people understand that the old ways are now neither effective nor viable.

4. Culture change need not take forever. Indeed, people who are told that there are to be lengthy periods of turbulence lose interest and motivation. The reality of change and development can be quickly conveyed through critical incidents: for example, the gain or loss of a major order; the collapse of a large firm in the sector; the entry of a new player into the sector; radical technological advances; and so on. Once this is understood, the attitudes, behaviour and orientation of the staff are given emphases in particular direction and the general positioning of their aspirations, hopes and fears is changed.

The ideal culture therefore, has its roots in the recognition of the nature, extent and influence of the pressures and constraints within which the organisation has to operate. It is essential also to recognise the influence of different aspects of organisation, design and operation:

- technology has influence on work arrangements and groupings, physical lay-out and the nature of the people employed;
- structure and hierarchy influence personal and professional interactions, personal and professional ambitions and aspirations;
- rules, regulations and systems influence attitudes and behaviour (positively or negatively) depending on how they are drawn up and operated and on their particular focus;
- leadership provides the key point of identity for everyone else, and from which people establish their own perceptions of the organisation's general standards;
- management style influences the general feelings of well-being of everyone else, and sets standards of attitudes and behaviour as well as performance;
- managerial demands, and the ways in which these are made, influence attitudes and behaviour also;
- hierarchical and divisional relations and interactions influence the nature of performance, attention to achievement and the value placed on achievements; this also applies to functional activities.

Where the need for culture change or development is apparent, interventions can be made into each or all of these.

The conclusion of this is an organisation culture which has the following elements:

- a positive aura, one to which people can subscribe and identify with confidence, pride and feelings of well-being, which in turn encourages positive views of the organisation and its work, and positive and harmonious working relationships;
- shared values and standards, capable of being adopted and followed by all concerned (this includes attention to high standards of integrity and morality; mutual concern and interest; and equity and equality);
- high levels of individuality, identity, motivation and commitment; high levels of group identity and mutual respect and regard;
- an organisation and management style that is supportive of everyone involved (whatever the style, whether autocratic or participative), and which concentrates on results and output, effectiveness and quality of performance and also on the development and improvement of the people;
- regular flows of high-quality information that reflect high levels of respect and esteem for the people on the part of the organisation.

Again, these can provide a useful point of reference for those concerned with the general well-being of the organisation, and when it becomes apparent that things are going wrong.

Much of this is clearly concerned with setting high standards and creating a positive general environment and background. This is to be seen in the context that where these elements are either not present or not attended to, or where the converse is present – a negative aura, one to which people do not subscribe, lack of shared values, or an unsupported management style, for example – there is no identity or common purpose. People seek refuge in groups or in their profession or technical expertise. Absenteeism and turnover increases, while performance declines. There becomes an ever-greater concentration on self and on individual performance, often at the expense of that of the organisation. Interpersonal and intergroup relationships also suffer.

Both the positive and negative feed off each other. Striving for a positive and ideal culture tends to reinforce the high levels of value placed on the staff and the more general matters of honesty and integrity. Similarly, allowing the negative to persist tends to mean that relationships will get worse, while aims and objectives become ever more fragmented or clouded, and the organisation purpose ever more obscured.

■ Conclusions

Effective organisation cultures are positive and designed rather than emergent. They must be capable of gaining commitment to purpose, the ways in which this is pursued and the standards adopted by everyone. Cultures are a summary and reflection of the aims, objectives, and values held. Where none of these are apparent, different groups and individuals form their own aims and objectives and adopt their own values; and where these are at variance with overall purpose, or negative in some way, they are dysfunctional and may become destructive.

BOX 14.7   Excellence and Culture

Without exception the dominance and coherence of culture proved to be an essential quality of the excellent companies [the 62 American companies studied by Peters and Waterman]. Moreover, the stronger the culture, and the more it was directed to the market place, the less need there was for policy manuals, organisation charts or detailed procedures and rules. In these companies, people way down the line know what they are supposed to do in most situations because the handful of guiding values is crystal clear.

From Peters and Waterman (1982).

For this to be effective, a strong mutual sense of loyalty and acceptance between organisation and people is essential. Employees exert positive effort on behalf of the organisation, making a personal as well as professional or occupational commitment. The reverse of this – the organisation's commitment to its people – is also essential. A strong sense of identity towards the organisation and its purposes and values is required, and this happens when these are clear and positive. Any commitment made by people to organisations (or anything else) is voluntary and personal, and can be changed or withdrawn. The best organisations produce cultures which are capable of generating this. They create the desire among their people to join, remain with and progress with them, recognising their mutuality of interest and the benefits available to everyone.

■ Questions

1. Outline the benefits and drawback of offering status symbols – for example, personal offices, car parking spaces, job titles – as marks of progress. What steps should be taken to ensure that, overall, benefits prevail and not the drawbacks?
2. What steps should organisations take to maintain and develop their culture in periods of a) rapid expansion and b) rapid shrinkage?
3. What does the work of Hofstede indicate about cultural similarities and differences? Why are some multi-national organisations so much more successful than others when operating away from their main locations and country of origin?
4. What changes are required in skills, knowledge, attitudes and behaviour for all groups of staff when moving from an archetypal role culture to an archetypal task culture?

CHAPTER 15
Technology

■ Introduction

All organisations use some form of technology and equipment in pursuit of their business and this has a basic and critical impact on the nature, design, structure and conduct of work. Technology also has implications for compartmentalisation, functionalisation and specialisation. Departments and divisions are created around the equipment used, whether for production, communications, information or control. It has an impact on the physical environment: particular processes determine the lay-out and format in which work is conducted, and the proximity of individuals and groups to each other. It therefore becomes a factor to be recognised in the creation of supervisory and managerial functions and activities.

Again, there is a historic background. Forms of technology and equipment were used in the construction of the great buildings, temples and monuments of the ancient world. Most of this was unmechanised, often requiring armies of people to move heavy blocks of wood and stone into place. Roman war galleys – fighting ships – used slave-driven banks of oars for propulsion and direction and to manoeuvre into fighting positions. In each of these cases a basic technology existed and was exploited, but using human, rather than mechanised, energy to make it effective. In each case, also, the task requirements meant that forms of organisation were required; and while in many cases the labour was composed of slaves, these nevertheless had to be sufficiently interested, motivated and directed to ensure that the product or output was both effective and of the required quality.

The relationship between people and technology in organisations and organised groups has therefore long been established and recognised. The effects of technology upon organisational behaviour become ever more apparent, however. This is especially true in the current environment of constant technological development and change.

The relationship between technology and organisational behaviour may be considered under the following headings.

1. **Approaches to production**: scientific management and its effects on production and behaviour; studies of groups in different working situations; the use of work groups in production.
2. **Levels and types of technology**: the effects of the size, scope and scale of operations; the use of production lines; the effects of mechanisation and automation on individuals and groups. This also extends to information technology.

3. **Organisational requirements**: the maximisation/optimisation of production; attention to standardisation, quality, speed, reliability and consistency of output.
4. **Human and behavioural implications**: boredom and alienation; health and safety and occupational health; stresses and strains; job and task division.

Organisational technology consists of:

- hardware: the capital equipment (computers, screens, robots, process machines);
- software: the packages needed to energise and direct the hardware profitably and effectively.

It also includes the following interrelated elements.

1. Production technology and equipment, which may be largely manual or mechanised, requiring human expertise, energy and input to make it effective and productive.
2. Largely automated, designed to produce products (or components of products) to uniform standards of quality, appearance and performance.

    In these cases the human input is often largely confined to switching the process on and off and monitoring (watching) the output flow. This includes production robotics and computerised manufacturing.
3. Support function technology: includes computer-aided design, desk-top printing and publishing, purchasing, stock room, storage and ordering systems.
4. Information systems: for the input, storage, retrieval, output and presentation of data in ways suitable to those using it; and the production of data for purposes of control, monitoring, evaluation and decision-making.
5. Specialised: for example, health equipment includes scanners, monitors, emergency equipment, laser technology for surgery and healing, heart, lung, organ and pulse monitoring equipment.
6. Generic: off-the-shelf computerised production and information systems that are of value to a wide range of organisations and activities.

All organisational technology is developed and improved along the following lines:

- that which is to be used in future supersedes that which was used in the past, either by improving quality or volume of output, or by reducing the time and resources (including human) taken to produce the existing levels;
- that which is to be used in the future has a greater variety of uses and applications than the existing technology, and may lead to the ability to gain entry into new markets and sectors, thus helping to secure the future of the organisation;
- fashion: everyone else in the given sector is using a particular form of technology and there is pressure to conform;
- the organisation itself has an accurate assessment of the nature of the technology required to produce its products to the required volume, quality and deadline and commissions the design and manufacture of the equipment to do this;

- organisations and the technology that they use must be capable of harmonisation with the given culture, values, attitudes, skills and qualities;
- items of technology must increasingly be capable of integration and interrelationship with each other.

■ Scientific management

This is the term used to describe the first major attempt to make effective the relationship between organisations and their technology. The approach taken by those who subscribe to this view was to try to break every task down into a set of routine, simple and ordered components. These would be quickly learned and repeated by the workers, who would become expert and excellent at their job. Attention was also paid to the design of equipment, making it as suitable as possible for the particular work in hand. A combination of the right equipment with people following simple, repetitive and routinised tasks would therefore lead to high standards of production, efficiency and effectiveness.

■ F. W. Taylor

The term scientific management is first ascribed to F. W. Taylor (1856–1915). He aimed to produce a science of management based on a detailed analysis of work. He took the view that few workers ever performed to the speed and capacity of which they were capable. This was due in part to bad supervision; nobody insisted that they worked any faster. The choice of work method was left entirely to the individual operator who also therefore set his own working speed. There was furthermore a perception among workers that by working slowly they ensured that large numbers of people continued to be employed; if they were to speed up, others would lose their jobs.

Taylor's approach was to bring efficiency, standardisation and discipline to each task (see Figure 15.1). He identified the planning of work as a management function, removing from the workers the choice of work method and work speed. The workers would carry out the work under the scrutiny of supervisors, whose key function was to ensure that efficiency and discipline prevailed.

In pursuit of efficiency, Taylor introduced methods of worker selection based on fitness, strength and capacity to do the job (hitherto people had joined companies largely on the basis of friendship or association with those already working there). He also ensured that a variety of equipment was available to suit the different sizes, strengths and physiques of the individual workers.

The other aspect of this was the motivation of the workers. Taylor invented the piece-rate system of payment. This was to ensure that the faster the work, the higher the output and the more the worker got paid. This in itself would eliminate the propensity to work more slowly.

1.

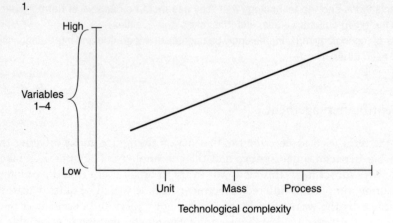

Variables: 1. Number of levels in management hierarchy
            2. Ratio of managers and supervisors to total staff
            3. Ratio of direct to indirect labour
            4. Proportion of graduates among supervisory staff engaged in
               production.

2.

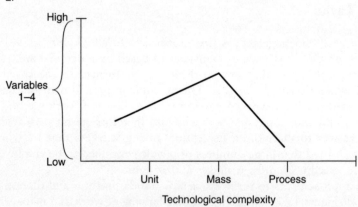

Variables: 1. Span of total of first time supervisors
            2. Organisation flexibility/inflexibility
            3. Amount of written communication
            4. Specialistion between functions of management, technical
               expertise the time–staff structure.

Figure 15.1 Organisations and technology

Source: Lawrence (1984). Used with permission.

He observed the work being carried out, noting the actions taken and the
speed with which they were performed. He selected 'good workers' as the

benchmark for speed and efficiency of production. He also paid attention to the size and usage of equipment.

By breaking each job down into simple repetitive tasks, all production would in any case become labour-intensive. Taylor foresaw happy, harmonious, productive and efficient groups of workers. Every person could conduct their part of the operation and hand it on to the next. The piece-rate system meant that there was a drive on the part of everyone to work fast. The correct equipment was present to ensure that this could happen and was available for everyone to use when it was needed.

The process of division and specialisation was extended to supervision and administration. Rather than having one person as a supervisor, responsible for overseeing all aspects of the work, this job was also broken down. Different individuals were employed to maintain discipline, keep time and inspect work. Huczynski and Buchanan (1993) describe this as follows.

The job of general foreman was distributed among eight separate individuals. Each of these would oversee a separate function of the work and would be called:

(a)   inspector;
(b)   order of work and route clerk;
(c)   time and cost clerk;
(d)   shop disciplinarian;
(e)   gang boss;
(f)   speed boss;
(g)   repair boss;
(h)   instruction card clerk.

BOX 15.1   Principles of Scientific Management

These are:

- efficiency – increasing output per worker; reducing worker control; reducing underworking; getting everybody to the standard of 'good workers';
- standardisation – of job performance; task performance; overall levels of activity;
- deskilling – reducing every activity to a set of simple tasks; removing the need for judgement; removing extraneous factors;
- discipline – based on a functionalised/divisionalised system of supervision;
- decision-making – to be left to supervisors and management; supervisors were responsible for seeing that decisions handed down from management were carried out by the workers.

There was thus a clear division of tasks and responsibilities between management and workers. Management and supervision were to be underwritten by a series of rules and regulations to give a formalised structure to the work to be carried out. In order to be effective, workers received 'job training' in their particular area of activity. In order for this to be effective, workers were selected and hired on the basis of capability and aptitude for the work.

Motivation of workers was entirely dependent upon money.

BOX 15.2   Consequences of Scientific Management

1. It assumed that the motivation of all employees was to secure the maximum earnings for the effort expended. It neglected the importance of the psychological aspects of work (job satisfaction, achievement, progress).
2. It neglected the interpersonal aspects of work: the fact that people require human interaction whether they are in a work situation or anywhere else.
3. It failed to recognise that this form of approach to work organisation would inevitably be regarded as coercive and divisive.
4. It ignored the psychological needs and individual capabilities of workers. Everything was based around the establishment of 'the one best way of doing the job'. The imposition of uniform methods of work both destroys individuality and also causes feelings of low self-esteem, frustration and alienation. The individual comes to be regarded purely as a cog in the machine, with no separate, personal and unique qualities.

In every case Taylor's purpose was to find 'the best way' of doing the job and of getting the highest possible output. The underlying reasoning was entirely positive: by compartmentalising every task, everyone involved would work together in efficient productive harmony, so output would increase; the wages of the workers would increase; and individual regulation of work would be eliminated. The key to this was the financial incentive: as long as money was available and paid for increased output, the workers would go faster.

■ Human performance and scientific management

The work of Taylor was developed by Frank and Lillian Gilbreth and Henry Lawrence Gantt. Gilbreth was a builder; Gantt worked for Taylor at the Bethlehem Iron and Steel Company in the USA.

The Gilbreths adapted scientific management to the building and construction sector. The approach was slightly different in that an 'optimum' level of performance was set, and refinements to the activities that were found would be used to make productive life easier, less stressful and less tiring. They identified a work–fatigue relationship and reasoned that, by allowing for fatigue and building in rest periods to the working day, efficient output would be achieved for longer periods of time. Their study of work concentrated on those elements that produced most fatigue and sought to eliminate or reduce these as far as possible. They also introduced the concept of the 'betterment' of work: improving the working environment and providing rest rooms with chairs.

Gantt looked at the humanisation of scientific management directly. He believed that the principles of scientific management had been taken and distorted by organisations. It was being used in practice by managers and supervisors as a system of oppression. Gantt produced a series of job instructions for workers in accordance with standard scientific management principles; into these he built discretion and leeway that allowed workers to organise and conduct the work as they saw fit. He divided the pay into two components: a wage or set rate for the day, and a bonus which was based on volume of output. By leaving a measure of autonomy with the workers, the achievement of maximum bonuses became (at least in part) their choice and responsibility. Once one person achieved maximum output, the rest normally were quickly found to have followed suit.

The contribution of Gantt and the Gilbreths was to begin to recognise the behavioural and psychological needs of those who worked on production lines and in other mass employment situations.

The principles first identified by the scientific management writers are apparent in the production organisations of today. Scientific management also identified fundamental behavioural elements of work organisation which again remained current.

The workers were not just workers who responded only to monetary incentives. They were (and remain) human beings with varying drives and motivations to work. These are related to the ways in which they conduct their lives and integrate work with their other interests, ambitions and aspirations. As with everyone, they have a fundamental need to be treated with fairness, respect and dignity.

The compartmentalisation and deskilling of work which Taylorism espoused also removed any feeling of job satisfaction, identity, achievement or recognition. The workers simply became the means of energising the production processes. This is emphasised today by the fact that so many of the jobs that were created along scientific management lines have been replaced by fully automated production processes.

Close observation of work and tight timing and scheduling activities are widely perceived to be punitive and oppressive by those being assessed. Close supervision is seen as intrusive at best and punitive and coercive at worst.

The removal of responsibility and personal contribution to the work (leaving this in the hands of managers) effectively meant that the individual had no involvement other than in terms of output and money. Again, this is widely perceived to be oppressive.

The driving force behind the concept of scientific management and production processes is the ability to turn out volumes of items of the same standard and – using current production technology – high quality. These operations are now highly automated over most of the industrialised world. The scientific management production concept therefore remains generally current. It is the growth and development of jobs and tasks around this together with the wider behavioural implications that require attention.

■ Size and scale of production

A variety of different scales of production and expertise may be identified and it is now necessary to define these. Each has behavioural implications.

Joan Woodward studied the impact of technology and behaviour on each other in a wide range of manufacturing organisations in Essex in the 1950s. From this work there has emerged a widely used classification of sizes and scales of production.

Unit

The production of individual, unique or specialised items. Resources are gathered together to produce these in response to demand and orders. To be successful in this a variety of conditions must exist. The technology and equipment used must be specialised. The expertise available must be both highly specialist in the given field and flexible, adaptable and responsive to individual demands. There must be commitment to quality and attention to details of the particular demands of customers. Scheduling and patterns of work will be flexible.

Most unit work is carried out by small organisations. Those who work in them must in turn be flexible in their attitude and approach to work. Many people involved in unit production bring with them high levels of technical expertise and this has to be integrated into effective output.

Mass production

The design of mass production operations was and remains based on the scientific management principles first developed by Taylor in the late nineteenth Century (see above). Work is broken down into simple and progressive operations. Large volumes are standardised and regular output is therefore produced. Automated and computerised production technologies are now widely used for this. The result has been to increase quality, volume, speed and reliability of output.

Mass production requires high and continuing levels of investment in the production technology of work premises. It also requires investment in the determination and management of scheduling, storage, marketing, sales and delivery and the organisation and training of the workforce. This normally means the employment of a wide range of distinctive, professional or semi-professional functional specialists and experts, and the creation of departments and divisions reflecting this. The contribution of each and their interaction with each other has to be managed and harmonised. Areas of conflict become apparent between the departments and divisions. There is also often the need to reconcile organisational priorities and directions with the demands of individuals to progress and develop their professional and technical expertise and their careers.

Batch production

This exists between the unit and mass scales of production. It draws features from each: the specialist quality output and the flexibility and responsiveness of the small producer, combined with the production standardisation and larger scales of activities. A batch is therefore a quantity large enough to require substantial technological investment in its production. This is limited by the size of demand for the product and one only of a range of outputs that a batch producer makes.

Organisations engaged in batch products require distinctive and appropriate technology and equipment and the expertise to use it effectively. They also need staff to be able to carry out the support functions indicated (for example, marketing and sales personnel) whether or not these are constituted into formalised departments.

Flow production

This is related to mass production in scale, but applies to areas of activity where the output is a continuous stream or flow, such as oil, petrol, chemicals, steel and plastic extrusion. The investment in technology is by far the greatest charge on organisations in these sectors. Input and expertise has to be scheduled in order to ensure a steady and correct flow of raw materials into the production and output processes. The second priority is the maintenance of the equipment used in order that there are as few breakdowns and stoppages as possible because the other critical level of charge comes from shutting down the processes and then restarting them.

For example, switching off a steel furnace normally means that it has to be relined with the fireproof heat retention and energy generation elements that are used to produce the extreme levels of temperature required. These cannot accommodate cooling-off after they have been operational. This therefore means substantial maintenance and refitting has to be accommodated if a shutdown occurs.

In flow production organisations, high levels of technology and process expertise therefore exist. Support functions have again to be created, harmonised and integrated.

This gives a general indication of the managerial and organisational behavioural issues that arise as a result of the adoption of particular types and scales of production and the technology used. There are implications for work division and allocation, work patterns, styles and methods of management, and supervision of operations. There are also production and operational pressures on those who actually conduct the organisation's primary activities.

■ **Expertise**

As with technology and equipment, different levels of expertise may be distinguished.

☐ *Professional*

The original professions were medicine, soldiering, priesthood and the law. They distinguished themselves from other occupations as follows.

1. They set their own entry barriers, normally in the form of pre-required levels of education or training which those who aspired to the profession had to have in order to be eligible for consideration for entry. This also limited the numbers in the profession and helped to keep reward levels relatively high.
2. They were self-regulating. There is a distinctive body of knowledge, skills and expertise required to be learned which is determined by the profession itself. The profession also set its own standards of expertise and integrity. It required those who came into it to follow courses of study and practice in order to achieve these standards. It also took responsibility for the disciplining and regulation of members' activities. Constitutions, councils or gatherings of elders or senior members of the profession were responsible for this.
3. They required regular updating and training to be undertaken to ensure that the service and expertise offered was current.
4. They set their own levels of pay and reward. For soldiering this normally meant participating in the spoils of victory. For medicine reward levels were based on the nature of the ailment being treated and the need of the patient to live. For the law this was based on the nature of the client being represented and the charges that had been levelled against them. For the priesthood this was based on the respect and love in which the priest was held by his (and it was normally male) congregation.
5. They carried a distinctive and high level of status and esteem. Professions were deemed positive and worthwhile by those who went into them. They were also held in high regard and respect by the rest of society.
6. They carried a commitment to serve, to provide the highest possible quality and level of service to those for whom they worked. They would do this regardless of whoever employed them or came to them for their services.
7. They had a loyalty to their profession itself, and to the other members of it.

Other occupations also aspire to professional status. These include teaching, social work, nursing, accountancy, building, construction, civil and chemical engineering. Most of these require some formal training and expertise in order to be able to practise, though none of them is entirely self-regulating. There are also limitations on the ability of individuals in these occupations to command reward levels.

Still other occupations, have developed themselves with the purpose of establishing a general body of expertise that the best practitioners in these sectors should have. These include personnel, marketing, general management, commodity sales and brokerage, central and local government, retail, travel and tourism.

☐ *Technological*

The basis of this is historically similar to that of the professions. Particular trades – for example, wheelwright, cooper, carpenter – required the acquisition of specialist skills and knowledge. They also had periods of articles or apprenticeship which meant that individuals had to be attached to someone already working in the trade to learn the expertise and its applications, and to undertake on-the-job training. The timescales involved – sometimes as long as seven years – also constituted an entry barrier.

Much of this still remains current today. Some engineering occupations, mechanics, cooks and catering, building and construction trades all require formalised qualifications and periods of on-the-job training if the individual is to be able to maximise the potential of her expertise.

In summary, at best high standards of commitment loyalty, expertise, training and development are both offered and expected. These have great implications for those who manage people from professionalised and expert occupations and for the organisations in which they work. In each case, the individuals concerned have a dual loyalty: to their profession or expertise, and to their organisation. This expertise is marketable and may be offered or sold to the organisation that makes 'the best bid'. This clearly concerns salary; it is likely also to include job interest, challenge, opportunities for development, the need for continuous training and updating.

The contribution of expertise also needs to be valued by organisations and their managers. There is no point for example, in hiring an expert (in whatever field) and then giving her tasks for which her skills are not particularly required. This is a waste of organisational resources and leads to frustration on the part of the individual concerned.

The need, therefore, is to assess the interaction between organisation, technology and expertise in order to be able to draw up effective methods of work that are both satisfactory and challenging to the experts and professionals involved, and also successfully and profitably integrated with the organisation's drives and purposes.

It is apparent from all this that there is a range of conflicting pressures which must be considered.

1. The scientific management and organisation of activities demands the standardisation and ordering of work in the interests of efficiency, speed and volume of output.
2. Outputs of the scale and scope of production dictates that the flow, mass and (to an extent) batch types of activities require this standardisation.
3. Professional and technical staff require variety, development and the opportunity to progress and enhance their work and expertise.

4. Everyone, whatever their occupation, has basic human needs of self-esteem, self-respect and self-worth.

The need is therefore, to be able to address and reconcile these issues.

The specific effects of developments, improvements and automation of technology seen in isolation are:

- to remove any specific contribution made by operators to the quality and individuality of production, whether real or perceived;
- to dilute or remove understanding of the production processes used and to remove any direct individual contribution that is made;
- to de-skill operations: operators become button pushers, machine minders and (when breakdowns occur) telephone users summoning specialist assistance;
- to create a feeling of distance – alienation – between the work and the people who carry it out;
- to create frustration which occurs when equipment is available but the expertise to use it is not; or when the equipment is not available but the expertise is; or when both are available but the organisation chooses not to have it available for use.

The result is again to underline feelings of low self-esteem and worth and to encourage boredom and dissatisfaction, and sow the seeds of conflict.

BOX 15.3   Alienation

Alienation is the term used to describe feelings such as the following.

1. Powerlessness: the inability to influence work conditions, work volume, quality, speed and direction.
2. Meaninglessness: the inability to recognise the individual contribution made to the total output of work.
3. Isolation, which may be either physical or psychological. The physical factors arise from work organisation requiring that people are located in ways that allow for little human interaction and feelings of mutual identity and interest. The psychological factors are influenced by the physical. They also include psychological distance from supervisors, management and the rest of the organisation.
4. Low feelings of self-esteem and self-worth arising from the lack of value (real or perceived) placed on staff by the organisation and its managers.
5. Loss of identity with the organisation and its work, the inability to say with pride 'I work for organisation X.' This is reinforced by the physical and personal commitment made by the individual to the organisation in terms of time, skill and effort and which does not bring with it the psychological rewards.
6. Lack of prospects, change or advancement for the future: feelings of being stuck or trapped in a situation purely for economic gain.

7. General rejection, based on adversarial managerial and supervisory styles and lack of meaningful communications, participation and involvement. This is increased by physical factors, such as poor working conditions and environment.
8. Lack of equality, especially where the organisation is seen (or perceived) to differentiate between different types and grades of staff to the benefit of some and detriment of others.

Alienation is the major fundamental cause of conflicts and disputes at places of work. It is potentially present in all work situations. Those who design and construct organisations need to be aware of it in their own particular situations and to take steps to ensure that ideally it can be eliminated, or at least kept to a minimum and its effects offset by other advantages.

BOX 15.4   Alienation and Rejection

In 1956 the Pilsbury Company, USA, produced an instant cake mix. It meant that those who wished to do so could bake perfect cakes every time, simply by adding hot water to the mixture, stirring it and putting it in the oven for a set length of time.

The product was rejected because there was no distinctive individual contribution. Literally 'anybody could do it'. No cake made this way was either special or unique.

The company redeemed the product by redeveloping the mix so that eggs as well as water had to be added. A distinctive individual contribution was therefore made and the product eventually became successful.

The example is not directly organisational or work-related, but useful lessons may nevertheless be drawn. People need to contribute positively and to feel and perceive that they have done so.

Where this contribution is either not possible or removed, rejection tends to take place, however much more simple life may actually become as a result.

On the other hand, food packaging and processing companies now produce 'instant meals'. These are kept in the freezer or packet until required and then put in a microwave oven or mixed with boiling water. The contribution of the individual is about the same as in the case of the instant cake mix. However, these meals are profitable for the companies that make them and highly satisfying to the individuals who buy them because they are marketed as a necessary and integral part of the busy pressurised (and therefore highly valuable and valued) lives that they lead. This may now be illustrated in organisational behaviour terms. The 'Affluent Worker' studies carried out in the 1950s and 1960s found high levels of alienation at the factories studied (Vauxhall/GM, Laporte and Skefco at Luton and Dunstable, Bedfordshire, UK). Those involved were prepared to put up with high levels of dissatisfaction and boredom at work as the price of having interesting,

> satisfying and fulfilled lives away from work – organisation alienation had its compensations elsewhere.

■ Effects of technological advances

Some further conclusions concerning the effects of technology upon worker morale may now be drawn.

1. Pay, at whatever level it is set, does nothing to alleviate any boredom or monotony inherent in the work itself. It may make it more bearable in the short to medium term. In many cases also, bonus systems are not within the control of the individual operator. Operators may work to their full capacity only to see their bonus fail because of factors further down the production process.
2. Insecurity, and related to this, the threat of insecurity and job loss used as a coercive management tool to try to bully the work out.
3. Poor working conditions, especially those that include extremes of temperature and noise, discomfort, lack of human content and warmth all contribute to poor morale.
4. Low status and esteem is generated through feelings of being 'only a cog in the machine'. This leads to feelings of futility and impotence on the part of the operator. It is from this that feelings of hostility towards the organisation start to emerge. This also leads to increases in strikes, grievances and disputes.
5. Mental health was identified as a feature by the 'Kornhauser' Studies, the results of which were published in 1965. Arthur Kornhauser studied car assembly workers at Ford, GM and Chrysler in Detroit, USA. A major conclusion was that basic assembly line work led to job dissatisfaction, which in turn led to low levels of mental health. This became apparent in the low self-esteem of the workers who also exhibited anxiety, life dissatisfaction and despair, and hostility to others.
6. Adversarial and confrontational styles of work supervision also contribute to alienation and dissatisfaction. This style of supervision tends to be perpetuated, even by those who have been promoted from among the ranks of operators. This is partly because it is all that they know and partly because of the pressure to conform that is exerted by the existing supervisory group. It is also apparent that supervisors themselves become alienated because of pressures from their managers, and also because of feelings of hostility towards them from the workers.

Approaches to the problems of dissatisfaction and alienation have taken three basic forms.

Attention to the work
Attention to the working environment
Attention to the people

☐ *Attention to the work*

Attention to the work has taken a variety of forms.

1. Job enrichment and enlargement, in which operators have their capabilities extended to include a range of operations. In some cases this has meant becoming responsible (with a group of others) for the entire production process in autonomous work groups.
2. Job rotation, in which operators are regularly rotated around different workstations and activities, making a different contribution to the whole.
3. Empowerment, in which the operator accepts responsibility for his own supervision of quality control as well as for the work itself.

Each of these also partly addresses some of the psychological and behavioural aspects of dissatisfaction and alienation. It is worth noting the experience of an electronics firm quoted by Handy (1993) as follows: 'Production went up only slightly but, more important from their point of view, quality was very high without the need for quality control experts, absenteeism and turnover went down to low levels, production flexibility was greatly increased and the job satisfaction of employees was higher.'

BOX 15.5   Semco

Semco is a Brazilian multi-national corporation that produces pumping and hydraulic equipment for the marine and civil engineering industries. As part of a radical transformation of the work methods and practices introduced by Ricardo Semler, the company proprietor and CE, workers were given full autonomy and responsibility for everything that they produced. They met the deadlines required of customers. They were to ensure that the equipment worked, exercising their own quality control function. They ensured that the equipment was delivered to the right place at the right time. They also fielded any subsequent customer complaints.

Levels of output and commitment soared. Company profits soared, ahead of the Brazilian hyperinflation of the 1980s and 1990s by a factor of 7. There is a waiting list to join the company at all levels and in all disciplines. People come from all over the world to study the company and its work methods and practices.

Source: from Semler (1992).

Attention to the work is a continuous process. Today's adventure becomes tomorrow's steady state and the monotony of the day after. There is a great propensity for development to occur in current production systems because of technological advances and also because the globalisation of competition has led organisations to seek new fields and new ways in which to operate.

There is clearly a mutual obligation in all of this for the organisation to provide continuous training and development and for the individual to accept and undergo it. Without this, effective organisation and job development cannot take place.

The question of pay must also be considered. If work enrichment is followed successfully, the outcome should be a highly skilled, highly motivated and well-paid workforce.

Multi-skilling and flexibility

Some versions of job enrichment and enlargement have sought to develop 'the fully flexible workforce' by ensuring that all those in a particular work group are capable of carrying out each of the activities required. This is a basic and integral job requirement. The obligation is placed on the organisation to provide increased levels and volumes of training and development and also to recognise and reward the additional value that the member of staff brings by being capable and flexible.

BOX 15.6   **Problems with Job Enrichment, Job Enlargement and Multi-skilling**

Expectations

Expectations placed on staff are raised and must be capable of being met. For example, people expect that when they are trained for something they will be able to practise it, and that it will lead to increased levels of performance, prospects and reward.

Conversely, people must have the potential for this increased level of performance and variety of occupation. It is both stressful for the individual and counter-productive to the organisation to place demands on the staff they simply cannot meet.

Management

It is counter-productive if people are chopped and changed about too often; flexibility needs integration and coordination with the operational demands of the organisation. The requirement is to produce both work interest and effective output.

It therefore becomes necessary for managers and supervisors to be trained in both behavioural and operational approaches to job enrichment if these approaches are to be effective.

BOX 15.7   Demarcation

Demarcation describes the boundaries of occupation and activity that exist between one worker (or group) and others. Based on Taylorism, the original purpose was to establish and describe who did what, and where this fitted into production processes.

Demarcation has become a means of job restriction (restrictive practices) and protection. A dispute with one element of the workforce meant that the whole production process would be brought to a standstill while this was resolved.

In the UK the phenomenon of job-specific and differentiated unions grew up on the back of demarcation. On the railways, for example, wheel tappers, shunters, siding men, foot plate men, drivers, guards and porters all originally had their own unions over the latter part of the nineteenth century and the first part of the twentieth (although most of these eventually either amalgamated or were taken over by larger generic unions).

As a general result, organisations that adopted these methods of working found themselves forever resolving disputes with different sets of staff. Nobody was allowed to cross demarcation lines, whether or not they were capable of doing the work. Demarcation was therefore often widely used as a means of regulating the work flow and pressure by the staff and their unions. It also led to the creation of large and sophisticated industrial relations systems. Organisations then needed personnel and industrial relations departments to manage, coordinate and maintain these systems and to resolve disputes as they arose.

The result was that demarcation (Taylorism) and its management came to be regarded as inefficient and ineffective, impossible to control and direct and requiring the creation in turn of specialist functions and posts to ensure that the procedures installed to uphold it could actually be made to work.

Autonomous work groups

The general attraction of autonomous work groups is that they appear to address both the operational and psychological factors. The giving of autonomy in deciding the allocation of work, organisation and production, attention to quality and output based on broad performance targets (for example, 'to produce x amount of product y by deadline z') leaves the group itself to arrange and determine how these are to be achieved. This involves:

- participation in determining and allocating the work, scheduling of priorities and activities, meeting preferences, and gaining commitment to meeting the targets;
- responsibility in ensuring that the broad targets are met and that stages along the total schedule are also reached;

- esteem, in that a complete output is seen at the end of activities with which the individual member of staff can identify;
- spirit and harmony, in that the contribution of everyone involved can be seen and valued.

For autonomous working groups to be successful, high levels of skill and flexibility are required. Production technology and processes must be structured to meet behavioural, as well as operational, needs. Individual and group training and development is essential in all aspects of the work. The process is also greatly enhanced if the group is able to participate (or at least be consulted) on the target-setting activities and to set its own means of quality control and assurance.

BOX 15.8   Alienation and Work: Newspaper Printing in the UK, 1880–1980

The printing of national newspapers in the UK used to be carried out by staff who operated a 'hot metal process'. This required the setting of the letters and words by hand in trays of molten metal. These were then cooled off to form a hard metal block on which the printing ink was poured. The sheets of newsprint were then pressed on to a block to produce the printed page.

The work was specialised, highly organised and unionised. Print workers set their own pace and worked to given volumes of output. If the newspaper companies needed any change to this – especially increased output – this had to be negotiated with the printers on the spot, which normally meant either increased staff for the shift or increased pay for the day. Newspaper proprietors took the collective view that the production of the paper was a critical factor, because they feared loss of market share to competitors if theirs failed to appear; because they feared loss of advertising revenue if this failure to appear became a habit; and because they perceived themselves as having a 'mission to inform and influence' through getting their own slant on the events of the world on to the streets every day.

The printers were extremely well paid. They were very important to the success of the paper. They had high levels of mutual identity, were well organised, and directly affected the volume and quality of work. They enjoyed high economic and personal status.

In the 1970s attempts were made, notably by *The Times*, to introduce computerised printing technology. This would enable anyone to produce material ready for printing simply by typing what was required into a computer. This would then be fed by the computer to its own printing process. The result would be to remove the need for any of the traditional printing process.

In spite of guarantees that wage levels would be maintained and that there would be no compulsory job losses, and promises of retraining as computer inputters for those printers who wanted it, the new processes were fiercely rejected and resisted by the staff. The newspaper proprietors were felt to be rejecting and un-valuing a hundred years of tradition and expertise. The printers themselves were also to lose status, importance, self-esteem and self-worth. Many rejected the chance to retrain because they felt that they would simply become typists. Unvalued and unwanted by the companies the printers and their unions engaged in bitter strikes and disputes. These were enjoined by News International, an Australian media multi-national which owned *The Times*, *The Sun*, the *Today* newspaper, *The Sunday Times* and *The News of the World*. News International at first went down the conciliation route, offering job security and retraining to all staff. When this was rejected, the company solved the problem in the most adversarial manner possible, by dismissing their printing staff and hiring non-union staff to use the computers.

The printers took refuge and found comfort among themselves. They and their unions eventually sued News International for breach of contract and won small amounts of compensation.

In terms of alienation and rejection, however, the lessons remain very strong. The organisation was able and willing to un-value the staff concerned once they had ceased to have useful functions to perform. The dispute was as much about status and importance as wages and money; if it had only concerned the latter all the printers would have retrained. It also centred around the rejection and ending of a whole way of life that had been built and developed over a hundred years.

BOX 15.9   Autonomous Work Groups: Saab

The Saab Company's best known experiment was in their engine factory at Sodertalje in Sweden. This began production in 1972. The company designed the factory lay-out of the work organisation from scratch. The lay-out consisted of an oblong conveyor loop which moved engine blocks to seven assembly groups, each with three members. An island of potted plants enclosing a café with telephone was placed alongside the assembly line. Each production group had its own U-shaped guide track in the floor to the side of the main conveyer loop. Engine blocks were taken from the main track, assembled by the group and then returned to the main track. They arrived with their cylinder heads already fitted and the group dealt with the final fitting of carburettors, distributors, spark plugs, cam shafts and other components. Each group assembled a complete engine and decided themselves how the work was allocated. The guide track of each group was not mechanically driven. The group was simply given 30 minutes to complete each engine and they decided how that time would be spent.

It was estimated in 1974 that Saab was saving around 65000 Swedish Kroner on recruitment and training costs and that reductions in absenteeism was saving another 5000 Kroner each year.

☐ *Attention to the environment*

The problems inherent in working environments were recognised by the Gilbreths and Gantt, who took steps towards organising basic comforts such as rest rooms, canteens and chairs at the places where they worked.

Attention to the work environment is now a vastly wider field. It stems from the recognition that people bring their full range of needs to work with them and that the more of these that are met, the lower the levels of personal dissatisfaction likely to arise (see also Herzberg). Basic and adequate levels of comfort are required. The opportunity to sit down at the workstation, unless this cannot (for overriding operational reasons) be provided, should always be offered. Temperature is to be controlled and extremes of heat and cold avoided or managed. Pot plants, the radio, pictures on the walls are all allowed and encouraged (and in some cases provided) wherever possible. Good quality furniture, decor and furnishings in all places of work reinforce the perceptions of value that organisations place on their staff; and bad quality or decrepit furnishings and tatty decor tend to lead to low feelings of perceived value.

BOX 15.10   Attention to the Work Environment: Mars Chocolate Ltd

A former Mars manager recounts the tale of Forrest Mars, the company founder visiting a chocolate factory in mid-summer. He went up to where the biggest chocolate machines were placed. It was very hot. He asked the factory manager why there was no air conditioning. The factory manager replied that it wasn't in his budget and he had to keep within his budget. Mr Mars acknowledged that this was true (the fellow had to keep within his budget). However, he asked the maintenance people to get all the factory manager's furniture and other things from his office and put them next to the big hot chocolate machine. A Mars under-manager said: 'The guy figured out that it was probably a pretty good idea to air condition the factory sooner rather than later.' Mr Mars told him that once that had been completed he could move back to his office at any time he wanted.'

From Peters and Austin (1985).

☐ *Attention to the people*

The view taken here is that dissatisfaction and alienation are removed from people if the behavioural causes are attacked. Extreme proponents of this point of view go a stage further, taking the view that if you genuinely respect and value people, they will do anything for you.

This approach is taken in different ways. The result is always to arrive at the point at which individuals know that they are valued for the contribution that they bring to the organisation and that this extends to all occupations.

Attention to people is a key point of inquiry of the 'Excellence' studies. It is central to the philosophy and ways of working of many high performing organisations.

The main features include:

- setting absolute standards of honesty, integrity, expectations of performance, quality of output, attitudes, values and ethics to which all those coming to work must aspire and conform;
- recognising that problems are inherent in all jobs and organising the work based around a philosophy of fairness and evenness that requires everyone to share in the problem areas and unattractive tasks;
- setting absolute organisational standards for managing the staff. These are based on high levels of integrity, support, equality, training and development. Pay and reward levels tend to be high in return for high-quality work. Pay and reward methods are honest, clear and unambiguous. Communications between organisation and staff, and the general information flows, are regular, continuous and open.

Rather than addressing the causes of alienation, or taking action to minimise their effects, these are removed altogether. Also removed are factors that differentiate between levels and standards of employee – for example, executive dining rooms and individual car parking spaces – to emphasise equality in both personal and occupational terms.

In some cases, this has extended to the structure and ownership of the organisation. For example, employees have become part-owners through company equity schemes (in the case of US Air, the majority shareholding is held by the staff). In others a proportion of pay is linked to the organisation's financial performance and the percentage of profits paid out to the staff. In the best cases this is paid as a percentage of individual salary so that everybody receives the same proportion of reward. This again underlines equality of treatment, contribution and value.

Whichever view is taken, the desired outcome is the reconciliation of the organisational and operational drives with the technology and equipment that is to be used, and the effects of these on the staff. The ability to do this stems from a recognition and understanding of the influences of the technology, both operational and behavioural. Each approach addresses this issue from differing points of view. It also provides a level of understanding of the underlying causes of conflict and dissatisfaction inherent in any work situation.

BOX 15.11   Removing the Causes of Alienation: Lessons from Japan

Sanyo UK Ltd base all staff/management procedures on simplicity, clarity and consultation. They are straightforward, easy to read and understand. Where problems do arise, the company undertakes to resolve them within two days. If formal grievances are taken out by the staff against the company, a full procedure, including ultimate appeal to the Managing Director, must normally be completed within ten working days unless circumstances do not permit this to happen.

Toshiba UK Ltd remove all doubts and uncertainties from new members of staff during their pre-induction course. In this the company undertakes to pay the employees well, to reward them for excellent performance and to treat them fairly and equally. A person is taken on because they have great value to the company. The member of staff is therefore expected to attend, to work hard and responsibly and to have a positive attitude.

The Sony Company Ltd does not have clocking-on procedures. The people are trusted to arrive on time and to go to their workstation to work. Apart from anything else, this removes several expensive layers of supervision. Above all, it emphasises the respect in which employees are held.

Nissan UK spent £6 million on induction and job training before commercial production was commenced. At the start of operations the company had a committed, able, versatile and motivated workforce.

Each of these organisations is a world leader in its field. Each uses highly automated and potentially alienating technology at the core of its activities. In recognising this, the organisations are able to take steps to minimise or remove the causes and symptoms, thus creating effective operations and committed workforces.

■ Conclusions

Overall, therefore, it is very difficult to understate the importance of attention to technology and its effects on organisational behaviour. In all circumstances, it affects organisation and work design and structure and therefore working relationships, patterns of supervision, control and management style. It also affects the wider strategic and contextual views adopted.

The key lies in the choice and effective usage of technology. This involves attention to volume and quality of production and output, the skills and qualities required to operate it effectively, and the quality of input and operation. Specific equipment must also be capable of harmonisation and integration with other technology that exists and is used.

Attention to investment, levels and frequency of investment, and attitudes to investment must also change. The best organisations concentrate on purpose, quality and suitability, as well as cost, durability and returns. Investing in technology and equipment is a consequence of engaging in particular activities.

Technological change, advance and innovation is also part of the equation. All organisations must be prepared to adopt, adjust, and even sacrifice, current equipment if and when others in the sector find better ways of doing things and better equipment to use. Again, there are implications for the skills, qualities and expertise required.

The impact of technology on organisational behaviour and performance is all-pervasive. This is both direct and indirect. It directly affects the size, nature and design of the environment and premises, the numbers of people required and their capabilities. It is also the focus around which support functions, processes and practices are devised and grouped. Moreover, it directly affects the behaviour, motivation and morale of individuals and groups.

■ Questions

1. Discuss the view that truly rewarding and satisfying work is impossible to achieve because of the constraints placed on all occupations and organisations by technology and equipment.
2. Consider Box 15.1. What criticisms can be made of the principles of scientific management? How much currency and validity do these principles still have?
3. Identify the opportunities and constraints placed on organisations by (a) the establishment and (b) the removal of formalised clocking-on procedures.
4. Outline the nature, approach and attitudes required to establish effective autonomous work groups.

CHAPTER 16

Organisation structure and design

■ Introduction

Organisation structures reflect the aims and objectives, the size and complexity of the undertaking, the nature of the expertise to be used, the preferred management and supervisory style and the means of coordination and control. Whatever arises as the result must be flexible, dynamic and responsive to market and environment conditions and pressures. It must provide effective and suitable channels of communication and decision-making processes; and provide also for the creation of professional and productive relationships between individuals and groups. Departments, divisions and functions are created as required to pursue aims and objectives, together with the means and methods by which they are coordinated and harmonised.

Structure also creates a combination of permanence and order. This is required to provide continuity for the organisation itself, and to generate the required levels of confidence and expectation in customers. It is also necessary to provide staff with (as far as possible) a settled and orderly working life. Means must also be found of ensuring the permanence and continuity of the organisation itself as people join or leave.

There are problems with structures. The history of organisation design indicates that structures are easier to put in place than to change, dismantle or rearrange. Long-standing organisations give the illusion of permanence to both staff and customers. Staff become accustomed to their position, and base their hopes and aspirations for the future on opportunities that are apparent within the structure. Many organisations have traditionally consciously provided career paths through the structure and this becomes one of the attractions to stay rather than seek opportunities elsewhere. Customers become used to dealing with a particular department or official; and, if they have problems, the structure traditionally provides a clear point of reference as to whom these should be addressed.

Pressures of economic turbulence and change, increased competition, diminishing resources and technological and expertise advances have all combined to cause a re-think of the ways in which organisations should be structured. The problem is to reconcile the qualities of flexibility, dynamism and responsiveness with the need for permanence, order and stability. This is the context in which the question of organisation structure should be seen.

Organisations are designed and structured in order to:

- ensure efficiency and effectiveness of activities in accordance with the organisation's stated targets;
- divide and allocate work, responsibility and authority;
- establish working relationships and operating mechanisms;
- establish patterns of management and supervision;
- establish the means by which work is to be controlled;
- establish the means of retaining experience, knowledge and expertise;
- indicate areas of responsibility, authority and accountability;
- meet the expectations of those involved;
- provide the basis of a fair and equitable reward system.

The general factors affecting organisation structure are:

- the nature of work to be carried out and the implications of this: unit, batch, mass and flow scales of production all bring clear indications of the types of organisation required, as do the commercial and public service equivalents; job definitions, volumes of production, storage of components, raw materials and finished goods; the means of distribution, both inwards and outwards; the type of support functions and control mechanisms;
- technology and equipment, the expertise, premises and environment needed to use it effectively; its maintenance; its useful life cycle; its replacement and the effect of new equipment on existing structures and work methods;
- the desired culture and style of the organisation and all that this means: it affects the general approach to organisation management; nature and spans of control; the attitudes and values that are established; reporting relationships between superiors and subordinates and across functions; staff relationships;
- the location of the organisation; its relationships with its local communities; any strong local traditions (for example, of unionisation, or not); particular ways of working; specific activities, skills and expertise;
- aims and objectives strategy; flexibility, dynamism, responsiveness, or rigidity and conformity in relation to staff, customers and the community; customer relations; stakeholder relations.

■ Structural forms

■ Tall structures

There are many different levels or ranks within the total. There is a long hierarchical and psychological distance between top and bottom. Tall structures bring with them complex reporting relationships, operating and support systems, promotion and career paths, and differentiated job titles. Spans of control (see below) tend to be small. The proportion of staff with some form of supervisory responsibility tends to be high in relation to the whole organisation.

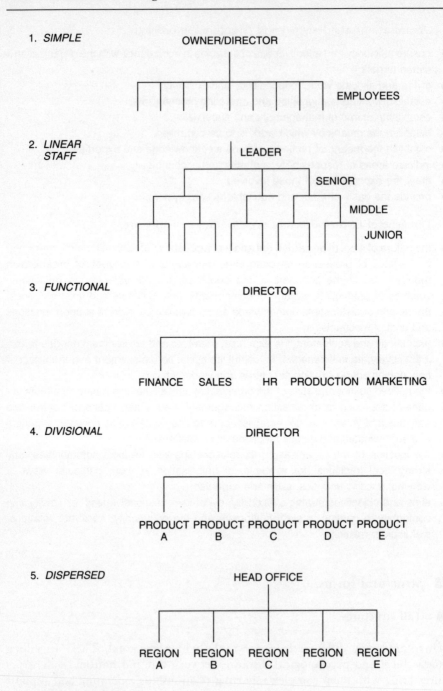

Figure 16.1   Organisation structures

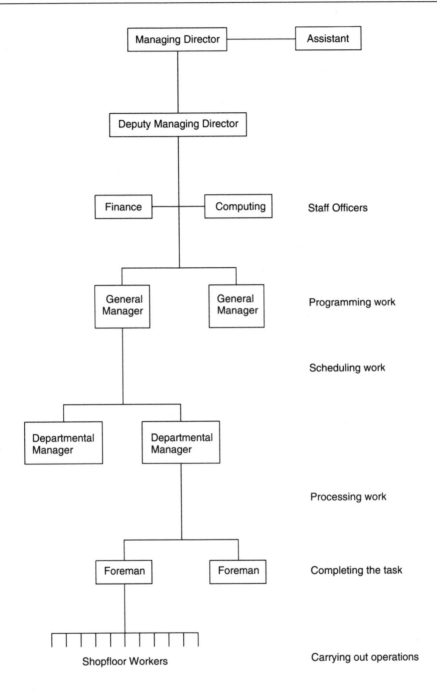

Figure 16.2 Traditional organisational model

■ Flat structures

There are few different levels or ranks within the total. Jobs tend to be concentrated at lower levels. There is a short hierarchical distance between top and bottom; this may reduce the psychological distance or it may not. Lower-level jobs often carry responsibilities of quality control, volume and deadline targets. Spans of control tend to be large. The proportion of staff with some form of supervisory responsibility (other than for their own work) tends to be small in relation to the whole organisation. Career paths by promotion are limited; but this may be replaced by the opportunity for functional and expertise development, and the involvement in a variety of different projects. Reward structures may not be as apparent as those offered alongside progress through a tall hierarchy. Reporting relationships tend to be simpler and more direct. There is a reduced likelihood of distortion and barriers to communications in a flat structure than in a tall one simply because there are fewer channels for messages to pass through.

■ Centralisation and decentralisation

■ Centralised structures

Centralisation is generally an authority relationship between those in overall control of the organisation and the rest of its staff. The tighter the control exerted at the centre, the greater the degree of centralisation.

The great advantage of centralisation is that top managers remain fully aware of the operational as well as strategic issues and concerns. There is relatively little likelihood that they will become detached from the actual organisation performance, or retain illusions of continuing excellence and high achievement for example, where the reality is very different (see Box 16.1).

■ Decentralisation

The converse is to delegate or decentralise. The role and function of the centre is therefore to maintain a watching brief, to monitor and evaluate progress and to concern itself with strategic rather than operational issues. The operations themselves are designed and allocated in accordance with overall aims and objectives, and the departments, divisions and functions given the necessary resources and authority to achieve them.

The advantages of decentralisation are as set out below.

1. The speeding up of operational decisions enables these to be taken at the point at which they are required, rather than having to refer every matter (or a high proportion) back to head office.

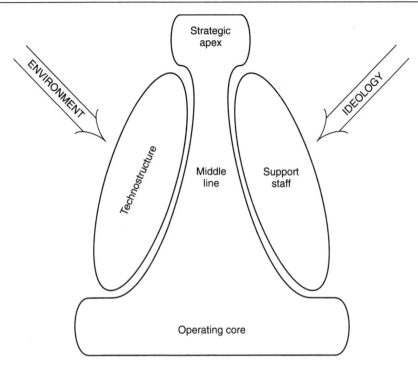

Figure 16.3   The Mintzberg model of organisations

2. It enables local management to respond to local conditions and demands, and to build up a local reputation for the overall organisation.
3. It contributes to organisation and staff development through ensuring that problems and issues are dealt with at the point at which they arise. This helps and enables organisations to identify and develop potential for the future.
4. By the same token it also contributes to staff motivation and morale. The exercising of responsibility and authority, and the opportunities for development, are more likely to filter through to all staff levels in a decentralised organisation.
5. It enables organisations to get their structures and systems right. Reporting relationships between functions and the centre still have to be designed for effectiveness; activities have to be planned and coordinated.
6. Consistency of treatment for both staff and customers has to be ensured across all functions and locations. However great the level of autonomy afforded to departments, divisions and functions, they have still to be contributing to the greater good of the whole organisation (they are not personal or professional fiefdoms).
7. It encourages organisations to continually assess the well of talent, its strength and depth. This is, above all, at managerial and supervisory levels; the greater the decentralisation, the more likely this is to be important at all levels. It is also essential in the identification and development of professional and other forms of expertise.

■ The role and function of Head Office

Head offices in all but the simplest structures have the responsibility for planning, coordinating and controlling the functions of the rest of the organisation; of translating strategy into operations; and of monitoring, reviewing and evaluating performance from all points of view: volume, quality, standards and satisfaction.

Whether a relative centralised or decentralised form of organisation is adopted, it is essential never to lose sight of this key range of activities. The problem lies in how they should be carried out and not in what should be done.

Table 16.1   Principles of organisation structure: a summary

	Operational constraints		*Key features*	
	Environment	*Internal*	*Structure*	*Activities*
Simple structure	Simple/dynamic Hostile	Small Young Simple tasks CEO control	Direction + Strategy	Direct supervision
Technocracy	Simple/static Conformist	Old Large Regulated tasks Technocrat control	Technostructure	Standardisation of work
Professional bureaucracy	Complex/static	Complex systems Professional control	Operational expertise Professional practice	Standardisation of skills
Divisionalised bureaucracy	Simple/static Diversity Hostile	Old Very large Divisible tasks Middle-line control	Autonomy Reporting relationships	Standardisation of outputs Sophisticated supervision
Ad hocracy	Complex/ dynamic Committed	Often young Complex tasks Expert control	Operational Expertise	Mutual adjustment
Missionary	Simple/static Committed	Middle-aged Often 'enclaves' Simple systems Ideological control	Ideology Standards	Policy, norms, Standards
Network organisation	Dynamic Committed	Young Reformed	Operational expertise Technostructure	Networking

Source: Based on Mintzberg (1979), Johnson and Scholes (1994).

In large, complex and sophisticated organisations – public, private and multi-national – the head office is likely to be physically distant from the main areas of operations, and this brings problems of communications systems and reporting relationships. Equally important, however, is the problem of psychological distance and remoteness. This occurs when the head office itself becomes a complex and sophisticated entity. This often leads to conflict between personal and organisational objectives, infighting, and concentrations of resources on head office functions rather than operational effectiveness. This is exacerbated when jobs at head office are, or are perceived to be, better careers and more likely to lead to personal opportunities than those in the field. In many cases the head office becomes so remote that it loses any understanding of the reality of activities. Cocooned by the resources that it commands for its own functions, it may preserve the illusion of excellence and dynamism often in the face of overwhelming evidence to the contrary (see Box 16.1).

BOX 16.1   IBM

In 1992 IBM declared the highest ever corporate loss in business history and John Akers, the CEO, was forced to resign.

The basis of the problem lay in the organisation's utter faith in its own excellence and infallibility. This was promulgated by head office in support of the company's main thrust of activities, mainframe computers and business operation systems. This was in spite of the fact that the emphasis of the computer world had switched to personal computers, for both business and private use.

Belatedly, during the 1980s, the company started to develop its personal computer division, but sales were disappointing (due to the long lead times on delivery and the high prices charged), and the market continued to be dominated by those organisations that took the fast moving consumer goods approach to computer sales. These companies produced equipment that was compatible with IBM business systems and effectively removed IBM from the market as the supplier of hardware.

The company failed to respond. It had been lionised in the 'Excellence' studies. It was a huge, multi-billion dollar corporation. Its technology and expertise were respected and held in awe the world over.

The organisation and its head office had lost sight of direction and contact with its markets. The 1992 loss led to a complete reappraisal of the whole company position. Departments, divisions and functions – and head office – were restructured and thousands of non-productive jobs were lost.

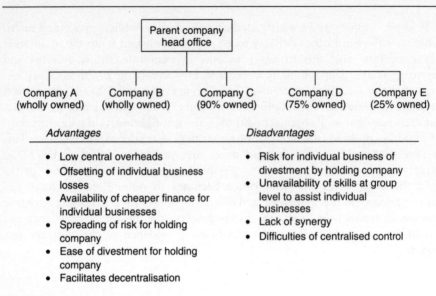

Figure 16.4   Holding company structure

■ Spans of control

'Spans of control' refers to the number of subordinates who report directly to a single superior, and for whose work that person is responsible.

Spans of control are defined in a broad to narrow spectrum. The narrower the span, the greater the number of supervisors required by the organisation in total. A workforce of 40 with spans of control of 4 (1 supervisor per 4 staff) needs 10 supervisors (see Figure 16.5). The same workforce with a span of control of 10 needs only 4 supervisors. If the principle is then developed as a hierarchy, it can be seen that in the first case additional staff are needed to supervise the supervisors.

The matter does require additional consideration, however. Narrow spans of control normally mean a tighter cohesion and closer working relationship between supervisor and group. They also give greater promotion opportunities. There are more jobs, more levels and more ways of moving up through the organisation, and this may be a driving force for those within it and one of their key expectations.

If this principle is followed in larger organisations, layers of management and hierarchy can be removed by increasing spans of control. An organisation of 4 000 staff would remove about 800 managers and supervisors by changing its spans of control from 4 to 1 to 8 to 1 (see Figure 16.6).

A. (4-person span of control)

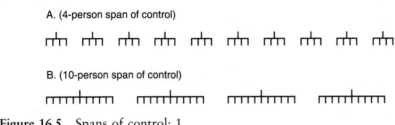

B. (10-person span of control)

Figure 16.5 Spans of control: 1

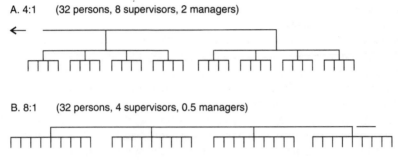

A. 4:1 (32 persons, 8 supervisors, 2 managers)

B. 8:1 (32 persons, 4 supervisors, 0.5 managers)

Figure 16.6 Spans of control: 2

On the other hand, the complex structures thus created tend to act as barriers and blockages to communications: the greater the number of levels that messages have to pass through, the more likely they are to become distorted and corrupted.

On the face of it there is, therefore, a trade-off between the effectiveness of the organisation and the satisfaction of staff expectations through the availability of promotion channels. Assuming that the effectiveness of the organisation is paramount, means are to be sought to enable expectations to be set and met in ways that contribute to this. The absolute effectiveness of the promotion channels must therefore be measured in this way and where necessary, different means of meeting staff expectations found.

Attention, then, has to be paid to operational factors. These are:

- the ability of management to produce results with spans of a certain size;
- the ability of the subordinates to produce results within these spans (in general, the greater the level of expertise held, the less direct supervision is required);

- the expectations of relative autonomy of the subordinates: for example, professional and highly trained staff expect to be left alone to carry out tasks as they see fit; while other types (for example, retail cashiers) need the ability to call on the supervisor whenever problems, such as difficulties with customers, arise;
- the expectations of the organisation and the nature and degree of supervision necessary to meet these, or the ability of the staff concerned to meet these without close supervision;
- specific responsibilities of supervisors that are present in some situations which gives the supervisor a direct reason for being there other than to monitor the work that is being carried out (the most common examples are related to safety: for example, on construction sites and in oil refineries, and in shops and supermarkets to handle customers, queries and complaints);
- the nature of the work itself, the similarity or diversity of the tasks and functions, its simplicity or complexity;
- the location of the work, whether it is concentrated in one place or in several different parts of one building or site, or whether it is geographically diverse (sub-spans are normally created where the location is diversified, even if ultimate responsibility remains with one individual and boundaries of autonomy are ascribed to one person and group in the particular location);
- the extent of necessity and ability to coordinate the work of each group with all the others in the organisation; to coordinate and harmonise the work of the individuals in the group and to relate this again to the demands of the organisation;
- the organisation's own perspective: the extent to which it believes that close supervision, direct control and constant monitoring are necessary and desirable.

■ Hierarchies

Spans of control create hierarchies. These reflect the level, quality and expertise of those involved and also the degree of supervision and responsibility of those in particular positions. These are underpinned by job titles that indicate both levels of position held in the hierarchy and also the nature and mix of expertise and responsibility.

Hierarchies are a familiar feature of all aspects of life. To turn a previous example around, if someone complains at the supermarket checkout and satisfaction is not forthcoming from the cashier, the person then asks to see the supervisor. If there is still no satisfaction then the manager will be called for; to be followed, if necessary, by a letter or approach to the CE. At each point, therefore, the approach is to the next person up the hierarchy in the hope/expectation that this person will be able to resolve the matter in hand.

Hierarchies form the organisational basis of public institutions, both for the ordering and management of services – national, military, civil and social – and also as points of reference for those who need to use them. Hierarchies tend to be formed or to emerge in all organisations for these purposes, and because it is a familiar structural form. From an organisational behaviour point of view, it also acts as the means of coordinating and integrating the activities of departments, divisions, groups, functions and individuals that have been separated out for the purposes of efficient and effective working.

☐ *Problems with hierarchies*

The general issue to be resolved is similar to that of spans of control: reconciling the need to divide and allocate work efficiently and effectively with the creation of blockages and barriers that the process of division tends to create.

Other problem areas include the following.

1. Divergence of objectives: for example, the marketing department may be asked to create marketing initiatives with which it has no sympathy; or it may create marketing initiatives at variance with the products, style and image of the organisation: it may seek, on the one hand, to enhance its own reputation, and yet to pursue organisation objectives which may be perceived as detrimental to this.
2. If one of the functions of hierarchy is to provide career paths, then these may be blocked by long-serving officials in particular jobs; or it may create vacancies which are either filled by people who do not yet have the required expertise or, where this is recognised by the organisation, they are filled by outsiders. Sudden departures, in particular, may leave a void which it is impossible to fill in the short term and which is then likely to lead to loss of departmental or organisation performance. In these cases outsiders may be brought in, again tending to lead towards frustration for those already in position.
3. Compartmentalisation: units and divisions tend to pursue their own aims and objectives as part of the process of competing for resources, prestige and status within the organisation rather than pursue the overall purpose.

    Similarly, individuals pursuing career paths take whatever steps are necessary to get on to the next rung of the ladder; and again this may be detrimental to overall requirements.
4. Responsibility: specific responsibilities are not always apparent. Things may not get done because nobody knows quite whose responsibility the matter in question is, or everyone involved may think that it is somebody else's area of operation. This is also a problem with the organisation's customers and clients, who may find it difficult to gain contact with the person specifically responsible for dealing with their problem.
5. Rigidity: hierarchies can be very difficult to move once they are established. They may continue to exist in a given form after the purpose for which they were specifically created has been served. They often hinder the organisation development process and may act as a barrier to the introduction of new technology, project activities and culture and behaviour change.

Those responsible for the creation of organisation structures have therefore to recognise that whatever is done must be capable of satisfying the organisation's purposes and reconciling these with the inherent problems and difficulties. Any organisation form that arises must be capable of flexibility and responsiveness, as well as creating order and stability.

In the 1990s the overwhelming drive of those responsible for the structure and design of organisations has been towards the enlargement of spans of control, the removal of tiers of supervision and management, and away from tight compartmentalisation. This in turn has led to the processes of job enhancement and enrichment to which reference has already been made, and this is especially true in terms of the extension of responsibility and accountability for those traditionally considered to be in lower grade and unskilled work. There is an economic benefit to those organisations that do remove levels of hierarchy and extend spans of control: the wage and salary bill is reduced. The expectations of those who come into the organisation for a career path, promotion and progress up through the hierarchy have also to be addressed, however; removal of these possibilities causes dissatisfaction if they are not replaced with something else. The streamlining of organisation structures is not therefore an end in itself: in particular, it brings specific responsibilities for training and development, and the offering of alternative forms of variety and enhancement that were previously available as the direct result of the hierarchical form.

■ Mechanistic and organic structures

Work carried out by Burns and Stalker in the 1950s identified distinctive variations in the components of organisation structure. These were affected by the nature of the work, the technology used, the rate and nature of change taking place, the stability or volatility of markets, and the nature and expertise of the staff. Their conclusion was that there were two distinctive forms of management system, mechanistic and organic.

■ Mechanistic systems

1. Degree of specialisation: very high, with specialised divisions and differentiation of tasks based on precise job descriptions and pursued on an operational rather than strategic basis.
2. Degree of standardisation: very high, with work methods prescribed and ordered.
3. Orientation of members: operational, attention to means and processes.
4. Conflict resolution: by the superior, and using procedures and channels.
5. Obligations: precisely defined, written in to each role.
6. Authority: based on hierarchy, reporting relationships, strictly delineated limitations; includes the setting of work standards and targets.

7. Communication: also based on hierarchy; patterns and interactions tend to be vertical; the content of communications tends towards instructions, directions and orders.
8. Loyalty: is to the organisation, based on obedience to superiors.
9. Status: from job title and the job held in the organisation.

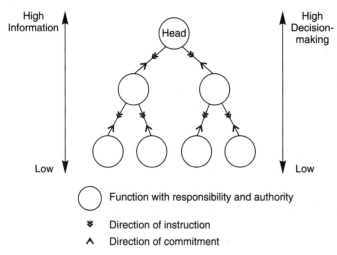

Figure 16.7 Organisation structures: mechanistic

Source: Lawrence (1984: after Burns and Stalker)

■ **Organic systems**

1. Degree of specialisation: low, little specialisation, few boundaries and divisions, low differentiation, no restrictive practices, work pursued on task and strategic basis.
2. Degree of standardisation: low, individual, interactive.
3. Orientation of members: towards aims and objectives, achievement, customer and personal satisfaction.
4. Conflict resolution: through interaction, discussion and debate.
5. Obligations: to task, output and satisfaction.
6. Authority: based on expertise, networks, availability, and accessibility.
7. Communication: based on strategic and operational need rather than hierarchy; lateral as well as vertical; content is based on advice, information, illumination and enlightenment.
8. Loyalty: to task and group as well as organisation.
9. Status: from personal contribution, results and achievements.

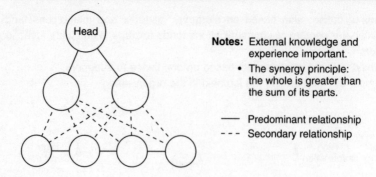

Notes: External knowledge and experience important.
• The synergy principle: the whole is greater than the sum of its parts.

—— Predominant relationship
- - - Secondary relationship

Figure 16.8   Organisation structures: organic/organismic

Source: Lawrence (1984: after Burns and Stalker)

The two systems are presented as polar opposites. However, Burns and Stalker found that individual organisations could accommodate both forms within their different divisions and operations and that this worked well in some circumstances. They also found that organisations could move from one to the other.

Burns and Stalker favoured neither one system nor the other. The important thing was to ensure that what was designed and introduced was appropriate in the circumstances. However, approaches tending towards mechanistic systems are likely to be more appropriate when the organisation uses long-standing technology to conduct activities in stable and steady markets, than in a highly volatile, changing and turbulent situation.

■ **Structural relationships**

■ **Line relationships**

This refers to the position of authority, responsibility, accountability and control of one position in relation to all the others in the hierarchy. A person occupying a given position or rank in the line hierarchy is deemed to have the authority to order and direct the activities of those beneath him, and to accept direction and control from those above. Line relationships are found within divisions, departments and functions; formal authority does not extend, for example, from the marketing director to the personnel assistant.

■ Staff and functional relationships

This occurs where someone is required to provide expert advice to another (of whatever rank). This advice may be acceptable or not, and accepted or not.

In some situations the staff relationship therefore acts as the means of bringing additional information and clarity to bear on a particular issue. This would occur, for instance, in discussions between the production manager and the production line maintenance supervisor when considering ways of increasing productive capacity or the potential for harnessing spare capacity.

In other situations the staff relationship acts as the focus for decision. The advice of the staff expert is likely to be the basis on which the decision is made. Where the production manager has an industrial dispute to resolve, the advice and guidance of the human resource or industrial relations specialist is likely to be sought and this will normally represent the way out of the situation.

Some managers use their secretaries, PAs and other closely linked staff in these ways. In these cases the role of the latter will be advisory or even simply acting as a sounding board for the manager in question. Their value lies in the ability to think clearly, to act as a focus for argument and where necessary, to go to find further information around the particular issue.

■ Authority

This plainly exists in the line relationship. Functional authority is harder to define. It occurs because of the inability to divide and compartmentalise work absolutely: there are marketing features in production processes (for example, design and packaging); there are human resource features in all activities; there are financial controls present in all functions. The problem arises over the extent of the influence of these different functions in the given area and the extent to which one function may be forced, coerced, required or advised to the follow the direction of the other.

Reference should also be made here to the 'influence without authority' role of the PA and secretary–manager relationship indicated above.

■ Control

This is the ability to influence and restrict the activities of others. Part of this is based clearly on line and authority.

Again, the issue is clouded where there is an interfunctional relationship. For example, Personnel may recruit and select staff for another function which the latter is then forced to accept for reasons 'beyond their control'. In this case,

Personnel has a form of control over the operations of the other function. Human resource functions may also insist on training and development, equality of opportunity and staff representation. Finance functions may insist on budget and resource reports made to particular deadlines that suit the finance rather than the other function.

■ Reporting relationships

Again, in the line relationship, these are clear; and again, they become clouded where the functional activities are carried out across departments and divisions. This also leads to questions of workload priority where, for example, an urgent job is required for one department and an important one for another.

Forms of informal authority may also have an impact. For example, the CEO may want a general request dealt with, the production manager an important request, and the finance assistant an urgent request.

Reporting relations centre around the achievement of aims and objectives, the completion of tasks and the use and presentation of information. There are also questions of management and supervisory and subordinate style, and the nature of delegation and job and task definitions to be considered.

■ Service relationships

These exist outside the line, functional, authority, control and reporting relationships indicated. Service departments gain and maintain their reason for being through the quality and value of the general contribution that they make to the work of others. There is no absolute obligation on the part of the rest of the organisation to avail itself of these services.

Service functions therefore gain an understanding of the requirements of the rest of the organisation for their activities. What is provided is a combination of service expertise, presented in ways useful to the receiving departments. This is enhanced and developed by making specific requests for the service in question in order to gain information or solve problems.

The most common forms are library and information services. These trawl the national and trade press, books, magazines and other publications and then provide synopses and summaries for particular departments. Others include catering services, research and development, design, premises management, cleaning and security. In UK public services, many of these have been put out to tender and placed in the hands of independent contractors with the stated purpose of ensuring that the relationship is productive and effective. It is said to be easier and more effective to define and manage in this way rather than retaining these services in-house.

■ **Core and peripheral organisations**

These forms of structure are based on a total reappraisal of objectives and activities with a view to establishing where the strategic core lies, what is needed to sustain this, and where, when and why additional support and resources are required.

The essential is the core. The rest is the peripheral and may be seen as a shamrock or propeller (see Figure 16.9). This may be viewed in the following ways.

(a) *The Shamrock Model*

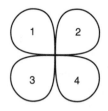

1. The core

2. Specialists

3. Seasonal staff

4. Staff on retainers for pressures and emergencies

(b) *The Propeller Model*

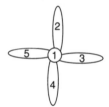

1. The core
2. Specialists
3. Sub-contractors
4. Research and development
5. Seasonal staff

Figure 16.9   Core and peripheral

1. Professional and technical services and expertise, drawn in to solve problems; designed and improved work methods and practices; all these manage, change and act as catalysts and agents for change. All of these functions are conducted by outsiders on a contracted basis. Areas include marketing, public relations, human resource management, industrial relations, supplies, research and development, process and operations management and distribution.
2. Sub-contracting of services, such as facilities and environment management, maintenance, catering, cleaning and security. These are distinctive expertises in their own right, and therefore best left to expert organisations.

    This form of sub-contracting is now very highly developed across all sectors and all parts of the world as organisations seek to concentrate on their given expertise and minimise areas of non-contributory activity.

3. Operational pressures, in which staff are retained to be available at peaks (daily, periodical or seasonal) and otherwise not present. This has contributed both to the increase in part-time, flexible and core hours patterns of employment, and also to the retention of the services of workforce agencies, who specialise in providing particular volumes of expertise in this way.

4. Outworking (often home working), in which staff work at alternative locations including home, avoiding the need for expensive and extensive facilities. This also enables those involved to combine work with other activities (parenting, study, working for other organisations).

   For this, people may be paid a retainer to ensure their continued obligation of loyalty. They may be well paid, or even overpaid to compensate for periods when there is no work. They may be retained on regular and distinctive patterns of employment (normally short time or part time).

The benefits lie in the need and ability to maximise resources and optimise staff utilisation. Rather than structuring the workforce to be available generally, the requirement for expertise and nature of operations is worked out in advance and the organisation structured from this point of view. All activities that are to be carried out on a steady-state daily basis are integrated into the core. The rest are contracted or retained in one of the forms indicated.

■ Federations

Federations are extensions of the core and periphery format. They tend to be more or less regularised between organisations with their own specialisms which are then harmonised and integrated in the pursuit of overall stated objectives. Within this, each organisation has its distinctive identity and full autonomy to pursue and conduct other work so long as it meets its obligations and makes its contribution to the federation.

The main problem lies in integrating, coordinating and controlling the relationships and activities required of each contributor. The critical factors are ensuring mutuality of interest, continuity of general relationship, communications and harmony. The reporting relationship is based on a combination of work contract (or contract for services) and measures of integrity, rather than on a bureaucratic or legal/rational format.

Operationally, the critical factors are meeting volume and quality requirements and deadlines. A much simpler and clearer form of direction and purpose is likely to emerge as a result and this is focused on performance overall rather than procedures and functions.

The likelihood is therefore that organisations will seek to simplify all of their features as they become involved in this form of activity. As well as clarifying purpose, it also frees up resources that would otherwise have to be used in accommodating staff and their equipment, supporting rules and procedures and the sub-functions that operate them.

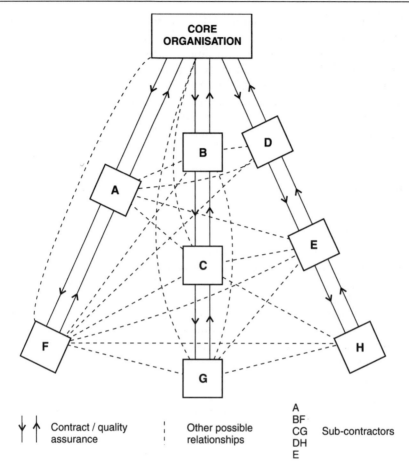

Figure 16.10   Federation

■ Ad hocracy

Ad hoc groups exist in all situations. The concern here is the extent to which and reasons for which they are encouraged or denied. When organisations use groups (including project groups, work improvement groups, quality circles and professional clusters) the need is to produce a format capable of sustaining and directing them, and giving them the space and resources and discipline.

There is a requirement for effective and flexible supervision that combines ensuring the best use of time and resources with the ability to let the group go its own way when it needs to do so. Attention is paid to results rather than processes, to aims rather than activities.

This form of structure and the ability of other structured approaches to accommodate this is dependent upon a corporate state of mind that is prepared to encourage people to take responsibility, use their talents, and generate effective activities. It also encourages respect, commitment, understanding and value across boundaries and divisions. It encourages greater ownership of problems and therefore a willingness to resolve them, producing results with which everyone can identify and understand. It also helps to develop positive and general feelings and attitudes, and specific qualities of flexibility and responsiveness.

■ Project groups and teams

The structural effects of these are lessened if the group is drawn from within one division. Where it is drawn from a range of different functions, problems arise when the work of the particular groups affects and conflicts with that of other functions involved. Again, problems of authority and functional relationship may arise; and again, there are questions of priority and workloads to be considered. The work of the group may be dearer to the heart of one contributing department than others. Some individuals may also be much more enthusiastic about participating than others.

Many of the problems of organisation structure stem from the term used – structure. In all other cases in life, structures are perceived to give a combination of stability, permanence and rigidity, and this is also what those in organisations ostensibly seek. The need for structural permanence springs however, from the opportunities that this provides to those who use the structure for other purposes, and this is the context within which organisation structures should be seen.

■ Bureaucracy

Bureaucracy means 'government by office'. The basis of the concept lies in the need to give organisations their own life, permanence and stability and to retain the fund of expertise and precedent that has built up over the period of existence, rather than being dependent on the personal knowledge of individuals. It also prescribes areas of authority and expertise and formalises the ways in which these are divided.

Every activity is therefore broken down into jobs, offices or positions. Each is formally described and its position in relation to the rest is determined and established. Each is given its own combination of expertise and authority, and its position in the organisation's hierarchy. The whole is then circumscribed by rules and regulations, indicating the relationship between each position, the bounds within which the office holder is to operate and the wider general standards by which people are to act and behave.

■ Legal and rational status

The position of jobs and offices has therefore a rationale based on the division of expertise and the rules drawn up. Authority for particular activities and people is accepted by post holders; and this also includes the relative positions in the hierarchy. Those dealing with the job holder from an external point of view accept that the person with whom they have contact is acting with the full support and backing of the organisation – in the name of the organisation – and that they have the expertise and competence to do so. Each individual is therefore expected to provide this level of capability and competence to the position and to be trained and developed to ensure that this remains so.

BOX 16.2   Louis XIV

According to Michael Albrow, the concept of bureaucracy was first defined by a Frenchman, Edmund de Gournay, in the eighteenth Century. He called it bureau-mania or the compulsion to organise everything into functions and compartments. This in turn had its basis in the approach of Louis XIV to his nobles. He kept them all around him at the huge Palace at Versailles and gave them menial and highly defined tasks that they each had to carry out every day. One would be responsible for example, for keeping the King's stockings clean; others for ensuring that he had a new nightshirt, his wig was powdered and so on. Each therefore had a distinctive and continuing responsibility and obligation to meet, and failure to do so was punished severely. Louis XIV took this approach in order to neutralise the individual power of the members of the French nobility, and to restrict and order their activities so that they had neither the resources nor the influence to threaten him. A similar approach was taken to his ministers and officials: the responsibilities of each were directly issued by the King and distinctly defined; exceeding these or failing to meet them also incurred the royal wrath.

BOX 16.3   The Work of Max Weber, 1864–1920

If the concept of bureaucracy was first articulated by de Gournay, the definitive work was carried out by Weber. Weber was a sociologist who studied the organisation forms and rules of government offices, the army and the Catholic Church. He used the term to describe a type of formal organisation based on rules and capabilities rather than personal connections and preferences. The highest form of organisation was that which led to efficient use of time and resources. By structuring organisations around offices and positions rather than around individuals, a logical and impersonal (rather than preferential) structure would be created allowing the pursuit of desired efficiency.

Bureaucracy therefore had the following characteristics:

1. Specialisation: each position has a clearly defined sphere of competence and activity.
2. Hierarchy: a firmly ordered system of supervision and subordination in which lower offices accept direction from those higher up.
3. Rules: the organisation follows general rules which are more or less stable, more or less comprehensive and which can be learned by everyone.
4. Impersonality: impersonality is the spirit in which the ideal functionary conducts business. Everyone is subject to equality of treatment. An official has no partiality or favouritism, either for subordinates or customers.
5. Appointments: people are selected for offices on the basis of their expertise and qualifications. They are appointed and not elected or brought into the organisation as a matter of favour.
6. Full-time: officials are employed on a full-time basis and this is reflected in the nature and volume of work.
7. Careers: the job constitutes part of a career path. There are systems of promotion based on a combination of seniority and achievement.
8. Separation: bureaucracy separates official and functional activity as something distinct from private life. Wages and salaries are paid in return for the work. An obligation is placed on the organisation to provide all necessary equipment and facilities.
9. Permanence: the expertise of the organisation is retained in a system of files so that achievements, precedent and previous activities can be referred to. For each recorded transaction a copy or note is kept for the files.

This approach offered guidelines and patterns for the organisation and distribution of work and the structuring of organisations. It also ensured impersonality and permanence above the particular contributions of individuals. Bureaucracies in this form have sprung up all over the world, and in all sectors and industries. Many people believe that this is the only suitable structural form for large and sophisticated organisations; and that in any case the principles of retention and impersonality need to apply to all organisations, however small.

■ Problems of bureaucracy

The main problem lies in the maze of offices and functions created, and their interactions and relationships. At worst, this leads to a proliferation of the papers, systems and procedures that govern every aspect of work and which in turn require monitoring and supervision.

From an internal point of view, this causes chains of command and communication to become clogged up and overloaded. Matters have often to be referred through several tiers for decision and then handed back to the originator.

Comprehensive sets of rules invariably do not cover every eventuality. The more they set out to do this, the more likely anomalies and contradictions are to occur. This leads to the need to refer matters again for decision, and again leads to delays and frustration.

Bureaucracies tend towards tall hierarchical structures and top-heaviness. Too many offices are either procedural or non-productive. Pressure is exerted on those who do work at the front line, both from customers and clients, and also from the higher ranks supervising them.

Bureaucracies are stable and permanent, and the converse of this is inert. They tend to greatest efficiency and effectiveness when working in a stable work environment with relatively permanent operations, technology and markets. Long-established bureaucracies are often themselves barriers to change and development (whatever the feelings of the job holders within them) when these become necessary.

Bureaucracies are not customer-friendly. They work best in this respect when the demands of the customer are regular and universal. Problems arise when this is not the case and when individual sets of circumstances have to be taken into account. Again, this causes frustration if decisions are not readily available.

■ Rules and regulations

These are created to support structures and practices, to establish general standards of behaviour, and to provide boundaries for operations, activities and functions.

The simpler the rules, the more likely they are to be understood, accepted and followed. The drive is therefore away from long and complex manuals designed to cover every eventuality (this is in any case impossible) and towards much shorter, crisper and clearer guidelines which set general and absolute standards.

The benefits of the simple approach lie in the ability of all concerned to take a flexible and judgemental view of problems and situations as they arise. Energies are not spent on searching exhaustively for precedent, or in interrupting different clauses according to the point of view adopted (see Box 16.4, and the section on Bureaucracy above). The onus is placed on managers and supervisors to set standards of fairness and equality: this has to be done anyway, whatever the complexity or otherwise of the rule book. The position adopted concern the exercising of judgement and dealing directly with problems however, rather than in searching out and administering the appropriate rule or clause.

The organisation itself must have some degree of permanence in order that confidence in it can be generated on the part of both customers and staff. The relationships that are built on that permanence are always based on a combination of expectations, continuity and satisfaction, and this is only achieved if the organisation is flexible and progressive enough to develop itself and its staff to ensure that this happens. Structure therefore becomes a basis for their development just as a house, for example, becomes the basis of personal comfort and satisfaction to the owner or user: the structure is stable, and the opportunities and usage afforded are almost infinitely variable. What is required, therefore, is a genuine understanding and realisation of the purpose of structure and the opportunities afforded by an adequately and effectively structured organisation. Functions, ranks, hierarchies, bureaucracy and relations are not ends in themselves and neither are they required *per se*. They are components to be combined and used in ways suitable to, and supportive of, the stated purposes.

BOX 16.4   Rules and Regulations in the NHS in the UK

Since its creation in 1944, the NHS has grown 74 distinctive sets of rules and regulations all of which are current in March 1995. These run to about 83 000 pages. They set out to cover (often in exhaustive detail) all aspects of work practice, industrial relations, staff relations, customer and patient care, organisation structures (both total and for individual units), reporting relationships, committee structures, the political interface, the role and organisation of trusts, human resource management, health and safety, total quality management and so on.

The problem is not with the coverage, but with the means adopted. Whenever there is a problem, armies of researchers and administrators set to work to trawl the 74 manuals and 83 000 pages for precedents, near-equivalence and guidance. The process can take months depending on the nature of the inquiry. During that time the problem is not effectively resolved but rather held on ice, while those involved seek and produce the parts of the manuals that are most supportive of their case.

This approach has led to the creation of departments whose sole purpose is learning and interpreting these procedures. Recognised unions, and professional and employers' associations in the NHS also employ officials full-time for this purpose so that they are able to provide effective services to their members and those who come to them in countering any alleged breaches of rules and procedures and advising on any general anomalies.

Rules and regulations on this scale clearly lose the purpose of giving support, guidance and boundaries for activities. The operation becomes an end in itself. Large administrative superstructures are created that have themselves to be staffed, maintained and serviced. The end result is the diversion of resources that could otherwise be used for primary functions into the maintenance of rules and regulations.

■ Procedures

Procedures are drawn up as the means by which rules and regulations are administered. They set standards of fairness and equality. In many cases (for example, trading standards, product quality, marketing, industrial relations) they are bounded by legal constraints. The ways in which they are drawn up and written up emphasise management style and attitudes. In general, again, the emphasis is placed on simplicity, clarity and precision for greatest effectiveness.

The aim, therefore, is to design and produce an organisation that is capable of accommodating every purpose and pressure. It is essential to recognise this at the outset. Organisations that do not do so normally find themselves creating additional systems and sub-functions to try to compensate for their imperfections.

These systems include, for example, quality control and industrial relations arrangements that in turn tend to compound the problems rather than resolve them. Both quality control and industrial relations also tend to be cross-functional and therefore bring with them a multiplicity and complexity of reporting relationships that invariably lead to different pressures and priorities. They are also extremely costly, especially if they become distinctive functions in their own right, carrying levels of supervision and departmental overheads for themselves.

The same approach is taken to the creation of all organisation functions. The clearer the purpose, the greater the chance of accommodating the pressures. There is also a much greater likelihood of creating departments, divisions and functions that work successfully towards the overall purpose, and the need for additional systems then diminishes or is removed altogether.

In absolute terms, the greater the numbers and levels of supervision, the greater the proliferation of rules and regulations, the higher the on-costs of the organisation. However, this has again to be seen in context: do the costs incurred in these ways contribute or detract from the total performance of the organisation? Is, for example, a greater degree of supervision worth having in order to minimise production or service defects, reduce customer complaints, ensure that staff problems are dealt with instantly, and so on? Or, conversely, would satisfaction, motivation, morale and output all rise if people were given responsibility and autonomy in their own areas, especially if this was underpinned by training and development, job enhancement and job enlargement and enrichment approaches?

Other factors must now be considered.

☐ *Structures and expectations*

Reference has already been made to the need to match people's expectations with the opportunities that the organisation can offer. The traditional way of making progress through the ranks of organisations is well understood and has hitherto been a strong driving force, especially for those in administrative, professional and technical grades. This has also opened up expectations for those in less skilled, front-line and clerical jobs. As organisations drive towards simpler forms, federations, reduced hierarchies and scalar chains, and increased spans of control, there are fewer of these avenues available and competition for each position becomes greater. There is also therefore, likely to be an increase in the quality of candidates from which to choose as each seeks to maximise her chance of gaining the particular position.

On the one hand, therefore, there is a great opportunity for organisations to choose excellent, high-quality staff for key positions. On the other, there is the question of what to do with those who do not achieve these positions, bearing in mind that this may affect a large number of staff and lead to wider general dissatisfaction.

The matter is partly resolved by ensuring that expectations are set at realistic levels at the outset. The nature of the avenues available, and whether these are available on the basis of promotion or variety, development, location and project work has to be made clear. The rewards to be gained through the pursuit of each should also be made clear. Organisations must also recognise that, if these are higher for one path than for others, then individuals will gravitate towards this in preference to the others.

☐ *Structure and career development*

In terms of organisation structure, the purpose is to make the combination of expectations and anticipation for advancement that the individual brings compatible with the prospects that the organisation can offer, and translate these into a productive and positive relationship. For this to happen the position of each is to be set clearly at the outset. There is no point in the organisation expecting loyalty and long service from the individual who anticipates rapid progression through the ranks if these channels are either not open to all, or are very restricted. Similarly, there is no point in the individual expecting this form of progression if the organisation has made it quite clear that this is not open and that progress is based on variety and development rather than promotion through the ranks.

Organisations have therefore to establish the basis on which variety and progress is to be offered, what they expect of their staff in this context and where they place value on them.

Other points may usefully be made. Programmes of organisation and professional development must be seen as leading to goals and objectives. Staff who are given training and development normally expect to be able to practise their new skills and qualities and to attain some reward or enhancement as a result. In very few cases at present are organisations able to be certain that people have reached the absolute pinnacle of their potential, education, training or development, or be certain that they have a particular niche for a long period of time. Even if this is the case, the niche is invariably subject to pressures of continuous improvement and development, and this again places obligations on the long-term post holder. Successful people at all levels both raise their own expectations and have raised expectations placed on them by their organisation.

☐ *Structure and reward*

A traditional driving force of the promotion path was normally that increased pay, salary and therefore better standards of living accrued as the result of progression upwards through the hierarchy. It was also a means of ensuring general measures of organisation talent and potential development and of meeting the general expectations of enhancement of the staff. Moreover, it was seen to reward loyalty and commitment.

Today, two assumptions are regularly challenged. The first is that those at the top of the hierarchy should receive greater rewards than those lower down (see Box 16.5). The second is that this is the only way of developing and rewarding loyalty and commitment.

Certainly, adequate means of reward have to be established. The organisation structure must be capable of doing this so that the contribution of everyone is seen to be valued. Once the connection is removed between rank and reward however, opportunities become available to assess this on the basis of whatever is of absolute value to the organisation (whether this is loyalty, output, professional development, invention, creativity or whatever).

The overriding concern is to ensure that rewards are targeted, paid out for achievement, give satisfaction and meet expectations. Rewards are not ends in themselves. People expect both continuity and improvement. In steady-state and rank structured organisations especially, people forgo measures of instant or short-term reward in return for, and in expectation of, this continuity and enhancement. In more turbulent organisations, the expectations relate to shorter term and enhanced levels of reward.

BOX 16.5   Rewards

There are lessons to be learned from many sectors. The best paid people in the entertainment sector are the entertainers themselves. Professional sportsmen and women earn more than tournament and competition managers and promoters.

In many cases labourers on construction sites earn more than site managers and supervisors. This is partly because of the hours that they have the opportunity to work and partly also because supervision is likely to be divided between several persons.

Productivity and output bonuses are often made available to factory and retail workers enabling them to earn more than those on equivalent or higher (but non-front-line) grades.

This has implications for promotion and development structures. People do not wish to lose money as the result of change (especially promotion), except where this is known to be a short-term disadvantage and that the prospects over the long term are greatly improved.

Rewards must also meet basic expectations and be seen to be placing adequate levels of value on the efforts of the staff. A mail order company based in Stoke-on-Trent, UK, asked its telesales staff to promote a distinctive range of kitchen products as part of their general work load. The initiative was highly successful, and the 22 women involved sold one million pounds' worth of products. The staff received a letter from the managing director of the company thanking them for their efforts. Enclosed with the letter was a small bar of chocolate. All of the staff felt insulted by this gesture; none found it to be an adequate expression of their efforts. Most said that they would rather have received nothing than such a slight gesture and token. The whole approach was perceived by the staff to be disrespectful and to belittle and denigrate their efforts.

■ Conclusions

Organisations are designed for particular purposes and circumstances and when these change, the structure should move on also. The concept of organisation structure has come full circle: from the position of having a structure and seeking uses for it, to having a purpose and seeking the means and order for pursuing it effectively.

Related to this is the expense of carrying sophisticated support functions, hierarchies and administrative superstructures. It is also often very difficult to coordinate and harmonise these with the organisation's main purposes. They tend to generate lives of their own – aims and objectives, results areas, systems and reporting relationships – which are both time and resource-consuming, often out of all proportion to the actual purpose served or envisaged.

It is clearly necessary that organisations retain their permanence and their knowledge and expertise, in spite of the comings and goings of the staff. It is also necessary to coordinate and control activities, operations and resources. Most of the principles indicated therefore remain sound. However, the creation of bureaucracies, human structures and pyramids, ranks and hierarchies, administrative systems and reporting relationships in the pursuit of permanence and order is not conducive to effective performance, clarity of purpose or optimum resource usage.

■ Questions

1. In what ways do personnel and finance functions contribute to overall organisational effectiveness and performance? How is their contribution measured for success and failure, and how should this be measured?
2. Outline the main problems associated with bureaucracies and state how these might be overcome, while at the same time ensuring that the needs for permanence and retention are satisfied.
3. What are the likely effects on the motivation and morale of those affected of:

   (a) a reduction in the number of levels in a hierarchy from 12 to 3 with no redundancies;

   (b) a reduction in the number of levels in a hierarchy from 12 to 3 with redundancies?

   Are there any differences between the two situations? What steps should be taken to address the problems of motivation and morale that you have identified?
4. Outline the main issues to be addressed when establishing a core and peripheral, or a federated, working relationship.

CHAPTER 17

Change

■ Introduction

Current political and economic turbulence, the globalisation of business and competition has called into question all the hitherto accepted ways of organising and conducting affairs, making products and delivering services. This has been fuelled by advances in all forms of technology, such as production, service, consumer and information. There is a much greater capacity for producing products more quickly, more uniformly and to higher standards of quality and reliability. The result of this has been to transform consumer expectations. With the ever-greater choices afforded by the internationalisation of activities, no organisation, company, industry or sector is immune from these pressures.

It is clear that much of the order and stability of the 1950s and 1960s was brought about by what has turned out to be a global dominance–dependency relationship; the dominance of manufacturing and production by Western industrialised nations serving ever-expanding and almost guaranteed markets. The entry of organisations from the Pacific Rim into this area with advanced technology and attention to product quality and reliability has brought further transformations. There are now more organisations from more countries competing for the same markets.

Those responsible for designing organisations have therefore to create the conditions in which change is a fact of life. This consists of fostering attitudes of flexibility, dynamism and responsiveness; seeking structures and cultures which are positive and organic; and developing the human resource to its maximum capacity. It also includes providing space and resources for creative and high-quality individuals and groups to pursue projects and other developments; and to continually develop and improve skills, knowledge, qualities, processes and practices. Innovation, development and change have to be accepted and valued in the future, just as order and steadiness were in the past.

■ Changing the status quo

Changing the status quo is a process. It is not enough to destroy the existing order (however desirable that might be); that simply causes chaos. It is also not sensible to take the first steps towards changing and dissolving the old order without considering what happens next. The process must have a view of 'from and to' in order to be effective. People will not willingly step off the kerb of a pavement if they do not, or cannot, see how far down it is to the road; much less will they willingly follow major disruptions to any part of their lives, including work, if they cannot see where this is supposed to lead.

The 'change from' part of the process therefore requires the recognition of the behavioural and psychological barriers that will present themselves when the change is first proposed. The 'change to' part is to create knowledge,

Figure 17.1   Barriers

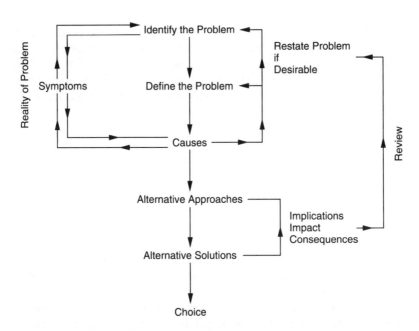

Purpose: to ensure that a rigorous and disciplined approach is recognised and understood as being necessary in all situations; or that it is adopted.
Points for consideration throughout the process must also include: the context and nature of it, when it is occuring; where it is occuring; why; its impact on the rest of the organisation, department or division, the extent to which it can be avoided; the extent to which it can be controlled; the consequences and opportunities of not tackling it (which is always a choice).

Figure 17.2   Simple change model

understanding and acceptance by those involved, and to present the desired result in terms of the benefits, enhancement and enrichments to working life that are to accrue.

■ Change catalysts

Catalysts are events – often crises or dramas – that cause organisations to question the wider situation. They may also take the form of technological advance, changes in ownership, function or activity, or the activities of a competitor.

In each case the outcome is the appraisal of the current position as unsatisfactory and the determination to do something about it.

■ Change agents

Change agents are those who energise, direct and drive the processes. They include key appointments (people brought in to give particular emphases); outsiders (where the need is for acceptable or where the views of the insiders are unacceptable for some reason); and distinctive experts (who bring confidence and credibility, understanding and acceptability by virtue of their level of skill or knowledge).

■ Behavioural barriers

■ Familiarity

At the point at which change is proposed, boring, mundane and routine activities and operations take on a whole new positive life of their own, precisely because they are familiar and because they are to cease or alter. As established and comfortable ways of doing things, they represent familiarity, certainty and confidence.

This also applies to the work environment. If this is to be disrupted by technological change or change of usage, for example, then the status quo becomes an object of affection because it is familiar.

Those involved also invest parts of themselves in the routines and the environment. They have normally at least accepted these as part of the conditions and bargain involved in working for the given organisation. If they have internalised these or become institutionalised into them, personal and psychological trauma is potentially that much greater, especially if they are unsure or unconvinced of the benefits that the changes are supposed to bring.

■ **Comfort**

A different slant on the familiarity aspect is comfort. People create habits and routines that enable them to manage many different parts of their lives (for example, meal times, bed times, social visits, the television). If everything is left purely *ad hoc* and the subject of fresh hourly/daily/weekly programmes, this is energy-consuming and can be stressful. Routines of this sort therefore create comfort, and a by-product of the routines created by organisations for their own efficiency and effectiveness is that people become comfortable with them. The perceived effective change is therefore to create discomfort.

■ **Stuck**

This is a more entrenched view of familiarity and comfort. Its roots are normally in some form of negativity or crisis. People have spent so long fighting against the odds – keeping a small company afloat against global or multi-national competitors for example – that this has become their way of life and way of working. Feeling stuck is akin to fighting trench warfare with the staff dug in and grittily determined not to be defeated and with some vision of ultimate success. The pressure, discomfort, stress, long hours and energy that are expended constitute a heavy personal investment. It brings its own familiarity and comfort. Any proposed change must address this investment in terms acceptable to those involved.

BOX 17.1   TINA

TINA stands for 'There is no alternative.' The phrase was coined by Margaret Thatcher during the 1980s. Recognising that many economic and social aspects of the UK needed to be changed, and having her own vision of the future status and greatness of Great Britain, she instituted major change programmes in public bodies and institutions and also in the attitudes of people.

Her efforts were resisted (and some would say fell far short of success) on the grounds that the people's support for the changes that she wished to make was never fully generated. The use of the phrase 'There is no alternative' simply became a challenge to people to dream up alternatives (however suitable or unsuitable these might have been). Even where there is truly no alternative, people have to be convinced of the need to change and to understand, accept and participate in it.

■ **Fear**

This is the human response to any concept or situation that is uncertain or unknown. It is the initial response to any change that is proposed unless it is accompanied by proper briefings and explanations. If fear and anxiety get out of hand, this becomes an exercise in devising and enlarging the most extreme forms of hypothetical scenario; and if this is allowed to persist it becomes both consumptive of organisation resources, and extremely damaging to collective morale and confidence. Fear is alleviated only by removing ignorance and substituting knowledge and understanding.

BOX 17.2   Channel Tunnel and Safety

During the conception and construction of the Channel Tunnel between Folkestone and Calais much was made of the safety aspects. It is clearly absolutely necessary for any such undertaking to be operationally safe and sound.

Much of the debate around this concerned the potential threat from terrorist attacks. The Tunnel was deemed, or perceived, to be especially vulnerable to this, and the potential scenario was much more frightening because of the enclosed space of the Tunnel itself and because of the sea above (which might come rushing in if the sea bed through which the Tunnel was drilled was breached).

Much of this debate and discussion was conducted around a series of 'What if?' scenarios. As well as:

'What if it was attacked?'
'What if it was flooded?'

people came up with:

'What if there was another European war?'
'What if there is a steady stream of illegal immigrants?'

Much of the debate was therefore clearly fanciful. However, this is extremely understandable from the point of view of general human behaviour. It always emerges when people do not receive adequate volumes or quality of information to enable them to make proper choices and decisions, especially on something that is to have a great effect on their lives.

■ **Perfection**

Wherever change is proposed, everything related to the status quo suddenly becomes perfect. Changes are seen as attacks on the status quo and therefore to be resisted. Again, if allowed to persist the perfection barrier becomes the focus for the drawing up of lobbies and vested interests, and again becomes expensive in terms of both time and resources.

Perfection also besets the 'change to' parts of the process. If whatever is proposed falls even a small way short of full success it is denigrated because it is not perfect.

■ Comparison

These occur in the context of, for example, 'This is exactly what Organisation X proposed to do and look what happened to them'; and 'This is what Retail Group Y set out to do and we are a hospital.' Effective change patterns are always specific. This does not prevent people from making the comparisons, and again they become destructive and debilitating if they are not addressed.

■ Expert opinion

This can come from a variety of sources: not all organisational, and not all legitimate. They can be exaggerated by social gossip, newspapers and the media, all of which from time to time change new policies and activities into major dramas, crises and upheavals.

Expert opinion may be drawn in by a vested interest to give a degree of legitimacy to its own point of view. 'Expert opinion' may also be given by a vested interest (a group that stands to lose influence if the change is successful, for example).

■ Contradiction

This happens when change proposals are unclear, or badly or inadequately presented. Different groups and individuals place their own interpretation on what is proposed and what this will mean for them. Contrasting views therefore emerge from the same information. Again, expert opinion and media coverage may be drawn up to support a particular point of view.

■ Letting go

Once the change is determined, as short a timescale for its implementation as is practicable should be drawn up. Failure to do this, or any delays that are faced, simply make it harder for people to let go of the old and accept the new. The issue here is to gain acceptance and create the reality of the new. If acceptance is gained then it makes no sense to delay implementation anyway; and, conversely, any delay limits and dilutes the extent of this acceptance.

■ Trust

People have to be convinced that what is proposed or presented is indeed that which is intended to happen. People tend to assume that there are hidden objectives if the change proposal is not straightforward or if this is what has happened in the past, and they will look for these as part of any process of resistance.

■ Self-respect and self-esteem

The barrier here occurs when those affected are faced with a perceived or actual change or loss of the identity with which they were familiar and comfortable. This especially occurs when identity and comfort has been built up over many years and has been internalised and adopted as part of their own wider life pattern and incorporated often into their personal values (and sometimes beliefs). Steps have therefore to be taken to remedy this by replacing the old as far as possible with something of equal or superior worth and value; or by changing positively the outlook of the people towards the organisation so that this can be accommodated effectively into the wider self-perception of the individuals.

■ Loss of influence

This barrier is normally a catalyst for lobbies and vested interest groups to emerge. It takes the form of resistance to the proposed change until new means of influence can be found.

This may in turn conflict with an organisational position of seeking change in order to reduce the influence of overmighty groups, departments and subjects. It is often allied in these circumstances with changes in work organisation and practices and procedures in order that dependence on such people is reduced.

The organisation may also at the same time seek to reduce the influence of trade unions, special interest groups and other forms of *ad hocracy*; and, again, it may expect resistance if this is the case.

■ The will to change

A factor common to each of these barriers is the will to change. People only change if they feel it to be in their interests to do so; and they will readily accept change if they believe it to be in their interests to do so. Whatever is proposed must take account of this. The processes and mechanisms devised for implementation can then be drawn up in terms that are understandable and acceptable to all, while at the same time meeting organisational objectives.

■ Drives for change

The need for organisational change is created by the following.

■ Changes in ownership

These may come about through takeovers, mergers, acquisitions; through the privatisation of public services; or through changes in the balance of shared ownership. In each case the new owners will normally bring their own views on the present and desired performance of the organisation, and this invariably affects many of the other areas indicated below.

■ Changes in management style

Such changes are driven by a general organisational recognition that the current approach is not right. This is normally accompanied by training developments and familiarisation programmes and briefings for all staff. It may also lead to some restructuring of patterns of supervision, allocations of responsibility and divisions of work.

■ Changes in technology

These are driven by the need to improve product, volume and quality and to maintain and improve the given competitive position. This normally leads to retraining, redeployment, transfers, and also often to redundancies. It may well lead to the redesign and restructuring of the work environment and, again, this is likely to affect patterns of supervision and management and work group cohesion.

■ Changes in markets

Changes in markets are driven by current levels of activities in relation to desired or required levels. This may also be driven by the need to seek new outlets for existing activities or new ranges of activities. The likely effects are again retraining and redeployment. There may also be issues of identity to be overcome. (See Box 17.3.)

BOX 17.3   Mitsubishi

Mitsubishi Heavy Industries is a typical Japanese company. It offers lifetime employment to its employees; in return for this the employees accept full flexibility of working. This means an acceptance and commitment to be retrained and redeployed to any part of the works where their presence is necessary. The attitude and approach of members of staff to their work is therefore 'I work for Mitsubishi', rather than 'I am a manager/technician/canteen assistant.'

This enabled the company to get over a serious commercial crisis successfully. In the early 1970s there was a slump in the shipbuilding industry, brought on by the oil crisis; Mitsubishi was the largest shipbuilding company in Japan and one of the largest in the world. However, at about the same time, the motor manufacturing arm of the company was experiencing a rapid growth in its business. The company resolved the problem of how to keep its shipbuilding labour force usefully employed by transferring them at very short notice from building ships to building cars. The location of the shipyard and the car plant were not particularly close together, so for some people this involved a geographical disruption as well as retraining and reskilling. However, because of the strong paternalistic approach taken by management (reflected in the concern for the employees), this was successfully achieved. Above all, the view that the employees worked for the company rather than followed a particular trade or occupation greatly reduced the behavioural barriers to this very essential change.

■ Jobs and work organisation

Here, change is driven by the need to improve production and output, and enhance the working environment. This normally means the creation of flexible patterns of work, offering increased levels of responsibility and broadening, enlarging and enhancing individual jobs. This, in turn, has the purpose of leading to increased identity with the organisation, greater levels of commitment, greater levels of volume and quality of output, and better wages and salaries for the staff.

■ Changes in structure

These are driven by assessments which conclude that the current structure is not as effective as it might be. This is normally arrived at by identifying blockages – in production, output, systems and communications – and relating these to structural factors. Restructuring will therefore be designed to ensure that these are removed. Restructuring also covers work practices. They also may include changes in work organisation as for example, with the move from production lines to work groups at Saab and Volvo (see Chapter 15).

■ Changes in culture, value, attitudes and beliefs

Here again, such changes are driven by the fact that these are inappropriate or not contributing fully and effectively to the organisation and situation. This is addressed through major communications, retraining, redeployment, organisation and personnel development, and enhanced by other related activities such as the changes in technology structure and work patterns indicated.

■ Obsolescence

This change may be driven by the entry of a new player into the sector who has found radical new ways of operating that are much more effective than the status quo. Others either have to make the same shift or else reposition their existing activities (or else cease business).

BOX 17.4   Obsolescent Swiss Watches

This happened to the Swiss wrist-watch industry in the 1970s. Based at Chaux-de-Fonds near the border with France, the industry had a name and reputation for high quality products at medium to high prices. The region was the main supplier of watches to the middle classes and professional segments of the world.

In the 1970s and 1980s, Japanese countries successfully adapted their electronic calculator technology to produce high quality wrist watches at low to medium prices (and at a fraction of Swiss production cost).

The Swiss ceased to be the major supplier. The Swiss industry survived through a combination of technological and production transformation, and taking its products up market and into the luxury goods range.

The usual immediate effect is to destabilise the whole sector, while all the players come to terms with the new ways of working. This form of change has occurred throughout the car and electrical goods industries, driven by the Japanese approach and ways of working.

Obsolescence may also be brought about by government action. For example, the sudden placing of legal restrictions or taxation charges on particular products and activities may cause people to turn away from them, leaving the organisations hitherto involved highly at risk.

Obsolescence in one organisation also occurs when others come along with substitute products and services. This is then taken up by the customers of the first organisation, again leaving it vulnerable.

In each case, obsolescence may come about very suddenly. It may also be due to circumstances over which the organisation has little or no control.

■ Managerial drives

These come about as the result of concerns by managers that the status quo will not serve the organisation forever, and are often hard to accept when the organisation is ostensibly going along extremely effectively and profitably; harder still, when this is allied to high levels of motivation, commitment and identity. These drives question and address each of the areas indicated. They come from within the organisation rather than outside. They are also likely to come from the point of view of taking preventative action rather than having to respond to crises.

■ Performance indicators and outputs

The assessment of these by managers leads to drives for change if either the operational or behavioural indicators give cause for concern (see Box ??). In these cases, the causes of each will be assessed and addressed. They, in turn, lead to change programmes which remedy the total performance of the whole organisation and the contribution of each department, division and function.

BOX 17.5   Performance Indicators

These are divided up as follows.

Strategic	Related to successful and effective performance over the life-time of an organisation.
Operational	Related to the success and profitability of products and services; product mixes and portfolios; productivity and output.
Specific	Including organisational income or profit per member of staff, per customer, per offering, per outlet, per square foot; returns on investment; density/frequency of usage; longevity of usage; speed of response; product durability and longevity of usage; volume and quality targets.
Behavioural	Related to the perceptual and staff management aspects; desired and prevailing attitudes and values; the extent of strikes, disputes, absenteeism, labour turnover and accidents; harmony/discord, cooperation/conflict; the general aura of well-being.
Confidence	The relationship between the organisation and its environment, its backers, its stakeholders, its customers, and its communities.
Ethical	The absolute standards of behaviour and performance that the organisation sets for itself and its acceptance in both markets and communities.

These form the basis on which organisation performance may be analysed, and help to pin-point its strengths, weaknesses and areas for concern.

■ Continuous improvement and development

The drive here stems from the recognition that there is no such thing as the perfect organisation and that the environment within which it operates is continuously fluctuating and changing. New and improved methods of work and constant attention to the behaviour and functioning of the individuals and groups therefore become a key feature of all effective organisations. The logical conclusion is thus that everything is subject to potential change and that even if something is seen and known to work extremely effectively, it may still be improved if the right means can be found.

The approach to continuous improvement and development is therefore as much attitude and state of mind as operational. As such it needs feeding, supporting and nurturing to ensure that everyone involved adopts the approach. The desired output is a combination of flexibility, dynamism, responsiveness, proactivity and pioneering, leading to enhanced business performance and greater levels of personal identity with, and commitment to, the organisation.

These drives stem from a combination of organisational effectiveness and behaviour. They reinforce the point made at the outset that neither can be achieved in isolation from the other. Any change programme that arises must address both; achieving effective results is only possible if the staff are also committed to the chosen direction.

■ Dissatisfaction with the status quo

Whatever the apparent strength of the familiarity, comfort and vested interest barriers, general and overwhelming dissatisfaction has to be changed. This is normally mainly behavioural, though the outputs of high levels of dissatisfaction are likely to be found in poor volumes or quality of products and increasing levels of customer complaints.

■ Crises and conflicts

Where an organisation is perpetually in crisis, radically different ways of working and patterns of behaviour are required and must be sought.

■ Lack of clear direction

In this case the situation is analysed and the clarity of purpose sought and established. This, again, is likely to lead to changes in attitudes, values and beliefs (indeed, it is often likely to fill a void in these). It also normally leads to the establishment of firm absolute standards of behaviour and performance.

■ **Taking control**

This drive refers especially to taking control away from vested interests, overmighty departments, divisions, groups and subjects and other lobbies and influences (for example, trade unions and consumer groups).

These drives stem from a combination of organisational effectiveness and behaviour. They reinforce the point made at the outset that neither can be achieved in isolation from the other. Any change programme that arises must address both: achieving effective results is only possible if the staff are also committed to the chosen direction.

Reasons for organisational change normally fall into one of these categories. Each also has present most of the drives indicated above, though the actual emphasis and mixture of these varies between and within organisations.

A summary framework may now be drawn up.

Why change:	What are the reasons and the drives; what are the barriers; what are the desired outcomes?
What to change:	Technology, jobs, structure, style, attitudes, values, beliefs, culture.
How to change:	What is the route to be followed between the present and what is required?
When to change:	What is the deadline for implementation and when must interim activities be completed?
Who to change:	Retraining, redeployment, redundancy; job titles and descriptions; areas of responsibility; areas of activity; changing aspirations, expectations, hopes and fears.
What to change to:	Benefits and consequences; advantages and disadvantages; for the organisation and for all concerned.

BOX 17.6   Unfreezing, Change, Refreezing

An early model of the change process is the 'unfreezing-change-refreezing' approach. This approach remains most useful in the recognition that the first stage requires specific addressing. With change comes a measure of upheaval and disruption. This is most likely to arise because not enough attention is paid to the unfreezing stage. It is one thing to recognise that the status quo is to be changed, but upheaval can be minimised if the 'what to change to' aspect is clearly understood and promulgated at the outset.

This model is less useful in the concept of 'refreezing'. A new status quo is clearly desirable; from a behavioural point of view an integral part of this is likely to be the acceptance of change, flexibility and dynamism as part of the new way of life. Refreezing rather implies that a new version of the old order is to be achieved.

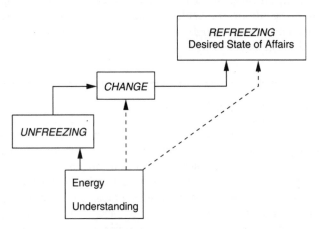

Figure 17.3   Unfreezing–change–refreezing

It is a useful analogy on the whole. For example, the effective unfreezing of water requires heat (that is, energy) to be applied and this is certainly the case with the instigation of the organisational change. It will not happen by itself, except at the whim and in the preferred direction of those being unfrozen. The result is, therefore, the equivalent to the block of ice left on the kitchen worktop to defrost of its own accord: it will gradually turn to water and spread wherever the contours of the surface allow it. It is much more effective to place the ice in a pot or pan and thaw it over a source of heat. In this way the unfreezing effects are controlled; and, again, it also emphasises the fact that changing to something is as important as changing from something.

■ **Skills, knowledge and expertise**

With very few (and increasingly few) exceptions these forms of change are facts of business and commercial life. The requirement for training, continuous professional and technical development, updating and enhancement are absolute. Closely related are concepts of job enlargement, enrichment and empowerment, behind all of which is the increasing recognition that the talents and capabilities of everyone are to be engaged and used to the full in working situations as in other aspects of life. Potential rewards to organisations are enormous. The converse where staff are not developed and enhanced, increasingly leads to loss of competitive position as well as to disillusion, alienation and loss of self-esteem on the part of the staff.

Use of the development of skills, knowledge and expertise is in itself therefore, a major force for change and development. Where this development is an obligation, an integral part of the contract of employment, this may be engaged to bring about the wider changes in attitudes, values, beliefs and expectations. This is increasingly a key and central feature of the development of the organisation as a whole.

BOX 17.7   Organisation Development

Organisation development (OD) is the term used to describe strategies and initiatives for improving organisational effectiveness through emphases on the capabilities, capacities and qualities of the human resource and approaches based on behavioural sciences. It stems from a corporate commitment to 'doing things this way'. It is an organisation-wide process, part of the strategy and endemic and integral to all activities that go on within it. It depends for success on resources, and on its adoption and absorption across all departments and functions and by everyone involved.

The process is aimed at changing and forming culture, values, attitudes and beliefs, as well as developing qualities and expertise.

The precise nature of the process varies between organisations that adopt OD as a strategy. In general, the key values and qualities reflect:

- a measure of conformity and willingness of staff to go down the paths indicated;
- obsession with product and service quality;
- obsession with high levels of motivation, enthusiasm and commitment on the part of the staff;
- strong customer orientation;
- setting a moral and value-led example and taking an active pride in the organisation and its activities.

OD strategies require:

- the setting of aims and objectives;
- devising processes, approaches and sub-strategies;
- addressing particular problems and issues;
- setting timescales and deadlines;
- establishing means of implementation, monitoring, review and evaluation of activities.

The benefits to be realised are as follows:

- commitment: a strong sense of identity and purpose that rises above any divergent individual aims and objectives;
- enhancement of style and values;

- improvements in understanding effective communications, and generation and enhancement of levels of motivation;
- promotion of harmony between normally or traditionally divergent business, sectoral or functional interests;
- constant openings and opportunities along the way for projects, initiatives, ad hocracy; and continuous enhancement and improvement;
- development of behaviour, structure, role and function;
- creative and positive environment for the approach to, and solution of, problems and blockages; under no circumstances should the training and development activities commissioned by OD programmes and initiatives lead to disciplinary activities, as part of the commitment required by these activities is that the organisation learns from failures rather than punishes them.

OD and the techniques related to it work effectively only where there is full corporate commitment. It is, above all, a business and managerial philosophy. It is both a manifestation of, and a developer of, the organisation's culture and beliefs. It requires a full level of understanding on the part of everyone in the organisation at the outset. There is inherent in OD a universal overall purpose which solves problems and addresses issues from the point of view of the organisation itself, and this is the approach to be taken.

■ **Key appointments**

Organisations give emphases to particular directions and initiatives through the title, nature and profile of certain appointments. For example, appointing an equal opportunities director tends to emphasise the importance placed on this area; and many UK public service organisations have created marketing and public relations positions to ensure that this aspect of work is effectively carried out following changes in their constitution and orientation.

High profile and high reputation individuals are appointed to existing positions in order to give these a boost and to increase the morale and confidence of those already in the function.

Low-profile appointments may also be made to decrease the influence of a given function, and key dismissals may occur for the same reason. Organisations may also take the opportunity to restructure an operational function in the wake of the resignation of the key figure.

■ **Expertise and management style**

Changes here are required when the current style is either not appropriate or else it has ceased to be effective for some reason. It may have become apparent, for example, that there has been a steady increase in the number of disputes and grievances and that an objective analysis of these has produced the conclusion that they have mostly been caused by a lack of managerial expertise or an inappropriate management style.

Changes in management style normally require managers and supervisors to become more approachable, accessible and visible to the staff; and more honest, open and direct in their dealings with people. This in turn, often requires a shift in attitude on the part of the managers concerned. It may also indicate the need for training in communication skills and human and organisational behaviour.

The general expertise of the manager is constantly being developed and tested in the conduct of the job. Specific training and development is required to increase this capacity, to improve current performance, to establish potential and to instil the qualities needed for the future.

■ Relationships

The most common reason to change relationships between groups and individuals arises from the need to break down the barriers that exist between them or, where the barriers largely concern physical distance, to find alternative means of getting over the problems that this presents.

The main issue is to ensure that common interests, aims and objectives exist, and that specific group and individual needs can be accommodated as far as possible. Part of the process of changing relationships may require a restatement of expectations and obligations to ensure that everyone understands the true position and nature of the organisation and their roles. Related to this are matters of mutual trust, respect and dependency and, again, the normal requirement is for these to be improved.

■ Structures

Every aspect of organisation structure may be called into question. The most obvious is the functional/hierarchical, as shown on the organisation chart: changes will be sought in this when the divisions and reporting relationships no longer serve current requirements, and when blockages in interdepartmental communications are identified as currently causing problems.

■ Changes to committee structures

This is where groups and meetings have lost their value and effectiveness.

■ Changes to employee representation

This is where that which is currently used is no longer useful to the organisation and staff purposes. This has happened in areas where unionism, and especially multi-unionism, was traditionally very strong. Organisations have sought to streamline the complex procedures and sub-structures that this has brought, to reduce the number of unions involved, and to streamline, simplify and clarify the whole representation process.

■ Sub-contracting

This consists of specialist functions, seasonal fluctuations and other areas of work pressure, in the pursuit of creating propeller-type organisations (see Chapter 15).

■ Work patterns

These also affect structure: again, especially where forms are flexible or distant (for instance, home working) work patterns are involved.

■ Behaviour

This may be changed from the current form to whatever is desired. Behavioural changes include for example, the adaptation of new safety procedures; responses to emergency alarms; and the introduction of no smoking policies. Behavioural changes also reinforce and energise other desired changes such as in attitudes, values and patterns of work. For example, those who take time off work due to sickness subsequently may be required to have an interview with their supervisor on their return; the interview is the behaviour, representing the attack by the organisation on absenteeism and this emphasises its own standards.

BOX 17.8   Behaviour Change: Accidents

A study by the Royal Society for the Prevention of Accidents (RoSPA) was carried out in 1982 concerning accidents and injuries in office environments. The main conclusion was that in the vast majority of cases people who worked in offices had a cavalier attitude to safety: they did not see any connection between themselves and health and safety requirements, believing that accidents were things that happened on building sites. Many ignored fire bells when they went off and emergency drills when they were supposed to take place. Many others failed to hold fire drills at all. Accidents – cuts, bruises and other injuries caused by tripping up, carelessness, kitchen utensils and so on – were rarely noted or reported.

Acting on the survey the Ceramics, Glass and Mineral Products Industrial Training Board brought in an order requiring all employees to report and record every single accident and injury, no matter how small. These were logged in the same way as factory accidents, and those with persistent and regular entries would be referred onwards for occupational health treatment, and possibly also other counselling.

> The result was a massive decline in the number of accidents and injuries and a complete rethink of the importance of health and safety at work in this environment. Accidents effectively became too much trouble to have. The procedure was rigorously supervised and the record book checked every week. After three months the rate had halved; after a year the volume had dropped by 90 per cent. The behavioural approach made everyone think a little before they acted. The result as well as the reduction in accident rates was to greatly increase the capability for work.

■ Work practices

This refers to improving the existing operations as the result of some other change, whether in technology, location, workplace design or reorganisation. The main impact again, is likely to be on behaviour; and this normally affects the habits, procedures, routines and general activities of those concerned.

It may also affect reporting relationships, management and operational structures and style, and staff representation procedures and methods.

■ Technology

Radical changes in technology – information or production – bring with them additional needs for retraining, redeployment, the reorganisation of work and the restructuring of functions. The operational rationale for technological change is clearly always based on the need for improved efficiency and effectiveness of work, and is usually related to market pressures: for example, the need to remain competitive and to improve quality and volume of output to become more flexible and to respond to opportunities. This can only be fully successful if attention is paid also to the behavioural aspects.

Furthermore, change in the usage of existing technology may be required. This occurs where new and better methods are found of organising and arranging the work around it, or where better operational software becomes available or where better ways of using the equipment itself are established. Again, there is invariably a requirement to train and brief as a result in order to gain both understanding and commitment.

■ Location

A major relocation – from one part of the country to another, for example – causes large upheavals. These invariably include redundancies for those unable or unwilling to make the move, and relocation for those who are to go with the organisation.

There are also wider community pressures. There are, first, anxieties on the part of the area that is to lose the organisation and the vacuum that this may create, not to mention the effects on purchasing power and volumes of business that are conducted at present. There is also anticipation of new opportunities on the part of the new location, together with some feelings of trepidation, especially relating to competition for labour, effects on house prices and the general approach of the organisation to its new environment and habitat. This will be exacerbated where the new location has had particular experiences of incomers in the past which were either strongly negative or positive. Where past experience has been negative the new location may put up social barriers to those coming into the area; where this has been positive, the new area will tend to welcome the incomer with open arms.

If relocation is to be managed successfully, organisations normally take it upon themselves to organise trips and breaks for the staff to the new area. This is so that they can gain at least an initial feeling of familiarity, see some of the opportunities and amenities provided, and look at house prices, schools for children, leisure facilities and so on. This approach also underlines the organisation's concern and respect for those who have served it well over the previous period.

■ Redundancy

Redundancies come about when particular forms of work cease. Jobs affected become obsolete. This occurs because of reorganisation, new technology or relocation. It is always traumatic for those affected. When redundancies take place, those at risk should be notified as early as possible. This at least is a mark of respect which can be given to people who have hitherto served the organisation well.

Alternatives should be offered wherever possible. The chance to retrain or relocate is often acceptable once people understand the opportunities and benefits that are to arise as a result. Where staff loss is unavoidable, its effects should mitigated as far as possible through the use of early retirement and voluntary severance arrangements. The best organisations create their own job clubs and employment agencies with the purpose of doing everything possible to find new employers for the staff that they have to shed.

DHL, the global courier and private postal organisation, placed adverts in the employment columns of both national newspapers and professional journals offering 'excellent and top quality staff in all areas of expertise' when it closed down its base in south-east England.

BOX 17.9   Redundancy Horror Stories

Television news

Hearing of redundancy through national television broadcasts is much rarer than it used to be in the UK. In the past, staff at British Leyland, British Telecom, the

National Coal Board, Ford and many county, district and borough councils have all found out about proposed redundancies via the television news before they were notified by their organisations.

Instant departures

The stress of redundancy is greatly enlarged if those concerned are to leave instantly, whatever the size and generosity of the severance payment. Instant departure happens in many areas – journalism, sales, banking and finance, for example – and is practised ostensibly to protect the organisation from disaffected redundant staff taking trade secrets or customer and client bases with them to new employers, or from sabotaging or corrupting databases before they go. This attitude says most about the value placed on the staff by the organisation.

Differentials

Redundancies have recently also taken place at times when others in particular organisations have received large pay rises. The reaction among those affected is always that different grades and occupations have varying degrees of value. Again, the effect on the those to be laid off is traumatic and exacerbated by feelings of loss of self-worth and self-esteem. This has occurred in the UK in the 1990s, especially in privatised utilities – the regional electricity companies and British Telecom, for example – and also in the national clearing banks.

■ Work patterns

The normal change in work patterns is from restricted to flexible with benefits for both the organisation and the staff. Attendance at the place of work comes to be governed by:

- core time, when those involved are required to be present because of work pressures;
- flexitime, when people may attend and get on with the remainder of their workload;
- overtime, when people are required or requested to attend for specific periods outside their core and flexitime, again because of particular pressures.

The combination of each element represents the total working hours for the period (day, week, month or year) and the basis on which the wage or salary is paid. Extended working of overtime or flexitime normally leads to additional pay and/or holidays or time off (the benefit to staff).

Attendance times may also be varied as, for example, with the development of twilight shift patterns (6 o'clock onwards in the evening), or by manufacturing and retail organisations extending their production times and opening hours.

Shift patterns also change according to the nature and volume of work envisaged.

Home working is also increasingly popular among those in information and service activities. In these cases the staff log on to their organisation's systems through equipment that has been provided for their use at home.

The main problem that the introduction of these forms of work patterns brings is that of perceived fairness and equality. People who are allowed or encouraged (or directed) to work at home may be regarded by the rest of the organisation as having an unfair advantage, preferential treatment or a soft option if this is not carefully and thoughtfully managed. Those not given this opportunity then become resentful. Any differentiated patterns of attendance have therefore to be carefully explained at the point of their introduction if this is to be avoided.

■ **Business**

Changes in business potentially bring both operational and behavioural problems, especially where the transformation is radical. Operationally, there is the necessity to gain both a commercial foothold and a reputation in new sectors, and this will bring feelings of anxiety on the part of the staff if the promised or anticipated rewards are not forthcoming. Behaviourally, the staff need to have their current feelings of confidence from being in Business X translated into the equivalent that are now to come from being in Business Y.

This is not such an issue if the staff have strong loyalty to and identify with, the organisation. The Virgin Group has been able to make its many transformations – from music retail to travel, to airlines, to cola – because of this strength of identity. Mitsubishi (see Box 17.3) were able to transform from ship to car manufacture, again because of the loyalty and confidence of the workforce.

The greatest problems occur when staff identify overwhelmingly with the sector and its work: 'I'm in insurance', or 'I'm in the rag trade', for example. The change must take account of this and accommodate it as far as possible if it is to be successful.

What is generally required in these circumstances is for the staff to receive recognition from the organisation that they are both skilled and valuable. The expression 'You are a skilled person' recognises the contribution of one part of the individual's talents; while the expression 'You are a valuable person' applies to the whole person as well as their talents and skills.

■ **Name**

Name changes occur for a variety of reasons. In the main it is to get over negative connotations held about the organisation in the past (see Box 17.9).

This also takes place as part of the process of updating the image of the organisation. For example, the Spastics Society of Great Britain changed its name to SCOPE in 1994 to give itself a brighter, more direct and assertive image. It also occurs when one organisation is taken over by another, or where a merger takes place; in both cases this must be incorporated into the structure of the new ownership. It occurs through a change of organisation status: for example, the privatisation of public industries, utilities and services or the flotation of shares on the stock exchange of a hitherto private company. In these cases, the greatest attention is paid to staff and customer identity to gain familiarity and acceptance for the new name as soon as possible.

BOX 17.10   Negative Connotations

The Windscale Nuclear Power Station and Energy Reprocessing Plant at Barrow, Cumbria, England, had its name changed to Sellafield following a long history of pollution and discharge scandals.

Ratners, the UK retail jewellery chain, lost its separate identity in the H. Samuel conglomerate because of persistent bad feelings arising from the 'off-the-cuff' disparaging remarks about its products by the then Company Chairman.

The Gateway food supermarket chain changed its name to Somerfield in 1993, and at the same time went through a major programme of staff training, store refurbishment, marketing strategy and product range extension to bring it up to the standards and perceptions of the best operators in the UK.

The various activities of British Rail have been through the change process *ad infinitum.* The South East region became Network South East and this in turn changed to Kent Coast and Network South Central. This in general tends to betray a lack of complete confidence, and such a feeling is nearly always passed on to both staff and customers.

As a contrast, the British Rail marques Pullman and Intercity have survived for long periods of time; moreover, Pullman is used to describe many forms of luxury travel (for example, on ocean liners and Concorde).

BOX 17.11   The Change Process

The process by which particular changes are to be achieved arrive from assessment of the components of the framework and elements indicated above. There are certain essentials.

1. Organisation commitment must be absolute.
2. Aims and objectives are to be clearly stated in terms that all affected understand.
3. Resources are required for all aspects of the process and each of the activities conducted in its pursuit.

4. Continuous monitoring, review and evaluation processes are to be conducted in the name of those responsible for designing and implementing the change programme.
5. Recognition of the expectations, hopes, fears and aspirations of all affected will themselves be changed and these require understanding and satisfaction.
6. Recognition that the process itself will generate its own life; that it will bring opportunities and problems that are not apparent at the outset; and that part of the successful management of change lies in assessing these as they arise and having the capacity to take whatever steps are necessary as the result.
7. The process requires leadership and direction, and general and specific responsibilities allocated to everyone.
8. Recognition that the unfreezing of the status quo is potentially destabilising and leads to chaos if it is not a part of the complete process and targeted.
9. General organisation support is required for all those affected. This is necessary in the form of communications, counselling and empathy based on an understanding of the situation of those involved; and also in providing retraining, redeployment and time off to look for alternatives.
10. Recognition that change is not an end in itself and that it will lead to further opportunities.

Attitudes and values

Attitudes and values are normally instilled at the induction and orientation phase of employment. In the same way, if they require to be changed, reinduction and reorientation (or the equivalent) must take place. The process of attitude formulation and development then remains in the control of the organisation rather than being allowed to emerge of its own volition.

This takes place in response to analyses which show that something is wrong in these areas. It may occur because it has never been considered before. It also arises because of shifts in general attitudes and expectations of the sector concerned: for example, one organisation gaining market share at the expense of others because of its attention to product quality and customer service. The others have therefore to reposition their whole view in order to respond effectively. This involves changing the attitudes of the staff in order to ensure that they, too, value these aspects and that it is critical to continued commercial success.

Attitude and value change is normally underpinned by obligations to train and develop, both in skills and expertise and also behaviour and demeanour. It is strongest in unitary organisation where it tends to be related to high levels of mutual identity and commitment.

■ Beliefs

Changes in belief are much more difficult and nearly always traumatic for those involved. People who have worked for a long time in organisations and who are suddenly made redundant have something akin to their beliefs shattered: the belief that the organisation is eternal and that it will look after them forever. Long periods of continuity and prosperity lead also to illusions of immortality, and this too becomes very akin to belief. People who conduct their affairs from the highest moral and ethical standpoint and who then find that this is not valued, or that they lose out to deviousness and expediency, also have some-thing akin to their beliefs shattered.

This is most difficult when the current and prevailing attitudes, values and beliefs are strong, positive, distinctive and subscribed to by all. Again, the desired outcome must both transcend and enhance these if it is to be successful. In many cases, this made easier by virtue of the fact that such positive attitudes, values and beliefs contain within them commitments to the well-being of the organisation and its customers, and changes presented and delivered in ways that address this directly. This form of attitude often includes qualities of flexibility and dynamism, and the need to undergo change may be apparent in any case.

It is more difficult, however, when no clear universal set of attitudes, values and beliefs exist. The result is that different groups will have adopted their own customs and norms. The sudden imposition of a universal set is therefore likely to generate initial resistance at least and during the change process steps may have to be taken to ensure that a parallel culture does not continue to exist to the detriment of the new.

Much of this therefore refers to the processes of attitude formation referred to elsewhere (see Chapter 4). However, there are additional features.

1. Acceptance and recognition of the fact that those prevailing are unsatisfactory for whatever reason.
2. Recognising and understanding the ideal and desired attitudes.
3. Taking responsibility for effecting the change and instigating change processes to ensure that this happens.
4. Identifying the barriers to attitude change that are present or likely to occur.
5. Identifying the drives that can be energised.
6. Identifying the resistances of particular groups and individuals.

■ Unsatisfactory attitudes

These generally take the form of being negative, indifferent or not positive enough. Negative attitudes especially arise as the result of a lack of clarity of purpose and where the organisation has paid insufficient attention to the standards of behaviour, performance and output that are required.

Negative attitudes may also arise as a result of the influence of different groups and individuals. This occurs when these groups and individuals have some cause for dissatisfaction and seek to influence others as the result. A form of siege mentality may develop (a negative form of group-think in organisational behaviour terms).

Negative attitudes also develop alongside work structuring and organisation and the management style that has been devised to support it; and, where this is alienative based on status differentials, a lack of respect and esteem and absence of equality of treatment.

■ Ideal and desired attitudes

As stated in Chapter 4 these are always positive and reflect the levels of commitment and demeanour necessary to productive and harmonious performance. One must therefore recognise the desired ideal and the current state so that a path from one to the other may be found.

Processes of attitude formation are then to be engaged with the stated purpose of achieving the ideal.

■ Responsibility

The first part of this involves accepting that change is to take place and accepting the responsibility that goes with this. It has then to be addressed in the same way as any other change. Strategies are devised with the goal of achieving the desired attitudes and with monitoring, review and evaluation processes established to ensure that the changes taking place are those required, and also the rate at which change is taking place and its effects on organisation performance.

■ Barriers

The main barriers to attitude change are as follows.

1. Prior and current commitments – occurring where people are unwilling to change because they have invested energy and expertise in the status quo and perceive or understand it to be working well and in their own interests.
2. Ego-protection – occurring where people are unwilling to admit that there is something wrong with the situation and especially that they have made mistakes or committed themselves to faulty courses of action.
3. Value defence – occurring where there is a strong group or individual identity with prevailing values, whether or not these are effective and successful from the organisation's point of view.
4. Lack of information – this is where people will not change their attitudes because they do not see it as being in their interests to do so, because of a lack of information

in relation to the imperfections of the status quo and because there is insufficient information made available about the purpose of the required and desired changes.

5. Fear – this is, above all, fear of the unknown; it engages defensive and protectionist attitudes on the part of those involved.

6. Influences of individuals – occurring especially where strong and dominant personalities tell others that the desired change is not required or that it is to be punitive or coercive (or negative or detrimental in some other way). This is reinforced if the particular individual has a history or reputation for having been right about these things in the past.

7. Influences of groups – the influences here are similar to those of particular individuals. People have a strong tendency to conform to group-think and group norms. This is exacerbated if the group in question has a high status or reputation. The group also has influence if the individual has taken a conscious decision to join it (such as with a trade union or professional association). In these cases the stated views of the group in relation to a particular situation are perceived to have a high degree of substance and credibility, and again this is enhanced if a group has a history of having been right about such matters in the past.

■ Drives for attitude change

Radical changes in attitude will only take place if each of these aspects is addressed effectively. The means of achieving this therefore involve the following elements.

1. Addressing prior and current commitments as stepping stones on the path of progress rather than seeking to deny or destroy them, and recognising and valuing the level of commitment that individuals have placed on these. If that has been largely of self-interest then means must be found of harmonising this with the commitment to the organisation that is now required.

2. Addressing ego-protection from the point of view of ensuring again, that what has been done was not of the order of fatal or mortal error (unless it was based on vanity, arrogance or incompetence). More positive still, recognition must be given for the value and effectiveness of whatever was done and achieved in the past; and even where this is minimal or lacking it may still be represented as a stepping stone.

3. Addressing values from the point of view again of building on the past and present rather than destroying it; this is likely to be most effective where the organisation repositions or restates its shared values and other absolute standards of policy and behaviour at the same time, taking active and positive steps to ensure that these are accepted and adopted; and furthermore, that any sanctions used are given to those who do not, or will not, respond positively.

4. Overhauling channels of communication to ensure that what is put out is of quality and value, as well as volume, and to address the basic problem of ignorance that is the barrier here.

5. Addressing fear from the twin standpoint that it is a barrier to attitude change and that it can also be used to change attitudes. Fear as a barrier normally constitutes

fear of the unknown and is thus largely addressed by attention to the channels of communication activities indicated above.

Fear as a drive for attitude change has to strike a balance between stating, on the one hand, that the status quo can no longer go on, with the converse on the other that something which is too threatening simply leads to a negative response (normally rejection). This is compounded by the fact that too little emphasis on the fear factor means that people perceive that there is nothing to be fearful of (see Box 17.4).

BOX 17.12   Attitude Change and Fear

In the 1970s and 1980s the UK glass industry commissioned a series of films, the purpose of which was to raise general awareness of the importance of safety in the industry. They also sought to change the prevailing attitudes to safety from those of complacency and indifference to one of acknowledgment and recognition. The ideal was to instil a much greater awareness of the damage and destruction caused both to individuals and factories by bad attitudes to safety.

The first of these films, *In the Dock*, centred around the inquest into an accident. While the message was generally clear, it was delivered in terms that were so bland and anodyne that it had little effect.

The second film was called *Intensive Care*. It showed in graphic detail the causes and effects of accidents. This included one character having a sliver of glass removed from her eye. The main accident shown, however, was the factory supervisor having a giant stack of glass tumblers come crashing down on top of him. This was so horrific that those who watched the film simply shut the message out: it was too traumatic to believe that such an accident would occur in their own places of work.

The third film, *Talking of Safety*, centred around the functioning of a safety committee. It struck a reasonable balance between the potential for accidents to occur and their devastating effects, and the need to adopt a preventative standpoint.

Cigarettes

Another example is provided in the case of anti-smoking messages and commercials. Cigarette packets in the UK now carry health warnings along the lines of:

- smoking when pregnant can harm your unborn baby;
- smoking causes cancer;
- smoking causes heart disease;
- tobacco seriously damages health.

This is more than offset by the images of luxury and glamour, and the level and volume of sports sponsorship in which the tobacco industry is involved.

Other anti-smoking initiatives have focused on documentary evidence of those dying of smoking-related cancers; the testimony of Roy Castle, who never smoked in his life but who died in 1994 of lung cancer related to passive smoking; and graphic pictures of raw, diseased and blackened lungs. Many of these have also been found to be so extreme and threatening to smokers that they simply shut off and refuse to listen or accept. As a result the commercials and initiatives have not had the desired effects; and, again, the balance has to be found between getting the right level of fear that ensures the maximum effect on attitude and behaviour without being either too bland or too threatening.

■ Other means

■ Coopting

This is the process of getting highly influential groups and individuals involved in the change process. Those who defend the status quo and the prevailing attitudes and values are invited to participate in the drive for change, and to suggest and devise means by which the changes required can be implemented successfully, while at the same time having regard to their own needs.

■ Use of operational change

Operational changes are also used to affect attitudes by emphasising and enhancing the opportunities that are to become available to staff as a result. This is part of the process of addressing the fear and ignorance elements. A relationship between the future ways of working and the general interest of those affected is defined. This is likely not to be an end in itself. Opportunities for training, occupational variety and redeployment normally have to be offered alongside operational change if new attitudes are to be formed effectively.

■ Use of technological change

Changes in all organisation technology – operational, production and information – invariably lead to attitude change because of the need to be retrained in order to be able to use the new equipment effectively. The result is the development of new outlooks as well as skills and knowledge, enhancement and proficiency, opening up new horizons, possibilities and potential.

■ Restructuring

Coopting, operational and technological change may all lead to, and contribute to, restructuring. The process can also be used to break up resistant groups and departments, as well as addressing operational effectiveness. It is also often possible to redefine relationships with trade unions and professional bodies and associations during restructuring on the grounds that, while the old ways may have been suitable in the past, they are no longer relevant to the new style of organisation.

■ Cooperating with the inevitable

If something is certain to happen, if the decision to change has already been taken, there is no point – and no honesty – in giving any other impression. Indeed, to do so is detrimental to the quality of future relationships. It also contributes to any prevailing negative attitudes. People who are given to understand that they have some say in matters, and then subsequently find that this is not so, generate feelings of mistrust and of negativity towards the organisation.

Positive attitudes are generated in response to the inevitable by presenting the benefits of the new situation, by dealing with negative aspects in open and straightforward ways and reinforcing each with necessary activities. Above all, this means attention to communications and the ways in which these are delivered and presented. It also means giving the organisation's support to groups and individuals who are to feel particular effects – especially negative effects, such as job loss – in the form of retraining and redeployment where possible. This should always be supported in terms of counselling, help, support and advice. It demonstrates respect and esteem for the staff. It acknowledges their past contribution and is a mark of value. It is also of benefit to those who remain, even if they have not been directly affected by the changes because it proves the organisation's care, concern and respect for all staff.

■ Letting go

Prevailing attitudes – both positive and negative – are familiar and therefore comfortable. Part of the process of changing attitudes is therefore concerned with generating acceptance of, and comfort with, the new. It may be possible to gain a general acceptance that the new is highly desirable, but the old has still to be left behind: people have still to 'let it go'.

Again, the likelihood of this is greater the greater the level of direct and active involvement taken by the organisation and generated in the people. The value and quality of communications and counselling, attention to groups and individuals, and reinforcement of respect and esteem are critical. In addition, the overall need is to persuade people to adopt and internalise the required attitudes and to let go of the old because it is in their interests to do so; they will be better served by the new than the old.

■ Strategies for the management of change

Successful organisational approaches to change therefore arise from an understanding of the elements and barriers that exist in particular situations and an appreciation of the ways in which people react when faced with change. Everyone concerned must be made aware of the drives, necessities and reasons for change from the organisation's point of view; and these have then to be related to the needs and aspirations of the rest of the staff. It is essential also to understand that people will be fearful and anxious about what is to happen until they understand that it is in everyone's best interests.

The key to successful change is communications. Change programmes require communications in the following forms.

■ Education

The need is to enlighten everyone concerned about the reasons and necessity for change, and the benefits that are to accrue as the result; the advantages to the staff (and disadvantages and threats if these are present also); the obligations of the organisation to the staff and vice versa; and the new or envisaged nature of the working relationship.

■ Consultation

Consultations will begin to take place at the point at which proposals for change become clear. The purpose is to ensure that initial familiarity with the idea is generated as quickly as possible (a form of ice-breaking).

Subjecting proposals to a wider audience is also likely to ensure that any absolute objections are raised as early as possible. This in turn identifies the nature and location (and the likely strength) of potential lobbies and vested interests. It may also draw in concerned responses with real problems that nobody so far concerned had hitherto considered.

Consultation will therefore be as wide as possible drawing everyone involved (and any representative bodies such as trade unions and professional associations) into the process. It is the first step towards identity, internalisation, ownership – and acceptance – by all concerned.

■ Participation

Genuine participation in the determination of change is unlikely. In most situations this is the key task and responsibility of top managers. Participation in the implementation of change is essential. The process will be much smoother and more effective if what is proposed is accepted and internalised by those directly concerned. These are the direct results of effective participation. Participation in change is also conducted through all the instruments available within the organisation, such as staff meetings, briefing groups, work improvement groups, quality circles and quality assurance groups, any trade unions and other staff representative committees. The role of each is to accept and adopt the change processes, give them life and energy and ensure that everybody is involved.

■ Facilitation

This refers to the provision of specialist and directed support to groups and individuals throughout the process. It is especially important if there is to be a major restructuring, or if redundancies, redeployments and retraining are to take place. Those affected in these ways have special needs and anxieties which must be supported.

There may also be problems with 'pockets of resistance'. Individuals and groups which refuse to accept the proposals need special counselling and additional support.

Specific individual problems may also need to be addressed in this way, such as the provision of company transport to enable people to get to a new location not on public transport routes, for example.

■ Negotiation

Again, general negotiation is unlikely in determining the aims and objectives of changes. It is, however, likely to feature in the implementation, especially on operational matters such as timescales and retraining.

Representative bodies, especially trade unions, may seek to negotiate the best possible deal for themselves and their members when facing change; but again, in the best managed situations this is most likely to be concerned with seeking extra money and better benefits for those affected rather than in diluting the proposals themselves.

It is in any case very dangerous for organisations to negotiate away part of their overall direction. Operationally, this is likely to dilute the effectiveness of the outcome and may seriously hinder its chances of success. Behaviourally, it tends to indicate a lack of absolute conviction that what is being done is right and may, in turn, lead to reduced levels of confidence.

■ Assertiveness

The greater the assertiveness, the more direct and 'adult' the language and approach used, the greater propensity of the receivers to understand and therefore accept what is being proposed. If the approach and language are not direct, the integrity of the proposals will in any case be called into question: those who are to be affected will instantly look for hidden agenda and objectives.

Proposals are also put in the language of the receivers for best effect and, again, anything that is clouded in jargon or 'bureaucrat-speak' is instantly suspect.

■ Organisation development

The establishment of programmes of organisation development, learning cultures and programmes of continuous development and improvement both create and reinforce the environment within which changes take place. In these situations participation in the programmes is normally an absolute requirement. Skills and knowledge are therefore changed and developed first. This leads to changes in behaviour, expectations and aspirations; and in turn again, prevailing styles, relationships, attitudes and values are affected.

This is reinforced through the use of quality circles, work improvement groups, briefing groups and targeted group and staff meetings.

■ Other groups

A key benefit of the creation of *ad hoc* and project groups, problem-solving teams and brainstorming sessions (as well as work improvement groups and quality circles) is that they help to break down barriers, misunderstanding and misconceptions. They enhance the general development of the organisation as well as addressing specific issues.

BOX 17.13   A Note on Failure

'Failure is a subjective or value judgment based on an event or activity.'

At times of change the ability to recognise failure is heightened by the general level of hope, fear and anxiety that is present. The failure of one initiative in the change process may cause the validity of the whole to be questioned and called into doubt.

This underlines the necessity for problem monitoring and review processes. A bad event can only be assessed as such if these are in place and if proper aims and objectives have been set for the whole process. Only through the use of these can it be satisfactorily determined whether or not the whole process is flawed or whether it was just simply an element that went wrong.

■ Coercion

This is used where there is no prospect of a positive, productive and participative relationship between organisation and employees. At its most positive, coercion underlines the fact that the proposals have been well thought out and that the organisation is determined to go ahead with them.

Negative coercion is more generally present. It is required to overcome entrenched resistance when all other approaches have failed. At its most extreme it includes threats of dismissal or discipline to the recalcitrants. Otherwise the coercive approach is best used through isolating the recalcitrants through persuading everyone else of the benefits and opportunities that are to arise.

Coercion generally is negative and to be avoided except as a last resort. It nearly always leaves some bad feeling and resentment, which may resurface at a later date and in a different form.

In most situations a combination of these approaches is required. The purpose is to engage a full understanding of the organisation's purposes as early as possible and follow this up with gaining full commitment. This is best achieved in most circumstances by having recourse to all the approaches indicated, and being prepared to be forceful and coercive as a last resort.

BOX 17.14   The Coercive Approach

Rosabeth Moss-Kanter suggests the following techniques for overcoming resistance and apathy to the introduction of new ideas, ways of working, attitudes and values. These apply in particular to blockers and interferers; they may be summarised as manipulative/coercive.

1. **Wait them out:** they might eventually go away.
2. **Wear them down:** keep pushing and arguing and being persistent.
3. **Appeal to higher authority:** gain the support of those in higher authority.
4. **Invite them aboard:** have them join the party, be coopted.
5. **Get friends in the camp:** get friends in whom they believe to talk to them.
6. **Support and promotion:** make sure that the drivers and instigators of change are present and active at key meetings and committees.
7. **Reduce the stakes:** emphasise the positive.
8. **Reduce the threat:** emphasise the volume and quality of knowledge available.
9. **Warnings:** let them know that senior management are committed to these courses of action.

Remember always that only afterwards does an innovation look like the right thing to have done all along. (Based on Moss-Kanter, 1983.)

BOX 17.15   Resistance Lowering: Rules for Overcoming Resistance to Change

---

Sources of Change

1. Resistance will be less if administrators, teachers, board members, managers and community leaders feel that the project is their own and not one devised and operated by outsiders.
2. Resistance will be less if the project clearly has wholehearted support from top officials and the resources and backing to match.

Change Benefits

1. Resistance will be less if participants see the changes reducing rather than increasing their present workload.
2. Resistance will be less if new ways of working accord with prevailing attitudes, values and beliefs.
3. Resistance will be less if new ways of working are seen as benefits and not threats.
4. Resistance will be less if those involved feel that their autonomy and security is not threatened.

Procedures in Instituting Change

1. Resistance will be less if those involved have been involved and consulted, and have participated in the change process.
2. Resistance will be less if those involved are made to feel critical to the eventual success of the proposals.
3. Resistance will be less if what is proposed is universally adopted.
4. Resistance will be less the more positive the relationship between the proponents of change and those who are to be affected.
5. Resistance will be less if fear of the unknown and the uncertain are addressed and clarified; and where people feel that there is a reduced level of risk.
6. Resistance will be reduced if continuous monitoring, evaluation, review and feedback is given.
7. Resistance will be reduced if particular groups and individuals require further or continuous clarification.
8. Resistance will be reduced if participants gain enhanced acceptance, support, trust, respect and confidence in their relationships with each other.
9. Resistance will be reduced if what is proposed is kept open to revision and reconsideration if the need for these becomes apparent.

From: Huczynski and Buchanan (1993), p. 544.

■ Conclusions

■ Future trends

Luthans (1990) identifies the following considerations for the future of organisational behaviour and human resource management.

1. The best and brightest will be drawn to organisations that foster personal growth.
2. The new role of managers is that of coach, teacher or mentor.
3. The best and brightest want ownership (both psychological and actual) in their organisation.
4. Organisations will increasingly turn to outside contractors for their people, shifting from hired staff to contract staff, creating propeller and federated organisations.
5. Authoritarian management styles will give way to a networking people-oriented style.
6. Intrapreneurship is creating new products and new markets and revitalising organisations from within.
7. Quality will be the dominant thrust of organisations.
8. Intuition and creativity are challenging the quantitative approach adopted by business schools.
9. Large organisations are learning from and copying the positive and productive qualities of small organisations.
10. The coming of the information economy has fostered a massive shift from infrastructure to quality of life.

It is clear that not all those affected by change efforts programmes will be positively affected; there will be winners and losers. Attention must be paid to the losers, as well as to the winners. This is especially important for long-serving employees who came into the organisation under one set of circumstances and who are now being required to adapt to others, or even to face the fact that their skills, qualities and expertise are no longer required. It should always be remembered that their contribution was valuable in the past and this should form the basis of the attitude adopted towards them for the future, whether or not they are to be kept on.

All change processes and programmes require wholehearted organisation commitment, supported by adequate levels of resource and time.

Successful change only comes about where managers successfully energise and drive each of the elements indicated. They key issue, therefore, is for organisations to adopt attitudes of flexibility, dynamism, responsiveness and positiveness, and the drive to maximise output and resource usage.

Change is a process; it is also a state of mind (just as order and steadiness were in the past). It therefore requires active involvement and direct and positive participation rather than simple acquiescence, and this should apply to everyone. Hierarchical progressions, steady jobs and administrative functions, and their historic output of satisfactory performance and results, are all being questioned, and often abolished, in the pursuit of direct contribution to performance and continued improvement and development.

Above all, the role of managers and supervisors must change from the operation of systems and procedures to the development of expertise, skills, knowledge and qualities in their people. The new manager will be a leader, director, developer and coach of the human resource, and the creator of conditions in which this can be successful. This, above all, is why an understanding of the behaviour of organisations and those who work in them is so valuable.

■ Questions

1. What do you foresee to be the most important global changes over the coming ten years? How is this likely to affect the behaviour of organisations?
2. Identify the main problems with introducing flexible patterns of work and state how organisations should seek to overcome these.
3. What elements should be contained in a management training programme under the title of 'The Management of Change'? What is the purpose of including these elements? How would you evaluate such a programme for success/failure?
4. Identify the major trends emerging in organisational behaviour. State why you believe these to be important. What actions are required by organisations to ensure that these are successfully and effectively adopted?

Conclusions: managing organisations for the future

■ Introduction

Most organisations and their managers today recognise the inevitability of change. All organisations are subject to the influence of competitive, economic, political and social forces, and to pressures brought about by changes and advances in technology and knowledge. Products and services have shorter life cycles resulting from these technological advances, and also wider choice, availability and access, and increased consumer expectations. The ability to remain in existence therefore depends on the capability to seek, identify and maximise opportunities and respond to threats.

No sector, organisation or occupation is immune from this: for example, in the UK, the armed forces and civil service have both been affected by redundancies and there is currently discussion of enforced job losses among the Anglican priesthood.

The obsolescence and passing of accepted and understood ways of doing things has affected social, as well as business and economic relationships. This includes the concept (some would say illusion) of steady permanent lifetime employment (see Box 18.1).

BOX 18.1   FT Share Index Line Up 1935: The Illusion of Immortality

An indication of the illusion of immortality was given by Caulkin (1995) in a discussion of the 30 companies that made up the original FT Ordinary Share Index. These were:

- Associated Portland Cement: survives, but changed its name to Blue Circle in 1978;
- Austin Motor: now owned by BMW;
- Bass: survives intact;
- Bolsover Colliery: nationalised in 1947;
- Callenders Cables and Construction: now part of BICC;
- Coats: now part of Coats Viyella;

- Courtaulds: survives;
- Distillers: bought by Guinness in 1986;
- Dorman Long: part of British Steel;
- Dunlop Rubber: now owned by BTR;
- EMI: merged with Thorn in 1979 to form Thorn EMI;
- Fine Spinners and Doublers: taken over by Courtaulds in 1964;
- General Electric Company: survives;
- Guest, Keen and Nettlefolds: survives as GKN;
- Harrods: taken over by House of Fraser in 1959;
- Hawker Siddley: taken over by BTR in 1991;
- Imperial Chemical Industries: survives intact, but demerged into ICI and Zeneca in 1993;
- Imperial Tobacco: bought by Hanson in 1986;
- International Teat Company Stores: lost its identity in the 1970s, following takeover by Gateway;
- London Brick: bought by Hanson in 1984;
- Murex: now owned by ESAB (Sweden) since 1983;
- Patons and Baldwins: merged with Coats in 1960;
- Pinchin, Johnson and Associates: taken over by Courtaulds in 1960;
- Rolls-Royce: now owned by Vickers;
- Tate & Lyle: survives;
- Turner & Newall: survives;
- United Steel: now part of British Steel;
- Vickers: survives;
- Watney, Combe & Reid: taken over by Grand Met in 1972;
- Woolworth: now part of the Kingfisher Group since 1989.

The overwhelming conclusion is that, in the given or current format at least, most organisations do not last long.

People's expectations of the organisations for which they work are therefore constantly changing and being changed. The ever-changing nature of activities and occupations requires continuing attention to training and development. Workforces have been restructured to accommodate the flexibility and dynamism required, above all in the creation of 'core and peripheral' approaches to organisation and in increases in the numbers of flexible hours and part-time members of staff. People have a general inclination towards earning high current levels of reward, rather than trading this off for a stability and permanence of relationship which no longer exists. Increased importance is also attached to the quality of working life: to the satisfaction of people's needs and expectations at work; to such factors as stress, frustration and alienation; to managerial and supervisory behaviour; and to job and work design. This also includes the relationship between employee commitment and levels of output and performance.

From this, a range of issues may be identified.

1. The concern of organisations to improve, maximise and optimise performance to ensure their continued ability to carry out effective and productive – and profitable – activities in markets which are no longer protected or guaranteed and which are subject to competition, threat and entryism from all parts of the globe.

2. The ability to reconcile short-term demands with the need for long-term permanence and stability. This is, above all, a problem for the provision of adequate and effective public services where the demands of those in overall control (especially politicians) are for instant and short-term results in the pursuit of political agenda. This directly conflicts with the need for a long-term perspective on service outputs (for example, in many cases health care and social support may be required for months; the output of education provision may not be apparent for 15–20 years). This is also true for commercial organisations which have to reconcile long-term and continuous profitable existence with the need to maintain the confidence in stock markets and among other backers, many of whom have short-term pressures to which to work.

3. Attention is required to the changing nature of investment based on technological advances and the needs of organisations to remain competitive. For example, the ability to commit an organisation to a form of production or information technology for a period of ten years is no longer tenable as an absolute; it is possible in practice only as long as nobody invents something else which does the job even better. On the other hand, the absolute commitment to the principle of investment is essential. This now represents the context in which all flows of capital investment have to be seen: the requirement for the outlay remains, but the view taken has radically altered. It also underlines the need for constant attention to the education, training and development of the people concerned (technology and equipment are only as good as the people using it).

4. The concern for continuous education and training for everyone, and the obligation of both organisation and the individual to ensure that it happens. This arises from the sheer rate of the advance of knowledge and understanding, and its application in work situations. An education for life – both working and general – is no longer possible during the formative years. They key feature of organisations that are successful over the long term is the attention that they pay to the education, training and development of all their people, and the priority that this is given.

From this arises a more universal understanding of a 'truth' that some organisations have long recognised and which others have yet to learn.

1. People in organisations are assets; people employed as assets give much better returns than those who are not. All assets require nurturing, maintenance, monitoring and improvement if adequate and improved returns are to be achieved. All assets also require a fundamental understanding of what makes them work, the conditions under which they work best, and how, where and why the best returns are made.

2. The management of these assets – that branch of general management referred to as personnel, human resource management, welfare and industrial relations – requires much greater attention and development, and a much deeper understanding of the keys to its effectiveness. Much of this has hitherto been based on a combination of systems and procedures arising from a fundamental lack of understanding of human behaviour or any notion of ordinary common decency.

3. Attention to management development to improve skills, knowledge, attitudes, behaviour and expertise; to improve the effectiveness of individual managers and teams of managers; and to improve organisational performance. Much greater attention is required to the training of those in managerial and supervisory positions to ensure that they can carry out fundamental managerial tasks of planning, organising, motivating, developing and evaluating people and performance. The contribution made by effective and professional managers to successful organisation performance is critical.

■ Personal obligations

Increasingly, the responsibility to have skills and expertise that are useful to organisations lies in their own hands. Some personal development is undertaken by organisations; this is certain to increase in the future. In the wake of technological change and advance, new jobs are created, new skills required and old jobs and old skills become obsolete. A much greater part of the individual's life is therefore likely to be taken up in education, training and development in the future.

■ Fashions and fads

Fashions and fads in management arise as organisations strive for continuous improvement. They are also often seen as panaceas and cures for organisational maladies.

The greatest contribution, however, is to fuel the debate, to ensure that it continues so that both people and their organisations pursue the means of continuous improvement. In particular the greatest contribution of the 'Excellence Studies' was to popularise and demystify many of the myths and legends surrounding management. The fact that fashions and fads continue to arise is itself an indication that no absolute truth exists in this area, that everything is capable of improvement and development.

■ Finally

The key to effective organisational performance lies in the people. The key to effective and successful management lies in understanding the nature of people, their behaviour, drives, hopes, fears and expectations; and the circumstances and activities necessary to bring the best out of them. To like, respect and value people is a basic prerequisite for effective management. Creating the conditions in which liking, respect and value exist, together with flexibility, dynamism and responsiveness, is the basis of effective and successful organisations and performance.

BOX 18.2   Fashions and Fads

Examples of current managerial and organisational fashions and fads are:

- **empowerment:** the addition of authority and responsibility to otherwise limited jobs;
- **total quality management:** attention to product and service quality based on staff training, technological excellence and customer responsiveness;
- **business process re-engineering:** continuous attention to processes, practices and procedures in the search for ever more effective and efficient use of resources;
- **excellence:** analysis of organisations considered to be high performers through attention to structure, style, strategy, shared values, staff, skills and superordinate goals;
- **core and peripheral organisation:** the organisation of key and continuing, and transient or occasional, tasks into a federated or contracted organisational structure;
- **benchmarking:** the identification of key roles and tasks within organisations and the establishment of performance targets around these as a guide to the rest of the organisation.

Bibliography

J.H. Adair (1975)   *Action-Centred Leadership*, Cambridge University Press.
——————— (1986)   *Effective Team Building*, Gower.
I. Adams, S. Hamil and A. Carruthers (1990)   *The Future of Organisations*, Free Press.
M. Argyle (1989)   *The Social Psychology of Work*, Penguin.
C. Argyris (1957)   *Personality and Organisations*, Harper & Row.
M. Armstrong (1993)   *Personnel Management*, Prentice-Hall.
M.K. Ash (1985)   *On People Management*, McDonald.
R.M. Belbin (1986)   *Superteams*, Prentice-Hall.
E.H. Berne (1984)   *Games People Play*, Penguin.
D. Biddle and R. Evenden (1989)   *Human Aspects of Management*, IPM.
R. Blake and J. Mouton (1986)   *The New Managerial Grid*, Gulf.
E. de Bono (1984)   *Lateral Thinking for Managers*, Pelican.
T. Burns and G.M. Stalker (1968)   *The Management of Innovation*, Tavistock.
D. Carnegie (1936)   *How to Win Friends and Influence People*, Simon & Schuster.
S. Caulkin (1995)   'Hooked on High Tech', *Business International*.
C.R. Christensen (1980)   *Business Policy*, Irwin.
G.A. Cole *et al.* (1994) (ed.)   *Management Theory and Practice*, DPP.
D. Drennan (1992)   *Transforming Company Culture*, McGraw-Hill.
P.F. Drucker (1955)   *Management by Objectives*, Prentice-Hall.
——————— (1986a)   *Drucker on Management*, Prentice-Hall.
——————— (1986b)   *The Practice of Management*, Prentice-Hall.
——————— (1988)   *The Effective Executive*, Fontana.
——————— (1990)   *Frontiers of Management*, Heinemann.
——————— (1993a)   *The Ecological Vision*, Transaction.
——————— (1993b)   *The Post-Capitalist Society*, HarperCollins.
G. Egan (1994)   'Cultivate your Culture', *Management Today* (April).
A. Etzioni (1964)   *Power in Organisations*, Free Press.
F.E. Fielder (1967)   *A Theory of Leadership Effectiveness*, McGraw-Hill.
J. French and B. Raven (1959)   'The Bases of Social Power', in D. Cartwright (ed.), *Studies in Social Power*, University of Michigan.
W. Goldsmith and D. Clutterbuck (1990)   *The Winning Streak*, Penguin.
J.H. Goldthorpe *et al.* (1968)   *The Affluent Worker*, Vol. 3, Cambridge University Press.
C.B. Handy (1984)   *The Future of Work*, Penguin.
——————— (1988)   *The Age of Unreason*, Penguin.
——————— (1990)   *Understanding Organisations*, Penguin.
——————— (1991)   *The Gods of Management*, Penguin.
——————— (1992)   *The Empty Raincoat*, Penguin.
——————— (1993)   *Understanding Organisations*, new edn, Penguin.

———— (1995)   *Beyond Certainty*, Macmillan.
———— *et al.* (1981)   *Making Managers*, Penguin.
P. Harris and R. Moran (1991)   *Managing Cultural Differences*, Gulf.
J. Harvey-Jones (1990)   *Making it Happen*, Fontana.
J. Henry (1992)   *Creative Management*, Open University.
F. Herzberg (1960, 1974)   *Work and the Nature of Man*, Granada.
F. Herzberg *et al.* (1959)   *The Motivation to Work*, Chapman & Hall.
G. Hofstede (1980)   *Culture's Consequences*, Sage.
P. Honey (1986)   *Learning*, UMIST.
A. Huczynski and D. Buchanan (1993)   *Organisational Behaviour*, Prentice-Hall.
J. W. Humble (1972)   *Management by Objectives*, BIM.
L. Iaccoca (1985)   *Iaccoca*, Bantam.
A. Jay (1967)   *Management and Machiavelli*, Holt, Rinehart & Winston.
G. Johnson and K. Scholes (1994) (eds)   *Exploring Corporate Strategy*, Prentice-Hall.
D. Katz and R. L. Kahn (1978)   *The Social Psychology of Organizations*, Wiley.
J. Kenney and R. Reid (1992)   *Training Interventions*, IPM.
D. A. Kolb (1985)   *Experience as the Source of Learning and Development*, Prentice-Hall.
D. A. Kolb *et al.* (1984)   *Organisational Psychology: An Experiential Approach to Organisational Behaviour*, Prentice-Hall.
D. R. Koontz *et al.* (1984)   *Organisations*, Longman.
P. A. Lawrence (1984)   *Management in Action*, Routledge & Kegan Paul.
P. A. Lawrence and K. Elliott (eds) (1988)   *Introducing Management*, Penguin.
P. A. Lawrence and R. Lee (1986)   *Insights into Management*, Oxford University Press.
P. R. Lawrence and J. W. Lorsch (1967)   *Organisation and Environment*, Harvard.
R. S. Lessem (1985)   *The Routes of Excellence*, Fontana.
———— (1987)   *Intrapreneurship*, Wildwood.
———— (1989)   *Managing Corporate Culture*, Gower.
———— (1990)   *Transforming Management*, Prentice-Hall.
R. Likert (1961)   *New Patterns of Management*, McGraw-Hill.
———— (1967)   *The Human Organisation*, McGraw-Hill.
B. Livy (1987)   *Corporate Personnel Management*, Pitman.
T. Lupton (1963)   *On the Shop Floor*, Pergamon.
———— (1984)   *Management and the Social Sciences*, Penguin.
F. Luthans (1989)   *Organisational Behaviour*, McGraw-Hill.
M. H. McCormack (1983)   *What They Don't Teach You at Harvard Business School*, Fontana.
———— (1989)   *Success Secrets*, Fontana.
D. C. McClelland (1988)   *Human Motivation*, Cambridge University Press.
D. McGregor (1961)   *The Human Side of Enterprise*, Harper & Row.
I. McGregor (1987)   *The Enemies Within*, Fontana.
N. Machiavelli (1993)   *The Prince*, Penguin Classics.
J. G. March and H. A. Simon (1958)   *Organisations*, Wiley.
A. Maslow (1960)   *Motivation and Personality*, Harper & Row.
———— (1987)   *Motivation and Personality*, Harper & Row.
H. Mintzberg (1973)   *The Nature of Managerial Work*, Harper & Row.
———— (1979)   *The Structuring of Organisations*, Prentice-Hall.
G. Morgan (1986)   *Images of Organisation*, Sage.
A. Morita (1987)   *Made in Japan: The Sony Story*, Collins.

R. Moss-Kanter (1983)   *The Change Masters: Corporate Entrepreneurs at Work*, George, Allen and Unwin.

L. Mullins (1993)   *Management and Organisational Behaviour*, Pitman.

A. Mumford (1989)   *Management Development*, IPM.

W. G. Ouchi (1981)   *Theory Z*, Avon.

H. Owen (1985)   *Myth Transformation and Change*, Collins.

R. Pascale (1989)   *Managing on the Edge*, Simon & Schuster.

R. Pascale and A. Athos (1983)   *The Art of Japanese Management*, Fontana.

M. Pedler *et al.* (1991)   *The Learning Company*, McGraw-Hill.

L. J. Peter (1970)   *The Peter Principle*, Penguin.

T. Peters (1989)   *Thriving on Chaos*, Macmillan.

————— (1992)   *Liberation Management*, Macmillan.

————— and N. Austin (1985)   *A Passion for Excellence*, Collins.

————— and R. Waterman (1982)   *In Search of Excellence*, Harper & Row.

R. Pettinger (1994)   *Introduction to Management*, Macmillan.

L. W. Porter and E. E. Lawler (1968)   *Managerial Attitudes and Performance*, Irwin.

————— *et al.* (1975)   *Behaviour and Organisations*, McGraw-Hill.

D. S. Pugh (1992)   *Writers on Organisations*, Penguin.

W. Reddin (1970)   *Managerial Effectiveness*, McGraw-Hill.

M. Reddy (1991)   *The Manager's Guide to Counselling*, Methuen.

W. D. Rees (1990)   *The Skills of Management*, Routledge.

A. Roddick (1992)   *Body and Soul: The Body Shop Story*, Ebury.

A. Rodger (1958)   *The Seven Point Plan*, National Institute of Industrial Psychology.

C. Rogers (1947)   'Observations on the Organisation of Personality', *American Psychologist*, Vol. 2.

G. Salaman (1981)   *Class and the Corporation*, Fontana.

————— (1992)   *Human Resource Strategies*, Open University.

M. Salamon (1992)   *Industrial Relations*, Prentice-Hall.

E. Schein (1988)   *Organisational Psychology*, Prentice-Hall.

E. F. Schumacher (1986)   *Small is Beautiful*, Oxford University Press.

R. Semler (1992)   *Maverick*, Free Press.

H. A. Simon (1969)   *The New Science of Management Decision*, Harper & Row.

E. Sternberg (1995)   *Just Business*, Warner.

R. Stewart (1963)   *The Reality of Management*, Park.

G. Suetonius (1969)   *The Twelve Caesars*, Penguin Classics.

R. Tannebaum and W. Schmidt (1958)   'How to Choose a Leadership Pattern', *Harvard Business Review*.

B. Taylor and G. Lippett (1984)   *Management Training and Development Handbook*, McGraw-Hill.

F. W. Taylor (1947)   *Scientific Management*, Harper & Row.

J. L. Thompson (1990)   *Strategic Management*, Chapman & Hall.

D. Torrington and L. Hall (1992)   *Personnel Management: A New Approach*, Prentice-Hall.

————— (1994)   *Human Resource Management*, IPM.

M. Trevor (1992)   *Toshiba's New British Company*, Policy Studies Institute.

E. Trist *et al.* (1963)   *Organisational Choice*, Tavistock.

B. Tuckman (1965)   'Group Development', *Psychological Bulletin*, Vol. 63.

L. F. Urwick (1947)   *Elements of Administration*, Pitman.

V. Vroom (1964)   *Work and Motivation*, Wiley.

C. R. Walker and R. H. Guest (1952) *The Man on the Assembly Line*, Harvard.

C. R. Walker and R. H. Guest (1956) *The Supervisor on the Assembly Line*, Harvard.

D. Walton and A. McKersie (1965) *A Behavioural Theory of Labour Negotiations*, McGraw-Hill.

P. Warr (1987) *Psychology at Work*, Penguin.

P. Wickens (1992) *The Road to Nissan*, Collins.

A. Williams *et al.* (1993) *Changing Culture*, IPM.

J. Woodward (1970) *Industrial Organisation: Behaviour and Control*, Oxford University Press.

P. Zimbardo *et al.* (1973) 'A Study of Prisoners and Guards', US Naval Research Review.

Index